MICROBIAL
AUTECOLOGY

MICROBIAL AUTECOLOGY
A METHOD FOR ENVIRONMENTAL STUDIES

Edited by
Robert L. Tate III
Department of Soils and Crops
Cook College
Rutgers, The State University of New Jersey
New Brunswick, New Jersey

A Wiley-Interscience Publication
JOHN WILEY & SONS
New York · Chichester · Brisbane · Toronto · Singapore

Library of Congress Cataloging in Publication Data:

Microbial autecology.

   "A Wiley-Interscience publication."
   Includes indexes.
   1. Microbial ecology.   I. Tate, Robert L.,
1944–

QR100.M48   1986   576′.15   86-15810
ISBN 0-471-80922-5

Printed in the United States of America

10 9 8 7 6 5 4 3 2 1

CONTRIBUTORS

PAMELA E. BELL, Department of Environmental Sciences, University of Virginia, Charlottesville, Virginia

CHARLES W. BOYLEN, Fresh Water Institute, Rensselaer Polytechnic Institute, Troy, New York

RITA R. COLWELL, Department of Microbiology, University of Maryland, College Park, Maryland

CHARLES HAGEDORN, Allied Corporation, Syracuse Research Laboratory, Solvay, New York

MAXINE A. HOLDER-FRANKLIN, Department of Biology, University of Windsor, Windsor, Ontario, Canada

DAVID H. HUBBELL, Department of Soil Science, University of Florida, Gainesville, Florida

AARON L. MILLS, Department of Environmental Sciences, University of Virginia, Charlottesville, Virginia

RICHARD Y. MORITA, Department of Microbiology, College of Science and College of Oceanography, Oregon State University, Corvallis, Oregon

E. RUSSEK-COHEN, Department of Animal Sciences, University of Maryland, College Park, Maryland

REGINALD J. SORACCO, Fresh Water Institute, Rensselaer Polytechnic Institute, Troy, New York

ROBERT L. TATE III, Department of Soils and Crops, Cook College, Rutgers, The State University of New Jersey, New Brunswick, New Jersey

PREFACE

Although many of the classical microbiological studies are prime examples of autecological research, microbial autecology must still be considered to be a science in its infancy. This is not the result of limited interest in the subject but rather the situation is derived primarily from the lack of readily available techniques for the study of individual microbial populations in situ. Until recently, microbial autecological research was, with some notable exceptions, essentially synonymous with laboratory or test tube studies with axenic cultures of microorganisms believed to be responsible for environmental processes of interest. The vision of the scientists involved with such research has in recent years been expanded by the introduction of fluorescent antibody and radioautographic procedures. Although the procedures are complex, microorganisms can finally be observed in samples of native habitats. With the development of automated laboratory and field analytical procedures and the incorporation of microcomputers into data analysis, we have approached the technical expertise that will allow the science to grow into maturity. This growth will include an expansion of the vision of the scientists conducting the research so that instead of being limited to evaluation of the behavior of one or a few microbial species in an ecosystem, they will be able to observe concurrent population fluctuations of entire communities.

With past limitations in mind, the authors and subjects were selected for this project with the objective of demonstrating the status — informational as well as technical — of microbial autecology. The goal was to demonstrate the utility of autecological research in developing an inclusive picture of ecosystem dynamics. Authors were selected for their past accomplishments in environmental microbial autecology and/or experience with promising techniques. The only limitation placed on the authors was that their chapters stress autecological relationships. The members of the team have both diverse opinions on the applicability of some of the experimental procedures as well as major philosophical differences. Thus, the reader should gain a more complete view of the subject than is provided by a group of scientists who basically agree on the fundamentals and future of their research area.

Because of the "youth" of the discipline, methods are stressed in this treatise. Chapters dealing with basic data collection and analysis follow the brief introduction. Once a background on available techniques has been provided, three rather broadly based chapters are presented to provide an overview of the accomplishments and future of autecological research in soils and waters. The length of the presentations varies with the quantities of autecological studies that have been conducted, the history of the technique, and the "whims" of the author. Some of the chapters are more philosophical, others more technical. This mixture was chosen again to stimulate new research and to provide a strong basic background for this research. If our objectives are accomplished, we will be able to review the literature in a few years and find a wealth of new information where we currently encounter a dearth.

The editor acknowledges support for a portion of his time devoted to the project from the following source: New Jersey Agricultural Experiment Station, Publication No. C-15187-1-85, supported by state funds.

ROBERT L. TATE III

New Brunswick, New Jersey
May 1986

CONTENTS

MICROBIAL
AUTECOLOGY

1 IMPORTANCE OF AUTECOLOGY IN MICROBIAL ECOLOGY

Robert L. Tate, III
Department of Soils and Crops
Cook College
Rutgers, The State University of New Jersey
New Brunswick, New Jersey

Many early microbiological studies, such as Henrici's evaluation of the microbial flora of Minnesota and Wisconsin lakes and Pasteur's studies of disease (human and wine) causative agents, can be loosely considered to be autecological research. This interest in population ecology of individual microbial types or species was, in many cases, quickly supplanted by a more generally applicable evaluation of overall microbial processes. A cursory examination of the literature suggests that the general science of microbiology has developed along two major, divergent pathways — basic physiologists with their interests in specific processes catalyzed by named organisms and the environmental scientist's quest into what perhaps would now be classified as process microbiology. An exception to this conclusion is found in the area of pathology where the behavior of readily identified pathogens is studied in a variety of ecosystems. In recent years, much of the environmental microbiological literature has related to studies of environmental processes such as various aspects of biogeochemical cycles in selected ecosystems. This specialization of our science has developed mainly because of the complexities encountered in environmental, autecological studies, and the fact that, in many cases, a more inclusive study of the microbial aspects of the ecosystem provided a better understanding of the system as a whole than would have been gained from study of an individual

This is New Jersey Agricultural Experiment Station Publication No. F-15187-2-84, supported by state funds.

1

microbial population. It is frequently easier to quantify the extent of an overall process, and, at least initially, it may be of greater interest or economic value, than it is to isolate and identify an individual microbial species and to justify its presence and function in situ. Work with individual species may also be compromised by discrepancies between culturable members of the community and those that are functioning in situ. That is, the most readily isolated microbes or those that catch our attention may not necessarily be the dominant contributors to successful ecosystem development. An exception to this observation involves the situation where the importance of a given species relates more to its metabolic capabilities in culture than in its native site. There has always been an interest in the "mining" of soils and waters to isolate new and exotic species for general interest (physiological and otherwise) and taxonomic purposes. But to be truly an ecological study, this work must involve some degree of evaluation of the microbe's role or function in situ.

In many cases, the complexity of the microbial community and the difficulties associated with detection and identification of microbial species in situ has discouraged a detailed evaluation of the individuals functioning therein. One could reasonably conclude that it is easier for the ecologist to recognize and study lions or ants in their native habitat than it is for a microbiologist to evaluate the behavior of a microbial species. Indeed, the simple task of defining the microbial species and validating that definition is difficult if not at times impossible. As will be documented herein, a complete understanding of the environmental limitations of microbial processes and the development of generally applicable models now requires a return to the more complicated autecological research. Hence, this chapter is presented with the twofold objectives of (1) delineating the realm, the problems, and the future of environmental microbial autecology; and (2) providing a basic introduction to the more detailed presentations that follow. This contribution is not considered to be or is it intended to be an exhaustive review of the literature. Instead, a limited number of papers are presented to exemplify the author's thesis and to provide an entry to the literature for those interested in inquiring further on the subject.

1.0. WHAT, WHERE, AND WHY

Autecology is defined by ecologists as the study of individual organisms or species within an ecosystem. Aspects of the work include evaluation of microbial life cycles and behavior as a means of adaptation of the individuals to the environment. This is contrasted with *synecology*, which involves the study of groups of organisms that are associated together as a unit (Odum, 1971). Alexander (1971) adapted these definitions to microbial ecology by defining synecology as the study of "the relationships between the environment and the different organisms that make up a biological complex in a single locale" and autecology as the study of "a single species and the influence of environmental factors on that species." Thus, the synecologist would evaluate the processes and the consortia conducting the processes in a given ecosystem, whereas the autecologist would be primarily interested in the individual and the pressures controlling the growth and function of that individual. I must add that current interest would expand this definition to include the concept of the contribution of the individual population to the community and the ecosystem taken as a whole. Those studies that most readily come to mind as examples of autecology involve pathogen, *Rhizobium,* or *Nitrosomonas* behavior in a variety of ecosystems.

Considerable confusion has existed in the definition of autecology and in the extent of such studies. In a recently published book (Lynch, 1984), autecological research was defined as consisting of experiments conducted with laboratory cultures of individual microbial species. Indeed, with past technical limitations relating to identification of individual microbial species in situ, this may be a practical definition, but with the advent of a number of more modern techniques, which shall be discussed briefly herein and described in detail in later chapters, this definition is unnecessarily restrictive. For example, with such tools as highly specific fluorescent antibodies, it is quite plausible to study an individual species, and perhaps individual bacterial strains in complex soil and water systems. Another error that has clouded our concept of microbial autecology relates to the breadth of the research. In this case, the location of the work is not the contention, but rather the difficulty lies with the extent of the study. As indicated previously autecology involves not only the study of the individual but also the study of the influence of the ecosystem on the individual. Simply, this means that to demonstrate the presence of a microorganism in a certain ecosystem is only the beginning of the research. The impact of the individual on the ecosystem as a whole as well as the impact of the ecosystem on the individual must be determined. This distinguishes the science of microbial autecology from that of "pure biology" or "look-see" microbiology.

1.0.1. Direction of Ecological Research. Odum (1971) observed that ecological research appeared to be evolving from predominantly autecological studies to more synecological work. This resulted from greater emphasis by modern ecologists on developing a total ecosystem approach. This trend is even more obvious today.

Microbial ecology followed a similar developmental pathway. With the increasing need to explain or model a variety of ecosystems, the future in microbial ecology must involve more autecology research. For example, identification of the limits of a given process in a specific ecosystem, such as organic matter accumulation in a subtropical swamp, provides a clear understanding of the basic functions in the ecosystem of study. This, however, provides little basis for extrapolation on a broader scale, say perhaps to organic matter accumulation in agricultural land. The difficulty stems from the versatility of the microbial community. Although the same reactions may occur in two totally different ecosystems, the microbes and the abiotic limitations to these microbes may be quite different. This results in principles developed from studies of microbial limitations in one ecosystem, soil type, or climatic region not necessarily being widely applicable. This difficulty may be alleviated by modifying the view point of the research to include an evaluation of (1) the specific microbial species involved, (2) the effect of various environmental parameters on the function of these microbes, and (3) the properties of the microbes catalyzing the process under a wide range of environmental parameters. Models more predictive of the occurrence of microbially mediated reactions in a variety of situations could then be developed. But, a major pitfall of autecological research must be avoided. The behavior of the particular microbial species studied must be evaluated in conjunction with the overall ecosystem function. If not, the data become rather esoteric and the applicability to the understanding of the process in question is lost. With this caveat in mind, autecological research will allow for major advances in microbial ecology.

1.0.2. Importance of Autecological Research. It is relatively easy to evaluate the practical value of a synecological research project that provides numbers descriptive of the extent and magnitude of nutrient cycling. Autecological projects involving behavior and survival of human, plant, and animal pathogens or readily identifiable participants in economically important biogeochemical cycles in soils and waters are equally easily justified. Greater difficulty is found in putting studies of more specialized microbes into perspective. The danger is always present that the role of the organism in the ecosystem may be so minute that full knowledge of its behavior is only of limited applicability to the system under study. So, with the problems associated with identifying a specific microbial species in a complex community and this question of applicability of the results, why study autecology? This question is perhaps most easily answered through evaluation of existing autecological research projects. Three environmentally significant applications that exemplify the importance of autecological studies come readily to mind. These are the occurrence of nitrification in acid ecosystems, survival of various laboratory selected *Rhizobium* strains in soil, and impact of ecosystem perturbation on ecosystem function.

Nitrification is known to be primarily catalyzed in soils and waters by obligatorily aerobic autotrophic bacteria, the ammonia oxidizers and nitrite oxidizers. These organisms only grow and function in soils and waters with a pH greater than 5.5, yet nitrification occurs in a variety of soils with pH values much below this threshold (Ishaque and Cornfield, 1972 and 1974; Remacle, 1977; Van De Dijk and Troelstra, 1980). Based on our knowledge of the autecology of the autotrophic nitrifiers isolated to date, several hypotheses may be developed to explain this discrepancy between cultural pH limitations and the occurrence of the process in acidic soils. These include the possibility that either the pH limitations measured in the laboratory are not operative in native systems (i.e., some factor in situ is compensating for the pH limitation) or that previously unidentified microbes are functioning in the acidic ecosystems. The latter alternative includes the potential activity of heterotrophic nitrifiers (Castellvi and O'Shananan, 1977; Doxtander and Alexander, 1966; Eylar and

Schmidt, 1959; Hirsch et al., 1961; Tate, 1977; Verstraete and Alexander, 1973), or the existence of autotrophic nitrifiers with pH optima in a more acid range than those currently known (Dommergues et al., 1978). Armed with these hypotheses, the microbial autecologist can further examine the acidic sites for specific microbial populations fitting the limitations of each hypotheses to clarify the situation.

Due to the high expenses associated with use of anthropogenically produced fixed nitrogen, there is intense interest in developing more efficient diazotrophs, including the symbiotic nitrogen fixers of the genus *Rhizobium*. But, development of more efficient *Rhizobium* strains is only the first step in meeting plant nitrogen needs. Once the more efficient strain is developed in the laboratory, it must be tested in the soil to evaluate its survival capability and its ability to compete with indigenous rhizobia in the formation of effective nodules on legume roots. The complexity of such tests, especially from the view of developing a general model for the behavior of the auxotroph in a variety of ecosystems, is indicated by simply listing the factors known to affect *Rhizobium* survival in soil. *Rhizobium* spp. survival in soil is affected by soil pH (Keyser et al., 1979; Lowendorf et al. 1981; Lowendorf and Alexander, 1983a and 1983b; Dughri and Bottomly, 1983; Barber 1980), aluminum levels associated with this soil acidity (Keyser and Munns 1979a and 1979b; Hartel et al., 1983; Hartel and Alexander, 1983; Franco and Munns, 1982), soil moisture and desiccation (Chao and Alexander, 1982; Mahler and Wollum, 1980 and 1981; Osa-Afiana and Alexander, 1979; Pena-Cabriales and Alexander 1979 and 1983a), carbon amendments (Pena-Cabriales and Alexander 1983b), temperature (Munevar and Wollum, 1981; Osa-Afiana and Alexander, 1982a; Boonkerd and Weaver, 1982), nitrate levels (McNeil, 1982), clay content (Osa-Afiana and Alexander 1982b), and cultivation practices (Robert and Schmidt, 1983).

Aside from the practical need of providing more economical plant nitrogen sources, autecological *Rhizobium* research has been stimulated by development of techniques to detect specific strains in situ. These procedures involve fluorescent antibodies (Crozat et al., 1982; Kingsley and Bohlool, 1981; Hughes et al. 1979; Bohlool and Schmidt 1970 and 1973; Vidor and Miller, 1980), antibiotic sensitive mutants discussed in Chapter 3 and in Hagedorn (1979), Kuykendall and Weber (1978), and Materon and Hagedorn (1982), as well as the more traditional soil inoculation methods. Noel and Brill (1980) have also developed a gel electrophoresis procedure that may prove useful in differentiating *Rhizobium* strains from infected nodules in field studies.

Considerable effort is currently being devoted to evaluation of environmental impact of ecosystem modification. This modification can consist of direct anthropogenic intervention, such as is involved with reclamation site management, or indirect contact, as exemplified by the studies of acid rain. In any case, the overall question relates to the effect of the modifications on ecosystem stability and the capability of the microbial community to adapt to the new environmental parameters. An example of drastic soil manipulation and the effects on the microbial community is provided by studies of mineland reclamation. The primary objective of site reclamation is to develop a stable, aesthetic above-ground plant community. General achievement of this goal is not possible, or it is at least limited, without a reasonable knowledge of the ability of the soil microbial community to adapt to the soil conditions resulting from the mining operation (Tate, 1985). With soils impacted by acid mine drainage, this may include the capability of the microbes to neutralize the soil acid or at least develop populations capable of growing and functioning under the acidic conditions (Mills, 1985) whereas with oil shale wastes, populations of microbes capable of complexing or removing toxic metals from the soils must develop (Wildung and Garland, 1985). These problems may be examined from two viewpoints. Either each site, or ecosystem, can be studied individually, with site-specific recommendations for reclamation developed, or the behavior of the individual microbial populations responsible for establishing the biogeochemical processes can be studied under a variety of limiting conditions. The data from the latter autecological study would then be incorporated into a model that would be used to predict the probability of reclamation success in a variety of alternate sites.

These examples elucidate the need for extension of the more common process research by evaluation of the behavior of specific populations in situ. Further discussion of these and other studies are provided in Chapters 7–9.

1.1. Environmental Parameters Affecting Microbial Activity

Relating the growth and activity of a specific microbial population to the prevailing environmental conditions is a prime requisite for autecological research. With some simple ecosystems, this may not be difficult, but with such heterogeneous systems as soil even highly significant correlations between microbial growth or activity and variation in a specific environmental parameter may not provide a realistic indication of the contribution of the population of interest to the total ecosystem function or development. Since in many cases the environment may vary to such an extent that the exact conditions at the time of sampling may never be duplicated again, it is important when planning environmental sampling studies to collect as much in situ data as possible. The discussion that follows emphasizes the difficulties in selecting variables for study and manipulation of the data. Of the ecosystems studied by the ecologist, the soil sites are likely the most complex and troublesome. This results from the extreme heterogeneity of the soil matrix. Therefore, since this would in all likelihood represent the extreme situation of study and the author's bias lies with that ecosystem, examples provided in these sections will deal primarily with soil studies.

1.1.1. Microsite versus Macrosite. The differences between the microsite where the microorganism is functioning and the macrosite in which the ecologist is functioning must be of foremost consideration in experimental design. This need results from the disparity between the size of the microorganisms (a few microns at most for bacteria) and the smallest sample that can be analyzed (a few milliliters in most cases). Hence, the physical and chemical parameters measured pertain to the system as a whole and in reality may be quite different from those actually encountered by the microorganism. Soil provides a prime example of such variation (Fig. 1). Soil is a mixture of solid particles (clay, sands, silts, rocks, etc.) air pores, and water. Heterogeneity of composition is also common within these fractions. The air composition varies within the soil matrix dependent upon the proximity to carbon dioxide generating sites (i.e., respiring plant roots, actively decaying organic matter, etc.), sites of nitrous oxide generating activity (denitrification or nitrification), and sulfate reducing or methane generating activity. Soil solution contents depend upon the solubility and diffusion rate of the soil mineral inclusions, source of the water, and biotic activity. Microbial growth and activity are also affected by water activity or availability in the soil (Orchard and Cook, 1983; Wildung et al., 1975; Wilson and Griffin, 1975). Excess water results in oxygen deficient conditions that encourage anaerobic or anoxic metabolism, whereas insufficient water to form a surface film on particulate soil components severely limits or even totally precludes microbial growth. As will be discussed in Sections 1.1.2 and 1.1.3, measurement of the various physical and chemical parameters in the bulk sample may or may not provide an indication of the effect of these parameters on the microbe in situ.

A less complex, but perhaps equally difficult ecosystem to describe at the microsite level is plant tissue. *Acremonium* sp. growing within the tissue of perennial ryegrass (*Lolium perenne* L.) is shown in Figure 2. This fungal endo-

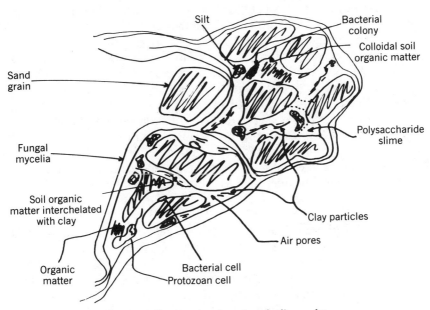

Figure 1. Heterogenous character of soil granules.

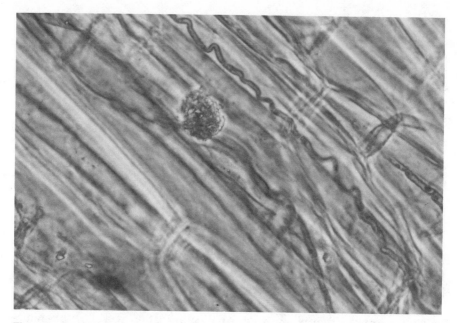

Figure 2. Growth of the endophytic fungus, *Acremonium* sp. in leaf sheath tissue of perennial ryegrass. (*Lolium perenne* L.).

phyte is only found growing intracellularly in grass tissue (Bacon et al., 1977; Lloyd, 1959; Neill, 1941). Since no damage to the growth of the host is detected, the fungus must be metabolizing the nutrients leaking from the host cells. Except for limited ability to measure metabolism with autoradiography and some electron microscopy techniques, the capability of describing the chemical and even the physical site of growth of this fungus and how it contributes to the survival and function of this microorganism is severely limited. In this case, macrosite measurements (plant tissue analysis) are of limited value.

Even with these difficulties in measurement and perhaps in conceptualizing of the microsites, microbiologists interested in evaluating the autecology of specific organisms and relating their behavior to realistic measurements of the environmental parameters must deal with this heterogeneity. The sections that follow document some variations in abiotic and biotic factors in soils and waters and provide some indication as to how this variation has been overcome in past experiments.

1.1.2. Abiotic Effectors. Many physical and chemical factors limit or control microbial activity. The relative importance of each individual factor in ecosystem function depends upon the amount of variation within the site (i.e., physical heterogeneity), as well as the magnitude of the variation. For example, temperature differentials in subtropical regions, such as southern Florida would have less effect on soil microbial activity than this parameter would in a soil site located in more temperate regions. This conclusion is based on biologically catalyzed processes generally having a Q_{10} of 1.5–3.0 and the small temperature range occurring under subtropical or tropical climates. In temperate sites, microbial activity could range from near zero during winter months to maximal activity levels during the warm, moist periods of the early and late summer. In subtropical or tropical soils, except in the harsh environment of the soil surface layer, the soil temperature is most likely within the optimum range for microbial activity throughout most of the year. Hence, environmental physical parameters selected for study in individual experiments must vary depending upon the location and type of ecosystem under study. For our present analysis, temperature gradients, nutrient source, pH variation, clay interactions, and heterogeneity in free oxygen levels and redox potential will be used as examples of the complexity of the effect of environmental conditions on experimental design.

1.1.2.1. Temperature Relationship. The overall ecosystem temperature is proportional to the difference between energy input and energy lost from the site. Thus, it logically follows that within an ecosystem, temperature variation results from any factor that limits either in-coming or out-going heat transfers. Similarly, temperature gradients exist within the ecosystem due to heat transfer rates from the warmer to the cooler areas. These general statements can be clarified by examining the heat variation in soil.

Two major types of temperature variation that are encountered in a soil ecosystem must be accommodated in the experimental design. These are (1) variation within the soil profile due to heat transfer down from the soil surface and (2) horizontal variation due to shading of the soil surface, that is, diminishing of heat input into the system. Fluker (1958) in an extensive study of soil temperature variation under a bare ground surface at College Station, Texas, demonstrated that a temperature gradient occurred in the top 305 cm of soil (Table 1) and that the temperatures and shapes of this gradient varied with the season (Table 2). Several factors of interest to the soil microbiologist are shown in these data. First, the maximum average temperature for the top 90 cm of soil was greater than the mean air temperature. Average minimum temperatures were greater than the average minimum air temperatures at all depths. Thus the microbe residing in the surface layers of this soil profile would experience a wider temperature range than would the organism deeper in the soil profile. The microbe in the surface of the soil would become active earlier in the spring and face a temperature related decline in activity earlier in the fall as a result of faster response of the surface soil to air temperature changes in the surface as opposed to subsurface soils. The potential also exists in warmer climates for development of soil surface temperatures exceeding the optimum for microbial activity. Hence, microbial activities may actually be lower in the top few centimeters of soil than in the deeper soil layers (e.g., see Tate, 1979). In the Fluker study, the minimum temperature of the top 13 cm of the soil profile occurred approximately 1 month earlier than in the 13 cm to 79 cm layer. Similarly, the

TABLE 1. Summary of the Variation of Soil Temperature within the Soil Profile

Depth (cm)	Temperature (°C)		
	Maximum	Minimum	Average
Air	30.0	10.5	20.8
5	35.2	11.1	24.1
30	33.9	13.9	23.9
61	32.9	15.0	23.8
91	31.9	16.0	23.6
122	30.8	16.6	23.6
152	30.7	17.6	23.6
183	28.7	18.5	23.5
244	27.1	19.5	23.4
305	26.3	20.3	23.4

Source: Reproduced by permission from Fluker, B.J., (1958). Soil temperatures. *Soil Sci.,* **68**:43. Copyright 1958 by The Williams & Wilkins Co., Baltimore.

top horizon reached its temperature maximum about a month before the next depth sampled. Diurnal variation in the soil temperature has also been recorded (Unger, 1978). Fluctuations are more rapid in the air than in soil. With a clear sky, the air temperature in temperate regions reaches a maximum at about two o'clock, but due to a lag in the response of the soil temperature, the soil does not reach a maximum temperature until later in the afternoon (Brady, 1984). Fluker (1958) found that the diurnal variation of soil temperature only extended to a depth of 60–90 cm below the soil surface. The implication of these data on the growth of microorganisms in soil relates to the zone of maximal soil microbial activity. In mineral soils, maximal microbial activity is generally

TABLE 2. Seasonal Occurrence of Minimum and Maximum Soil Temperatures

Depth (cm)	Month of Occurrence
	Minimum
0–13	December
13–79	January
79–198	February
198–305	March
	Maximum
0–13	July
13–142	August
142–274	September
274–305	October

Source: Reproduced by permission from Fluker, B.J. (1958). Soil temperatures. *Soil Sci.,* **68**:43. Copyright 1958 by The Williams & Wilkins Co., Baltimore.

found in the top few centimeters of soil (Alexander, 1977). In organic soils, this activity may extend from 60 to 70 cm before appreciable declines occur (Tate, 1979). In the latter case, these declines may be more in response to soil moisture changes due to water table placement than to any other effector of microbial activity (Tate and Terry, 1980). Thus, for the more commonly occurring mineral soils, the bulk of the microbial activity is found in that portion of the soil profile experiencing greatest temperature variation. Therefore, due to temperature variations with depth and time and the fact that soil temperatures may exceed air temperatures, care must be taken to record a meaningful soil temperature in relationship to in situ estimates of microbial activity. For situations where direct measurement of soil temperature is impractical, several models have been developed to predict soil temperature and moisture profiles (e.g., see Lascano and Van Bavel, 1983). The author has had no direct experience with extrapolating from these models, but in cases where no other practical means exists for collecting the data, such models may prove useful.

Along with the vertical, seasonal, and diurnal variation of soil temperature, soil surface cover may also result in a horizontal temperature gradient. This is best exemplified by data collected to evaluate the effect of no-till cropping on soil temperature (Bennett et al., 1976; Gupta et al., 1983; Unger,1978). These studies were conducted primarily as the result of crop yield problems encountered if the soil temperature rise to optimal levels for seed germination is inhibited by surface mulch layers. Gupta et al. (1983) examined the effects of tillage and surface residue interactions on soil upper boundary temperatures. They found that soil surface temperature variations between the various residue and tillage treatments were primarily the result of the differences in surface residue cover. The effect of leaving crop residue on the soil surface as opposed to turning the residues under is shown in Figure 3 (Unger, 1978). The maximum soil temperature was reached earlier and was lower in the residue covered soil as opposed to the bare soil surface. Again, these variations in soil temperatures in the horizontal plane require careful experimental design. Merely collecting all soil samples on the same day, at approximately the same time may not insure sample temperature uniformity. Type of soil cover, amount of soil cover, and even variations in soil moisture as it affects the soil thermal conductivity must be considered. The example used here pertained primarily to the soil environment, but it is not too difficult to extrapolate the concepts to other ecosystems, such as lakes and streams, or even the artificial ecosystems of sewage treatment facilities. Again, the vertical variation of the ecosystem temperature depends upon the intensity of energy striking the surface (including amount of shading), the thermal conductivity of the solid components of the ecosystem, and, in the case of aqueous ecosystems, the thermal conductivity and the amount of mixing of the water. All this can make experimental design frustrating to the microbial ecologist, to say the least.

The significance of these problems of soil temperature variation on experimental design in all actuality can vary from essentially insignificant to being the major contributor to sample variation. This conclusion is derived from consid-

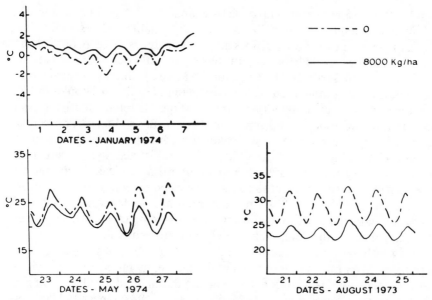

Figure 3. Effect of surface layer of 8000-kg/ha mulch on soil temperature. Reproduced from Agronomy Journal, Volume 70, 1978, pages 858–864 by permission of the American Society of Agronomy. P.W. Unger, author, Figure 4, page 861, Figures 5, and 6, page 863.

eration of the relationship of temperature to rate of microbial activity. Two considerations are of importance here. The first involves the temperature extremes at which microorganisms can function and the second relates to the actual effect of temperature on the rate of biological reaction. First, microorganisms have been found to be active essentially at any temperature where free water exists. Psychrophilic microorganisms commonly grow at temperatures of 0 °C or lower (Innis, 1975). Growth at temperatures below the -10 °C minimum now recorded may be possible if antifreeze substances needed to maintain free water are developed that are not toxic to microorganisms at the concentrations needed to prevent freezing at the lower temperatures (Innis, 1975). The most commonly studied natural ecosystem in evaluation of adaptation to high temperatures is the hot spring (Brock and Darland, 1970; Kristjansson and Alfredsson, 1983; Sandbeck and Ward, 1982). In each of these studies, maximum growth temperatures were between 70 and 80 °C. In culture, *Bacillus caldolyticus* has been shown to grow at 105 °C with increased pressure (Heinen and Lauwers, 1981). The record temperature for microbial growth appears to have been recorded by Baross and Deming (1983) in their study of barophilic thermophiles in deep Pacific hydrothermal vents. The organisms were capable of multiplying under pressure at over 250 °C. Thus, the temperature limit for detection of active microorganisms apparently relates primarily to the maximum and minimum temperature at which free water exists under the limits imposed by the other environmental factors.

Of greater importance in developing a model of microbial activities within most ecoystems is the effect of temperature variation on the microbial activity. The practical significance of this activity–temperature relationship relates to the determination of the range of temperature variation that can occur before a significant change in microbial activity is measured. Other means of answering this question have been demonstrated (Ratkowsky et al. 1982), but probably the most commonly used procedure involves the Q_{10} relationship. Although high Q_{10} values have been detected for such processes as petroleum decomposition (Atlas 1981), generally most microbial processes have a Q_{10} between 1.5 and 3.0. Frequently, values outside this range relate to temperature effects on the physical state of the substrate (e.g., the change in petroleum viscosity and water solubility with increasing temperatures). Thus, the amount of change in the reaction rate within the range of site temperature variation can be estimated. Should this value be insignificant compared to the variation caused by other environmental variables, then at least in the first cut, extreme accuracy in temperature measurement may not be necessary.

1.1.2.2. Nutrient Source. Of prime interest in consideration of nutrient availability is the heterogeneity in distribution of nutrient sources within a given ecosystem. Effects of phytoplankton or detritus distribution in aquatic sites and the rhizosphere effect in soil ecosystems are easily evaluated, but such nutrient distributional effects may not be so easily recognized in other ecosystems. For example, nutrients, interchelated with soil clay minerals or coating sand or silt particles, although of limited availability to the microbial community, may still materially contribute to microbial growth. Practical implications of nutrient location heterogeneity relate to the sample size chosen for study. For total ecosystem studies, samples must be of sufficient volume to be representative of the ecosystem as a whole. Such variables as within and between row sampling for cropped soils, or distance from the nutrient source must be recorded. Due to the obvious effect of an influx of a metabolizable energy source, the experimental design must account for such variations. This may be difficult for the microbial autecologist because the site of interest is that microzone surrounding the individual microbial cell. Thus, when recording activities of microorganisms in situ (such as with fluorescent antibodies or autoradiography), some observation of the type of inanimate material around the cell may be necessary. Due to the lack of or difficulty in the general use of techniques to measure substrate distribution in situ this is likely one of the more commonly overlooked aspects of microbial ecology.

The plant rhizosphere provides an example of a site with a soluble nutrient source as well as an insoluble source. The soluble nutrients are those nutrients leaching from the roots, whereas the insoluble material consists of the root cellular material itself that becomes available to the growing microbial community as cells are sloughed or as the roots die and decay. The impact of the water soluble nutrients on microbial growth and metabolism decreases with distance from the point of origin. The concentration gradient varies with the diffusion rate of the substrate as well as the microbial metabolic rate.

Plant roots are a well documented source of microbial nutrients (Alexander, 1977; Paul and Schmidt, 1961). Paul and Schmidt (1961) identified about 15 free amino acids totaling $2-4\,\mu g/g$ of soil. Numerous other unidentified organic compounds were detected. Barber and Lynch (1977) demonstrated that the soil microbial community actually stimulates carbohydrate leakage from the plant roots because they found that the numbers of bacteria in the rhizosphere of barley plants exceed the size of the biomass that could be produced from those carbohydrates leaking from the roots of plants growing in the absence of microorganisms. Procedures for studying this interesting ecosystem and the behavior of specific organisms therein have included classical procedures of measuring *(R)/(S)* values, electron microscopy (e.g., see Rovira and Campbell, 1974), and assay of soil enzymatic and other metabolic activities. The isolation of the rhizosphere influenced soil microbial community from nonrhizosphere soil has been made easier by development of techniques reported by Smith and Tiedje (1979) and Helal and Sauerbeck (1983).

1.1.2.3. pH. The difficulty of microsite variation and interpretation of microbial activity in situ was discussed previously in relationship to the role of autotrophic nitrifiers in acid soils. pH measurements are of necessity an indication of macrosite pH values rather than microsite variations. Thus, molecular changes in the environs of the individual bacterium may result in an in situ pH value different from the macrosite pH. This discrepancy results from acidic by-products of microbial metabolism as well as from chemical interactions resulting from charged soil colloids. With the former, the microbial colony serves as a point source of the acidic product. Effect of the metabolic product on neighboring populations depends upon their sensitivity to the acid and the concentration of the acid. The latter are affected by the quantities of acid produced and the diffusion rates. An interesting indirect effect of soil pH can be an inhibition of microbial metabolic activity by the organic acid itself and not the pH resulting from the presence of that acid. Kilham and Alexander (1984) recently postulated that organic acid production is a mechanism for stimulating organic matter accumulation in flooded, acidic soil systems. The inhibitory effect of the acid results from the un-ionized acid interacting with the microbial cell. Thus, the indirect pH effect relates to the conversion of the negatively charged acid anion to the uncharged species at pH values below the acid pK_a.

A similar effect on microsite pH results from charged colloids, such as soil clays and humic acids. The most common clay materials, silicate clays (Brady, 1984) ordinarily carry a negative charge. Thus, in an aqueous suspension, a cloud of hydrogen ions is formed around the clay particle. An enzymatic reaction catalyzed in the vicinity of the clay particle in actuality occurs at a more acidic pH value than is indicated by measurements of the overall soil pH. These differences explain, at least in part, such contradictory data as the minimum pH for autotrophic nitrification being pH 5.5 yet autotrophic nitrifiers can be detected in soils with pH values of $4.5-5.5$ (Dommerges et al., 1978) as well as much of the variation of enzyme optimum pH values recorded in the literature.

1.1.2.4. Clay Interactions. Clay interactions are of paramount importance to the microbial activity in any ecosystem containing appreciable concentrations of these minerals. Because clay minerals are negatively charged and microbial cells, enzymes, and many substrates and products are also charged, interaction with clay minerals are expected to have some effect on microbial function in soil. Although at the prevailing soil pHs, both the clay minerals and microbial cells and enzymes are negatively charged, adsorption of the organic materials to the clay can occur through physical adsorption (van der Waals' forces), electrostatic attraction or chemical adsorption, hydrogen bonding, and coordination complexes (Stevenson, 1982). The interaction of clay minerals and soil organic components have been extensively reviewed (Stevenson, 1982; Marshall, 1971), hence the discussion herein is limited to indicating that clay minerals can and will interact with the microorganism and its substrate or products in a manner that may stimulate, retard, or even have no effect on the rate of growth and function (Lynch, 1984).

1.1.2.5. O_2 (Redox Potential). The role of free oxygen levels and redox potential in selection of microbial populations is unquestioned. Of interest to the present discussion is the variation of these parameters within a given microsite and the resultant effect on the growth and activity of the microbial community. Probably the most commonly cited example of soil heterogeneity involves the concurrent occurrence of nitrification (an obligatorily aerobic process) with denitrification (an anoxic process) in a soil sample. Early postulates of *aerobic denitrification* (Broadbent and Stojanovic, 1952) were clarified by subsequent delineation of the relationship of soil granular structure and microsite variation (Greenwood, 1962). These studies demonstrated that the soil granular structure is such that aerobic processes can occur on the granule surface concurrent with the existence of anoxic sites and processes within the granule. Tiedje and co-workers (Tiedje et al., 1984; Sextone et al., 1985) have recently shown through the use of microoxygen probes that such anoxic sites can exist in soil granules. The occurrence of this phenomenon in situ may be more common than Tiedje's data suggest in that the internal granular oxygen levels would not only be determined by diffusion limitation but also by oxygen consumption rates of the surface microbial population. Thus, in an ecosystem with an active nitrogen mineralizing population providing ammonium for the autotrophic nitrifiers, a sufficient autotrophic nitrifier population could develop to limit the quantities of oxygen reaching the interior of the granule.

1.1.3. Biotic Interactions. The range and implications of biological interactions in a variety of ecosystems was recently reviewed by Alexander (1981). The topic is presented herein only as a reminder that such interactions may retard or stimulate the growth and function of the microbial population of interest to the autecologist. Readers are referred to the previously cited review for an inclusive evaluation.

Biotic interactions include predator – prey and parasite – host interactions as well as the variety of effects on microbial growth due to the excretion of a variety of microbial products into the soil. These factors may stimulate microbial growth through the production of carbon and/or energy sources or through population control as a result of predation or parasitism. The impact of these observations is that ecologists must always remember that their interesting microbes do not exist in a vacuum and that other, perhaps less interesting organisms, may be impacting the microbial population in a manner to cause anomalous behavior. The practical consideration resulting from this observation is that for a complete understanding of the behavior of individual microbial species in an ecosystem, population densities of a variety of microbes must be analyzed. This necessitates utilization of some of the factorial analysis, computer modeling, and other procedures discussed in the next section.

2.0. LABORATORY METHODS FOR AUTECOLOGY STUDIES

Past studies of individual species in complex ecosystems have generally been limited to those organisms that can be easily recognized or to where the needs for the study were sufficient to spur development of the necessary specialized analytical techniques, such as the use of fluorescent antibody procedures. Yet, with the development of rapid identification procedures and the spreading use of microcomputers, analyses of greater complexity will become common. The next few chapters of this monograph demonstrate the available techniques as well as some of the developing tools for examination of population dynamics of individual microbial species. Since the details of these procedures and their usage will be presented in the appropriate chapters, the discussion here is limited more to the philosophical basis for such procedures and an evaluation of past problems and limitations that may be overcome by the developing procedures.

Five major areas of study or discussion are apparent in evaluating an autecology project. These are (1) definition of the species or functional entity, (2) visualization or detection of this entity in a complex environmental sample, (3) separation of the active from the inactive individuals, (4) evaluation of the role or impact of the species unit in the ecosystem, and (5) analysis of the data (modeling).

2.1. Problems of Species Identity

Autecology was defined initially in this discussion as "the study of the relationships between the environment and the different organisms that make up a biological complex in a single locale." Therefore, the first decision to be made in initiating an autecology study is to decide whether to evaluate named taxonomic units (species diversity Chapter 6) or individual biochemical or functional taxa (Mills, 1985). Advantages and disadvantages are found with either choice. The more traditional procedure is the isolation and analysis of individual species in that such analyses can be compared with the literature pertaining to the species in question. A major assumption in use of taxonomically defined units is that these units, be they genera or species, are stable as defined. A significant limitation in species diversity studies is the number of taxonomic tests that must be conducted to assure that the organism(s) isolated are indeed the species of interest. This is simplified where the microbes exhibits a unique property or where it has been possible to develop highly specific serological tests, for example, detection of *Salmonella* using specific antibodies or rhizobia or nitrifiers with fluorescent antibodies. In contrast, the evaluation of the variation in populations of functional taxa avoids the taxonomic questions of species identification. Thus, the number of biochemical or morphological traits analyzed to group the organisms may in general be reduced. The latter procedure while providing meaningful data for the specific site and perhaps closely related situations is hampered when it comes to comparing the results to other unrelated systems. Perhaps a valid compromise between these two extremes of taxonomic analysis—none versus total species identification—would be to include a limited number of known species in the functional taxa analysis. In this case, some of the diversity could be attributed to variation of known species and those that are closely related.

2.2. Visualization of Species or Taxa

Once the species unit has been defined, a marker or means of identification of the organism in mixed culture must be developed or selected. For plant or animal pathogens, such traits may be as simple as measuring host–pathogen interactions. With other less distinct microorganisms, this task may be more difficult, if not seemingly impossible. Where such phenotypic traits as pigment production or a distinctive morphological characteristic cannot be used, antibiotic sensitive mutants or fluorescent antibody procedures have proven to be quite valuable. As will be discussed in Chapters 2 and 3, these techniques do have their limitations. With the former, the antibiotic auxotroph selection must be demonstrated to have no effect or minimal effect on the survival and function of the microbe in situ. For example, antibiotic resistant *Rhizobium* mutants must retain the survival, nodulation, and nitrogen fixation capacity of the parent. Among the complications of the fluorescent antibody procedures are those associated with the specificity of the antibody. The antibody must be sufficiently specific to label only the species or strain of interest, yet not so specific as to label only a subset or strain of the species of interest.

Species and functional analytical procedures obviously necessitate collection of large masses of data. With the objectives of noting how individual populations vary with time in relationship to many other taxa in an environmental sample, the task of data collection and analysis becomes nearly insurmountable. Relief is found in the adaptations of computers to data collection and analysis (Chapter 4). With automated procedures, the amount of data that can be collected with the standard materials and personnel commitments is vastly increased. The introduction of computer assisted data collection and analytical procedures has made detailed microbial autecological research a realizable goal.

2.3. Separation of Active from Inactive Individuals

Although the general tendency of a microbiologist exploring a new ecosystem is to count microbes present using some relatively nonselective medium such as nutrient agar or soil extract agar, such data are frequently of little or no value. This conclusion is based upon the observation that microorganisms may exist in a variety of resting stages; spores, conidia, sclerotia, endospores, and so on. Thus, generalized plate counts are only of value where it can reasonably be concluded that the microorganisms are actively growing in situ and that representative microbial populations are capable of growth on the isolation medium. Microorganisms may be anticipated to be actively growing in pioneer communities, such as during the colonization of volcanic ash, during the invasion of susceptible tissues (as is shown by invasion of tissue by pathogenic organisms), or following the drastic perturbation of the ecosystem. This disturbance involves release of the chemical or physical limitations to microbial growth and activity. For example, oxygen and organic matter availability limitations are reduced when a virgin soil is plowed. The above-ground biomass is incorporated into the soil and the soil structure and oxygen regime is disrupted by the mixing of the soil. The resultant burst of microbial activity combined with the reduced input of fixed carbon causes a dramatic decline in the concentrations of colloidal soil organic matter within the soil matrix (Tate, 1985).

   Most communities contain actively growing, resting microbial propagules, and inactive microorganisms. The analytical difficulties associated with occurrence of these inactive or resting organisms are demonstrated quite vividly by the problems of assessing the impact of fungal activity in a soil system. Fungi may exist as active mycelia or in a variety of resting stages. With many of the more commonly observed genera (i.e., those readily noted on laboratory agar), millions of conidia or spores for every mycelial unit per gram of soil are detected. Hence, simply counting colonies that grow on a general fungal enumeration medium, such as rose bengal agar (Menzies, 1965), vastly overestimates the role of such organisms in the soil ecosystem. For accurate determination of fungal activity, the use of specific antibiotic inhibitors (Nakas and Klein, 1980; Tate and Mills, 1983) or direct observation of fungal hyphae is necessary. The more accurate but rather time-consuming procedures are the direct microscopic techniques (Van Veen and Paul, 1979). A similar situation exists with soil bacteria. In a study of microorganisms within the profile of Pahokee muck, a drained organic soil, it was noted that the metabolic rate for a variety of carbonaceous substrates per 1000 bacteria increased with soil depth (Tate, 1979). Thus, although greater bacterial populations were found within the top few centimeters of soil, many of the bacteria were inactive. As the environmental pressures of reduced oxygen and metabolizable substrate input and elevated soil moisture increased, the number of total bacteria present decreased as the proportion of the bacteria that were active increased.

The direct observation of microbial propagules in a sample gives a better estimate of microbial contribution to soil respiration, but simple direct observation techniques do not differentiate between living, living but inactive, and dead cells. Similarly, use of fluorescent antibody procedures allows estimation of population densities of specific taxa but reveals nothing concerning the activity of the microbe. Vital stains and autoradiographic procedures have been developed to demonstrate respiration of individual microorganisms in situ. The combination of fluorescent antibodies and vital stains has proven to be quite useful in determining active microorganisms in aquatic samples (Mills and Wassel, 1980). The details of the procedure are discussed in Chapter 2. Essentially the fluorescence associated with the labeled antibodies separates the microbes of interest from others present in the sample whereas the presence of the vital stain within the cell divides the populations into active and inactive propagules. Although this procedure retains the difficulties associated with the use of specific antibody preparations, which were discussed in part previously, use of this technique has become relatively common in aquatic studies. It would be interesting to determine the value of the procedure with the more complex soil ecosystems where complexing of the stain with soil colloids may be a problem.

A further refinement of the immunofluorescence procedures involves the use of autoradiographic techniques to label metabolically active microbes. This study has the advantage that not only are the actively respiring microbes labeled, but a measure of the extent of the metabolism and the substrate(s) oxidized is provided. Also, the relative contribution of the species under study to total metabolism of the substrate in the site is indicated by comparing nonfluorescing microbes containing the silver grains indicative of presence of the radioactive substrate in their cells with fluorescing populations containing the silver grains. The immunofluorescent–autoradiographic procedure is limited by the fact that if the microbes are not metabolizing the ^{14}C-labeled substrate amended to the sample, then their metabolic activity remains undetected. This difficulty is lessened by the fact that the metabolic capabilities of the taxa of interest are likely well known and therefore radiolabeled substrates could be selected, which the microbe should be metabolizing in situ. Where this is not possible, a variety of radiolabeled substrates will have to be used. These are only two currently available procedures used to determine the activity of specific microbial populations in situ. Both suffer from the fact that they are relatively laborious. Thus, the number of samples that can be analyzed in a reasonable time frame is limited. Perhaps as interest in this type of study expands, and the computer data collection capabilities become more commonly available, some automation of the procedure will be possible. It should be reasonably easy to develop a computer assisted procedure for enumerating fluorescent cells and for counting silver grains on the slide.

2.4. Evaluation of the Role or Impact of the Species Unit

Because of the existence of inactive microbes in most ecosystems as well as their metabolic versatility, it is incumbent upon microbial ecologists to relate their microbes to a role or function within the site. In many instances, the organism may be merely supplying an exogenous nutrient source, such as occurs during the die-off of sewage organisms in soil ecosystems, or the microbes may be existing in a resting state until a suitable host for propagation is encountered (as is observed with the overwintering of sclerotia of plant pathogenic fungi). Alternatively, the microorganisms may be actively growing and reproducing in the site. This potential for growth and function may or may not relate to the biogeochemical process of interest to the microbial ecologist; that is, a microorganism present in a sample may be phenotypically capable of catalyzing a given reaction but the activities may not be induced under the prevailing environmental conditions. For example, because of the obligatory linkage of ammonium or nitrite oxidation with energy generation by obligate autotrophic nitrifiers, it is reasonable to assume that the presence of metabolically active nitrifying bacteria in a sample indicates that the organism is contributing to the soil nitrification capacity. These organisms have no other mechanism for energy generation. This is not the situation with heterotrophic nitrifiers, in that the organisms exist quite well without the electrons supplied during nitrification. Thus, these organisms may be present and contribute nothing to the quantities of oxidized nitrogen in the site. Similar data analysis problems result from the respiratory diversity of denitrifiers. These bacteria can use molecular oxygen or nitrogen oxides as terminal electron acceptors. Thus, their presence in the soil samples is not an indication of their role in denitrification. Denitrifier population densities may not even correlate with the denitrification potential of the soil sample (Terry and Tate, 1980).

The current state of the art in this portion of microbial autecological research is rather limited. At this time, many of the conclusions are related to speculation and extension of test tube studies to native ecosystems. Hope is seen for those studies where radiolabeled substrates may be used, but direct measurement capabilities for other processes are more limited. A viable option, at this time, involves the concurrent analysis of the population dynamics of a number of microbial species. Through the combination of actual observations in situ and the knowledge of the metabolic capabilities of each of the species, a coherent model could be developed. With the experience and methods currently available, such studies would seem unwieldy and rather insurmountable to the individual seeking to finish graduate studies in a reasonable time or the professor desiring tenure or promotion, but as microcomputers and laboratory automation becomes more common, these barriers will be removed.

2.5. Data Analysis

Data analysis and development of total ecosystem models are of little interest if autecology research does not contain a mandate to explain the presence of the microbial species in situ. That is, if the objective is to simply develop a list of sites where a specific microorganism could be found or isolated, sophisticated data analysis is not needed, but if the objective is to determine the role or impact of the presence of the microbe in situ, data analysis can become quite complicated. As was indicated previously, with the development of factorial analysis (Chapter 5) and species diversity (Chapter 6) procedures, large quantities of data are amassed. Such data needs to be reduced to a coherent model of the microbial community of the site.

Comparison of community structure models and observing the changes of this structure with environmental perturbation provides a measure of the role of the various organisms in situ. Tate and Mills (1983) used this sort of procedure to evaluate the effect of cropping on bacterial community composition of Pahokee muck. In their study, functional units rather than bacterial species were studied. Obviously similar procedures could be used with species as the taxonomic unit. Several examples of such studies are provided in Chapter 6. The Mills and Tate work was limited by the number of samples that could be processed in the laboratory, hence average diversity of the soil sites was examined. With automation of the laboratory procedures, changes in the species diversity and behavior of populations of individual species of interest could be easily followed.

These few comments are provided simply to indicate the importance of collecting as much data as possible from a given site and the need of complex analytical procedures to develop descriptive models of the ecosystem from the data. The reader is referred to the chapters that follow to gain a more meaningful discussion of this subject.

3.0. CONCLUSIONS

Microbial autecology has been defined as the evaluation of the behavior of the population of a single species within an ecosystem. Implicit within this definition is the fact that this study must include a determination of the effect of the species in question on the biotic and abiotic parameters of the behavior of the organism. Thus, by definition "mining expeditions" into an ecosystem for unique microorganisms, are not autecological research. Recent trends in microbial ecology have been away from autecology research and towards synecology or process microbiology. Major impetus for this change in focus is the result, at least in part, of the great difficulty associated with the visualization and identification of individual microbial species in a complex ecosystem sample. Where this limitation has not been encountered; such as within the discipline of plant pathology, in the study of those physically unique organisms, or with the identification of organisms for which specialized techniques have been developed, autecological research is flourishing. Growth in developing an understanding of the behavior of most other microbes in situ has awaited the evolution of more specialized techniques. With the development of techniques to observe the individual cells of many species of bacteria and fungi (e.g., fluorescent antibody techniques) and the growing availability of computerization of data collection and analytical procedures, these limitations to the science are being alleviated. As documentation of this conclusion, the following chapters are presented. The techniques described are in many cases borrowed from other areas of study; but, as each author has adequately demonstrated, the procedures are quite readily adaptable to the study of microbial autecology. The reader is thus invited to evaluate the methods sections plus those chapters describing the current state of environmental microbial autecological research and the future for such research. It is my sincere hope that study of these chapters will spur the adventurous scientist into opening the "black box" of process microbiology and delving into the inner workings of our ecosystem.

REFERENCES

Alexander, M. (1971). *Microbial Ecology*, Wiley, New York.

Alexander, M. (1977). *Introduction to Soil Microbiology*, Wiley, New York.

Alexander, M. (1981). Why microbial predators and parasites do not eliminate their prey and hosts. *Ann. Rev. Microbiol.*, **35**:113–133.

Atlas, R. M. (1981). Microbial degradation of petroleum hydrocarbons: An environmental perspective, *Microbiol. Rev.*, **45**:180–209.

Bacon, C. W., J. K. Porter, J. D. Robbins, and E. S. Luttrell (1977). *Epichloe typhina* from toxic tall fescue grasses. *Appl. Environ. Microbiol.*, **34**:576–581.

Barber, D. A. and J. M. Lynch (1977). Microbial growth in the rhizosphere. *Soil Biol. Biochem.*, **9**:305–308.

Barber, L. E. (1980). Enumeration, effectiveness, and pH resistance of *Rhizobium meliloti* populations in Oregon soils. *Soil Sci. Soc. Am. J.*, **44**:537–539.

Baross, J. A. and J. W. Deming (1983). Growth of "black smoker" bacteria at temperatures of at least 250°C. *Nature (London)*, **303**:423–426.

Bennett, O. L., E. L. Mathias, and C. B. Sperow (1976). Double cropping for hay and no-tillage corn production as affected by sod species with rates of atrazine and nitrogen. *Agron. J.*, **68**:250–254.

Bohlool, B. B. and E. L. Schmidt (1970). Immunofluorescent detection of *Rhizobium japonicum* in soils. *Soil Sci.*, **110**:229–236.

Bohlool, B. B. and E. L. Schmidt (1973). Persistence and competition aspects of *Rhizobium japonicum* observed in soil by immunofluorescence microscopy. *Soil Sci. Soc. Am. Proc.*, **37**:561–564.

Boonkerd, B. and R. W. Weaver (1982). Survival of cowpea rhizobia in soil as affected by soil temperature and moisture. *Appl. Environ. Microbiol.*, **43**:585–589.

Brady, N. C. (1984). *The Nature and Property of Soils*, Macmillan, New York.

Broadbent, F. E. and B. F. Stojanovic (1952). The effect of partial pressure of oxygen on some soil nitrogen transformations. *Soil Sci. Soc. Am. Proc.*, **16**:359–363.

Brock, T. D. and G. K. Darland (1970). Limits of microbial existence: Temperature and pH. *Science*, **169**:1316–1318.

Castellvi, J. and L. O'Shananan (1977). Nitrificacion heterotrophica par bacterias marines. *Invest. Pesq.*, **41**:501–507.

Chao, W. -L. and M. Alexander (1982). Influence of soil characteristics on the survival of *Rhizobium* in soils undergoing drying. *Soil Sci. Soc. Am. J.,* **46**:949–952.

Crozat, Y., J. C. Cleyet-Marel, J. J. Giraud, and M. Obaton (1982). Survival rates of *Rhizobium japonicum* populations introduced into different soils. *Soil Biol. Biochem,* **14**:401–405.

Dommergues, Y. R., L. W. Belser, and E. L. Schmidt (1978). "Limiting factors for microbial growth and activity in soil," in M. Alexander, ed., *Advances in Microbial Ecology,* Vol. **2**, Plenum, New York, pp. 49–104.

Doxtander, K. G., and M. Alexander (1966). Nitrification by heterotrophic soil microorganisms. *Soil Sci. Soc. Am. Proc.,* **30**:351–355.

Dughri, M. H. and P. J. Bottomley (1983). Effect of acidity on the composition of an indigenous soil population of *Rhizobium trifolii* found in nodules of *Trifolium subterraneum.* L. *Appl. Environ. Microbiol.,* **46**:1207–1213.

Eylar, O. R. and E. L. Schmidt (1959). A survey of heterotrophic microorganisms from soil for ability to form nitrite and nitrate. *J. Gen. Microbiol.,* **20**:473–481.

Fluker, B. J. (1958). Soil temperatures. *Soil Sci.,* **68**:250–254.

Franco, A. A. and D. N. Munns (1982). Acidity and aluminum restraints on nodulation, nitrogen fixation, and growth of *Phaseolus vulgaris* in solution culture. *Soil Sci. Soc. Am. J.,* **46**:296–301.

Greenwood, D. J. (1962). Nitrification and nitrate dissimilation in soil. II. Effect of oxygen concentration. *Plant Soil,* **17**:378–391.

Gupta, S. C., W. E. Larson, and D. R. Linden (1983). Tillage and surface residue effects on soil upper boundary temperatures. *Soil Sci. Soc. Am. J.,* **47**:1212–1218.

Hagedorn, C. (1979). Relationship of antibiotic resistance to effectiveness in *Rhizobium trifolii* populations. *Soil Sci. Soc. Am. J.,* **43**:921–925.

Hartel, P. G. and M. Alexander (1983). Growth and survival of cowpea rhizobia in acid, aluminum-rich soils. *Soil Sci. Soc. Am. J.,* **47**:502–506.

Hartel, P. G., A. M. Whelan, and M. Alexander (1983). Nodulation of cowpea rhizobia in acid, aluminum-rich soils. *Soil Sci. Soc. Am. J.,* **47**:514–517.

Heinen, W. and A. M. Lauwers (1981). Growth of bacteria at 100°C and beyond. *Arch. Microbiol.,* **129**:127–128.

Helal, H. M. and D. R. Sauerbeck. (1983). Method to study turnover processes in soil layers of different proximity to roots. *Soil Biol. Biochem.,* **15**:223–225.

Hirsch, P., L. Overrein, and M. Alexander (1961). Formation of nitrite and nitrate by actinomycetes and fungi. *J. Bacteriol.,* **82**:442–448.

Hughes, T. A., J. G. Lecce, and G. H. Elkan (1979). Modified fluorescent technique using rhodamine for studies of *Rhizobium japonicum*-soybean symbiosis. *Appl. Environ. Microbiol.,* **37**:1243–1244.

Inniss, W. E. (1975). Interaction of temperature and psychrophilic microorganisms. *Ann. Rev. Microbiol.,* **29**:445–465.

Isaque, M. and A. H. Cornfield (1972). Nitrogen mineralization and nitrification during incubation of East Pakistan tea soils in relation to pH. *Plant Soil,* **37**:91–95.

Isaque, M. and A. H. Cornfield (1974). Nitrogen mineralization and nitrification in relation to incubation temperature in an acid Bangladesh soil lacking autotrophic nitrifying organisms. *Trop. Agric.,* **51**:37–41.

Keyser, H. H. and D. N. Munns (1979a). Effects of calcium, manganese, and aluminum on growth of rhizobia in acid media. *Soil Sci. Soc. Am. J.,* **43**:500–503.

Keyser, H. H. and D. N. Munns (1979b). Tolerance of rhizobia to acidity, aluminum, and phosphate. *Soil Sci. Soc. Am. J.,* **43**:519–523.

Keyser, H. H., D. N. Munns, and J. S. Hohenberg (1979). Acid tolerance of rhizobia in culture and in symbiosis with cowpea. *Soil Sci. Soc. Am. J.,* **43**:719–722.

Kilham, O. W. and M. Alexander (1984). A basis for organic matter accumulation in soils under anaerobiosis. *Soil Sci.,* **137**:419–427.

Kingsley, M. T. and B. B. Bohlool (1981). Release of *Rhizobium* spp. from tropical soils and recovery for immunofluorescence enumeration. *Appl. Environ. Microbiol.,* **42**:241–248.

Kristjansson, J. K. and G. A. Alfredsson (1983). Distribution of *Thermus* spp. in icelandic hot springs and a thermal gradient. *Appl. Environ. Microbiol.,* **45**:1785–1789.

Kuykendall, L. D. and D. F. Weber (1978). Genetically marked *Rhizobium* identifiable as inoculum strain in nodules of soybean plants grown in fields populated with *Rhizobium japonicum*. *Appl. Environ. Microbiol.,* **36**:915–919.

Lascano, R. J. and C. H. M. Van Bavel (1983). Experimental verification of a model to predict soil moisture and temperature profiles. *Soil Sci. Soc. Am. J.,* **47**:441–448.

Lloyd, A. B. (1959). The endophytic fungus of perennial ryegrass. *N. Z. J. Agric. Res.,* **2**:1187–1194.

Lowendorf, H. S. and M. Alexander (1983a). Identification of *Rhizobium phaseoli* strains that are tolerant or sensitive to soil acidity. *Appl. Environ. Microbiol.,* **45**:737–742.

Lowendorf, H. S. and M. Alexander (1983b). Selecting *Rhizobium meliloti* for inoculation of alfalfa planted in acid soils. *Soil Sci. Soc. Am. J.,* **47**:935–938.

Lowendorf, H. S., A. M. Baya, and M. Alexander (1981). Survival of *Rhizobium* in acid soils. *Appl. Environ. Microbiol.,* **42**:951–957.

Lynch, J. M. (1984). *Soil Biotechnology: Microbiological Factors in Crop Productivity,* Blackwell, Oxford.

Mahler, R. L. and A. G. Wollum II (1980). Influence of water potential on the survival of rhizobia in Goldsboro loamy sand. *Soil Sci. Soc. Am. J.,* **44**:988–992.

Mahler, R. L. and A. G. Wollum II (1981). The influence of soil water potential and soil texture on the survival of *Rhizobium japonicum* and *Rhizobium leguminosarum* isolates in the soil. *Soil Sci. Soc. Am. J.,* **45**:761–766.

Marshall, K. C. (1971). "Sorptive interactions between soil particles and microorganisms," in, A. D. McLaren and J. Skujins, ed., *Soil Biochemistry,* Vol. 2, Dekker, New York, pp. 409–445.

Materon, L. A. and C. Hagedorn (1982). Competitiveness of *Rhizobium trifolii* strains associated with red clover (*Trifolium pratense* L.) in Mississippi soils. *Appl. Environ. Microbiol.,* **44**:1096–1101.

McNeil, D. L. (1982). Variations in ability of *Rhizobium japonicum* strains to nodulate soybeans and maintain fixation in the presence of nitrate. *Appl. Environ. Microbiol.,* **44**:647–652.

Menzies, J. D. (1965). "Fungi," in C. A. Black, ed., *Methods of Soil Analysis,* Part 2, Am. Soc. Agron., Madison. pp. 1502–1505.

Mills, A. L. (1985). "Acid mine drainage: microbial impact on the recovery of soil and water ecosystems," in R. L. Tate III and D. A. Klein, ed. *Soil Reclamation Processes: Microbiological Analyses and Applications,* Dekker, New York, pp. 35–81.

Mills, A. L. and R. A. Wassel (1980). Aspects of diversity measurements for microbial communities. *Appl. Environ. Microbiol.,* **40**:578–586.

Munervar, F. and A. G. Wollum II (1981). Effect of high root temperature and *Rhizobium* strain on nodulation, nitrogen fixation, and growth of soybeans. *Soil Sci. Soc. Am. J.,* **45**:1113–1120.

Nakas, J. P. and D. A. Klein (1980). Mineralization capacity of bacteria and fungi from the rhizosphere-rhizoplane of a semiarid grassland. *Appl. Environ. Microbiol.,* **39**:113–117.

Neill, J. C. (1941). The endophytes of *Lolium* and *Festuca. N. Z. J. Sci. Technol. Sect. A,* **23**:185–193.

Noel, K. D. and W. J. Brill (1980). Diversity and dynamics of indigenous *Rhizobium japonicum* populations. *Appl. Environ. Microbiol.,* **40**:931–938.

Odum, E. P. (1971). *Fundamentals of Ecology,* Saunders, Philadelphia.

Orchard, V. A. and F. J. Cook (1983). Relationship between soil respiration and soil moisture. *Soil Biol. Biochem.,* **15**:447–453.

Osa-Afiana, L. O. and M. Alexander (1979). Effect of moisture on the survival of *Rhizobium* in soil. *Soil Sci. Soc. Am. J.,* **43**:925–930.

Osa-Afiana, L. O. and M. Alexander (1982a). Differences among cowpea rhizobia in tolerance to high temperature and desiccation in soil. *Appl. Environ. Microbiol.,* **43**:435–439.

Osa-Afiana, L. O. and M. Alexander (1982b). Clays and the survival of *Rhizobium* in soil during desiccation. *Soil Sci. Soc. Am. J.,* **46**:285–288.

Paul, E. A. and E. L. Schmidt (1961). Formation of free amino acids in rhizosphere and nonrhizosphere soil. *Soil Sci. Soc. Am. Proc.,* **25**:359–362.

Pena-Cabriales, J. J. and M. Alexander (1979). Survival of *Rhizobium* in soils undergoing drying. *Soil Sci. Soc. Am. J.,* **43**:962–966.

Pena-Cabriales, J. J. and M. Alexander (1983a). Growth of *Rhizobium* in soil amended with organic matter. *Soil Sci. Soc. Am. J.,* **47**:241–245.

Pena-Cabriales, J. J. and M. Alexander (1983b). Growth of *Rhizobium* in unamended soil. *Soil Sci. Soc. Am. J.,* **47**:81–84.

Ratkowsky, D. A., J. Olley, T. A. McMeekin, and A. Ball (1982). Relationship between temperature and growth rate of bacterial cultures. *J. Bacteriol.,* **149**:1–5.

Ramacle, J. (1977). The role of heterotrophic nitrification in acid forest soils— preliminary results. *Ecol. Bull. (Stockholm),* **25**:560–561.

Robert, F. M. and E. L. Schmidt (1983). Population changes and persistence of *Rhizobium phaseoli* in soil and rhizospheres. *Appl. Environ. Microbiol.,* **45**:550–556.

Rovira, A. D. and R. Campbell (1974). Scanning electron microscopy of microorganisms on the roots of wheat. *Microbial Ecol.,* **1**:15–23.

Sandbeck, K. A. and D. M. Ward (1982). Temperature adaptations in the terminal processes of anaerobic decomposition of Yellowstone National Park and Icelandic Hot Spring Microbial Mats. *Appl. Environ. Microbiol.,* **44**:844–851.

Sextone, A. J., N. P. Revsbech, T. B. Parkin, and J. M. Tiedje (1985). Direct measurement of oxygen profiles and denitrification rates in soil aggregates. *Soil Sci. Soc. Am. J.,* **49**:645–651.

Smith, M. S. and J. M. Tiedje (1979). The effect of roots on soil denitrification. *Soil Sci. Soc. Am. J.,* **43**:951–955.

Stevenson, F. J. (1982). *Humus Chemistry,* Wiley, New York.

Tate, R. L. III (1977). Nitrification in Histosols: A potential role for the heterotrophic nitrifiers. *Appl. Environ. Microbiol.,* **33**:911–914.

Tate, R. L. III (1979). Microbial activity in organic soils as affected by soil depth and crop. *Appl. Environ. Microbiol.,* **37**:1085–1090.

Tate, R. L. III (1985). "Microorganisms, ecosystem disturbance, and soil-formation processes," in R. L. Tate III and D. A. Klein, ed. *Soil Reclamation Processes: Microbiological Analyses and Applications,* Dekker, New York, pp. 1–33.

Tate, R. L. III and A. L. Mills (1983). Cropping and the diversity and function of bacteria in Pahokee muck. *Soil Biol. Biochem.,* **15**:175–179.

Tate, R. L. III and R. E. Terry (1980). Variation in microbial activity in Histosols and its relationship to soil moisture. *Appl. Environ. Microbiol.,* **40**:313–317.

Terry, R. E. and R. L. Tate III (1980). Denitrification as a pathway for nitrate removal from organic soils. *Soil Sci.,* **129**:162–166.

Tiedje, J. M., A. J. Sextone, T. B. Parkin, and N. P. Revsbech (1984). Anaerobic processes in soil. *Plant Soil,* **76**:197–212.

Unger, P. W. (1978). Straw mulch effects on soil temperatures and sorghum germination and growth. *Agron. J.,* **70**:858–864.

Van De Dijk, S. J. and S. R. Troelstra (1980). Heterotrophic nitrification in a peat soil demonstrated by an in situ method. *Plant Soil.,* **57**:11–21.

Van Veen, J. A. and E. A. Paul (1979). Conversion of biovolume measurements of soil microorganisms, grown under various moisture tensions, to biomass and their nutrient content. *Appl. Environ. Microbiol.,* **37**:686–692.

Verstraete, W. and M. Alexander (1973). Heterotrophic nitrification in samples of natural ecosystems. *Environ. Sci. Technol.,* **7**:39–42.

Vidor, C. and R. H. Miller (1980). Relative saprophytic competence of *Rhizobium japonicum* strains in soils as determined by the quantitative fluorescent antibody technique (FA). *Soil Biol. Biochem.,* **12**:483–487.

Wildung, R. E. and T. R. Garland (1985). "Microbial development on oil shale wastes: influence on geochemistry," in R. L. Tate III and D. A. Klein, ed., *Soil Reclamation Processes: Microbiological Analyses and Applications,* Dekker, New York, pp. 107–139.

Wildung, R. E., T. R. Garland, and R. L. Buschbom (1975). The interdependent effects of soil temperature and water content on soil respiration rate and plant root decomposition in arid grassland soils. *Soil Biol. Biochem.,* **7**:373–378.

Wilson, J. M. and D. M. Griffin (1975). Water potential and the respiration of microorganisms in the soil. *Soil Biol. Biochem.,* **7**:199–204.

2 DETERMINATION OF INDIVIDUAL ORGANISMS AND THEIR ACTIVITIES IN SITU

Aaron L. Mills and Pamela E. Bell
Department of Environmental Sciences
University of Virginia
Charlottesville, Virginia

1.0. INTRODUCTION AND BACKGROUND

1.1. Importance of the Individual Microorganism

Even more than for the plant and animal kingdoms, questions about the behavior and distribution of individual species of bacteria relate directly to the activity of the organisms and their function in the ecosystem. Autecological studies, therefore, are based on the individual species and its relationship to its environment irrespective of relationships with other organisms. Clearly, interspecific interactions are important, but they are of autecological importance only insofar as they effect the function of the microbe of interest. The environmental impact of microbial processes is invariably the sum of the contribution of each individual organism of the same or different *species*, located in close physical proximity. Microbiologists, rarely, if ever, deal with individual organisms (cells), except to quantify the total population density catalyzing a reaction of interest. Because of the difficulties in defining microbial species, microbiologists must depart slightly from the classical definition of autecology. Whereas autecology normally refers to studies of a population of a defined species and its environment, we will expand the usage to include functional groups defined as guilds (see Section 1.2).

This chapter deals with microbiological research methods and studies that are perhaps the closest to autecology in its classical usage. We will explore methods for identifying individual cells and for determining specific types of

27

activity. As will be seen, the sole purpose in this effort is to obtain a quantitative view of the numbers and distribution of individuals in situ. Often it is the distribution of an activity rather than a species that is of interest. Using the techniques described here, those activities can often be quantified using basic autecological concepts. The problems of defining species relationships in procaryotes are substantially greater than for the other kingdoms (see Section 2.0). This "problem" often benefits microbial ecology, however, for it tends to direct attention away from a species-centered approach, and instead allows us to focus on the important activities and functions carried out by the microbes.

1.2. Taxonomic Considerations

The fact that microbial autecology necessarily deals with individuals as units of a single group creates a serious problem in terms of identifying the group being examined. Numerical methods of grouping organisms are clearly superior when looked at from a genetic viewpoint. They allow examination of a large number of characteristics of isolates and determination of those with phenotypic similarities. However, such a classification scheme is not always relevant and is rarely useful in ecosystem ecology. Studies of microorganisms in the environment relate to what the cells do; specifically, what functions the organisms carry out. Innumerable studies revolve around the question, "How many cells are doing (or are capable of doing) the specific function that I am interested in without regard for the genetic label (species name) that a numerical analysis of a large number of isolates may provide?" In fact, it is only in certain studies that the species name has great relevance to any ecological question. For example, species identification can be important if the reactions of interest are unique to a single or few species. This would include environmental studies of pathogen behavior, of indicator organisms, or of functional types represented by a genetically limited collection of microbes such as the methanogens or autotrophic nitrifiers.

Ecosystems tend to be biologically redundant, that is, several mechanisms for accomplishing an essential function are generally available. Therefore, if environmental conditions change, a different set of organisms may become the dominant mediator of the reaction of interest. For example, in anaerobic habitats, many fermentors generate acetate from higher molecular weight substrates. To keep the process of organic matter decomposition operating, the acetate must be further oxidized. Two major groups of organisms carry out this function, the sulfate reducers and the methanogens. Although both groups of organisms can oxidize hydrogen, they also support the acetogenic proton reducers. If adequate sulfate is available, the sulfate reducers are the primary group responsible for acetate catabolism, whereas if sulfate is absent, methanogens convert the acetate to carbon dioxide and methane. Because several different "species" capable of carrying out the same reactions (even at the same time) may coexist in a habitat, grouping of those organisms by major function is often desirable. Root (1967) used the term "guild" to describe groups of birds with similar feeding habits, although they were of different species. Wassel and Mills (1983) used the term to describe groups of bacteria clustered by numerical techniques, where the number of characters tested for the isolates was insufficient to claim relatedness near the species level. Guilds are often appropriate means of naming and considering functional groups in microbial ecology. Such terminology should be considered to replace the often misused term "population" when speaking of groups of organisms sharing the same function, for example, the guild of sulfate reducers, *not* the population of sulfate reducers. We shall use the term population to describe only those organisms that have such a high degree of phenotypic similarity as to be considered as species. We will use the term interchangeably with species, much as is done for the higher kingdoms. We suggest that others do likewise to avoid the confusion that microbial ecologists frequently encounter as a result of overuse and misuse of population.

The direct methods outlined in the later portions of this chapter often aid in the escape from the idea that we must give the organisms names. On the one hand, if we use some specific measure of activity, we can examine all the cells possessing that activity (all members of the guild) without regard for the "taxonomic label." This type of study must also be classified as autecological research. On the other hand, given an isolate that possesses a certain trait, use of specific identifying techniques, namely, immunofluorescence assays, can help us evaluate the behavior of that population (species) in complex ecosystems. Ultimately, it is necessary to combine identification techniques with activity measurements. It is essential to quantify the proportion of a population that is active. It is also important to know how many cells catalyzing the same reaction are of a specific guild.

Direct, sensitive assays are available for quantifying the activities of both guilds and populations. Several of the techniques are being widely used. A few research groups have taken the logical step and combined activity measures with species specific assays to begin to carry out the first true autecological studies that have accurate quantitative methodologies included as part of their protocols. Our purpose here is to provide a description of the techniques that are available at this time for use in direct examinations of individual cells in situ. Our treatment does not pretend to include all of the examples that could have been used. Many of the procedures are well documented and reviewed in other places, and we have sought to provide an entry into that literature, as opposed to inclusion of an exhaustive literature survey. We attempt here to make a case for the role of the direct, in situ procedures in the autecology of microorganisms, but we also include the appropriate warnings of the major limitations of methods currently being used. Further research on, and use of, the approaches outlined here will help to establish these methods as the most acceptable means of examining specific groups of microbes in the environment.

1.3. Importance of Quantitative Considerations

Once a property of interest has been ascribed to an organism, whether the property is pathogenicity or some other function important within an ecosystem, the most frequently asked ecological questions are operational — is the organism of interest present and how abundant is it? Questions of the effect of various parameters, environmental and biological, are often answered by looking for changes in the abundance of the organism of interest. The first question, that of presence or absence, may be seen as a qualitative one, that is, the answer is either yes or no; however, it is obvious that the quantitative aspects of the method used to search for the microbe will determine whether presence of a very few cells or a great many cells will be required for detection. In the case of an organism that causes a disease, demonstration of presence is often adequate to answer the most pressing questions about it, while for organisms with more subtle activities, such as the oxidation of ammonium to nitrite, the abundance is of prime consideration.

If it is assumed that each cell contains the same amount of enzyme (a fact never conclusively demonstrated), then it follows that total activity should be directly proportional to the abundance of the organism. As we will see later, not all individuals of a population or guild contain the same levels of activity. The relative proportion of those containing the activity to the total number provides information as to the nutritional status of the group, be it population or guild, in that specific habitat. Accurate assessment of changes in either total numbers or in the percentage of active cells with time can lead to an understanding of the dynamics of the group, and how various conditions affect growth and survival of the population or guild in the habitat.

1.4. History of Enumeration

Plate counts have been the "mainstay" of quantitative microbiology since shortly after Mrs. Hesse suggested agar as a solidifying agent for Koch's cultural investigations. While a variety of methods are used to get the appropriate number of organisms on or in the medium, the basic principle of dilution to physically separate individual cells followed by counting of colonies that presumably arise from single cells can be attributed to Koch's early efforts in isolation of pathogens. Two general types of enumerations have been devised for the plate count (and its cousin, the most probable number technique — MPN), selective and nonselective. The selective counts assume that some material added to or deleted from the growth medium enhances development of a single type of organism while inhibiting the growth of all others. Included here for the purposes of this discussion are the differential media that allow growth of many organisms, but which induce a pigment formation or cause some visible change in or about the colony so that individuals of one type are highlighted. Nonselective media, in theory, allow growth of all organisms present. The underlying objective for using the latter media is to enumerate total microbial (bacterial) communities. To this end, a variety of rich media have been used including yeast extract, animal and vegetable protein extracts, and mixtures of sugars and amino acids. Evaluations of effectiveness of various media has been in terms of those that produce the highest counts of total organisms, or of the organism in question.

Many individuals have decried the use of plate counts (and similar methods) even to the extent of saying that ". . . the plate count is the worst thing that ever happened to marine microbiology because it is so misused," (Hamilton, 1979). In many cases this observation is well founded, nevertheless, cultural counts remain the most frequently used means of gathering information on either total or specific microbial abundance. The use of plate counts in certain situations appears to be warranted by cost and time considerations, and, in many cases, provides a useful means of predicting some factor or determining some limit on use of microbiologically contaminated materials. This utility more likely relates to the good correlation of some symptom (such as increased occurrence of a disease or other perturbed state) with a reproducable colony count than to accurate quantification of the numbers of individuals.

Early microscopic observations indicated that there are more microbial cells in samples than are accounted for by plate counts or MPN enumerations (Starkey, 1939). Some feel that many of the cells observed with the microscope are nonviable or dormant (Jannash, 1965; Stevenson, 1978), but maybe not all of the organisms present are capable of growth on the medium used. Most recent research has shown that, while not all cells observed by direct counts are alive or active, the inability of many organisms (individual cells) to produce visible colonies on plates or turbidity in broth is the largest source of inaccuracy in cultural methods. It has been suggested, therefore, that all direct cell counts are overestimates of the true numbers of viable cells, while cultural counts are underestimates.

Differences between direct microscopic results and cultural counts may range, anywhere from 2 to 4 orders of magnitude. Even if only 10% of all the bacteria observed with a direct count method are viable, the differences between the two procedures can not be explained by viable versus nonviable cells; clearly the cultural methods fail to detect a tremendous number of bacteria in soil and water samples.

The search has thus begun for reasonable direct count methods. A variety of stains have been used, but direct visualization is often confounded by particles in the samples that react with stains and mimic bacteria. (This, of course, provides ammunition to those who contend that direct counts represented little or no advantage over cultural techniques.) The advent of the use of fluorescent dyes provides an advancement in our ability to directly observe microbial cells.

Particularly important are those chemicals that combine with biological materials, such as nucleic acids, with a high degree of specificity. Use of compounds such as acridine orange has permitted greatly improved differentiation of most bacteria (and other microbes) from particulate matter. But, quantitation is still a problem.

Initially, microscopes used routinely for fluorescence microscopy employed substage illumination. Thus, to be seen, samples had to be held on a transparent material, namely glass slides. While substage illumination is adequate for many stained preparations (e.g., tissue sections for histologic examination, or classical bacterial stains), resolution is reduced by the requirement for the light generated by the fluorochrome to pass through the cell body as it was directed toward the objective. Furthermore, estimating the number of bacteria in a volume of liquid smeared on a slide is neither accurate nor precise. A major breakthrough in enumeration of microbial populations came with the use of incident illumination, or epifluorescence. In this method the excitation beam is directed at the specimen from above, allowing the full fluorescence to be visualized. Extraneous light is excluded from the observer by a series of beam splitters and filters. This modification not only allowed for a brighter image, but also meant that opaque surfaces could be used to hold the cells (Mills and Maubrey, 1981). Using epifluorescence, a suspension can be quantitatively filtered, the surface of the filter examined, the particles present counted, and the numbers accurately extrapolated to the original sample.

Another modification in direct microbial counts came with the use of Nuclepore filters (Hobbie et al., 1977; Bowden, 1977). Tortuous pore filters often yield counts that are variable and usually lower than anticipated due to loss of cells into the depths of the filter. With Nuclepore membranes, the cells are retained on a flat surface. This simple fact increases both the yield and the precision of the direct count method.

While most investigators accept the fact that direct count methods are preferable in terms of accurately estimating the total abundance of microbes, it is clear that if the approaches and studies described in this chapter are truly representative of microbial ecology, the plate count will continue to be a very important tool. Any technique that examines a population requires, at some time or another, the isolation of organisms. Dilution-culture methods, such as are employed with plate counts, are the only means available for isolations. Even the most advanced methods, such as the fluorescent antibody (FA) techniques, require isolation of the organism presumed to be the one of interest. Difficulties with that presumption will be presented as part of the discussion of the FA technique.

As direct methods become more widely studied, modified and used, plate count and other cultural assays will likely be used primarily as rapid survey techniques, as a means of obtaining isolates for production of antibodies employed in direct assays, and as experimental analytical tools. Other uses would certainly include those such as water quality monitoring where large data sets on performance of the tests have been established.

2.0. INDIRECT METHODS

2.1. Use of Cultural Methods

While this chapter's purpose is to describe direct methods for the examination of the dynamics of guilds and populations in situ, it is useful to preface that discussion with one of the indirect assays provided by cultural methods. The reasons for doing so are twofold: (1) the direct and indirect techniques address the same questions, and (2) direct assays that utilize a single population or serotype rely on an initial survey by cultural methods followed by isolation of the organism of interest by classical plating or other dilution methods. A brief presentation of autecological approaches using plate counts or other cultural methods appropriately introduces the direct techniques for examining natural samples for the abundance dynamics of a specific population or guild.

Although frequent references are made to selective media, few media exist that truly inhibit growth of all organisms not of immediate interest. Most selective media have been developed in response to the need to isolate and enumerate pathogens from environmental samples. For example, Bordet-Gengou agar amended with penicillin inhibits growth of normal flora while allowing the growth of *Bordetella pertussis* (Krieg, 1981). Addition of sodium tellurite to agar suppresses growth of most Gram-positive and Gram-negative organisms with the exception of the *Corynebacterium* sp. Furthermore, the medium has the ability to differentiate among organisms that can grow successfully on the medium; *C. diptheriae* and similar organisms produce colonies that are black as a result of reduction of the tellurite (Krieg, 1981).

Some organisms are conveniently enumerated due to the extreme conditions in which they are active. For example, populations of the autotroph *Thiobacillus ferrooxidans* are most often quantified by an MPN technique using an organic-free medium containing abundant ferrous iron (as an energy source) at a pH of about 2.5 (Silverman and Lundgren, 1958). This is a highly selective medium for enumeration, although recent studies have demonstrated the ubiquitous presence of a heterotrophic contaminant that lives on the excretions of the autotroph (Harrison et al., 1980).

A simpler matter than looking for an individual population is the enrichment method for counting guild members. In fact almost all cultural techniques "select" for guild members rather than for a specific taxonomic group. For example, the ability to use a specific saccharide or amino acid as a sole source of carbon and energy can be used as a convenient selection criterion, simply by providing that substance as the only source of carbon and energy in the plates (this can be difficult in many marine situations where the agar itself may be metabolized by many of the organisms present in the sample). For those organisms that can utilize a compound in the presence of another carbon or energy source materials can be added to the medium to give direct evidence of the activity. Clear zones surrounding colonies catabolizing a lipid emulsion or a cellulosic substance in agar suspension are often used to enumerate individuals

TABLE 1. Examination of Various Guilds of Bacteria Existing in Beach Sands in the Straits of Magellan 2 yr After the Grounding of the VLCC Metula[a]

Guild	Sampling Date			
	May 19	June 3	June 19	August 13
Total	$4.0 \times {}^6$	2.7×10^7	3.9×10^6	9.9×10^6
Starch	—	0	0	9.7×10^5
Chitin	5.2×10^5	7.7×10^5	2.7×10^5	2.0×10^5
Casein	—	6.0×10^5	4.0×10^5	7.1×10^5
Tween 20	—	7.3×10^6	4.0×10^5	1.6×10^6

[a]"Total" refers to counts made on a nonselective medium containing yeast extract and the guilds listed refer to the ability of colonies growing on the agar plates to produce a clearing zone in medium containing the indicated polymer. Unplublished data from the study reported in Colwell et al. (1978).

containing lipolytic or cellulolytic enzymes (Colwell et al., 1978). While these organisms may be from a variety of populations, the questions asked of the guild are identical to those asked of a species. For example — what is the effect of a pollutant on the numbers in the guild (and ultimately on the functions of the guild)? An example of the type of data collected in this manner is shown in Table 1 for a time course study of effects of crude oil on bacterial guilds in beach sands.

Direct plating techniques generally cannot be used to determine how population composition of the guild is altered, although some information is occasionally obtained by observing differences in colonial morphology. To answer questions such as this one, the numerical taxonomic approach is often employed, but the question is one of synecology rather than autecology, namely the relationship of the populations, one to another, and how the structure of the community may be altered.

Cultural methods are often used for autecological studies in laboratory simulations. If an organism is seeded into an environment or a sample of that environment in a laboratory situation, it is often possible to follow the dynamics of the population and correlate the results with measures of appropriately selected activities in the samples. If the sample is sterilized prior to inoculation, a nonselective medium may be used to provide information on the changes in numbers of the organism with time. If a selective or differential medium is used, a population can often be followed in the presence of other organisms. Some authors have utilized antibiotic resistant mutants of the organism of interest to mark the population inoculated into nonsterile samples (Danso et al., 1973). This method represents only a modification of the selective medium approach to following the dynamics of a population and is commonly used in attempts to trace the viability of genetically modified bacteria in the environment.

2.2. Problems with the Use of Cultural Methods

Despite the best efforts of scientists employing cultural techniques, the results, although often informative, are never accurate, and can easily lead to misconceptions about the organisms being considered. Many of the problems associated with the use of cultural counts in autecological studies are the ones leveled against the use of the plate count in general; that is, inaccuracy due to clumping of the cells, failure to spread the cells sufficiently on the plate, intercolony interactions, counting difficulties with spreading organisms, questions of counts of vegetative cells versus germinated spores, and so on. However, the major weakness of the cultural approach is that it is an indirect measure. While the question may be asked "How many members of the species or of the guild are present?" the actual question answered by any cultural technique is "How many organisms (or propagules) present are capable of growth on the medium I have chosen?" At best, the method provides information on the potential for organisms to carry out a specific function, whereas if properly used, the direct assays can tell which cells are actually carrying out a reaction in situ, or if the cells of a given population are viable.

Comparisons of results obtained with direct and indirect assay methods for individuals of a population or a guild suggest that the answers to the aforementioned questions are rarely, if ever, the same. Early work (Trolldenier, 1973) suggested that cultural counts could be related to direct counts by a scaling factor, that is, cultural counts recovered a constant fraction of the total number of cells present (see Fig. 1). This plot yielded a regression equation ($y =$

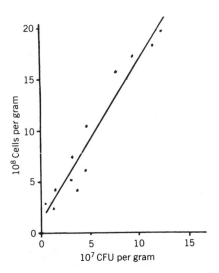

Figure 1. Recovery of microbes from soil by direct count (y axis) versus plate count (x axis). Figure redrawn from Trolldenier (1973).

$900.2 + 15 [x - 49.5]$) with $r = 0.970$. Several papers since that time have suggested that the relationship is not constant. Sample data in support of this concern are provided in Table 2. The good fit observed by Trolldenier (1973) is rarely seen. In the sample data, the regression actually has a substantially different form ($y = 4.37 \times 10^6 + 393.1x$) and $r = 0.07$, the r value indicates little relationship between the two counts.

While enumerating *T. ferrooxidans* in acidic to circumneutral waters, Baker and Mills (1982) found that the conventional MPN method employing the modified 9K medium (Silverman and Lundgren, 1958) underestimated the number of viable cells present at all sites tested. No cells were observed by the cultural method in the circumneutral waters even though the direct methods (described later) indicated the presence of viable organisms. It was further determined that if the appropriate preincubation procedures were conducted, namely, centrifugal separation of bacterial cells and sequential resuspension in liquid of progressively lower pH, *T. ferrooxidans* could be isolated from the higher pH environments. Thus, it became clear that *T. ferrooxidans* could survive periods of exposure to high pH waters and could be easily transported from one site to another in normal lake waters. This concept had not been previously realized, because MPN determinations in circumneutral waters always indicated that no organisms were present. Furthermore, it was the use of a direct assay for active cells of the population that disclosed this misconception.

Despite the lack of accuracy, cultural approaches in experimental situations usually produce results that successfully delineate overall trends in guild or population dynamics. As compared to the direct examination methods, the cultural techniques are less laborious and are often less expensive. Consequently, the classical methods, with appropriate modifications as new information becomes available, will continue to be utilized in many laboratory simulation exercises.

TABLE 2. Comparison of Direct (AODC) and Plate Counts at Stations in Lake Anna, Virginia in 1978[a]

Station	June	July	August	September
C1	8.1×10^5	9.4×10^5	5.1×10^6	4.8×10^6
	2.5×10^1	1.3×10^2	5.0×10^0	2.7×10^2
F1	1.5×10^6	1.0×10^6	6.3×10^6	6.7×10^6
	9.3×10^2	—	3.4×10^1	7.6×10^2
A2	1.8×10^6	6.6×10^5	6.1×10^6	1.1×10^7
	6.0×10^2	2.0×10^3	4.0×10^2	2.0×10^1

[a]Plate count enumerations employed one-half strength nutrient agar. The first of the two numbers given is the direct count in cells per milliliter, and the lower number is the number of colony forming units per millilter.

3.0. DIRECT METHODS

3.1. Direct Assays for Cellular Activity and Identity

Direct assays are of two types: those that are designed to determine the number and distribution of organisms capable of catalyzing a specific activity, for example, uptake of an amino acid, and those that are designed to determine the number and distribution of cells of a specific population, for example, *Legionella pneumophila*. There are some techniques that examine the numbers of total organisms, for example, the AODC (acridine orange direct counts) method; however, these methods have autecologic significance only when used in conjunction with another of the techniques, for example, to help show that silver granules formed during the microautoradiographic process are truly associated with cells. As stated previously, the purest autecological methods employ two types of assays, a population specific assay, namely, immunofluorescence (FA), to determine the total number of cells of a population present in the sample, and a direct activity-specific assay to determine how many of those organisms are active (viable). We will detail each of the assay types; activity measures being guild specific and FA techniques being population specific, and we will demonstrate the utility of each used alone or the two types together. We will describe several techniques that are considered to be general measures of microbial activity; that is, that ask how many cells in general are viable. These techniques may have great autecological significance if combined with the use of immunofluorescence (FA) techniques to examine a specific population. Those that have already been combined with FA methods will be detailed as such in Section 3.3. Because Jones (1979) published an excellent monograph covering the precise methodologic details of many of the techniques described herein, including appropriate filters, optics, vacuum pressures, and so on, we will not discuss such details.

3.1.1. Synthetically Active Bacteria.

3.1.1. Synthetically Active Bacteria. Synthetically active bacteria (SAB) are those that continue to enlarge when in the presence of nalidixic acid (NA) and yeast extract. NA inhibits DNA synthesis within 15 min of exposure while only slightly inhibiting RNA and protein synthesis (Goss et al., 1965). The net effect is that cells continue to grow but are prevented from dividing. The cells appear enlarged as compared to the inactive cells present. Cells are visualized by acridine orange staining (other stains could be used) and epifluorescence microscopy.

Kogure et al. (1979) first used NA and yeast extract to examine bacteria near the Kuroshio current. He found that the numbers of SAB were 10–300-fold greater than colony forming units (CFU) obtained by the classical viable plate count method (CFU about 0.1% of SAB). Although this was an improvement over plate count recoveries, only 5–10% of the total AODC were active.

Kogure called the number of positive cells a "direct viable count" (DVC) as opposed to the "total direct count" (TDC) obtained with the AODC. The term

DVC implies that cells unaffected by either the NA or yeast extract are nonviable. This is probably not true as NA is generally more inhibitory to Gram-negative cells than to Gram-positive or eukaryotic cells, and not all bacteria are stimulated by yeast extract.

The effect of Kepone on the activity of the general community of Chesapeake Bay microbes was evaluated using SAB and ^{14}C amino acid uptake (Orndorff and Colwell, 1980). By this measure, the microbial community was apparently not affected by the in situ concentrations (< 0.01 ppm). However, when the concentration of Kepone was raised to 0.2 ppm, there was a 85 – 90% inhibition of amino acid metabolism measured by radiolabeled amino acid uptake and a 45 – 97% reduction in observed SAB.

Maki and Remsen (1981) compared SAB with INT (an indicator of cytochrome activity—see Section 3.1.4) in four different aquatic systems and found no significant difference in the abilities of the two methods to determine the percentage of active cells. A range of 4.3 – 14.7% active cells was obtained from both oligotrophic and eutrophic lentic freshwater systems in Wisconsin. Neither increasing the incubation time for the INT stain nor incubating INT with yeast extract plus NA significantly changed the percentage of active cells.

Tabor and Neihof (1984) recently compared SAB, INT, and microautoradiography (Section 3.1.5) using ^{3}H-acetic acid, ^{3}H-amino acids, and methyl-^{3}H-thymidine at the surface (1.0 m) and at depth (8.5 m) in Chesapeake Bay. They found from 3 to 77% SAB with the lowest values at both depths in March (3% at 1 m, 7% at 8.5 m). SAB in the surface water peaked at different times than those at depth, with 77% active at the surface in August and 50% active at 8.5 m in July and September. The correlation between the number of SAB and amino acid microautoradiographically active cells was higher than that between SAB and direct counts, and SAB and INT active cells. The proportion of SAB was found to be a significant function of temperature.

It is interesting to note that surface bacteria tended to give higher percentages of SAB than those at depth. The authors suggest that the anoxic hypolimnion is responsible for the decrease in activity. However, anoxic conditions encourage an increased number of fermentors and anaerobes, many of which may be killed or inhibited by the incubation conditions used for these tests.

While the SAB technique has been applied to general considerations of viable cells in the bacterial community, it could provide a valuable means of examining a population as well. If a fluorescent antibody method were coupled with the incubations, the number of synthetically active cells of that population could readily be determined. As with all immunofluorescence assays, this assumes that SAB cells are antigenically stable, that is, that the cells used to elicit the specific antibody response do not lose their reactive antigens (unlikely using polyclonal antibody) and that cells of other populations are unlikely to acquire cross reacting antigens. The SAB technique allows determination of those cells that are actively growing in the habitat. Thus questions about growth and reproduction of the population could be addressed directly by this means.

3.1.2. Frequency of Dividing Cells. Hagstrom, et al. (1979) introduced frequency of dividing cells (FDC) as an indirect method of measuring growth rate in aquatic environments. This would greatly expand the value of AODC in estimating productivity. The method assumes that growth rate (and therefore cell activity) is related to a cell cycle event (septum formation) (Woldringh, 1976). A positive relationship was demonstrated between FDC and growth rate with pure and mixed cultures isolated from the Baltic Sea, and seasonal changes in FDC covaried with ^{14}C-phytoplankton exudate uptake.

Newell and Christian (1981) used FDC to predict growth rates of coastal marine bacterial communities. Samples were filtered to exclude bacteriovores, although some bacteriovores may have passed the filters (Fuhrman and McManus, 1984), and the nutrient concentrations were manipulated. Regressing the natural logarithm of the growth rate (ln μ) on FDC gave a better fit (coefficient of variation = 7%) than did a regression of the untransformed growth rate on FDC. Newell and Christian (1981) suggested that Hagstrom's (Hagstrom et al., 1979) straight–line fit with untransformed data was fortuitous and would not have been found if higher growth rates were examined.

There are problems with measuring the growth rate of a natural population. The large amount of point scatter around the regression line of ln μ on FDC suggested that it might be difficult to predict the growth rate of field samples using this method. Prediction of growth rates from FDC also assumes that the system is in a steady state, a tenuous assumption for a large pool of organisms with relatively short generation times. A further problem deals with starving cells that fragment and decrease their cell volume. Are these cells growing? FDC may be a valuable tool to estimate growth rates in nature, but many questions remain to be answered.

As with SAB, the FDC technique could also be applied to specific populations through the use of a fluorescent antibody to distinguish individual cells. The information gained would be largely the same as with the SAB method, except that there could be no possibility of inhibition of the cells by NA. This method holds promise, because it would require no manipulation of the samples. The FA could be applied to a sample in a manner similar to the acridine orange now used. The major drawback would be in finding adequate numbers of rare cells to provide a statistically valid sampling. That problem is, however, endemic to nearly all the FA methods.

3.1.3. Fluorescein Diacetate. Fluorescein diacetate (FDA) is a nonpolar, nonfluorescent derivative of fluorescein. Because of its nonpolar nature, the molecule is fat soluble and passively diffuses across the lipid phase of cell membranes (Rotman and Papermaster, 1966). Once inside the cell, nonspecific esterases deacetylate the compound. The deacetylated molecule (fluorescein) is fluorescent, polar, and will accumulate in intact cells. However, once cells are injured, (from ageing, freezing, puncture, surfactants, etc.) the dye leaks out and general background fluorescence is observed.

This technique was originally used for fluorometric assays of membrane-bound esterase (Rotman and Papermaster, 1966). It was considered to work only in intact membranes, and therefore fluorescence implied living cells. Schnurer and Rosswall (1982) observed that FDA is also hydrolyzed by proteases and lipases, as well as esterases. Brunius (1980) found that nonbiological hydrolysis occurs at high and low pH, in fresh uninoculated nutrient broth, and in inoculated nutrient broth. Furthermore, the presence of EDTA (ethylene-diaminetetraacetic acid) increases cell permeability to FDA. Several workers have found that FDA may be useful for evaluating living fungal biomass (Schnurer and Rosswall, 1982; Swisher and Carrol, 1980; Soderstrom, 1977, 1979).

FDA does not seem to work as well with bacteria as with fungal hyphae, though Newell and Fallon (1982) observed a strong correlation between FDA positive bacterial cells and cells incorporating ^{3}H-thymidine ($r = 0.97$) in coastal water column and sediment samples. The FDA counts were 2–7 times higher than those obtained with the labeled nucleoside. Chrzanowski et al. (1984) used this method to detect active cells in fresh water. The FDA method gave estimates that 6–24% of the total cells were active. This was less than the estimate given by INT in the same study. The difference may have been due to a low permeability of FDA through the outer membrane of Gram-negative cells; the ester seems to penetrate Gram-positive bacteria, fungi, and other eukaryotic cells better than Gram-negative bacteria.

The FDA method of estimating active cells may be best for soils where fungi and Gram-positive cells are numerous. Bacterial cultures and mixed populations are quite variable in their ability to take up the stain (Jones and Simon, 1975).

This method has little hope of being combined with FA techniques, because the two fluorescences would compete. The only possibility for success would involve conjugation of the antibody with a fluorochrome that was excited by light from a different part of the spectrum than fluorescein. Such an adaptation would require switching illumination, but this is already done for combined methods such as FA and INT. In light of the several other methods that provide more information than FDA, combination of this method with FA is probably not worth pursuing.

3.1.4. Tetrazolium Salts.

Tetrazolium salts serve as alternate electron acceptors, the reduced product being an insoluble pigmented formazan (Tsou et al., 1956; Nachlas, 1957). Originally, these compounds were used in histologic studies of eukaryotic cells (Kun and Abood, 1949; Cooperstein et al. 1950; Novikoff, 1959), where it was ascertained that the amount of formazan produced is a linear function of the amount of dehydrogenase present. Using plant cells and a variety of dyes [TNBT, NBT, MTT, INT, NT, BT, and TTC (see Table 3)], Gahn and Kalina (1968) found that all reductions were inhibited by the addition of malonate, a specific inhibitor of succinate dehydrogenase. Trevors (1984) compared INT and TTC (triphenyltetrazolium chloride) in soils

TABLE 3. Chemical Names for the More Common Tetrazolium Salts

Compound Abbreviation	Name
TTC	Triphenyl tetrazolium chloride
NT	2,2'(p-Diphenylene)-bis-(3,5-diphenyl)tetrazolium chloride
NT(BT)	Methoxy-derivative of NT
INT	2-(p-Iodophenyl)-3-(p-nitrophenyl)-5-phenyl tetrazolium chloride
NBT	2,2'-Di-p-nitrophenyl-5,5'-diphenyl-3,3'-(3,3'-dimethoxy-4,4'-biphenylene)ditetrazolium chloride
MTT	3-(4,5-dimethyl-thiazolyl-2)-2,5-diphenyl tetrazolium chloride
TNBT	2,2'-5,5'-Tetra-p-nitrophenyl-3,3'-(3,3'-dimethoxy-4,4'-diphenylene)ditetrazolium chloride

and found that the use of INT always resulted in higher activities than did TTC.

Packard (1971) estimated total combined phytoplankton and zooplankton respiration and found that maximum activity occurred when samples were incubated with NAD(P)H and succinate. He proposed that INT measured succinate dehydrogenase. Curl and Sandberg (1961) developed a quantitative method with INT to be used on shipboard. Optimum conditions were described (pH, temperature, reagents, concentrations, time, etc.) along with his finding that succinate enhanced the reaction. Although the method requires extraction of the reduced formazan, the paper is a valuable reference for experimental conditions.

Kenner and Ahmed (1975) found that diatoms and green algae did not reduce INT when tested in the presence of antimycin A, rotenone, or amytal. The authors suggested that the active site of formazan formation is the electron transfer from the cytochrome b–ubiquinone complex to cytochrome c_1.

Zimmerman et al. (1978) was probably the first to apply the technique to look directly at individual cells. This procedure allowed simultaneous determination of the percentage of respiring cells and the size distribution of respiring and nonrespiring cells. In the Baltic Sea coastal areas, most cells were $0.4\,\mu m$ or less and 6–12% were actively respiring. In comparison, most cells in freshwater lakes and ponds were 1.6–2.4 μm with 5–36% respiring. Zimmerman raised the question of whether INT-negative cells are truly not actively respiring or are merely respiring at a rate below the limits of detection.

Other workers have found excellent correlation between INT reduction and oxygen consumption in a variety of systems including sediments (Jones et al., 1979), freshwater benthic and planktonic samples (Jones and Simon, 1979; Christensen and Packard, 1979), and sedimenting particulate material (51). Jones et al. (1979) found sediment results to be variable and not correlated with the trophic status of the lake. Iturriaga (1979) found that while the total numbers of bacteria exhibited no seasonal tendency, the percentage of INT positive cells was highest in the late summer and lowest in the spring. The study also showed that the respiratory activity of sedimenting particles was lower than that of planktonic particles.

No information is available to determine if fermentors or anaerobes reduce INT. Since fermentors conserve energy by substrate phosphorylation and anaerobes tend to use electron carriers of lower potential than cytochrome b and cytochrome c_1, it is likely that these physiologic groups are INT negative. This may account for the apparent lower activities observed in sediments and on sedimenting particulate material. Alternatively, Baker and Mills (1982) observed that INT was rapidly reduced in the presence of ferrous iron. Formation of formazan prior to incorporation by the microbes would result in a lack of uptake and an artificially low number and size of crystals. Tetrazolium salts are known to be reduced to formazan in the presence of dithionite, diammonium sulfide, ascorbate, cysteine, glutathione, pyridine nucleotides, and several dehydrogenases (Nineham, 1955). The rate and extent of the reduction is a function of the specific Eh–pH conditions. Use of INT in any anaerobic environment or aerobic environment containing Fe^{2+} must be approached with caution.

Pamatmat et al. (1981) attempted to find a correlation between heat production in sediments and ATP or electron transport system (ETS) activity. There was no relationship between heat production and either ATP or ETS activity; however, there was a correlation between ATP and ETS activity in surface sediments. In 1980, two separate groups used INT to investigate microbial activity in marine systems (Harvey and Young, 1980; Christensen et al., 1980). Harvey and Young (1980) determined that the surface layer of a salt marsh estuary contained 16% respiring cells while subsurface water contained only 5.14%. Christensen et al. (1980) used pure cultures of marine pseudomonads to relate ETS activity to changes in physiologic state such as energy charge [(ATP + 1/2 ADP) / total adenylates]. As energy charge decreased, ETS activity measured by INT reduction concommittantly decreased, suggesting reduced cellular activity.

Tabor and Neihof (1983) recently suggested improvements to increase the sensitivity of the direct INT method. When formazan containing cells are examined, over 70% of the positive cells may be lost due to dissolution of the formazan crystal in the immersion oil, this problem was circumvented by isolating the organisms from the oil with a thin gelatin film. Clarity of the image may also be enhanced by transferring organisms collected on a filter to a gelatin film followed by an additional coating of gelatin. Using this method 61% of the total direct count of estuarine organisms examined by Tabor and Neihof were INT positive. The gelatin stripping method was used by Baker and Mills (1982) to demonstrate that in varying environmental conditions, from 1 to 80% of *T. ferrooxidans* cells were INT positive.

The reduction of INT has already been successfully coupled with the FA technique to produce a method for examining viable cells of a specific population (Baker and Mills, 1982; Fliermans et al., 1981). These techniques and their usage will be discussed in Section 3.3.

3.1.5. Microautoradiography. Microautoradiography (MARG) is potentially the most powerful method for the determination of single cell activity in situ. It is the most appropriate method for enumerating cells of guilds where members are delineated on their ability to incorporate a radiolabel. Major limitations involve the lack of suitable isotopes for some activities, for example, inorganic nitrogen incorporation and situations in which the important activity is determined as formation of a specific product. In such cases, MARG is unlikely to be of value.

There is extensive literature on the use of radioisotopes including a book by Rogers (1979) that provides a detailed discussion of theoretical considerations and technical problems of autoradiography. The most common activities evaluated include nucleic acid synthesis (Furhman and Azam, 1982; Bern, 1985; Karl, 1982; Moriarty and Pollard, 1982; Pollard and Moriarty, 1984), uptake of soluble organic matter (Ramsay, 1974; Ward et al., 1971; Stanley and Staley, 1977; Wright and Hobbie, 1965; Wright and Hobbie, 1966; Munro and Brock, 1968), and amino acid uptake (Tabor and Neihoff, 1984, Hoppe, 1976, Bright and Fletcher, 1983).

Brock and Brock (Brock and Brock, 1966; Brock, 1967; Brock and Brock, 1968) were the first to apply MARG to questions of microbial activity in situ. They found that the heaviest colonization of bacteria was in the axillary region of *Leukothrix mucor* where diffusion is limited and organic material may accumulate. Briefly, the method involves exposing a sample to a radiolabeled substrate, filtering the sample, and imbedding it in a gelatin matrix on a microscope slide. The slide is then coated with a photographic emulsion that is exposed by the radioactivity for approximately 1 week. After developing the emulsion, the silver grains associated with bacteria are counted. This is a fairly expensive and labor intensive procedure, but the activity defining the guild is probably more closely determined using this method than with any others.

Recently Tabor and Neihoff (1982) reported improvements in the MARG techniques and compared their results to those of Meyer-Reil (1978). The improvement is similar to the gelatin stripping procedure developed for the INT reduction assay. It leaves the cells imbedded in a gelatin matrix before exposure to the photographic emulsion. The resulting microautoradiogram is much clearer than that generated while the filter is in place. Tabor and Neihoff (1982) found 49, 50, and 73% of the direct count community active in the uptake of acetate, amino acids, and thymidine, respectively. When the specific activity of the amino acids was doubled, 94% of the cells become active in amino acid uptake. Substrate concentration is also an important variable when using this method and several concentrations should be evaluated. It may be difficult to compare results from one study to another in the absence of some standardized test concentration of both substrate and radioactivity.

Some common general problems with autoradiography include loss of activity due to chemical fixation of cells (Silver and Davoll, 1978), energy loss from beta particles from heat, pressure, or chemical reactions, chemography (Rogers, 1979), and inappropriate incubation times. Knoechel (1976) found that effects of source geometry must be corrected for. A common simplifying assumption is that the grain count over a cell is proportional to the cell's radioactivity. This assumption is almost never realized with a mixed population, resulting in overestimation of the activity of large cells and underestimation of the activity of small cells. Relative grain densities around organisms are a function of cell geometry, specimen density, energy of tracer, and sensitivity of the photographic emulsion (Faust and Correll, 1977). Aggregating cells may contribute to underestimation of unlabeled cells.

There are numerous reports of methods for obtaining some kind of activity index. The simplest is the percentage of active cells (Faust and Correll, 1977; Fuhrman and Azam, 1982; Hoppe 1976). Ward (1984) devised relative activity as an index of CO_2 fixation on a per cell basis. He defined relative activity as the mean number of silver grains per cell ÷ the number of grains in a similar area of background. This measure is a relative one, and is not an absolute measure of CO_2 fixation.

3.1.5.1. Nucleoside Uptake. Incorporation of nucleosides, especially thymidine and adenine, has been used extensively as a measure of bacterial productivity. Concerns with measures of total uptake of labeled nucleosides have been voiced because of theoretical problems. It is generally assumed that only nonphotosynthetic bacteria will incorporate exogenous thymidine since those cells contain the enzyme thymidine kinase (Fuhrman and Azam, 1982; Bern 1985; Moriarity and Pollard, 1982; Grivell and Jackson, 1968). Organisms lacking thymidine kinase incorporate radiolabeled thymidine with less specificity than those having preferred salvage pathways.

Some general processes that must be considered when examining uptake of nucleosides are (1) community potential for assimilating exogenous precursors, (2) intracellular and extracellular pools of structurally related compounds that may dilute the radioisotope, (3) balance between *de novo* and salvage pathways, (4) specificity and extent of macromolecular labeling (Wright, 1978; Karl, 1982). Qualitative and quantitative patterns of labeling may be influenced by the position of the label (Karl, 1981a). For example, a greater percentage of thymidine goes into DNA when the molecule is labeled with ^{14}C, than with methyl-[3]H (Karl, 1982). Thymidine has been found to be incorporated into yeasts, slime molds, algae, and protozoa in nanomolar concentrations (Karl, 1982), and there are also reports of marine pseudomonads (Pollard and Moriarity, 1984) and anaerobes (Moriarity and Pollard, 1982) that do not incorporate exogenous thymidine. Lack of incorporation by some bacteria might be a severe problem in MARG assays; however, uptake by eucaryotes would present no problem since they are easily discernible microscopically from the bacteria.

Karl (Karl, 1981a; Karl et al., 1981b; Karl 1982) has examined the utility of 2 – [3]H – adenine for detecting active cells in situ. Some of the major assumptions made when labeling populations with adenine are (1) most cells must transport and assimilate exogenous adenine, (2) addition of exogenous adenine must not expand the ATP pool, luxury uptake, or in situ stimulation of the rate of RNA synthesis, (3) there should be no compartmentalization of ATP (an immediate precursor to RNA). Karl validated assumption (2) and found that 49 out of 50 random isolates were able to incorporate exogenous adenine. It was also found that the proportion of cells able to assimilate ^{3}H-adenine was greater than that of cells able to assimilate ^{3}H-amino acids.

3.1.5.2. Uptake of Organic Carbon Compounds. Using ^{3}H-glucose Meyer-Reil (1978) found no correlation between standing crop values (CFU, biomass, AODC) and the number of glucose-active cells in samples from Kiel Fjord beaches and Kiel Bight. While glucose is obviously not a suitable substrate for determining the relative number of active cells in the general community, it could be used effectively in a scheme combined with a fluorescent antibody to estimate viability in a population known to oxidize glucose. Several ^{14}C organics have been used to examine the activity of organisms in leaf litter (Ward et al., 1971) attached to sand grains (Munro and Brock, 1968), and in aquatic environments (Stanley and Staley, 1977). The results also lead to the conclusion that while a single compound might not be appropriate for general community work, guild examinations with or without a fluorescent antibody is certainly feasible.

Uptake kinetics of organic compounds need to be considered when estimating heterotrophic activity. Bacteria tend to have specific transport systems that become saturated at low nutrient concentrations while algae transport by Fickian diffusion with velocity of uptake increasing with increasing substrate concentration (Wright and Hobbie, 1965; Wright and Hobbie, 1966).

3.1.5.3. Other Labels. Labeled amino acids (Hoppe, 1976), and phosphorus (Faust and Correll, 1979) have also been used to assess microbial activity in situ. Hoppe (1976) used ^{3}H-amino acids to evaluate active heterotrophs with distance from shore. He found that the number of colony forming units from plate counts was from 0.01–6% of the total active heterotrophs determined using labeled amino acids (100% active), glucose (29%), aspartic acid (30%), and thymidine (81%). The amino acid mixture was taken up by the largest proportion of the total cells. The incubation time with the labeled compound must be long enough to label but short enough not to allow cells to multiply. Use of a labeled amino acid mixture tends to produce the highest percentage of active cells of all the labeling techniques (Tabor and Neihoff, 1984).

Using $^{33}PO_4^{3-}$, Faust and Correll (1977) compared the relative importance of bacteria and algae in phosphorus cycling. They found that, overall, 95% of the phosphorus was assimilated by bacteria with algae being significant in phosphorus uptake only in the summer.

Obviously, activity or viability is actually defined by the conditions of the assay being used. Depending on which of the above techniques is used, the data vary widely (Table 4). This variation is understandable when the organismal capabilities needed to generate positive results in any given test are examined. Tests in which the cells expand in size (SAB) or divide (FDC) require the

TABLE 4. Various Estimates of the Percentages of Active Cells in Several Environments as Determined with Different Direct Assays[a]

Method	Saline Water		Freshwater		Soils/Sediments
FDA			6–24	(9)	2–83 (12)
INT	6–12	(1)	5.2–14.7 (10)		25–94 (13)
	5–16	(2)	5–36	(1)	20–90 (14)
	5–10	(3)			
	61	(6)			
SAB	5–10	(3)	4.3–9.7	(10)	
MARG + AODC	20–80[b]	(4)			
	28–50[b]	(5)			
	95[c]	(6)			
	2.3–56.2[c]	(7)	air/water 22–59 (10)		
MARG	63–85	(8) bacteria (^{33}P)			
+ SAFRANIN	28–42	(8) phytoplankton (^{33}P)			

[a]Values given are the percentages based on a direct count (usually AODC). Numbers in parentheses represent the literature citations:

[b] ^{3}H-thymidine.
[c] ^{3}H-amino acids.
[d] ^{3}H-glucose.
(1) Zimmerman et al. (1978).
(2) Harvey and Young (1980).
(3) Kogure et al. (1979).
(4) Riemann et al. (1984).
(5) Furhman and Azam (1982).
(6) Tabor and Neihoff (1982).

(7) Meyer-Reil (1978).
(8) Faust and Correll (1977).
(9) Chrzanowski et al. (1984)
(10) Maki and Remsen (1981).
(11) Hermansson and Dahlbak (1983).
(12) Lundgren (1981).
(13) Tabor and Neihoff (1984).
(14) Iturriaga (1979).

greatest integrated activity on the part of the cells. Measures of specific enzyme activity (FDA) or cytochrome activity (INT reduction) theoretically require that cells be intact and functional at some level and would be intermediate in terms of demands on the cells (Table 5). MARG techniques could be the least rigorous of all, since some labeled compounds may be passively transported across the membrane resulting in the enumeration of nonactive cells. The latter statement hinges, of course, on the compounds used in the studies, and on the general state of the samples. Nevertheless, it is clear that viability (or activity) may have different meanings, dependent on the test used. Individuals seeking to investigate cell specific activity in situ should select techniques based on the level of activity they wish to examine in the habitat being studied.

3.2. Population Specific Assays

3.2.1. Nonspecific Fluorescent Stains. The only direct assay for members of a population is by the immunofluorescence or FA technique. In order to place this method in its proper context, and also to provide a bit of information on the techniques used to examine guilds, especially with MARG assays, we will briefly discuss nonspecific stains as well.

3.2.1.1. Acridine Orange. Acridine orange (AO) is currently the most common nonspecific stain used to obtain total counts of bacteria. Acridines form random complexes with DNA and RNA by intercalating between stacked base pairs. This reaction separates the base pairs by twice their normal distance making acridines powerful mutagens, usually inducing frame-shift mutations (Mandelstam and McQuillen, 1976). Stained bacteria appear red or green when illuminated by epifluorescence microscopy. AO fluoresces green when it is complexed as the monomer with double stranded DNA and fluoresces red when it is complexed as a dimer to single-stranded RNA (ss RNA) or DNA (ss DNA), (Daley, 1979). Originally, it was thought that the color of fluorescence could be used to determine viability of the cells, namely, green cells should be the normal viable condition (not actively engaged in protein synthesis, that is, nonlog phase) and red cells should be dead and decomposing (ssDNA) or rapidly growing (ssRNA). Experience rapidly showed that this differentiation was so inconsistent as to be worthless in evaluating the physical status of cells.

Direct counting by any method is dependent on the quality of the microscope and the microscopist (Brock, 1984). Daley and Hobbie (1975) compared epifluorescent microscopic methods for determining numbers of marine and freshwater microorganisms. The size and nature of the filter used to trap bacteria (Fuhrman, 1981; Azam et al., 1983) are also very important, and prestaining filters with Irgalan Black helps to increase the visibility of the organisms by eliminating or reducing interfering fluorescence (Hobbie et al., 1977). Good agreement has been documented among AODC and scanning and transmission electron microscopic counts (Bowden, 1977; Larsson, 1978), suggesting that AO counts produce an accurate estimate of the true standing stock of bacteria. Bowden (1977) found that there was no significant difference in SEM and AO counts when 0.2-μm Nuclepore polycarbonate filters were used.

Daley (1979) has written as extensive review of the methodology and results

TABLE 5. Viability as Defined by the Several Direct Examination Techniques for Activities[a]

Techniques	Measures	Implications
MARG	Uptake	Indicates transport of a compound into the cells—active or passive
INT Reduction	Functioning cytochrome system	Indicates that the organism is currently respiring
SAB	Biomass accretion	Indicates that the cells are, in fact, growing larger—the biomass of the population is increasing
FDC	Growth rate	Indicates rate of cell division—increasing numbers

[a]The methods are ranked according to the level of activity measured, from general to specific.

obtained from direct epifluorescence microscopy. AO has been successfully used for enumeration of bacteria in water column (Moriarity, 1979), sediments (Rublee and Dornseif, 1978), and decomposing plant material and detritus (Robertson et al., 1982, Rublee et al. 1978).

3.2.1.2. Use of Other Fluorochromes. Two other fluorescent stains not extensively used for enumeration of bacteria are DAPI (4′6-diamidino-2-phenylindole), which is a DNA stain and may improve visualization of small ($< 1\,\mu$m) cells (Porter and Feig, 1980), and FITC (fluorescein isothiocyanate). FITC stains proteins and is used extensively in immunology (see FA methods). Karl et al. (1981b) found that individual cells were easier to visualize in microautoradiographs when stained with DAPI than when stained with AO. It is likely that the use of DAPI will increase greatly, especially in marine studies where cells tend to be substantially smaller than in freshwater or soil habitats.

3.2.2. Immunofluorescence Assays. Antibody techniques take advantage of the antigenic diversity of organisms along with the immunologic specificity of antibodies. Antibodies were first used to identify the *Salmonella* serotypes responsible for human infection (Garvey et al., 1977). Once an organism is isolated, production of the antibody in a rabbit is fairly straightforward since bacteria tend to elicit a strong antibody response in rabbits. Briefly, whole cell suspensions are injected into the rabbit's marginal ear vein at 4-day intervals for a period of 16 days. The animal is rested for a week and the titer against the antigen is determined. If the titer is high, indicating a strong antibody response was achieved, the blood is harvested and the antibody is purified from the serum. The antiserum is termed polyclonal since antibody is made against more than one antigenic determinant site if whole cells are used. The antiserum must be tested against many strains of bacteria to determine its specificity and adsorbed with any cross-reactive strains. For example, there are over 200 serotypes of *Salmonella,* but only a few are generally important in human infection. At the same time *Pseudomonas* species tend to be very cross reactive. This is probably an extension of the general genetic plasticity of this genus. Testing antisera for cross-reactive populations isolated from the system of interest cannot be overemphasized. If cross-reactive species are found, then a decision must be made whether or not to adsorb the antisera. There are many good immunology texts that describe appropriate methods and controls necessary in all steps of antibody preparation (e.g., Garvey et al., 1977; Carpenter, 1975).

Bacteria to which the antibody is made are visualized by conjugating the antibody with a fluorescent dye (direct method), or by using a fluorescent tagged antibody against the rabbit antibody (indirect method). The indirect method is more sensitive and does not require much more time. An additional advantage to the indirect method is that one fluorescent tagged antibody may be purchased (usually goat anti-rabbit IgG) and used to visualize many specific rabbit antibodies made to different organisms.

Bohlool and Schmidt published an excellent review on the uses of the FA method to enumerate bacteria in environmental samples (Bohlool and Schmidt, 1980). Counts of individuals using FA are generally one to three orders of magnitude greater than those generated using the most probable number method (Baker and Mills, 1982). Investigators have used FA to study the distribution of bacteria in a variety of aquatic and terrestrial environments (Gates and Pham, 1979; Apel et al., 1976; Ward and Frea, 1980; Stanley et al., 1979; Fliermans and Schmidt, 1975; Hermansson and Dahlbak, 1983).

The approach to quantifying cells with FA is similar to that used with other fluorescent dyes except that numbers of FA positive cells may be substantially less than the total count and more efforts must be made to concentrate and find the cells. This can become a problem when working in sediments or soils where cells tend to be attached to particles. There is also a problem with nonspecific fluorescence due to charge interactions of antibody and other particles, although this may be overcome by first staining the preparation with fluorochrome-conjugated gelatin (i.e., if FITC-conjugated antibody is used, counterstaining with Rhodamine-conjugated gelatin results in a brownish background with green fluorescing cells) (Bohlool and Schmidt, 1968).

Some disadvantages of FA are: (1) Because of the specificity of the stain, only one population (species, serotype) is detected. It is difficult to determine if the species is, in fact, environmentally important; and, (2) The stain also tags dead or inactive cells. To our knowledge, no one has determined how antigens disintegrate as cell function ceases.

The greatest weakness of the FA technique is the requirement for pure cultures of the organism of interest. For examination of the in situ distribution of an organism that is well known and characterized, this presents no problem. For example, studies of *Legionella pneumophila* proceed without difficulty, because the major biotype in the population has already been isolated, although new serotypes continue to appear in the literature. In cases where the organism of interest is one of the components of a natural assemblage, it is difficult to assess the importance or ecologic function of the isolate in the original sample. For studies that rely on obtaining an isolate from natural samples prior to making the antibody, the success of the entire study hinges on the ability of the investigator to get the "right" organism. For example, in studying the distribution of methanogens and sulfate reducers in an acidified lake, we have prepared antibodies to one isolate of each type. Unfortunately we do not know if the sulfate reducer is responsible for most or even a significant part of the sulfate reduction occurring in those sediments. We can make some statements about the likelihood of importance of the isolate after the study, when the sulfate reduction rates are correlated to the numbers of the isolate present in the sample. At that time (and not before) will we truly know if this organism is a good tracer of the sulfate reducing guild in these sediments. Of course, the same concerns can be raised for the methanogen. It is certainly possible to make antibodies against type strains available from various culture collections, but there is still a question of the relevency of that strain to the system under examination.

3.3. Combined Population and Activity Specific Assays

The FA technique is the key to population based autecological studies, but the greatest potential comes from combining two or more of the direct microscopic methods described previously. With the combinations we have essentially come full circle and are able to directly address the question of the abundance of active (viable) cells of a population in situ that was first addressed over 100 years ago with crude cultural methods. Unfortunately we have spent many pages building to this section, which will be one of the shortest. The use of combined methods for assaying the presence of viable cells of a specific population has barely been touched. The few available examples will be given here, along with an implicit demand for more research along these and similar lines.

Baker and Mills (1982) combined FA with INT (and called it the FAINT assay) to examine changes in the number of respiring *T. ferrooxidans* as distance from the source (pyrite mine tailings) increased. They found that the number of respiring organisms dropped more rapidly than the total number of *Thiobacillus* as the pH of the water increased (Table 6). Simultaneously the total number of cells and the number of actively respiring cells was found to increase. As pointed out earlier, the finding of viable *T. ferrooxidans* in circumneutral water, and the ability to isolate the organism whenever observed with the FAINT assay provides new information on how this bacterium moves from one source of energy to another.

Using the FAINT approach (Baker and Mills, 1982), Scala et al. (1982) examined the numbers of both *T. ferrooxidans* and *T. thiooxidans* in acid mine drainage from a variety of sources including metal sulfide ores and coal mines. Their results (Table 7) indicated that the two organisms occurred in roughly equal proportions at all of the 16 sites evaluated. The FA portion of the assay determined that the two organisms together accounted for only about 12 to 20% of the total numbers present by AODC determinations. The proportion of *Thiobacillus* sp. shown to be actively respiring by the FAINT procedure varied

TABLE 6. Distribution of Respiring Bacteria in Lake Anna, Virginia, as Determined by Combined Epifluorescence Staining and INT-reduction[a]

	Station[b] (10^3 cells mL)		
	C1	C3	A2
AODC	370	390	920
AODC + INT	74	230	580
FA	38	18	13
FAINT	30	9.2	2.9
MPN	0.0033	0	0
pH	3.2	4.2	6.9

[a]Comparisons are given for total cells by AODC and *Thiobacillus ferrooxidans* FA, FAINT, and MPN (Baker and Mills, 1982).
[b]Zero indicates below limit of detection, not true 0.

TABLE 7. Numbers of Total Cells, Respiring Cells, and Total and Respiring *Thiobacillus Ferrooxidans* and *Thiobacillus thiooxidans* in Several Samples of Acid Mine Drainage Waters from Different Mineral Sources[a]

Site	AODC 10⁴ cells/ mL	FFA 10³ cells/ mL	TFA 10³ cells/ mL	FINT % of FFA	TINT % of TFA
Balaklala[b]	8.82	3.06	14.14	48.30	29.17
Weil[b]	82.20	57.77	50.13	51.25	46.90
Squaw Creek[b]	9.83	17.50	3.70	20.00	35.30
Mammoth[b]	10.24	2.45	4.96	35.57	46.65
Argo[c]	6.99	7.24	6.74	31.63	31.02
Contrary Creek[d]	47.80	9.02	6.19	31.00	15.00

[a]AODC and FA counts are expressed as cells per milliliter. INT reduction results are expressed as a percentage of the FA counts. Standard errors have been omitted for the sake of simplicity, but were always on the order of 5–30% of the listed value. A total of 16 sites were visited, and data similar to those shown here were seen at all locations. Values of pH at the various sites were all below 3.0 at the time of sampling.
[b]Iron mines in West Keswick mining district of California.
[c]Gold mine in Colorado.
[d]Abandoned pyrite mine in Virginia.

from site to site and ranged from 19 to 74%. In general, high or low percentages of active cells of each of the species examined covaried, that is, they could not be shown to be significantly different.

At the same time that Baker and Mills (1982) were using the FAINT assay for *T. ferrooxidans,* Fliermans et al. (1981) independently adapted a combined FA and INT reduction technique to examine the distribution of viable cells of *Legionella pneumophila* in situ. In later studies, (Fliermans and Harvey, 1984) the combined technique was used to show that an industrial biocide reduced neither the numbers nor percentage of INT-positive cells in cooling tower applications. INT reduction has also been combined with malachite green (MINT) to look at the number of active bacteria in sewage (Dutton et al., 1983), although this assay is not truly population specific. Actually, the MINT assay represents no significant difference from staining with AO or any other general stain.

MARG and epifluorescence microscopy (AO) are often combined to look at specific guilds of bacteria (Wright, 1978, Hermansson and Dahlbak, 1983; Harvey et al. 1984) in estuarine and coastal waters, air–water interface, and aquifers. The combination of FA and MARG has also been combined to examine population specific activities. MARG and FA techniques were combined to look at the activity of nitrogen cycle bacteria (Fliermans and Schmidt, 1975; Ward, 1984). Fliermans and Schmidt (1975) made a specific polyclonal antibody against *Nitrobacter agilis* and *Nitrobacter winogradskyi*. Using $NaH^{14}CO_3$ and $^{14}CO_2$ to follow carbon fixation, they determined that log phase cells were not uniformly active and that the highest percentage of activity occurred in early log phase (84%). Fliermans and Schmidt correctly pointed out that theirs was a true study in autecology.

Ward (1984) used the antibody against *Nitrosococcus oceanus* and *Nitrosomonas marina* along with $^{14}CO_2$ to evaluate the autotrophic activity of ammonium oxidizers in seawater. Over 10^4 cells /L were found. Relative activity was positively correlated with the abundance of ammonium oxidizers, temperature, dark CO_2 assimilation, decreased oxygen concentration, and pheopigment concentrations in the upper photic zone. The relative activity peaked near the surface and again in the nitrite maximum region below the photic zone.

The frequency of dividing cells technique has also been combined with MARG (Riemann et al., 1984, Newell and Fallon, 1982) to produce quantitative growth data about the general community. Riemann et al. 1984 found that FDC activity approximated activity estimated from the uptake of (methyl-^{3}H) thymidine in Danish coastal environments with an increase in activity frequently occurring in the morning. Newell and Fallon, (1982) using similar methods in the water column and sediments of the Georgia coast, found a strong correlation between the two methods with FDC estimating two to seven times more activity than ^{3}H-thymidine. They estimated a secondary productivity of $2-4 \times 10^8$ cells $\cdot$ L^{-1} $\cdot$ hr^{-1} at 0.25-km offshore and $1-9 \times 10^7$ cells $\cdot$ L^{-1} $\cdot$ hr^{-1} at 15-km offshore. These studies, however, represent a comparison of methodologies rather than a combination for the purposes of autecology.

4.0. CONCLUDING COMMENTS AND SUGGESTIONS FOR FUTURE RESEARCH

It should be clear that a variety of techniques exist for approaching the original question of the distribution of active cells of a population or of a guild by examining individual cells in situ. What should also be clear is that use of these techniques is currently limited to a few research groups. The fact remains that fluorescent antibody work is tedious, and may border on impossible if large numbers of samples are involved. Furthermore, INT reduction and MARG are at least as time and labor consuming as FA procedures. Application of these methods, especially in combination, is not for the microbiologist looking for quick answers. The preparations for the experiments require a great deal of overhead in terms of operator time, and the analyses require time and effort devoted to, what must be candidly admitted, is very boring work. The results are, however, worth the time and effort. Direct examination of individual cells, especially when identified by immunofluorescence methods is the only way that truly accurate pictures of the behavior of populations and guilds in situ may be accomplished.

Data handling can often present problems. Most counts such as INT and MARG are made relative to AODC counts or FA counts made simultaneously on the sample. The AODC or FA counts are made on filtered samples allowing easy extrapolation of dilution factors, while the other counts are made on smeared or gelatin-stripped subsamples stained with AO or a fluorescent anti-body as a cell visualizer. The results are most often expressed as a percentage of the AODC or FA. Any attempt to convert this percentage to the total number of cells in a volume of sample presents difficulty. First there is a counting error associated with the original count (AODC, e.g.). Counting two or more inde-pendent samples allows a variance to be calculated for the counts. Similarly, if multiple samples are run for the activity measure, a variance can be calculated for the percentage of active cells. Combining those terms to produce a variance term for the number of FAINT cells, (e.g.,) is less straightforward. Baker and Mills (1982) approached the problem by randomly assigning each individual INT determination to an individual FA determination to get a series of FAINT values (in cells per milliliter) equal in number to the number of FA (and INT) determinations. These values were then used to calculate a variance for FAINT determinations. Scala et al. (1982) also used this procedure in their study of the distribution of *Thiobacillus* spp. (Those calculations are not shown in Table 7.) While the variance thus calculated was acknowledged to be contrived, its use in parametric statistics was considered to be conservative, and the fact that few significant differences were found in any comparisons except where the values were so widely separated as to preclude the use of any statistical analysis lent credence to the assertion that if an error arose it would have been a Type II error, that of accepting a false null hypothesis, the most conservative type of error. It is possible that an effect might be present but undetected, yet the authors would be unlikely to have claimed a difference that was not present. Figure 2 indicates the process used to obtain a variance for FAINT counts.

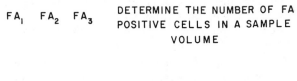

FA_1 FA_2 FA_3 DETERMINE THE NUMBER OF FA
POSITIVE CELLS IN A SAMPLE
VOLUME

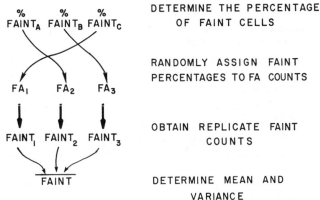

%   %   %   DETERMINE THE PERCENTAGE
$FAINT_A$ $FAINT_B$ $FAINT_C$ OF FAINT CELLS

RANDOMLY ASSIGN FAINT
PERCENTAGES TO FA COUNTS

FA_1 FA_2 FA_3

OBTAIN REPLICATE FAINT
COUNTS

$FAINT_1$ $FAINT_2$ $FAINT_3$

DETERMINE MEAN AND
VARIANCE

FAINT

Figure 2. Process for determining a mean and variance for FAINT counts. This scheme could be used for any similar assay in which percentages are multiplied by separate counts to obtain a final value. It is important that independent samples be used for the determinations.

While it may seem that several methods are available for examining populations and guilds, in situ, much work remains before the procedures will be commonplace. Methodological improvements are necessary. What, precisely, does INT reduction indicate about a cell in terms of viability versus activity? This question applies to any of the techniques. Does the SAB technique exclude slow growing organisms that may have an overwhelming effect on an important ecological transformation? What assurance is there that an organism enumerated by an FA technique is of quantitative significance in terms of the functions carried out by other members of the guild? There are many other questions appropriate to this area of microbial ecology, and more widespread examination of the techniques and their uses will not only reveal answers but additional questions as well. In the meantime, the data generated by users of these methods will continue to be recognized as the foundation of the future of microbial autecology.

REFERENCES

Apel, W.A., P.R. Dugan, J.A. Filppi, and M.S. Rheins (1976). Detection of *Thiobacillus ferrooxidans* in acid mine environments by indirect fluorescent antibody staining. *Appl. Environ. Microbiol.,* 32:159–165.

Azam, F., T. Fenchel, J.G. Field, J.S. Gray, L.A. Meyer-Reil, and F. Thingstad (1983). The ecological role of water-column microbes in the sea. *Mar. Ecol. Prog. Ser.,* 10,257–263.

Baker, K.H. and A.L. Mills (1982). Determination of the number of respiring *Thiobacillus ferroxidans* cells in water samples by using combined fluorescent antibody -2-(*p*-iodophenyl)-3(*p*-nitrophenyl)-5-phenyltetrazolium chloride staining. *Appl. Environ. Microbiol.,* 43,338–344.

Bern, L. (1985). Autoradiographic studies of (methyl-³H) thymidine incorporation in a Cyanobacterium *(Microcystis wesenbergii)*-bacterium association and in selected algae and bacteria. *Appl. Environ. Microbiol.* 49,232–233.

Bohlool, B.B. and E.L. Schmidt (1968). Nonspecific staining; Its control in immunofluorescence examination of soil. *Science,* 162,1012–1014

Bohlool, B.B. and E.L. Schmidt (1980). "The Immunofluorescence approach in microbial ecology," in M. Alexander, ed., *Advances in Microbial Ecology,* Vol 4. Plenum, New York, pp. 203–241.

Bowden, W.B. (1977). Comparison of two direct-count techniques for enumerating aquatic bacteria. *Appl. Environ. Microbiol.,* 33,1229–1232.

Bright, J.J. and M. Fletcher (1983). Amino acid assimilation and electron transport system activity in attached and free-living marine bacteria. *Appl. Environ. Microbiol.,* 45,818–825.

Brock, T.D. (1967). Bacterial growth in the sea: Direct analysis by thymidine autoradiography. *Science,* 155,81–83.

Brock, T.D. (1984). How sensitive is the light microscope for observations on microorganisms in natural habitats? *Microbial Ecol.,* 10,297–300.

Brock, T.D. and M.L. Brock (1966). Autoradiography as a tool in microbial ecology. *Nature (London)*, **209**, 734–736.

Brock, M.L. and T.D. Brock (1968). The application of microautoradiographic techniques to ecological studies. *Mitt. Int. Ver. Theor. Angew. Limnol.*, **15**,1–29.

Brunius, G. (1980). Technical aspects of the use of 3′,6′-diacetyl fluorescein for vital fluorescent staining of bacteria. *Curr Microbiol.*, **4**,321–323.

Carpenter, P.L. (1975). *Immunology and Serology*, 3rd ed., W.B. Saunders, Philadelphia.

Christensen, J.P., T.G. Owens, A.H. Devol, and T.T. Packard (1980). Respiration and physiological state in marine bacteria. *Biol.*, **55**,267–276.

Christensen, J.P. and T.T. Packard (1979). Respiratory electron transport activities on phytoplanton and bacteria, comparison of methods. *Limnol. Oceanogr.*, **24**,576–583.

Chrzanowski, T.H., R.D. Crotty, J.G. Hubbard, and R.P. Welch (1984). Applicability of the fluorescein diacetate method of detecting active bacteria in freshwater. *Microbial Ecol.*, **10**,179–185.

Colwell, R.R., A.L. Mills, J.D. Walker, P. Garcia-Tello, and V. Campos-P (1978). Microbial ecology studies of the Metula spill in the Straits of Magellan. *J. Fish. Res. Board Can.*, **35**,573–580.

Cooperstein, S.J., A. Lazarow, and N.J. Durfess (1950). A microspectrophotometric method for the determination of succinic dehydrogenase. *J. Biol. Chem.*, **186**,129–130.

Curl, H. and J. Sandberg (1961). The measurement of dehydrogenase activity in marine organisms. *J. Mar. Res.*, **19**,123–128.

Daley, R.J. (1979). "Direct epifluorescence enumeration of native aquatic bacteria: Used, limitations, and comparative accuracy," in J.W. Costerton and R.R. Colwell, eds., *Native Aquatic Bacteria: Enumeration, Activity, and Ecology. ASTM STP 695*, American Society for Testing and Materials, Philadelphia, pp. 29–45.

Daley, R.J. and J.E. Hobbie (1975). Direct counts of aquatic bacteria by a modified epifluorescent technique. *Limnol. Oceanogr.*, **20**,875–882.

Danso, S.K.A. and M. Alexander (1974). The survival of two strains of *Rhizobium* in solid. *Soil Sci. Soc. Am. Proc.*, **38**,86–89.

Danso. S.K.A., M. Habte, and M. Alexander (1973). Estimating the density of individual bacterial populations introduced into natural ecosystems. *Can. J. Microbiol.*, **19**,1450–1451.

Dutton, R.L., G. Bitton, and B. Koopman (1983). Malachite green-INT (MINT) method for determining active bacteria in sewage. *Appl. Environ. Microbiol.*, **46**, 1263–1267.

Faust, M.A. and D.L. Correll (1977). Autoradiographic study of detect metabolically active phytoplankton and bacteria in the Rhode River Estuary. *Mar. Biol.*, **41**, 293–305.

Fliermans, C.B. and R.S. Harvey (1984). Effectiveness of 1-bromo-3-chloro-5,5-dimethylhydantoin against *Legionella penumophila* in a cooling tower. *Appl. Environ. Microbiol.*, **47**:1307–1310.

Fliermans, C.B. and E.L. Schmidt (1975). Autoradiography and immunofluorescence combined for autecological study of single cell activity with *Nitrobacter* as a model system. *Appl. Microbiol.*, **30**,676–684.

Fliermans, C.B., R.J. Soracco, and D.H. Pope (1981). Measure of *Legionella pneumophila* activity in situ. *Curr. Microbiol.*, **6**,89–94.

Fuhrman, J.A. (1981). Influence of method on the apparent size distribution of bacterioplankton cells: epifluorescence microcopy compared to scanning electron microscopy. *Mar. Ecol. Prog. Ser.*, **5**,103–106.

Furhman, J.A. and F. Azam (1982). Thymidine incorporation as a measure of heterotrophic bacterioplankton production in marine surface waters: evaluation and field results. *Mar. Biol.*, **66**,109–120.

Fuhrman, J.A. and G.B. McManus (1984). Do bacteria-sized marine eukaryotes consume significant bacterial productivity? *Science*, **224**,1257–1260.

Gahn, P.B. and M. Kalina (1968). The use of tetrazolium salts in the histochemical demonstration of succinic dehydrogenase activity in plant tissues. *Histochemie*, **14**, 81–88.

Garvey, J.S., N.E. Cremer, and D.H. Sussdorf (1977). *Methods in Immunology.* Benjamin.

Gates, J.E. and K.D. Pham (1979). An indirect fluorescent antibody staining technique for determining population levels of *Thiobacillus ferrooxidans* in acid mine drainage waters. *Microbial Ecol.*, **5**,121–127.

Goss, W.A., W.H. Deitz, and T.M. Cook (1965). Mechanism of action of nalidixic acid on *Escherichia coli*. II. Inhibition of deoxyribonucleic acid synthesis. *J. Bacteriol.*, **89**, 1068–1074.

Grivell, A.R. and J.F. Jackson (1968). Thymidine kinase: evidence for its absence in *Neurospra crassa* and some other microorganisms, and the relevence of these to the specific labeling of deoxyribonuecleic acid. *J. Gen. Microbiol.*, **54**,307–317.

Hagstrom, A., U. Larsson, P. Horstedt, and S. Normark (1979). Frequency of dividing cells, a new approach to the determination of bacterial growth rates in aquatic environments. *Appl. Environ. Microbiol.*, **37**,805–812.

Hamilton, R.D. (1979). "The plate count in aquatic microbiology," in J.W. Costerton and R.R. Colwell, eds., *Native Aquatic Bacteria: Enumeration, Activity, and Ecology*, ASTM STP 695. American Society for Testing and Materials Philadelphia pp. 19–28.

Harrison, A.P., B.W. Jarvis, and J.L. Johnson (1980). Heterotrophic bacterium from cultures of autotrophic *Thiobacillus ferrooxidans*, relationships as studied by deoxyribonucleic acid homology. *J. Bacteriol.*, **143**,448–454.

Harvey, R.H., R.L. Smith, and L. George (1984). Effect of organic contamination upon microbial distributions and heterotrophic uptake in a Cape Cod, Mass., aquifer. *Appl. Environ. Microbiol.*, **48**,1197–1202.

Harvey, R.W. and L.Y. Young (1980). Enumeration of particle-bound and unattached respiring bacteria in the salt marsh environment. *Appl. Environ. Microbiol.*, **40**,156–160.

Hermansson, M. and B. Dahlbak (1983). Bacterial activity at the air/water interface. *Microbial Ecol.*, **9**,317–328.

Hobbie, J.E., R.J. Daley, and S. Jasper (1977). Use of nuclepore filters for counting bacteria by fluorescence microscopy. *Appl. Environ. Microbiol.*, **33**,1225–1228.

Hoppe, H.G. (1976). Determination and properties of actively metabolizing bacteria on the sea, investigated by means of micro-autoradiography. *Mar. Biol.,* **36,**291–302.

Iturriaga, R. (1979). Bacterial activity related to sedimenting particulate matter. *Mar. Biol.,* **55,**157–169.

Jannasch, H.W. (1965). Biological significance of bacterial counts in aquatic environments. *Proc. Atmos. Biol. Conf.,* pp. 127–131.

Jones, J.G. (1979). *A guide to methods for estimating microbial numbers and biomass in freshwater,* Vol. 16. Sci. Publs. Freshwat Biol Assoc., Titus Wilson and Sons, Ltd. Kendal, U.K.

Jones, J.G., M.J.L.G. Orlandi, and B.M. Simon (1979). A microbiological study of sediments from the Cumbrian Lakes. *J. Gen. Microbiol.,* **115,**37–48.

Jones, J.G. and B.M. Simon (1975). An investigation of errors in direct counts of bacteria by epifluorescence microscopy, with reference to a new method for dyeing membrane filters. *J. Appl. Bacteriol.,* **39,**317–329.

Jones, J.G. and B.M. Simon (1979). The measurement of ETS activity in freshwater benthic and planktonic samples. *J. Appl. Bacteriol.,* **46,**305–315.

Karl, D.M. (1981a). Simultaneous rates of ribonucleic acid and deoxyribonucleic acid synthesis for estimating growth and cell division of aquatic mircrobial communities. *Appl. Environ. Microbiol.,* **42,** 802–810.

Karl, D.M. (1982). Selected nucleic acid precursors in studies of aquatic microbial ecology. *Appl. Environ. Microbiol.,* **44,**891–902.

Karl, D.M., C.D. Winn, and D.C.L. Wong (1981b). RNA synthesis as a measure of microbial growth in aquatic environments. I. Evaluation, verification, and optimization of methods. *Mar. Biol.,* **64,**1–12.

Kenner, R.A. and S.J. Ahmed (1975). Measurements of electron transport in marine phytoplankton. *Mar. Biol.,* **33,**119–127.

Knoechel, R. and J. Kalff (1976). The applicability of grain density autoradiography to the quantitative determination of algal species production: a critique. *Limnol. Oceanogr.,* **21,**583–590.

Kogure, K.,U. Simidu, and N. Taga (1979). A tentative direct microscopic method for counting living marine bacteria. *Can. J. Microbiol.,* **25,** 415–420.

Kreig, N.R. (1981). "Enrichment and isolation," in P. Gerhardt, R.G.E. Murray, R.N. Costilow, E.W. Nester, W.A. Wood, N.R. Kreig, and G.B. Phillips, eds., *Manual of Methods for General Bacteriology.* American Society for Microbiology, Washington DC, pp. 112–142.

Kun, E. and L.G. Abood (1949). Colorimetric estimation of succinic dehydrogenase by triphenyltetrazolium chloride. *Science* **109,**144–146.

Larsson, K., C. Weilbull, and G. Cronberg (1978). Comparison of light and electron microscopic determinations of the number of bacteria and algae in lake water. *Appl. Environ. Microbiol.,* **35,**397–404.

Lennox, L.B. and M. Alexander (1981). Fungicide enhancement of nitrogen fixation and colonization of *Phaseolus vulgaris* by *Rhizobium phaseoli. Appl. Environ. Microbiol.,* **41,**404–411.

Lundgren (1981). Fluorescein diacetate as a stain of metabolically active bacteria in soil. *Oikos.* **36,**17–22.

Maki, J.S. and C.C. Remsen (1981). Comparison of two direct-count methods for determining metabolizing bacteria in fresh water. *Appl. Environ. Microbiol.,* **41**,1132–1138.

Mandelstam, J. and K. McQuillen, eds., (1976). *Biochemistry of Bacterial Growth.* Wiley, (1976). pp. 302–303.

Meyer-Reil, L.A. (1978). Autoradiography and epifluorescence microscopy combined for the determination of number and spectrum of actively metabolizing bacteria in natural waters. *Appl. Environ. Microbiol.,* **36**,506–512.

Mills, A.L. and R. Maubrey (1981). Effect of mineral composition on bacterial attachment to submerged rock surfaces. *Microb. Ecol.,* **7**,315–322.

Moriarity, D.J.W. (1979). Biomass of suspended bacteria over coral reefs. *Mar. Biol.,* **53**,193–200.

Moriarity, D.J.W. and P.C. Pollard (1982). Diel variation of bacterial productivity in seagrass *(Zostera capricorni)* beds measured by rate of thymidine incorperation into DNA. *Mar. Biol.,* **72**,165–173.

Munro, A.L. and T.D. Brock (1968). Distinction between bacterial and algal utilization of soluble substances in the sea. *J. Gen. Microbiol.,* **51**,35–42.

Nachlas, M.M., K.C. Tsou, E. deSouza, C.S. Chung, and A.M. Seligman (1957). Cytochemical demonstration of succinic dehydrogenase by the use of new *p*-nitrophenyl substituted ditetrazole. *J. Histochem. Cytochem.,* **5**,420–436.

Newell, S.Y. and R.R. Christian (1981). Frequency of dividing cells as an estimator of bacterial productivity. *Appl. Environ. Microbiol.,* **42**,23–31.

Newell, S.Y. and R.D. Fallon (1982). Bacterial productivity in the water column and sediments of the Georgia (USA) coastal zone: Estimates via direct counting and parallel measurement of thymidine incorporation. *Microbial Ecol.,* **8**,33–46.

Nineham, A.W. (1955). Chemistry of formazans and tetrazolium salts. *Chem. Rev.,* **55**,355–483.

Novikoff, A.B. (1959). "Histochemical and cytochemical staining methods," in R.C. Mellors, ed. *Analytical Cytology.* McGraw-Hill, New York.

Orndorff, S.A. and R.R. Colwell (1980). Effect of Kepone on estuarine microbial activity. *Microbial Ecol.,* **6**,357–368.

Packard, T.T. (1971). The measurement of respiratory electron-transport activity in marine phytoplankton. *J. Mar. Res.,* **29**,235–244.

Pamatmat, M.M., G. Graf, W. Bengtsson, and C.S. Nooak (1981). Heat production, ATP concentration and electron transport activity of marine sediments. *Mar. Ecol. Prog. Ser.,* **4**,135–143.

Pollard, P.C. and D.J.W. Moriarty (1984). Validity of the tritiated thymidine method for estimating bacterial growth rates: Measurements of isotope dilution during DNA synthesis. *Appl. Environ. Microbiol.,* **48**,1076–1083.

Porter, K.G. and Y.S. Feig (1980). The use of DAPI for identifying and counting aquatic microflora. *Limnol. Oceanogr.,* **25**,943–948.

Ramsay, A.J. (1974). The use of autoradiography to determine the proportion of bacteria metabolizing in an aquatic habitat. *J. Gen. Microbiol.,* **80**,363–373.

Riemann, B., P. Nielsen, M. Jeppeson, B. Marcussen, and J.A. Fuhrman (1984). Diel changes in bacterial biomass and growth rates in coastal environments, determined by means of thymidine incorporation into DNA, frequency of dividing cells (FDC), and microoutoradiography. *Mar. Ecol. Prog. Ser.,* **17**,227–235.

Robertson, M.L., A.L. Mills, and J.C. Zieman (1982). Microbial synthesis of detritus-like particulates from dissolved organic carbon released by tropical seagrasses. *Mar. Ecol. Prog. Ser.,* **7**,279–285.

Rogers, A.W. (1979). *Techniques of Autoradiography.* Elsevier/North-Holland Biomedical Press, Amsterdam.

Root, R.B. (1967). The niche exploitation pattern of the blue-gray gnatcatcher. *Ecol. Monogr.,* **37**,317–350.

Rotman, B. and B.W. Papermaster (1966). Membrane properties of living mammalian cells as studied by enzymatic hydrolysis of fluorogenic esters. *Proc. Natl. Acad. Sci.,* **55**,134–141.

Rublee, P., L. Cammen, and J.E. Hobbie (1978). *Bacteria in a North Carolina salt marsh: standing crop and importance in the decomposition of Spartina alterniflora,* UNC Sea Grant Pub. No. UNC-SG-78-11. University of North Carolina.

Rublee, P. and B. Dornseif (1978). Direct counts of bacteria in the sediments of a North Carolina salt marsh. *Estuaries,* **1**,188–191.

Scala, G., A.L. Mills, C.O. Moses, and D.K. Nordstrom (1982). Distribution of autotrophic Fe and sulfur oxidizing bacteria in mine drainage from several sulfide deposits measured with the FAINT assay. *Abst. Ann. Meet. Am. Soc. Microbiol.,* **N68**,189.

Schnurer, J. and T. Rosswall (1982). Fluorescein diacetate hydrolysis as a measure of total microbial activity in soil and litter. *Appl. Environ. Microbiol.,* **43**,1256–1261.

Silver, M.W. and P.J. Davoll (1978). Loss of ^{14}C activity after chemical fixation of phytoplankton: Error source for autoradiography and other productivity measurements. *Limnol. Oceanogr.,* **23**,362–368.

Silverman, M.P. and D.G. Lundgren (1958). Studies on the chemoautotrophic iron bacterium *Ferrobacillus ferroxidans.* I. An improved medium and a harvesting procedure for securing high cell yields. *J. Bacteriol.,* **77**,642–647.

Soderstrom, B.E. (1977). Vital staining of fungi in pure cultures and on soil with fluorescein diactate. *Soil Biol. Biochem.,* **9**,59–63.

Soderstrom, B.E. (1979). Some problems in assessing the fluorescein diacetate active fungal biomass in the soil. *Soil Biol. Biochem.,* **11**,147–148.

Stanley, P.M., M.A. Gage, and E.L. Schmidt (1979). "Enumeration of specific populations by immunofluorescence," in J.W. Costerton and R.R. Colwell, eds., *Native Aquatic Bacteria: Enumeration, Activity, and Ecology,* ASTM STP 695. American Society for Testing and Materials, Philadelphia, pp. 46–55.

Stanley, P.M. and J.T. Staley (1977). Acetate uptake by aquatic bacterial communities measured by autoradiography and filterable radioactivity. *Limnol. Oceanogr.,* **22**,26–37.

Starkey, R.L. (1939). Some influences of the development of higher plants upon the microorganisms in the soil: VI microscopic examination of the rhizosphere. *Soil Sci.,* **45**,207–249.

Stevenson, L.H. (1978). A case for bacterial dormancy in aquatic systems. *Microbial Ecol.,* **4**,127–133.

Swisher, R. and G.C. Carrol (1980). Fluorescein diacetate hydrolysis as an estimator of microbial biomass on coniferous needle surfaces. *Microbial Ecol.,* **6**,217–226.

Tabor, P.S. and R.A. Neihof (1982). Improved microautoradiographic method to determine individual microorganisms active in substrate uptake in natural waters. *Appl. Environ. Microbiol.,* **44**, 945–953.

Tabor, P.S. and R.A. Neihof (1983). Improved method for determination of respiring individual microorganisms in natural waters. *Appl. Environ. Microbiol.,* **43**,1249–1255.

Tabor, P.S. and R.A. Neihof (1984). Direct determination of activities for microorganisms of Chesapeake Bay populations. *Appl. Environ. Microbiol.,* **48**,1012–1019.

Trevors, J.T.(1984). Dehydrogenase activity in soil: A comparison between the INT and TTC assay. *Soil Biol. Biochem.,* **16**,673–674.

Trolldenier, G. (1973). The use of fluorescence microscopy for counting soil microorganisms. *Bull. Ecol. Res. Comm. (Stockholm),* **17**,53–59.

Tsou, K.C., C.S. Cheng. M.M. Nachlas, and A.M. Seligman (1956). Synthesis of some *p*-nitrophenyl substituited tetrazolium salts as electron acceptors for the demonstration of dehydrogenase. *J. Am. Chem. Soc.,* **78**,6139–6144.

Ward, B.B.(1984). Combined autoradiography and immunofluorescence for estimation of single cell activity by ammonium-oxidizing bacteria. *Limnol. Oceanogr.,* **29**,402–410.

Ward, J.S., K.J. Preston, and P.J. Harris (1971). A method to detect metabolically-active microorganisms in leaf litter habitats. *Soil Biol. Biochem.,* **3**,235–241.

Ward, T.E. and J.I. Frea (1980). Sediment distribution of methanobacteria in Lake Erie and Cleveland Harbor. *Appl. Environ. Microbiol.,* **39**, 597–603.

Wassel, R.A. and A.L. Mills (1983). Changes in water and sediment bacterial community structure in a lake receiving acid mine drainage. *Microb. Ecol.,* **9**,155–169.

Woldringh, C.L. (1976). Morphological analysis of nuclear separation and cell division during the life cycle of *Escherichia coli. J. Bacteriol.,* **125**,248–257.

Wright, R.T. (1978). Measurements and significance of specific activity in the heterotrophic bacteria of natural waters. *Appl. Environ. Microbiol.,* **6**,297–305.

Wright, R.T. and J.E. Hobbie (1965). The uptake of organic solutes in lake water. *Limnol. Oceanogr.,* **10**,22–28.

Wright, R.T. and J.E. Hobbie (1966). Use of glucose and acetate by bacteria and algae in aquatic ecosystems. *Ecology,* **47**,447–464.

Zimmerman, R., R. Iturriaga, and J. Becker-Birck (1978). Simultaneous determination of the total number of aquatic bacteria and the number thereof involved in respiration. *Appl. Environ. Microbiol.,* **36**,926–935.

3 ROLE OF GENETIC VARIANTS IN AUTECOLOGICAL RESEARCH

Charles Hagedorn

Allied Corporation
Syracuse Research Laboratory
Solvay, New York

The selection and use of bacterial genetic variants has emerged over the last two decades as a powerful research technique in autecological studies. Although this procedure has been most widely reported in association with *Rhizobium* ecological research, it has been exploited with a variety of other microbial species and strains. Generally, antibiotics are used to select genetic variants whose presence can be detected in a variety of ecosystems, although occasionally other types of materials (i.e., fungicides and antimetabolites) have been employed for this purpose. For example, in 1963 a strain of *Serratia marcesens* that was resistant to penicillin, aureomycin, actidione, and streptomycin was employed as a marker of water movement in an estuary as a measure of pollutant flow (Rippon, 1963). Similarly, antibiotic resistant *Serratia indica* was used to trace sewage in sea water and to determine mixing in an outfall along a bay (Ormerod, 1964). In early studies of antibiotic resistant mutants of *Rhizobium,* Schwinghamer (1967), and Schwinghamer and Dudman (1973) first described the loss of some physiological characteristics by the resistant mutants. In further studies, antibiotic resistant variants have seen use in all phases of *Rhizobium* research including survival (Brockwell et al., 1977), competitiveness (Skrdleta, 1970), nodule occupancy (Kuykendall and Weber, 1978) multiplication in soil (Chatel and Parker, 1973), symbiotic properties (Pankhurst, 1977), and carrier and inoculation methods (Hagedorn, 1979). Genetic variants continue to be employed in surface water studies (Pike et al., 1969; Wimpenny et al., 1972), biological disease control (Weller and Cook, 1983; Howell and Stipanovic, 1979), and groundwater translocation (Rahe et al., 1978; McCoy and Hagedorn, 1979).

With the widespread use of bacterial auxotrophs in ecological research, it is necessary, if not obligatory, to consider the advantages as well as the problems raised by this method. Topics to be evaluated are (1) guidelines (based on published reports) for selection, (2) auxotroph evaluation, (3) field testing, and (4) recovery of genetic variants from environmental samples. Basic issues to be addressed include the decision to use genetic variants, and requirements for additional research to expand the applicability of this procedure.

1.0. ADVANTAGE OF GENETIC VARIANTS FOR AUTECOLOGICAL RESEARCH

An advantage of the use of genetic variants is the capability for direct, quantitative recovery of the auxotrophs from a variety of native ecosystem types including aquatic, plant tissue and soil (Bushby, 1982; Danso et al., 1973). If it is desirable to demonstrate that the use of an amended bacterial strain has some particular function (such as nitrogen fixation), then precise recovery and identification of that specific strain is essential. Antibiotic resistance can provide a basis for this selection and recovery as well as for identification. In other approaches, the variant itself may be of only secondary importance compared to its performance as a biological tracer to study some phenomenon such as water movement (Hagedorn, 1979) or pollution dispersal (Johnston and Beringer, 1975). Basically the advantages of the use of antibiotic resistant mutants in ecological studies are that the selection and evaluation of variants is fairly straightforward, requires no sophisticated equipment, can be performed routinely in most laboratories, and has wide applicability to many ecological systems. Procedural details have been described recently by Bushby (1982).

2.0. PROBLEMS ASSOCIATED WITH AUXOTROPH USE

The most obvious problem that must be considered in the use of antibiotic resistant mutants is the stability of the genetic marker. If the resistant variant reverts to a sensitive condition at a high rate, then detection will not be possible in a complex microbial population even though the amended organism is still present. Also, selection procedures for obtaining mutants could result in strains that possess an unknown number of multiple mutations. Some of these could result in losses of specific metabolic functions that would be very difficult to detect (Hagedorn, 1979). Resistance to any one antibiotic (or antimetabolite) may induce multiple changes within a given gene or mutations on a number of different loci (Lewin, 1977). These gene alterations can each result in a change in some phenotypic characteristic, which may not be readily detectable. In addition, the possibility can never be completely eliminated that indigenous strains with identical resistance markers to the variant exist in any given habitat.

In many studies, mutagenic agents such as UV (ultraviolet) light or nitroso-quanidine have been employed prior to selecting mutants. The possibilities of inducing multiple mutations with these procedures are high, and considerable effort must be devoted to each isolate to ensure that major genetic damage has not occurred. Also, it has been relatively easy in several cases to isolate naturally occurring strains with the same resistances or metabolic capabilities as the selected mutants (Roy and Mishia, 1974; Bromfield and Jones, 1980).

Recently, there has been considerable discussion of the potential mobility of the mutant gene within the general microbial population. The issue is the transfer of the resistance element to other bacterial strains, thus dispersing into the environment resistance to clinically important antibiotics (Talbot et al., 1980; Stewart and Koditschek, 1980; Fontaine and Hoadley, 1976). There is also the remote but real possibility that such strains (or genetic recipients) could enter food chains and thus contribute to antibiotic resistance in microbes inhabiting the gastrointestinal tract (Cenci et al., 1980). Certainly the decision to use genetic variants requires careful judgment and exact testing procedures designed to assure complete environmental safety and confidence with result-ant data.

3.0. SELECTION OF GENETIC VARIANTS

Methods for the selection of resistant mutants have been adequately described in recent reports (Bushby, 1982; Danso et al., 1973; Hagedorn, 1979). Although many of these relate to *Rhizobium,* the following procedures could be em-ployed with most bacteria. Commonly employed procedures include selection of spontaneous mutants, intrinsic resistance, and new techniques made possi-ble with transposable elements.

3.1. Spontaneous Mutants

For mutants formed spontaneously prior to exposure to the selective agent, an antibiotic (or other compound) can allow isolation of the auxotroph from among a dense population of prototrophs (antibiotic sensitive microbes). Within bacterial populations, it has been estimated that one cell in every 10^6 cells is spontaneously resistant to any one antibiotic, whereas one cell in 10^{14} cells may be resistant to two combined antibiotics (Miller, 1982). Because of these low frequencies of occurrence, it may be necessary to prepare a centri-fuged suspension to obtain a sufficiently high cell density for detecting mutants resistant to multiple antibiotics. Generally, spontaneous variants are selected sequentially against each antibiotic rather than in combination. This allows larger numbers of mutant colonies to be detected, avoids simultaneous effects of combined antibiotics, and provides exact information on each resistant isolate.

The choice of antibiotics for selection is of critical importance to the success of obtaining genetic variants. The aminoglycoside antibiotics (i.e., streptomycin, kanamycin) have been widely used. Although early reports indicated that loss of desirable characteristics (such as nodulation) is associated with some classes of antibiotics, this has not been observed with aminoglycosides (Schwinghamer, 1964, 1967). A later report demonstrated that many bacterial strains react differently to common antibiotics and may not be adversely affected by selection for spontaneous mutants (Hagedorn, 1979). This implies that any antibiotic could potentially be used as a marker in a genetic variant as long as the mutant was examined for potential changes in other characteristics.

Closely related to antibiotic selection is the choice of microbial growth media. As more selective media are used (i.e., reduced nutrient content), the susceptibility of the auxotroph to the selective agent may increase. That is, the organism will be unable to tolerate as high inhibitor concentrations as in the rich medium (Barber, 1979; Armstrong et al., 1982). In most cases it is preferable to select mutants and pursue antibiotic screening on the same medium that will be used for recovery and identification in the planned ecological studies. For example, Rahe et al. (1978) used antibiotic resistant variants of *Escherichia coli* in conjunction with a selective medium (Eosin Methylene Blue Agar) for both mutant recovery and enumeration studies. It is also necessary to assure that a given medium does not contain materials that may partially inactivate or otherwise alter the agent incorporated to detect the variants.

The technical aspects of the plating procedures have been well described (Bushby, 1982). The gradient plate assay is most useful for rapid screening to determine the approximate selected level of resistance of the parent strain. Resistant variants are quickly selected over a wide range of antibiotic concentrations. However, each variant colony must then be evaluated to determine its inhibitor tolerance limits. Therefore, it is occasionally simpler to examine the parent strain on agar media that contains the exact concentration of the compound used as the selective agent. Again, to obtain a useable number of resistant colonies, it may be necessary to concentrate the cell suspension prior to plating.

To verify resistance and strain purity, isolates should be restreaked on media containing the selective agent. Cultures may then be stored on agar slants. The storage medium should be the same as the isolation and purification media until performance on other media formulations has been determined.

3.2. Intrinsic Resistance

Intrinsic resistance (to low concentrations of many antibiotics) has received considerable attention recently because its use allows identification of resistance – sensitivity patterns at low inhibitor concentrations, thereby avoiding the selection of mutants with high inhibition tolerance. Pinto et al. (1974) differentiated *R. meliloti* strains using natural resistance to low levels (2 – 10 μg/mL) aminoglycoside antibiotics as a selective factor. Josey et al. (1979) screened several strains of *R. phaseoli* and *R. leguminosarum* against various concentrations of eight antibiotics and found unique resistance patterns for all but one strain. Reliable strain identification with reference to stock cultures could be made on the basis of these patterns when examining nodule isolates from host plants. Kramer and Peterson (1981) incorporated this technique with both fast and slow-growing rhizobia and found that resistance–susceptibility patterns were reliable for identifying strains in field nodules. However, they reported that the rhizobia must first be isolated from the nodules to obtain a standard inoculum size and then be typed on antibiotic containing media. There are problems with native isolates possessing the same resistance patterns to strains being studied. It may also be necessary to examine the stability of each resistance–sensitivity characteristic in order to ensure its consistency over time (Miller, 1982). Certainly the uniqueness of the selected pattern must be fully examined before the technique of intrinsic resistance can be employed for any strain.

3.3. Transposable Elements

New developments in molecular biology offer a novel potential for use with genetic variants in autecological studies. The major advantage is that insertion mutants via transposable elements suffer one, and only one, mutational event. This avoids the isolation of mutants with multiple mutations and the difficulties of determining the effects of these secondary mutations. Antibiotic resistance has been the most frequently used marker to determine the successful insertion of recombinant vectors. This technique appears suitable in several species of bacteria and *Saccharomyces* (Mytton, 1975; Odeyemi and Alexander, 1977; Webster and Dickson, 1983). Concerns over stability of the inserted marker under various conditions and transmission of the resistance element to other organisms are as appropriate with recombinant mutations as with spontaneously derived mutants. Thus, appropriate control studies under laboratory and greenhouse conditions are necessary before field studies can be initiated.

3.4. Other Markers

There are occasional reports of genetic variants in autecological studies that do not involve drug resistance. Pigmented (red variants of *Serratia marcesens*) have been employed in water quality studies after selections for strains that did not revert to nonpigmentation (Ormerod, 1964). Rahe et al. (1978) and McCoy and Hagedorn (1979) developed strains of *E. coli* resistant to sodium azide, as well as a variety of antibiotics including streptomycin and nalidixic acid. The sodium azide resistance was particularly useful in that *E. coli* strains recovered from field sites possessed resistance to the same antibiotics (except nalidixic acid) as the selected variants, but were not resistant to sodium azide. Temperature sensitivity was found to be a useful marker in *Kluyveromyces lactis* as a tool for biochemical analysis and mutant recognition (Mayniroli and Puglisi, 1980), whereas Lighthart (1979) observed that cadmium-mediated antibiotic resistance could be used as an enrichment and selection tool. Other investigators have reported the use of resistance to a variety of heavy metals, toxic metabolites, and dyes as markers of specific strains (Pattison and Skinner, 1974; Gillberg, 1971).

Odeyemi and Alexander (1977) reported selection via enrichment culture for rhizobia (three species) resistant to seed coat fungicides. They selected for adapted cells from the parent cultures that were spontaneously resistant mutants present at very low levels in the population. The use of enrichment offers the advantage of recovering such strains as well as allowing large populations of cells to be exposed to the selective agent. This increases the probability of success in obtaining appropriate cultures. Odyemi and Alexander (1977) also found that several of their resistant strains actually metabolized the fungicides and converted them to products that were not toxic to sensitive rhizobia. This research led to practical applications that allowed for nitrogen fixation and seed protection of legumes by incorporating fungicide resistant rhizobia.

4.0. EVALUATION OF GENETIC VARIANTS

After appropriate auxotrophs have been isolated with a selective screening procedure, each mutant must be evaluated for similarity to the parent strain. The objective is to select a mutant with, if possible, a single difference from the parent, that is, the antibiotic sensitivity mutations. If multiple mutations must be accepted, the number should be minimized, and the *secondary* mutations must be in genomes with minimal impact on organismal behavior and function. Regardless of the manner in which the mutants are selected and the type of marker they contain, identical procedures are employed to determine phenotypic similarity to the parent strain. It would not be practical to examine every mutant against all criteria, but efforts should focus on those that provide the best comparison (depending upon the intended use of the mutants).

4.1. Cultural Tests

Initial tests should be performed with culture media because this is the simplest examination, and mutants not successful at this stage can be discarded, thereby avoiding unnecessary inclusion in more complex tests. Genetic variants should perform consistently with an adequate level of resistance over appropriate cultural conditions. This includes comparison to the prototrophic strain based on growth rates, generation times, growth over a range of temperatures and pH values, and utilization of carbon and nitrogen sources with minimal media and other pertinent biochemical tests. The mutant should be plated on media with and without the selective agent so that reversion frequencies and recovery efficiencies can be estimated. Reversion frequencies should be as low as possible, whereas recovery efficiencies need not be high, as long as this characteristic is sufficiently stable to allow accurate population estimates (McCoy and Hagedorn, 1979).

For genetic studies, cross reaction with other antibiotics is not desirable, although cross-reacting mutants can be useful as an aid in identification. Bushby (1982) found that cross resistance allowed a greater spectrum of antibiotics to be added to selective agar to reduce contaminant growth. Accurate plate counts of field populations of an amended *R. japonicum* strain could be obtained by employing multiple antibiotics conferred by selections against streptomycin (Obaton, 1971). Hagedorn (1979) reported that, with *R. trifolii*, cross-resistance patterns were generally restricted to those antibiotics with similar modes of activity. The development of cross resistance occurred in 5.7% of the possible resistance combinations. With any mutant, cross resistance is acceptable as long as the resistance levels to the other antibiotics are known.

Other characteristics that may be employed between genetic variants and parent strains are phage resistance patterns (Kowalski et al., 1974), colony morphology and/or pigmentation, and serological tests. Serological comparisons can be useful with techniques such as gel diffusion so that small differences in reactions to antisera can be detected (Diatloff, 1977; Vincent, 1970).

4.2. Growth Chamber or Greenhouse

Studies involving the effects of specific environmental parameters on selected variants are often valuable as predictors of variant behavior and survival in field trials. Such experiments are best performed in a growth chamber or greenhouse, where behavior of the parent strain can be compared against the variant in every case. Parameters to be studied depend upon the type of field environment under consideration. Such evaluations have been conducted in soil and rhizosphere (Pugashetti and Wagner, 1980; Johnston and Beringer, 1975), competition with mixtures of *Rhizobium* strains (Kuykendall and Weber, 1978), nodule occupancy in legumes (Materon and Hagedorn, 1983), survival in (Rahe et al., 1978; McCoy and Hagedorn, 1979), and on plant structures (Weller and Cook, 1983).

Depending upon experimental objectives, specific aspects of the intended environment such as moisture levels (Chatel and Parker, 1973), temperature (Hardarson and Jones, 1979), or acidity–alkalinity (Munns, 1970) may be examined. With such studies comparisons may include survival of the variant strain (McCoy and Hagedorn, 1979), nodulation (Bushby, 1982), nitrogen fixation (Brockwell and Hely, 1966), competition in nodule occupancy (Levin and Montgomery, 1974), or suppression of plant pathogens (Weller and Cook, 1983; Howell and Stipanovic 1979). Results may be difficult to interpret because it may not be possible to examine the parent strain since it carries no genetic marker and cannot be identified in the presence of natural populations. If interactions of the parent strain cannot be determined, then there is little to compare a genetic variant strain against. The best use of these tests is to observe for failure to nodulate, failure to fix nitrogen, rapid elimination of the introduced variant, or failure to exhibit some other type of activity by the variant. In spite of the difficulty in designing and pursuing such studies, discovering the failure of a genetic variant at this point is still preferable to conducting unsuccessful field studies.

4.3. Field Studies

The ultimate test for any genetic variant is in an unaltered, unrestricted enviroment; that is, in situ in a native ecosystem. In environmental studies, it is necessary to keep treatments to a minimum because of the effort involved in preparation and maintenance of field sites, especially in cropped ecosystems where a commitment to field operations may be as long as eight months per year (Materon and Hagedorn, 1983). In such cases amendment of the genetic variant to the soil can only be made once annually, so it is essential to use only those strains that have appeared suitable through every other examination. For example, many forage legume species (i.e., clovers and alfalfa) mature over a six to eight month period, yet inoculation, to be successful, can only be performed at planting. Correcting a failure at this point (i.e., poor nodulation) involves replanting the stand at the start of the next growing season (Hagedorn, 1979). Parent strains and genetic variants should be compared against each other in whatever evaluation is appropriate (i.e., disease suppression, crop yields). More specific comparisons can be performed if the parent can be detected by another method (i.e., serology) because persistance of both parent strain and variant may be important in evaluating the success of the field experimentation.

Sample storage should be tested before field studies are initiated. This is also true for recovery media, incubation conditions, and identification of the variant colonies. It is also advisable to examine isolates from nonselective media (where possible) to determine if portions of the genetic variant population cannot survive the transfer from an environmental sample to selective media. If such are found, then sample preincubation may be needed or initial isolation on a less specific medium followed by transfer onto a more selective formulation (McCoy and Hagedorn, 1979).

Finally, additional tests should be performed to determine if any obvious morphological or physiological characteristics have changed during the course of the environmental studies. These comparisons should be against variant stock cultures as well as the parent strain, and sufficient tests ought to be conducted to allow a reasonable assessment of whether any changes in the variant have occurred. These extra identification steps may be as straightforward as a series of biochemical tests or as elaborate as symbiotic efficiency on a host plant or protein band profiles (polyacrylamide gel electrophoresis) depending upon the desired level of sensitivity for examining the recovered variant strain (Vincent, 1970).

Although many reports deal with *Rhizobium* in competition and nodule occupancy studies with field grown legumes, there are a variety of examples of field research using genetic variants in several other ecosystems such as surface water (Ormerod, 1964), groundwater (Rahe et al., 1978), and for the suppression of plant pathogens in cotton (Howell and Stipanovic, 1979), or wheat (Weller and Cook, 1983; Weller, 1983). Regardless of the system, there are common aspects involving field site selection and experimental design.

Containment of the auxotroph at the experimental site is important. This may be difficult or at least of lesser importance to the outcome of the experiment in soil ecosystems, but containment is a primary concern with flowing water sites in that the amended bacteria could contaminate surface or shallow groundwater. Due to limitations of bacterial movement in soils because of various absorption phenomena, groundwater contamination is less likely. Careful monitoring of water flow is necessary to reduce this potential in aquatic ecosystems (Hagedorn, 1984; Wimpenny et al., 1972). In field studies, it may be desirable to dispose of crop residues or to examine such material for the presence of any of the amended bacteria. Limiting access to the experimental site and soil fumigation after completion of the research may also be appropriate if the test organism must be eliminated from the site.

Field experimental designs must also be chosen based both on the mutant's characteristics and the plant community to be studied. For example, in designing field trails involving annual crops, a randomized complete block design is generally appropriate. However, if the crop is a reseeding annual or a perennial where the sites are to be monitored for several years, it may be desirable to separate plots amended with the genetic variants from untreated plots (Hagedorn, 1979; Bushby, 1982). If not, the treatments will eventually become cross contaminated. This contamination can be confirmed by analysis for the genetic variant outside of the plots to which it was applied. It is often appropriate to include the parent strain in the study even though this strain cannot be detected in the field. This will allow comparison of the parent against the mutant (Vincent, 1970). This may include patterns in cross reactions with other strains by antisera prepared separately, against the parent strain and the genetic variant.

Finally, should plant–microbe associations be important in the field, *in planta* tests may be conducted. These tests may include comparisons of variant and parent strain in nodulation with symbiotic bacteria, i.e., *Rhizobium* (Mytton, 1975), nitrogen fixation rates in nodules (Phillips, 1974), or nodulation patterns (Levin and Montgomery, 1974). Such tests are usually run in sterile pouches or jar assemblies where contamination is kept to a minimum. However, the range of responses in such characteristics can be large due to variability within plant populations, so adequately large samplings with sufficient numbers of plants must be included.

5.0. CONCLUSIONS

5.1. Research Needs

A common observation that emerges from a literature study is the relative lack of evaluation of genetic variants prior to use in field studies. The extensive testing procedures described herein represent the total of what has been used in many different approaches. Certainly it is unrealistic to attempt such detailed examinations of every genetic variant, but it is possible to develop a consistent program of testing that includes appropriate evaluations of the variant at each step in a research program. In fact, such thorough testing may eventually be required by governmental regulations that will control the use of strains altered through molecular biology techniques. Even though such regulations may not directly affect spontaneously derived mutants, the use of genetic variants in uncontained environments is both politically and perhaps socially sensitive and will receive great attention in the future. Thus the need arises to focus on a more complete characterization of genetic variants prior to, during, and after their use in the field than may otherwise be considered appropriate. This will improve the quality of experimentation with variants in autecological studies as well as prepare for the level of environmental monitoring that may be required in the future.

5.2. Future Significance

The introduction of new genetic techniques to microbiology offers the potential for developing a wide variety of microorganisms that possess novel characteristics for use in a natural environment. The application of this technology emphasizes an expanded role for the autecological approach. Closer attention must be focused on recovery methodology, long-term survival of amended strains, transfer of genetic material to other microorganisms, and potential movement of the amended strain beyond the test site. These concerns are principally environmental. Whereas they must be addressed, the requirement of these extensive control studies should in no way discourage the utilization of genetically variant microbes as an important research tool to promote additional progress and understanding of microbial survival and function in native ecosystems.

REFERENCES

Armstrong, J. L., J. J. Calomiris, and R. J. Seidler (1982). Selection of antibiotic resistant standard plate count bacteria during water treatment. *Appl. Environ. Microbiol.,* **44**:308–316.

Barber, L. E. (1979). Use of selective agents for recovery of *Rhizobium meliloti* from soil. *Soil Sci. Soc. Am. J.,* **43**:1145–1148.

Brockwell, J., and F. W. Hely (1966). Symbiotic characteristics of *Rhizobium meliloti:* An appraisal of the systematic treatment of nodulation and nitrogen fixation: Interactions between hosts and rhizobia and diverse origins. *Aust. J. Agric. Res.,* **17**:885–889.

Brockwell, J., E. A. Schwinghamer, and R. R. Gault (1977). Ecological studies of root-nodule bacteria introduced into field environments. V. A critical examination of the stability of antigenic and streptomycin resistance markers for identification of strains of *Rhizobium trifolii. Soil Biol. Biochem.,* **9**:19–24.

Bromfield, E. S. P., and D. G. Jones (1980). Studies on double strain occupancy of nodules and the competitive ability of *Rhizobium trifolii* on red and white clover grown in soil and agar. *Ann. Appl. Biol.,* **94**:51–59.

Bushby, H. V. A. (1982). "Direct quantitative recovery of *Rhizobium* from soil and rhizosphere," in J. M. Vincent, ed., *Nitrogen Fixation in Legumes.* Academic, New York, pp. 59–67.

Cenci, G., G. Morozzi, R. Danielle, and F. Scazzocchio (1980). Antibiotic and metal resistance in *Escherichia coli* strains isolated from the environment and from patients. *Ann. Sclavo,* **22**:212–226.

Chatel, D. L., and C. A. Parker (1973). Survival of field-grown *Rhizobium* over the dry summer period in Western Australia. *Soil Biol. Biochem.,* **5**:415–423.

Chatel, D. L., and C. A. Parker (1973). The colonization of host-root and soil by rhizobia. I. Species and strain differences in the field. *Soil Biol. Biochem.,* **5**:425–432.

Danso, S. K. A., M. Hobto, and M. Alexander (1973). Estimating the density of individual bacterial populations introduced into natural eco-systems. *Can. J. Microbiol.,* **19**:1450–1451.

Diatloff, A. (1977). Ecological studies of root-nodule bacteria introduced into field environments—6. Antigenic and symbiotic stability in *Lotononis* rhizobia over a 12-year period. *Soil Biol. Biochem.,* **9**:85–88.

Fontaine, T. D., and A. W. Hoadley III (1976). Transferable drug resistance associated with coliforms isolated from hospital and domestic sewage. *Health Lab. Sci.,* **13**:238–242.

Gillberg, O. B. (1971). On the effects of some pesticides on *Rhizobium* and isolation of pesticide-resistant mutants. *Arch. Microbiol.,* **75**:203–208.

Hagedorn, C. (1979). Nodulation of *Trifolium subterraneum* L. by introduced rhizobia in southwest Oregon soils. *Soil Sci. Soc. Am. J.,* **43**:515–519.

Hagedorn, C. (1979). Relationship of antibiotic resistance to effectiveness in *Rhizobium trifolii* populations. *Soil Sci. Soc. Am. J.,* **43**:921–925.

Hagedorn, C. (1984). "Microbiological aspects of groundwater pollution due to septic tanks," in G. Bitton and C. P. Gerba, eds., *Groundwater Pollution Microbiology.* Wiley, New York, pp. 181–195.

Hardarson, G., and D. G. Jones (1979). Effect of temperature on competition amongst strains of *Rhizobium trifolii* for nodulation of two white clover varieties. *Ann. Appl. Biol.,* **92**:229–236.

Howell, C. R.,and R. D. Stipanovic (1979). Control of *Rhizoctonia solani* on cotton seedlings with *Pseudomonas fluorescens* and with an antibiotic produced by the bacterium. *Phytopathology,* **69**:480–484.

Johnston, A. W. B., and J. E. Beringer (1975). Identification of *Rhizobium* strains in pea root nodules using genetic markers. *J. Gen. Microbiol.,* **87**:343–350.

Josey, D. P., J. L. Beynon, A. W. B. Johnston, and J. E. Beringer (1979). Strain identification in *Rhizobium* using intrinsic antibiotic resistance. *J. Appl. Bacteriol.,* **46**:343–350.

Kowalski, M., G. E. Ham, L. R. Fredrick, and I. C. Anderson (1974). Relationship between strains of *Rhizobium japonicum* and their bacteriophages from soil and nodules of field-grown soybeans. *Soil Sci.,* **118**:221–228.

Kramer, R. J., and H. L. Peterson (1981). Nodulation efficiency of legume inoculation as determined by intrinsic antibiotic resistance. *Appl. Environ. Microbiol.,* **43**:636–642.

Kuykendall, L. D., and D. F. Weber (1978). Genetically marked *Rhizobium* identifiable as inoculum strain in nodules of soybean plants grown in fields populated with *R. japonicum*. *Appl. Environ. Microbiol.*, **36**:915–919.

Levin, R. A., and M. P. Montgomery (1974). Symbiotic effectiveness of antibiotic-resistant mutants of *Rhizobium japonicum*. *Plant Soil*, **41**:669–676.

Lewin, B. (1977). "Gene Expression," *Plasmids and Phages* Vol. 3. Wiley, New York.

Lighthart, B. (1979). Enrichment of cadmium-mediated antibiotic-resistant bacteria in a Douglas fir *(Pseudotsuga meniesii)* litter microcosm. *Appl. Environ. Microbiol.*, **37**:859–863.

Materon, L. A., and C. Hagedorn (1983). Competitiveness and symbiotic effectiveness of five strains of *Rhizobium trifolii* on red clover. *Soil Sci. Soc. Am. J.*, **47**:491–495.

Marmiroli, N., and P. P. Puglisi (1980). Antibiotic-resistant temperature-sensitive mutants in *Kluyveromyces lactis* as a tool for the analysis of nucleo-mitochondrial relationships in a petite negative yeast. *Mutat. Res.*, **72**:405–422.

McCoy, E. L., and C. Hagedorn (1979). Quantitatively tracing bacterial transport in saturated soil systems. *Water, Air, Soil Pollut.*, **11**:467–479.

Miller, J. H. (1982). Experiments in molecular genetics. Cold Spring Harbor Laboratory, Cold Spring Harbor.

Munns, D. N. (1970). Nodulation of *Medicago sativa* in solution culture. V. Calcium and pH requirements during infection. *Plant Soil*, **32**:90–94.

Mytton, L. R. (1975). Plant genotype × *Rhizobium* strain interactions in white clover. *Ann. Appl. Biol.*, **80**:103–107.

Obaton, M. (1971). Utilization de mutants spontanes resistants aux antibioti-ques pour letude ecologique du *Rhizobium*. *C. R. Acad. Bulg. Sci.*, **272**:2630–2633.

Odeyemi, O., and M. Alexander (1977). Resistance of *Rhizobium* strains to phygon, spergon, and thiram. *Appl. Environ. Microbiol.*, **33**:784–787.

Odeyemi, O., and M. Alexander (1977). Use of fungicide-resistant rhizobia for legume inoculation. *Soil Biol. Biochem.*, **9**:247–251.

Ormerod, J. G. (1964). *Serratia indica* as a bacterial tracer for water movement. *J. Appl. Bacteriol.*, **27**:342–349.

Pankhurst, C. E. (1977). Symbiotic effectiveness of antibiotic resistant mutants of fast- and slow-growing strains of *Rhizobium* nodulating *Lotus* species. *Can. J. Microbiol.*, **23**:1026–1033.

Pattison, A. C., and F. A. Skinner (1974). The effects of antimicrobial substances on *Rhizobium* spp. and their use in selective media. *J. Appl. Bacteriol.*, **37**:239–250.

Phillips, D. A. (1974). Factors affecting the reduction of acetylene by *Rhizobium*-soybean cell associations *in vitro*. *Plant Cell Physiol.*, **54**:654–658.

Pike, E. B., A. W. D. Bufton, and D. J. Gould (1969). The use of *Serratia indica* and *Bacillus subtilis* var. *niger* spores for tracing sewage dispersion in the sea. *J. Appl. Bact.*, **32**:206–209.

Pinto, C. M., P. K. Yao, and J. M. Vincent (1974). Nodulating competitiveness amongst strains of *Rhizobium meliloti* and *R. Trifolii*. *Aust. J. Agric. Res.*, **25**:317–329.

Pugashetti, B. K., and G. H. Wagner (1980). Survival and multiplication of *Rhizobium japonicum* strains in silt loam. *Plant Soil*, **56**:217–227.

Rahe, T. M., C. Hagedorn, E. L. McCoy, and C. F. Kling (1978). Transport of antibiotic-resistant *Escherichia coli* through western Oregon hillslope soils under conditions of saturated flow. *J. Environ. Qual.*, **7**:487–494.

Rippon, J. E. (1963). The use of a coloured bacterium as an indicator of local water movement. *Chem. Ind.,* March 16:445.

Roy, P., and A. K. Mishia (1974). The relative frequencies of spontaneous and UV [ultraviolet]-induced antibiotic resistant mutations in *Rhizobium lupini. Sci. Cult.,* **40:**373–378.

Schwinghamer, E. A. (1964). Association between antibiotic resistance and ineffectiveness in mutant strains of *Rhizobium* spp. *Can. J. Microbiol.,* **10:**221–223.

Schwinghamer, E. A. (1967). Effectiveness of *Rhizobium* as modified by mutation for resistance to antibiotics. *Antonie van Leeuwenhoek J. Microbiol. Seror.* **33:**121–136.

Schwinghamer, E. A., and W. F. Dudman (1973). Evaluation of spectinomycin resistance as a marker for ecological studies with *Rhizobium* spp. *J. Appl. Bacteriol.,* **36:**263–272.

Skrdleta, V. (1970). Competition for nodule sites between two inoculum strains of *Rhizobium japonicum* as affected by delayed inoculation. *Soil Biol. Biochem.,* **2:**167–170.

Stewart, K. R., and L. Koditschek (1980). Drug resistance transfer in *Escherichia coli* in New York bight sediment, *USA Mar. Pollut. Bull.,* **11:**130–133.

Talbot, T. W., Jr., D. K. Yamamoto, M. W. Smith, and R. J. Seidler (1980). Antibiotic resistance and its transfer among clinical and non-clinical *Klebsiella* strains in botanical environments. *Appl. Environ. Microbiol.,* **39:**97–104.

Vincent, J. M. (1970). *A Manual for the Practical Study of Root Nodule Bacteria,* No. 15. IBP Handbook Blackwell, Oxford.

Webster, T. D., and R. C. Dickson (1983). Direct selection of *Saccharomyces cerevisiae* resistant to the antibiotic G418 following transformation with a DNA vector carrying the Kanamycin-resistance gene of Tn903. *Gene,* **26:**243–252.

Weller, D. M. (1983). Colonization of wheat roots by a fluroescent pseudomonad suppressive to Take-All. *Phytopathology* **73:** 1548–1553.

Weller, D. M., and R. J. Cook (1983). Suppression of take-all of wheat by seed treatments with fluorescent pseudomonads. *Phytopathology* **73:**463–469.

Wimpenny, J. W. P., N. Cotton, and M. Statham (1972). Microbes as tracers of water movement. *Water Res.,* **6:**731–739.

4 INTRODUCTION OF THE COMPUTER INTO AUTECOLOGICAL STUDIES

Maxine A. Holder-Franklin
Department of Biological Sciences
University of Windsor
Windsor, Ontario, Canada

Robert L. Tate, III
Department of Soils and Crops
Cook College
Rutgers, The State University of New Jersey
New Brunswick, New Jersey

By its nature, microbial autecological research must involve the collection of vast quantities of data. Information necessary to reveal the role of a microbial species in an ecosystem should include descriptions of the physical, chemical, and biological ecosystem components. Problems relating to data handling and analyses have induced past researchers to limit the scope of the project and select one feature such as measuring population densities in sequestered ecosystems for study. A more complex project might include evaluation of strain activity within a given site. But, rarely could the totality of the system be considered. The exception may involve some simple pathogen–host interactions.

With the introduction of computers into science, especially the general availability of microcomputers for data collection and processing as well as report preparation, some major procedural restrictions in experimentation are being removed. We are now entering an era for microbial autecological research where scientific technical advances are outstripping the skills of the scientist. Thus, it could be concluded that the development of computer techniques in ecological research and, in particular, microbial autecology and the science of microbial autecology are coming to fruition in the same time frame. Currently, research design and the thought processes associated with ecological experi-

This is New Jersey Agricultural Experiment Station Publication No. F-15187-1-86, supported by state funds.

mentation are frequently connected by a computer. Even if the computer is not an integral part of the research, the processing of the manuscript requires computers at some stage.

Computerized publications and data processing have lifted a burden from the research team that is reminiscent of the arrival of the modern photocopy machines. Not only is data processed faster and more economically but multi-dimensional concepts can be simplified and brought within the constraints of the human brain. Students can visualize the components of an experiment or an ecosystem. Recordkeeping and literature reviews have lost much of their tedium. Image enhancement makes it possible to measure the components of a microscopic image. The word "graphics" has taken on a new meaning and this is only the beginning. The future holds the completely automated laboratory.

The remarkable use of computers in other research disciplines is an indication of the possibilities that are not only exciting but within the grasp of microbial ecologists. The discipline of microbial ecology benefits from the fact that computerization of data analyses and collection has been a *long-standing* process in other scientific disciplines. For example, the analysis of the algorithms used in autecology is very similar to that undertaken by chemical engineers in the study of chemical reactor theory. In the field of biotechnological ecology, it is fortunate that many equations of ecological interest have appeared first in the chemical engineering literature.

The following is not a thorough survey of the use of computers in microbial ecology but it is rather a selection of processes and programs that are in productive use for the researcher and teacher primarily in the practices of microbiology. The programs mentioned here are those that have been tested in ecological research or have potential in microbial autecology. Several review papers have outlined the broad spectrum of computer use in microbiology beginning with an early review by Colwell (1976) and a more recent and very thoughtful dissertation by Krishevsky (1982). Hampel (1979) described the interfacing hardware for the analysis and control of microbial growth and metabolic processes. Microscopic image analysis has been demystified by Caldwell (1985) in a review of the technique. These reviews provided a perspective on the wide-ranging application of computers; however, remaining current on the application of computers even within the discipline of microbial autecology is difficult. To keep abreast of current developments, the Microbiology Computer Users' Group of the American Society for Microbiology publishes a valuable newsletter, which enables users to exchange information on problems and solutions in an informal manner. Similarly, those who are initiating computerized research are also advised to enlist the aid of a programmer who is expert in writing computer programs. For the neophyte, Creekmore (1983) has prepared a primer (illustrated) which introduces the basic principles of the micromaze.

1.0. ALGORITHMS THAT HAVE BEEN COMPUTERIZED

1.1. Numerical Taxonomy

Many of the uninitiated have been introduced to computer technology through the study of numerical taxonomy. Not all of the new technology has received the enthusiasm that computerized numerical taxonomy now enjoys. This can be attributed to the pioneers in the field of computerized analysis as is noted in Chapters 5 and 6. Some of the developments in numerical analysis introduced originally for taxonomy have found a use outside of biological classification (Anderberg, 1973; Legendre and Legendre, 1983). The simpler forms of computer identification are becoming tools for the simultaneous teaching of Adansonian taxonomy and the underlying mathematical concepts. In addition, developing computer skills through the manipulation of the hardware (the computers and printers) and software (the disks and tapes) is a bonus in the pedagogical sense. The software also includes the program that gives the instructions to operate the system, process the words or the data, make the calculations, and store the results. Most of the programs originally written for numerical taxonomy require a lot of memory and a large computer, which is called a mainframe to distinguish it from the smaller types such as a mini and a microcomputer.

Sackin (1986) assembled a comprehensive overview of numerical taxonomy packages (a set of programs that interact) as well as specific programs related to numerical taxonomy. The packages are composites of several programs and perform a variety of functions within the envelope of taxonomy but also have a use in numerical analysis. Several of the programs that are in use at present by taxonomists were spawned from a few original programs, TAXMAP of Carmicheal and Sneath (1969), CLUSTRIT by Lefkovitch (1974), NT-SYS of Rohlf et al. (1971), Wishart's CLUSTAN (1969), and BOLAID by Hall (1965). Freidman et al. (1973) developed MICRO, the forerunner of TAXPAK, to assist in the identification of Gram-negative rods from clinical specimens using the Baysean formula. Lance and Williams (1966) and Goodall (1964) were among the first to develop programs for taxonomy.

Certain specialized programs within the envelope of numerical taxonomy include the hierarchical clustering programs of Milligan and Sokol (1980). After clustering by the unweighted pair group method with arithmetic averaging (UPGMA), the clusters are adjusted by the K-means program of Anderberg (1973) to make them more stable should perturbations occur in the data. Identification programs for the microcomputer only include ONTRACK (Rypka et al., 1982), which runs on a Hewlett-Packard 9845-9836. This program is used to find the successively most discriminating characters to use for the identification of an unknown. SAKID (Sackin, 1986), runs on a mainframe and the identification may be generated by TAXPAX. Other useful programs include MATIDEN and IDENMIX (Sneath, 1968), which compare the unknown isolate with all pairwise mixtures of taxa on the assumption that the unknown is a mixture of two bacterial cultures. This is particularly useful for identification of isolates from natural environments that are frequently difficult to purify and, therefore, may enter the identification process under the false assumption that they represent a single strain. The quality of the taxonomic data can also be examined by the program of Sneath (1968).

DINDEX is the computerized and modified discriminating index of Gyllenberg (Holder-Franklin and Wuest, 1983), developed for evaluation of the discriminating and thus clustering ability of each test. Following clustering by UPGMA using the NTZ package (Sakin, 1986) each test is indexed. The program eliminates those tests that are >80 and <2% positive, and indexes only the most discriminating.

Cluster analysis outside of numerical taxonomy has been used by Hada et al. (1983) to correlate bioluminescence, resistance to antibiotics, and resistance to heavy metal toxicity with plasmid occurrence in 512 strains of *Vibrio* isolated from sediments near Galveston Island. Cluster formation was associated with plasmid content. Those strains that demonstrated bioluminescence, antibiotic resistance, and resistance to heavy metals, which were plasmid-controlled traits, tended to show a high similarity. Strains with a low incidence of plasmids also clustered together. Relatedness of *Actinomyces* species was indicated by cluster analysis of polyacrylamide gel electrophoresis of whole cells by McCormick et al. (1985). The strains clustered according to serotype and then according to species. The taxonomic groupings were similar to those obtained by DNA – DNA homology. Protein and nucleotide sequences have been analyzed by Schulz (1983) using HAN 7. Amino acid sequence pairs were compared by sliding segments of one of the sequences along the others to find positions of insertions and deletions.

For taxonomic clustering of bacteria examined by protein or lipid analysis, the Commodore 3032/3040 computer provides high resolution color graphics of electrophoretic patterns of densitometer scans or gas – liquid chromatography traces. A number of software packages have been developed for analyses of such data. TRACETAX and PAGETAX include electrophoretic traces in bacterial taxonomy (Jackman, 1983). PAGE-PACK (Biomedical Computing Technology Information Centre, Rodbard and Graber, 1975) analyzes electrophoretic traces on an Apple II and IIe.

1.2. Mathematical Models

Mathematical models as described by Williams (1973) based on differential equations have expanded the projection of theories beyond the experimental limits. Ideas essential to the development of hypotheses and thus to experimental approaches can be formulated, tested, and reformulated within the rigors of mathematical design before the actual data collection occurs. Modeling is thought to be an abstract, even esoteric pursuit by the uninitiated but to the theorist this process is central to ecological research.

Howell (1983) reviewed the more commonly constructed models, most of which are first-order nonlinear differential equations that relate one strain to one substrate. The most popular in both teaching and research is the exponential growth model, which can be manipulated to demonstrate the effects of population density increases on growth rate or substrate limitation. The culture system can be open (continuous) or closed (batch), and a myriad of end products, intermediates, and processes can be modeled.

The Monod model (Monod, 1942) and its variations are the most commonly studied. A more complex model can be constructed from the growth and metabolism of microorganisms in films where the diffusion barrier, limiting nutrient and concentration gradient, controls the movement from the inner portion to the outer portion of the film (Characklis, 1983). The additional complexity requires the use of second-order differential equations. Bader (1982) described several models for elucidating the changes that occur with double substrate limited growth. The simplest model is the change in microbial population with time (dx/dt), which is directly related to the microbial population (x) multiplied by a specific growth rate constant (K); that is, $dx/dt = Kx$.

The many kinetic models available have helped our understanding of microbial growth. Modification of these models to include factors relating to the myriad of environmental variables impinging upon microbial population development in a native environmental site will allow a greater understanding of the behavior of individual microbial species within the ecosystem. The most important value of modeling can be observed when the theoretical forms the basis for the research design. There are some rather elegant examples of the successful testing of the model. May (1976) provided the criteria needed to evaluate these contributions. Only a few will be cited here. For example, Newman and Watson (1977) designed a computer model of the rhizosphere that relates the rate of change of the substrate with the biomass. Bazin and Saunders (1973) studied the dynamics of nitrification demonstrating the activities of *Nitrosomonas* and *Nitrobacter* in a predicted, open system.

Simkins and Alexander (1984) using their own program MARQFIT, fitted plots of the mineralization of benzoate by sewage bacteria to six kinetic models using nonlinear regression. Deductions on the behavior of bacteria in relation to several parameters including the presence and absence of protozoa could be made from the models. These experiments are an excellent example of the proof of a model by experimental data. Simkins and Alexander (1985) also demonstrated the mineralization of mixed substrates with mixed bacterial populations using the computer program MARQUANCOVA.

1.3. Factor Analysis

Multivariate statistics offers many algorithms that reveal the essential variation in a body of data. One of the most powerful is factor analysis. The matrix of coefficients, which represents a large number of variables, is reduced to a set of factors that profile the data set. All measurable parameters can be included; that is, those that represent the biological component, the physicochemical, or both in the same analysis.

The analysis of data in a study of population shifts of heterotrophic bacteria by Holder-Franklin (1984) was completely computerized. The model used was a succession of algorithms beginning with the positive response frequencies of the dichotomous database of numerical taxonomy. The matrix was factor analyzed and the most important factors scored. The factors provided a nutritional and physiological profile of the population that was not constrained by the taxonomic classification. When the physicochemical and other environmental features are factor analyzed, the scores of the two factor sets, the environmental and the bacterial, can be compared or correlated. The programs to complete the analysis are XFF, positive response frequencies, FACTOR (modified from NT-SYS), ROTATE, and PLOTTER (modified from SYMVU), which produces a three dimensional plot as shown in Chapter 5. The next stage in the model is path analysis (from the SPSS package, see Section 1.5), which indicated a causal relationship between the environmental parameters and the bacteria (Holder-Franklin, 1984). Path analysis is a selection of the best sequence of causes as performed on a set of regressions.

1.4. Time Series Analysis

All of the variables in an experimental data set are related to the independent variable, time. A time series is a collection of observations made sequentially in time in order to study the evolution of the dependent variables (Box and Jenkins, 1970; Chatfield, 1975).

Dalrymple and Crowther (1983) reviewed time-domain techniques as described by Box and Jenkins (1970) and recommended that this calculation be computerized. It is unlikely that one could complete the sequence of calculations required without a computer. The possible models of serial correlations can be tested and the most appropriate selected following the statistical testing. These authors suggest the ISCOL package. Fry et al. (1981) used time-domain analysis to study metabolic changes over a period of time in laboratory cultures.

Cyclical events in the populations of heterotrophic river bacteria were revealed by the SPECTRA procedure of the Statistical Analysis System (SAS) computer package (Holder-Franklin et al., 1980). The package uses fast Fourier transform to reduce computation time of the point estimates. Legendre et al. (1984) also analyzed the fluctuations of bacterial sewage populations using a computerized spectral analysis. The analysis indicated that the sewage bacteria were under the control of climatic factors and physicochemical changes as well as responses of the zooplankton and phytoplankton.

1.5. Systems for Data Analysis on the Mainframe

1.5.1. Packages with Multifaceted Abilities. SAS in addition to data storage, retrieval, modification, and programming, also performs a range of statistical analyses from the most simple descriptive statistics to complex multivariate techniques. Another useful package is the statistical package for the Social Sciences (Nie et al., 1975), SPSS.

1.5.2. Custom Programs for Data Processing. Processing of ecological data often requires a custom program to perform the desired set of functions. For example, Litchfield (1979), calculated heterotrophic uptake and analyzed mineralization data for waters and sediments in triplicate and four time periods using the program NAOH. The IBM mainframe calculated the T_t, V_{max}, $K_t +$ S_n, regression equation and r of the line as well as the first-order constants when Michaelis–Menton kinetics did not apply. This program is available by personal arrangements with the author.

2.0. IMAGE ANALYSIS

Image analysis is a new and potentially rewarding technique in microbiology but is still in the development phase. Several improvements have been made since the report of Pettipher and Rodrigues (1982) counting bacteria and somatic cells in milk using a television camera to detect the cells stained with the epifluorescent dye, acridine orange.

2.1. Computer-Enhanced Microscopy

Computer-enhanced microscopy has changed the analysis of microscopic images and is one of the few techniques that was developed as a computerized process. The use of these techniques does not require knowledge of programming. Caldwell (1985) in a recent review outlined the steps and rationale of current image analysis procedures including the digitization of the image and the eventual analysis. A scanning microspectrophotometer is incorporated into a microscope, which is connected to a photomultiplier based detector or photodiode detector. The information is fed into a computer that is equipped with an eight colorgraphic system. The scanning stage of the microscope moves at speeds of 0–250 steps/s. Three computer languages are most commonly used: FORTRAN, BASIC, and ASSEMBLER, depending upon the system. The more sophisticated systems permit a switchover from photometry to photomicrography or television camera. The latter is required for counting individual cells. The data is analyzed by the integrated software, that includes basic statistics, correlations, and particle size analysis. Histograms, scattergrams, and three dimensional plots of the correlation of any two parameters are displayed graphically.

Zeiss, Inc. and Leitz, Inc. have developed systems that perform a variety of image analyses including scanning of photographs, spectrophotometric analysis of the components of a cell, and enumeration of cells in a sample. As an alternative to these commercial techniques, some workers have developed their own systems (Costello and Monk, 1985; Sieracki et al., 1985). Most top grade research microscopes can become part of an image analysis system, but the resolution of bacteria by the microscope must be excellent. Generally, the resolution limit of light microscopes is approximately 0.2 μm, which is close to the size of some bacterial cells. With most systems, effective resolution is improved by the use of image enhancement to overcome the restrictions of the light microscope. The technique is widely used in several other disciplines but there are a few reports in microbiology. Caldwell and Germida (1985) used image analysis to demonstrate the growth of *Ensifer adhaerens* in agar slide cultures. The area of new growth and the original cell were discriminated in this study. Sieracki et al. (1985) developed a system to count planktonic bacteria on filters stained with the dyes, acridine orange, and 4,6-diamidino-2-phenyl oxide (DAPI). The latter, a vital stain for DNA, allowed detection of cells of $<0.2\,\mu m$ and helped to overcome the microscopic resolution limitations that persists below certain detection levels in specimens containing detritus.

Another limitation of image analysis is that instruments only "see" the samples as two dimensional objects, whereas the human eye views them three dimensionally. Thus, data interpretation still requires operator interface, that is, looking at the specimen at critical intervals.

Costello and Monk (1985) counted yeast cells using a hemocytometer, a video camera, monitor, and an Apple microcomputer. The yeast were distinguished and counted rapidly despite the presence of bacteria. The Olympus microscope was fitted with a dark field condensor to accentuate the contrasting cell images. The Apple IIe analyzed the images using the program Digisector DS-65 (The Micro Works, Del Mar, California). This relatively simple arrangement of instruments was used successfully for cell counts and more importantly was an improvement over the previous noncomputerized method.

2.2. Biomass Estimation

Microbial biomass may be estimated through measurement of cell volume. Krambeck et al. (1981) calculated biovolume by measuring the sizes of bacterial cells in scanning electron micrographs of filtered plankton. The micrographs were projected on a digitizer field that functions on the principle of magnetostrictive ranging. The cells, which are outlined manually with the cross-hair cursor that can be moved across the image like a computer "mouse," were selected by eye. (The human eye remains the superior instrument in making judgments of suitable images to record.) A microcomputer using the program BABI recorded two dimensions of each cell, length and width, and determined if the cell had been recorded previously in the same analysis. It then accepts or rejects the cell, eliminating duplicates and printing an analog trace of the omitted bacteria. The program interacts with the operator and calculates the biovolume with 95% confidence limits. The biovolume parameter can be used in studies of the responses of heterotrophic bacterial populations to spatial and temporal changes.

3.0. DATABASE MANAGEMENT

Buck (1985) used microcomputers in the clinical laboratory to record information on bacterial isolates in relation to source, biochemical tests, taxonomic data, and antibiotic susceptibility. Commercially available database management programs were modified for this task. Using a fixed disk storage (commonly called a hard disk), the data are retrieved and collated efficiently. Quality control results for media are stored and analyzed periodically. The files can be searched for a selected category of information that can eventually be analyzed statistically. The following integrated software can be used for storage in a multiplicity of research areas but are particularly useful for storage of information on single isolates: KNOWLEDGEMAN (MicroDataBase Systems, Inc.), FRAMEWORK (Ashton–Tate), and LOTUS and SYMPHONY (Lotus Development Corporation).

KNOWLEDGEMAN (Buck, 1985) is an integrated database management system with spreadsheet that consists of 5 modules, which work together: KNOWLEDGEMAN, K-TEXT, K-GRAPH, K-PAINT, and K-MOUSE. The information can be sorted, indexed, and retrieved in ascending or descending order and calculations can be done automatically on the fields. The management systems can also be used for literature storage. The database management system is similar to dBase II by Ashton–Tate but uses arrays. The language has functions for log and square root. LOTUS and SYMPHONY make graphs, perform numerical calculations, and edit text.

Many programs now available can be modified for the specific needs of the researcher. Minimal program changes can make the software tailormade. Not all programs will run on all computers. Compatability is more likely on a microcomputer, but there are still machine dependence problems. Certain mainframe programs need changes to run on another computer.

4.0. LITERATURE MANAGEMENT

The Institute for Scientific Information (ISI) has for many years, published CURRENT CONTENTS, a weekly survey of journal contents in specific fields. ISI has developed SCIMATE, which consists of three programs, the Personal Data Manager, editor, and the Online Searcher. The software runs on most of the major microcomputers using electronic indices (IBM, Apple IIe, and any Z-80 processor).

The Personal Data Manager (PDM), which substitutes for a card index to certain types of information collections such as reprints, reports, correspondence, manuscripts, and literature citations stores each reference by field; that is, by title, author, journal or book, data, keywords, and so on. The system accommodates up to 20 field options. There is space within each item to store the abstract and any other information with a maximum 1894 characters. The retrieval of a set of references can be obtained by access number or by a single word. The set is then sorted alphabetically using any field. The set can be displayed on the monitor and/or printed. A feature that makes the program attractive is that the set of references that have been selected can be transferred into the word processor program and added to the manuscript under preparation such as this one. It is possible to add a field where each reference is arranged in the order or sequence most commonly used in the microbiological journals. When the item is transferred into the word processor, the reference is in the correct order and sorted alphabetically.

The Online searcher is integrated with the PDM. The terminal must be connected to a telephone using a modem. Once connected to the host database, ISI, a search of designated information begins. The operator can screen the items and select those that are to be loaded into the operator's computer. The search can be updated regularly from the end of the last search from the same database. Most large institutions have professionals searching the informational databases, but the capability is within everyone's grasp with the menu-driven software. The Online searcher can examine other databases such as DIALOG, BRS, NLM, ORBIT, ERIC, BIOSIS, and MEDLINE.

5.0. INTERFACING OF APPARATUS AND DATA PROCESSING

One of the most useful laboratory advancements available to the microbial ecologist is computer directed data collection. Use of such procedures in physiological ecological studies is exemplified by the work of Simkins and Alexander (1985) (as was described in Section 1.2). They demonstrated the mineralization of mixed substrates with mixed bacterial populations using the computer program MARQUANCOVA. Similarly, Gordon and Millero (1983) measured the heat production of attached *Vibrio alginolyticus* as compared to free cells and found that the attached cells had a lower specific heat production when actively metabolizing glucose. The flow sorption microcalorimeter data was collected on a Hewlett–Packard 7101B strip chart recorder and by a Commodore 2001 microcomputer, which logged the data in digital form on a floppy disk.

Pickett et al. (1979) developed an interactive bioreactor that runs on a computer program. The examples of this type of system in the chemical engineering literature are too numerous to cite herein. A more direct relationship to microbial autecology is found with automated assessment of microbial population densities. Two groups of workers have described microcomputer programs for the computation of most probable number (MPN) using a Newton–Raphson interaction. The program of Clark and Owens (1983) calculates the estimates of MPN for any combination of dilution levels, numbers of replicates, and sample volumes. The program of MacDonnell et al. (1984) accommodates any number of replicates up to 10 dilutions and simultaneously prints the MPN, confidence interval, and goodness of fit. Both programs are listed in the publication and both avoid the use of tables.

The programs available vary from the statistically simple to the more complex. An example of a mathematically intricate program was reported by El-Shaarawi (1985) who examined data sets of *Escherichia coli* counts that had been statistically analyzed. The data were tested for the proportion of the material that was contaminated, uncontaminated, and the bacterial density in the uncontaminated part using goodness-of-fit methods for the Poisson plus added zeros distribution and the truncated Poisson distribution, providing another level of scrutiny for the statistics and an expansion of the information available for ecological interpretation.

Misri and Poole (1983) have described a flow dialysis apparatus that measures solute and O_2 uptake by growing cultures. The problem of premature anoxia in the system was avoided by computer control of the gas mixture and a link to a second O_2 electrode in the incoming gas phase.

A problem common in the laboratory is the multiplicity of instruments and the scarcity of computers. Accordingly, Fackrell and Glascow (1984) designed two simple components that allow a single microprocessor to monitor several analog instruments without losing signal resolution. A remote control box equipped with a speaker permits the operator to communicate with the microprocessor. These components are part of a sophisticated immunoassay, enzyme-linked immunoabsorbent assay (ELISA), which is useful in a wide variety of disciplines. This assay identifies antigens. Using the mathematical analyses developed for radioimmunoassay, the dose response curves are fitted to a series of models. The programs include X and Y transforms such as logit – log, 4-parameter logistic, and probit models. Fackrell et al. (1985) used programmable automatic dispensers – diluters, programmable microwell plate washers, programmable multiwell plate readers, and robot arms for transfer of the microwell plate to reduce tedious manipulation and ensure reproducibility in the measurement of optical density or absorbance due to the reaction of immobilized enzyme with its substrate. These workers advise that the user of data analysis packages work with a computer programmer who is knowledgeable in the mathematics. The program should include interaction between the user and the computer, be of the modular type, that is, allow data input from a variety of assays and be flexible in the use of algorithms, data storage, and input. These authors have found in analysis of staphylococcal alphatoxin that one should not rely solely on graphics or statistics and that evaluation of model fit should include visualization of the dose-response curve by an experienced analyst.

Many types of automated data collection and analysis systems are rapidly becoming available. These few examples are reported solely to indicate the utility of such procedures to ecological research.

6.0. BENEFITS OF COMPUTER ASSISTED LEARNING TO MICROBIAL AUTECOLOGY

A secondary limiting factor in the adaptation of computer skills to microbial autecology relate to the computer literacy of the scientist. Successful implementation of the skills requires program development, individual insight into ecological research needs, and the capability to understand the idiosyncrasies of computer controlled and, at times, generated data. The requisite training may be derived from computer assisted learning. In this situation, the student can become accustomed to the use of the computer and observe the direct application of the techniques to relevant study areas.

Whiting (1985) lists six topics where computer assisted learning may be most applicable:

a. Epidemiological investigations into infectious diseases.
b. Fermentor monitoring and control.
c. Taxonomy of bacteria.
d. Genetics of fungi and bacteria.
e. Bacterial metabolism.
f. Ecological simulation.

Several of these are of special interest to the microbial ecologist. For example, taxonomy lends itself well to the teaching sphere. Heimbrook (personal communication) used a mainframe program that matched characteristics of bacteria in percentages. This program has been used for several years and has been a successful teaching aid. For institutions that cannot offer mainframe space to students, the program BACTID written by Jilly (personal communication), which runs on most microcomputers, is an excellent alternative.

BACTID identifies unknown strains after comparing them with a known data set and is based on the Baysean theory of probability. The database is the test responses of known strains and the unknown test responses are compared to it. The probable identification, the likelihood, and the similarity of the unknown in relation to the suggested identifications are also calculated. The files are in ASCII format and are generated using a word processing program on a microcomputer.

There are several features that should encourage the use of computer assisted instruction. The student can pace the course of study and the instructor's time is saved, particularly if the program coaches the student at critical decision points, such as the selection of input parameters and procedures. Necessary changes of direction should be accompanied by instructions from the program.

Use of computer assisted learning may also aid in exposing students to complex experiments that ordinarily could not be conducted in a classroom situation. Frequently the cost of running an actual experiment is prohibitive. The expense of a computer simulation is considerably less. The development of microcomputers has placed computer assisted learning and its benefits within the reach of most post-secondary institutions.

Examples of programs that have been used in teaching with some success are FERMT by Bungay (1971) and CCSP written by Computers in the Undergraduate Science Curriculum under Bazin and Saunders (1973). FERMT is the simulation of an industrial batch fermentation where the input data is the amount of raw material used and the program calculates the profit. CCSP (continuous culture simulation program) is based on Monod kinetics and estimates the μ_{max} and K_s based on the following Monod equation:

$$\mu = \mu_{max}\, S/(K_s + S)$$

where μ = specific growth rate and S = concentration of limiting substrate.

The CCSP program can use competitive inhibition, noncompetitive inhibition, and substrate inhibition as well as Monod kinetics. The output can be biomass density, limiting nutrient concentration, and/or inhibitor concentration.

Heimbrook's (1984) advice on the use of microcomputers in education is as follows: Computers should be used as an aid and the programs should be designed to fit the needs of the course, the students, and the skills of the students. If the numbers of students are far in excess of the available hardware, alternative exercises that do not use computers may be necessary. With the growing number of computer literate students, this may cease to be an option. Flashy programs that don't contribute to the student's understanding are as ineffective as those that are oversimplified, repetitive, and dull. A successful program is one that the students enjoy, where the learning process is carefully controlled, and that has a component of unintended learning.

Microcomputers are well suited to the advanced class in microbial ecology, which are focusing on special topics. Most of the programs cited in this chapter could be useful for a research oriented class (particularly the MPN counting programs).

A science student should not leave the university without some minimal computer experience. If that seems a bit overstated, it would be similar to Thomas Paine saying that he didn't learn to write because pushing that scratchy quill pen was tedious and anti-intellectual.

7.0. CONCLUSIONS

Microbial autecology is in all reality an academic enigma. Few studies have been identified specifically as being in the autecological subdiscipline, but, in fact, much of microbial ecology reported to date falls within this category. Although many microbiological studies may be classified under this research heading, scientific advancement has been slow and at times progress is difficult to detect. Scientific limitations have resulted not from the lack of inquisitiveness but rather from limitation of the vision of these individuals by practical technical difficulties. Visualization of individual microorganisms in many fields, quantification or even the detection of their activity, and manipulation of the data necessary to describe totally the function of individual microbial species in situ was a seemingly insurmountable problem. The increasing availability of computers to bench scientists and the growing computer literacy of the scientific population has provided the means of overcoming these difficulties. This observation is most readily documented by the more frequent encounters with numerical taxonomic or species diversity studies in the literature and/or the common "harrassment" by salesmen wishing to provide the latest in computer assisted laboratory equipment. The examples provided in this chapter demonstrate that indeed great gains have been made in supplying the software needs of the microbial autecologist. These studies provide the base for a rapidly growing library of computer programs for data collection, analysis, and even publication. We may conclude, therefore, that the microbial ecologist is rapidly approaching the state of only being limited by intellectual capacities (and, of course, by funding). The question has changed from what can I do with the tools available to what do we really need to know about the behavior of the microbial populations in this ecosystem?

REFERENCES

Anderberg, M. R. (1973). *Cluster Analysis for Applications.* Academic, London.

Bader, F. B. (1982). "Kinetics of double substrate—limited growth," in M. J. Bazin, ed., *Microbial Population Dynamics.* CRC Press, Boca Raton, pp. 1–32.

Bazin, M. J. and P. T. Saunders (1973). Non-steady state studies of nitrification in soil: Theoretical considerations. *Soil Biol. Biochem.,* 5:45–57.

Bazin, M. J. and P. T. Saunders (1985). CAL in Microbiology: A note of caution. Collegiate Microcomputer III (2):145–147.

Box, G. E. P. and G. M. Jenkins (1970). *Time Series Analysis, Forecasting and Control.* Holden-Day, San Francisco.

Buck, G. (1985). A review of KNOWLEDGEMAN, an integrated information management system. Microbiology Division, Clinical Laboratories, The University of Texas, Medical Branch, Galveston.

Bungay, H. R. (1971). FERMT—a fermentation process game. *Proc. Biochem.,* 4:38–39.

Caldwell, D. E. (1985). New developments in computer-enhanced microscopy (CEM). *J. Microbiol. Meth.,* 4:1–10.

Caldwell, D. E. and J. J. Germida (1985). Evaluation of difference imagery for visualizing and quantitating microbial growth. *Can. J. Microbiol.,* 31:35–44.

Carmichael, J. W. and P. H. A. Sneath (1969). Taxometric Maps. *Syst. Zool.,* 18:402–415.

Characklis, W. G. (1983). "Process analysis in Microbial Systems: Biofilms as a case study," in M. Bazin, ed., *Mathematics in Microbiology.* Academic, London (pp. 171–234).

Chatfield, C. (1975). *The Analysis of Time Series: Theory and Practice.* Chapman and Hall, London.

Clark, K. R. and N. J. P. Owens (1983). A simple and versatile microcomputer program for the determination of 'most probable number'. *J. Microbiol. Meth.,* 1:133–137.

Colwell, R. R. (1976). "Computer science and technology in a modern culture collection," in *The Role of Culture Collections in the Era of Molecular Biology.* American Society for Microbiology, Washington, D.C. (pp. 9–20).

Costello, P. J. and P. R. Monk (1985). Image analysis method for the rapid counting of *Saccharomyces cerivisiae* cells. *Appl. Environ. Microbiol.,* 49:863–866.

Creekmore, W. (1983). *Through the micromaze. A visual guide from Ashton–Tate.* Ashton–Tate, Company Culver City.

Dalrymple, J. F. and J. M. Crowther (1983). "Theory and practice of time domain techniques," in M. Bazin, ed., *Mathematics in Microbiology.* Academic, London (pp. 233–285).

El-Shaarawi, A. A. (1985). Some goodness-of-it methods for the Poisson plus added zeros distribution. *Appl. Environ. Microbiol.,* **49**:1304–1306.

Fackrell, H. B. and A. H. Glascow (1984). An interface to input analog signals to a remotely located computer. *Int. J. Bio-Med. Comput.,* **15**:159–164.

Fackrell, H. B., O. P. Surujballi, and S. R. Burgess (1985). Eliza data reduction: A review. *J. Clin. Immunoassay,* **8**:213–219.

Freidman, R. B., D. Bruce, J. MacLowry, and V. Brenner (1973). Computer Assisted Identification of Bacteria. *Am. J. Clin. Pathol.,* **60**:395–403.

Fry, J. C., N. C. B. Humphrey, and T. C. Iles (1981). Time series analysis for identifying cyclic components in microbiological data. *J. Appl. Bacteriol.,* **50**:189–224.

Goodall, D. W. (1964). A probabilistic similarity index. *Nature (London),* **203**:1098.

Gordon, A. S. and F. Millero (1983). Measurement of the activity of attached bacteria using a sorption calorimeter. *J. Microbiol. Meth.,* **1**:291–296.

Hada, H. S., M. I. Krishevsky, and R. K. Sizemore (1983). The use of cluster analysis to help determine the function of plasmids in marine Vibrio species. *J. Microbiol. Meth.,* **1**:229–237.

Hall, A. V. (1965). The peculiarity index; a new function for use in numerical taxonomy. *Nature (London),* **206**:952.

Hampel, W. (1979). "Application of microcomputers in the study of microbial processes," in T. K. Ghose, A. Feichter, and N. Blakebrough, eds., *Mass Transfer and Process Control,* Vol. 13. Advances in Biochemical Engineering. Springer-Verlag, New York, pp. 1–33.

Heimbrook, M. (1984). Microcomputers in Education. *Microbiology Computer Users Group Newsletter,* **2**:11–14.

Holder-Franklin, M. A. (1984). Mathematical analysis of bacterial test responses. Bacteriologie Marine. *Colloq. Int. C.N.R.S.,* **331**:71–77.

Holder-Franklin, M. A., L. J. Wuest, and M. Franklin (1980). Oscillations in bacterial viable counts as revealed by time series analysis. Abstracts of the Annual Meeting, American Society for Microbiology. **61**:173.

Holder-Franklin, M. A. and L. J. Wuest (1983). Population dynamics of bacteria in relation to environmental change as measured by factor analysis. *J. Microbiol. Methods,* **1**:209–227.

Howell, J. A. (1983). "Mathematical Models in Microbiology," in M. Bazin, ed., *Mathematics in Microbiology.* Academic, London.

Jackman, P. J. H. (1983). A program in BASIC for numerical taxonomy of micro-organisms based on electrophoretic band positions. *Microbios Lett.,* **23,** 119–124.

Krambeck, C., H.-J. Krambeck, and J. Overbeck (1981). Microcomputer-assisted biomass determination of plankton bacteria on scanning electron micrographs. *Appl. Environ. Microbiol.,* **42**:142–149.

Krichevsky, M. I. (1982). Coping with computers and computer evangelists. *Ann. Rev. Microbiol.,* **36**:311–321.

Lance, G. N. and W. T. Williams (1966). A generalized sorting strategy for computer classifications. *Nature (London),* **212**:218–219.

Lefkovitch, L. P. (1974). "Choosing clustering levels for non-hierarchical procedures," in G. F. Estabrook, ed., *Proceedings of the Eighth International Conference on Numerial Taxonomy.* Freeman, San Francisco (pp. 132–142).

Legendre, L. and P. Legendre (1983). *Numerical Ecology: Developments in Environmental Modelling,* Vol. 3. Elsevier, Amsterdam.

Legendre, P., B. Baleux, and M. Troussellier (1984). Dynamics of pollution-indicator and heterotrophic bacteria in sewage treatment lagoons. *Appl. Environ. Microbiol.,* **48**:586–593.

Litchfield, C. (1979). Microbial contributions to organic mineralization in the waters and sediments of the New York Bight. Center for Coastal and Environmental Studies. Rutgers, The State University, New Brunswick, N. J.

MacDonnell, M. T., E. Russek, and R. R. Colwell (1984). An interactive microcomputer program for the computation of most probable number. *J. Microbiol. Methods,* **2**:1–7.

May, R. M. (1976). *Theoretical Ecology: Principles and Applications.* Blackwell, Oxford.

McCormick, S. S., H. F. Mengoli, and M. A. Gerencser (1985). Polyacrilamide gel electrophoresis of whole cell preparations of *Actinomyces* spp. *Int. J. Syst. Bacteriol.,* **35**:429–433.

Milligan, G. W. and L. M. Sokol (1980). *Educ. Psychol. Meas.,* **40**:755–759.

Misri, R. and R. K. Poole (1983). An apparatus for the continuous and simultaneous monitoring of oxygen and solute uptake by growing microbial cultures. Application to synchronous and asynchronous cultures of *Escherichia coli. J. Microbiol. Methods,* **1**:181–190.

Monod, J. (1942). *Recherches sur la Croissance des bacteriennes,* 2nd ed., Hermann, Paris.

Newman, E. I. and A. Watson (1977). Microbial abundance in the rhizosphere: a computer model. *Plant Soil,* **45**:17–56.

Nie, N. H., C. H. Hull, J. G. Jenkins, K. D. Steinbrenner, and H. Bent (1975). *Statistical Package for the Social Sciences,* 2nd ed. McGraw Hill, New York (pp. 383–397).

Pettipher, G. L. and U. M. Rodrigues (1982). Semi-automated counting of bacteria and somatic cells in milk using epifluorescence microscopy and television image analysis. *J. Appl. Bacteriol.,* **53**:323–329.

Pickett, A. M., H. H. Topiwala, and M. J. Bazin (1979). A new method of industrial bioreactor operation: The transient operation technique. *Proc. Biochem.,* **14**:10.

Rodbard, D. R. and L. G. Graber (1975) PAGE-PACK: Polyacrylamide Gel Electrophoresis. Biomedical Computing Technology Information Center, Vanderbilt Medical Center, Nashville.

Rolhf, F. J., J. Kishpaugh, and D. Kirk (1971). NT-SYS numerical taxonomy system of multivariate statistical programs. Technical Report. State University of New York at Stony Brook, Stony Brook.

Rypka, E. W., E. R. Fletcher, and R. G. Babb (1982). Unified systems approach to medical microbiology: 1. Introduction and methods. *J. Clin. Lab. Autom.,* **2**:191–200.

Sackin, M. J. (1981). Vigour and Pattern as Applied to Multistate Quantitative Characters in Taxonomy. *J. Gen. Microbiol.,* **122**:247–254.

Sackin, M. J. (1986). Computer programs for classification and identification. *Methods Microbiol.:* **19.** (in press). Academic, New York.

Schulz, G. E. (1983). In J. Felsenstein, ed., *Numerical Taxonomy.* Springer-Verlag, New York.

Sieracki, M. J., P. W. Johnson, and J. McN. Sieburth (1985). Detection, enumeration and sizing of planktonic bacteria by image-analyzed epifluorescence microscopy. *Appl. Environ. Microbiol.,* **49:**799–810.

Simkins, S. and M. Alexander (1984). Models for mineralization kinetics with the variables of substrate concentration and population density. *Appl. Environ. Microbiol.,* **47:**1299–1306.

Simkins, S. and M. Alexander (1985). Non-linear estimation of Monod kinetics that best describe mineralization of several substrate concentrations by dissimilar bacterial densities. *Appl. Environ. Microbiol.,* **50:**816–824.

Sneath, P. H. A. (1968). Vigour and pattern in taxonomy. *J. Gen. Microbiol.,* **54:**1–11.

Whiting, J. (1985). *Microbiological CAL. In Binary.* The Society for General Microbiology Computer Club, London.

Williams, F. M. (1973). Mathematical modelling of microbial populations. *Bull. Ecol. Res. Commun. (Stockholm),* **17:**417–426.

Wishart, D. (1969). An algorithm for hierarchical classification. *Biometrics,* **22:**165–170.

5 ECOLOGICAL RELATIONSHIPS OF MICROBIOTA IN WATER AND SOIL AS REVEALED BY DIVERSITY MEASUREMENTS

Maxine A. Holder-Franklin
Department of Biological Sciences
University of Windsor
Windsor, Ontario
Canada

1.0. AUTECOLOGY AND MICROBIAL DIVERSITY

The diversity dynamic is central to studies of natural microbial populations. Investigations into the factors that control the maintenance of individual species in an econiche will not be productive until we know the status of microbial populations and how they relate to each other. The isolation and identification of microbial strains, although far from perfect, is an essential part of microbial ecology. Without this form of basic information, population dynamics could not be elucidated.

Diversity measurements of natural microbial populations have been developed largely to demonstrate effects of perturbations of an econiche. A variety of biological parameters have been utilized in these studies and include microbial biomass, enumeration of colonies, colonial differentiation, microscopic cell counts, enumeration of species and genera as well as microbial profiles determined by cluster analysis and factor analysis. The improvement in computer programs for mathematical analysis has been reflected in the increase in research reports using these methods. The algorithms employed in microbial diversity studies now appearing in bacteriological literature have their origins in other fields, that is, the physical sciences, psychology, plant and animal ecology. The rationale for utilization of diversity formulas in ecology has been well described by Pielou (1975).

Biologists are constantly seeking mathematical analysis of qualitative data. This is particularly true when methods are required to evaluate the relative importance of individual species within community structure. One measure is diversity (Alexander, 1971). Bacterial diversity in natural environments can be measured by noting the variations in colonial morphology, by citing the species identified or by employing a diversity index or an algorithm of multivariate statistics. The diversity index can be calculated from the species numbers or the phenons created by cluster analysis. Diversity can also be measured by factor analysis that can utilize a wide variety of information sources, descriptors, or attributes to profile the biotic and abiotic components of the environment.

Studies of diversity in bacterial populations are frequently linked to the environmental parameters that created the diversity, temperature, nutrients, ion concentration, pH, and oxygen levels, as well as spatial and temporal parameters. This discussion of bacterial diversity within selected aquatic and terrestrial environments will focus on the analytical methods that have increased our understanding of the econiche. The studies to be reported are for the most part those using a numerical or mathematical measurement of the biological data. The possible uses of diversity measurements in microbial autecology have not been clearly demonstrated. However, there are several interesting and even provocative reports that employ diversity indices in this field (Hood et al., 1975; Gamble et al., 1977; Kaneko et al., 1977; Bell et al., 1982; Mok et al., 1984). The diversity index does not have the discriminating power of factor analysis for revealing the variance in representative samples from large areas but it could be the preferred algorithm for a study of succession in a limited econiche (Martin and Bianchi, 1980).

Odum (1969) described the process of succession as one of the binding concepts of ecology. This concept is particularly germaine to microbial ecology where constantly changing environments create pressure for change in the microbial population. Diversity indices can be used to measure this change. Microbial succession studies were described by Alexander (1971) as shifts in the species composition and abundance. This apparently simple definition describes the basic principles of diversity studies and should form the nucleus of the research design. The mathematical concept is also deceptively simple. Kempton defines a diversity index as a one dimensional representation of the species abundance vector (Kempton, 1979).

2.0. THE HISTORY AND STRUCTURE OF SPECIES DIVERSITY IN BRIEF

2.1. Concepts of Diversity

The concept of species diversity was introduced by Fisher et al. (1943) and has been refined over the years to accommodate many ecological information sets. The large body of literature that has accumulated in the fields of plant and animal ecology has consistently supported the use of several indices that appear to have ecological application. The controversy over the appropriateness of these indices has been partially resolved by plant and animal scientists but not by microbiologists.

Measurements of diversity in the ecology of macrobiota are reasonably precise and the recognition of subdivisions or species contribute significantly to studies of fluctuations in biota. In the disciplines dealing with microbiota, recognition of distinct genetic entities becomes less clear as the trophic level descends. The study of plants and animals using species diversity indices is extensive, and the refinements and understanding of diversity measurements comes from those sources (Routledge, 1979). The controversy over the use of mathematical formulas originally constructed to solve very different types of problems than those of species diversity created a literature of its own (Routledge, 1980; Hurlbert, 1971). Hairston et al. (1968) rejected the use of a diversity index that assumes that the distribution of individuals follows a mathematical form. In addition, they claimed that the variables are strongly influenced by the number of species and therefore not independent, creating an inherent flaw in the logic. Hurlbert (1971) does not recommend the use of species diversity indices to measure properties of a biological community and stated that the mathematical entity "diversity" does not exist because there is no diversity scale for comparison of all members of an econiche. The problem is compounded in bacterial taxonomy as common features for comparison are few, that is, the tests or features that describe one group may be very different from those used to describe another group. The lack of universal tests such as the Gram's stain could theoretically inhibit diversity measurement by indices. Numerical taxonomy does have the potential to approximate scalar dimensions or at least form the basis for a universal code of common attributes (Colwell et al., 1968; Sneath and Sokal, 1973).

One of the most important advances in microbial ecology was the development of computerized analysis of bacterial test data that was pioneered by Sneath and Sokal (1973), Gyllenberg (1963), Skyring and Quadling (1969), and Colwell et al. (1968) to name a few. Colwell's development of numerical taxonomy within the ecological context has contributed a valuable dimension to microbial ecology.

Many studies using these methods (including ours) were prompted by this early work. There were as many skeptics in 1968 concerning numerical taxonomy in ecological studies of bacteria as there are presently for species diversity.

Diversity studies within the general context of ecology rarely included bacteria even in multidisciplinary projects. One of the earliest reports that recognized the role of bacteria in the general context of ecology, that is, where detailed analyses of species were included in an ecological study was published by Patrick (1949). A large research group surveyed the biota of the Conestoga Basin, Lancaster County, Pennsylvania, in an extensive multidisciplinary study that included speciation of the bacteria. They concluded that the drop in species variety was attributed to pollution. The average numbers of species, fungal, algal, bacterial, protozoa, insect, and mollusc were calculated at each station. The physicochemical data collected at the same time were compared with the bacterial data. Some estimates could be made of the degree of pollution from the biota surveyed. The data were not analyzed by the diversity index but Patrick demonstrated that multidisciplinary surveys were needed to solve ecological problems and that observations on species diversity could supply information on the conditions of the environment.

2.2. The Species Diversity Index

A diversity index measures the relative numbers of groups in a population that have been classified. The classification system for plants is reliable and the information code is common and stable. Within the microbial world, the classification is not based on a common set of criteria. Therefore, the change in code from group to group introduces an error that has not been accounted for in the index formulas. However, Pielou (1966a) has suggested a solution (see Section 5.2).

A species is a stable entity with > 90% of its genome intact and in which the phenetic expression of the genome is clearly recognizable. The criteria for classification have been recently reviewed by Schleifer and Stackbrandt (1983) who recommend chemotaxonomy but admit that the inclusion of chemotaxonomic markers has not become universal. The best hope for revealing the phylogenetic relationships of procaryotes is the comparative analysis of oligonucleotide sequences of ribosomal 16S RNA. However, it will be some time before all groups have a revised classification based on analysis and hybridization of DNA and RNA. Other markers will be used until this task is completed since research on population changes based on genetic homogeneity cannot wait for the universal development of chemotaxonomy.

The term species diversity must be laid to rest in microbial autecology until the word species has been defined. Staley (1980) objects to species diversity measurements and proposes strain diversity. In essence, numerical taxonomy is a form of strain clustering. The term species diversity is comprised of species abundance, evenness, equitability, and richness. These attributes are compatible with microbial ecology. Perhaps it would be worthwhile to examine the principles of species diversity in order to know which are meaningful to the microbiologist and which must be set aside.

Why use a mathematical index, why not just make a quantitative assessment using simple averages and percentages? Why impose a mathematical formula on questionable numbers? Are we giving credibility to suspect information? Can microbiologists claim that diversity indices are measurements of community stability as other biologists do? Can diversity indices be related to other ecological parameters? Both the case for and the case against will be presented because the jury is still out on the value of diversity indices in microbial autecology, largely because of the small number of studies reported.

In the microbial world, the isolation and identification of individual organisms in a liter of water or 500 g of soil should be called species density to include the spatial component. The projection of the microbial content of a liter of water as representative of Lake Superior or the North Sea is not logical. The misconception is further exacerbated if the data on the microbiota is interpreted using a formula originally devised to analyze sound signals without regard to the nature of the original variables.

The measurement of diversity, the variety of flora or fauna in an econiche, requires an examination of these components.

1. Richness—the number of species per sample.
2. Evenness—the relative abundance of species (equitability).
3. Density—the total number of organisms per sample.

If the species diversity increases, it may be due to an increase in the number of species or due to an increase in the equitability, that is, the abundance of species becomes more even. De Jong (1975) demonstrated that the increase in diversity that follows the increase in species plateaus and attributes this to the mathematics rather than to ecological processes. However, observations of microbial behavior indicate that the plateau is quite possible on ecological grounds. At present, the restrictions on species numbers relate to the research methods rather than the intrinsic nature of the populations.

The diversity indices developed in plant and animal ecology and most commonly employed in microbial research are the Simpson (1949) and Shannon indices (Shannon and Weaver, 1959). De Jong has shown that the Shannon, McIntosh, and Simpson indices are linearly related to evenness and the $\log_2$ of the number of species. The Simpson and McIntosh indices are influenced more by evenness and less by richness than Shannon's index. The Shannon index was the most strongly correlated with species richness and the Simpson index the least.

2.3. Diversity According to Pielou

Pielou described the use of species diversity indices (Pielou, 1966a, 1966b, 1975) and classified the collections analyzed into the following types (Pielou, 1966c).

Type A   Collections small enough for a complete census of species.
Type B   Larger collections sampled randomly but completely censused.
Type C   Random sample with number of species unknown but with a smooth species abundance curve.
Type D   As in type C with variable species abundance.
Type E   Collections that cannot be sampled randomly.

The indices within these categories that have been applied to studies in microbial ecology are Shannon and Simpson, type B. An index with potential is Brillouin, type A.

2.4. Communities and Collections

The definition of community can vary and become any collection of organisms sampled, for example, a pail of water from the ocean is a random sample within the depth parameter. A fully censused community is called a collection. Pielou (1966c) and Wilhm (1968) regard biomass as an acceptable collection. Whether a water sample is representative of the whole econiche is in serious question.

2.5. Diversity Indices in Mixed Communities

Although organisms of many species that form a collection from one econiche cannot be ordered on a linear scale, diversity indices can be calculated on the basis of certain statistical properties. Hurlbert (1971), who does not agree with the use of diversity indices, has suggested a formula that measures the proportion of potential interindividual encounters assuming every individual in the collection can encounter all other individuals. The formula is the complement of the Simpson diversity index and is as follows (Pielou, 1966b).

$$\Delta_2 = 1 - \sum_{i=1}^{S} \pi_i^2$$

where $\pi = N_i/N$ and $S =$ number of species.

This formula is mentioned here as it has the potential to elucidate the frequency of transfer of genetic information in soil and aquatic bacteria due to conjugation.

2.6. The Shannon Index

The Shannon index was based on information theory or communication theory where the fundamental problem was to reproduce a message sent from another point. The information sources used to develop the theory are of various types, sequences of letters, as a function of time or functions of space, time, and light intensity as in television. In a discrete noiseless system there are restrictions on the type of information that can be analyzed as Weaver described in the classic volume on Shannon's theory of communication (Shannon and Weaver, 1959). Beginning with first principles, Weaver described the formulation of communication theory as based on the probability that one set of information is selected over another and is dependent on the sender, the transmitting medium and the receiver and, most importantly, assumes free choice. The information is measured by the log of the number of available choices. Weaver stressed that information must not be confused with meaning. In the diversity studies of most species, the meaning is introduced before the calculation is made, that is, everything is precoded by the technique (the tests selected, the sampling method, and the data analysis). Margalef (1951) introduced Shannon's information theory into the study of mixed populations and has transposed this theory into ecological concepts chiefly relating to phytoplankton, but the information concept is so universal that it can also be transposed into the calculation of microbial diversity.

In microbiological research, the information source is the phenome, the transmitter is the observer, and the receiver is the database. The interference with the signal is the environmental conditions that supress or stimulate certain species. The selection of operating genome and resulting phenome are both governed by the law of probability, which depends on the successive choices — gene operating or not operating. For instance, if an organism is fermenting glucose, the probability is low that it is utilizing glucose aerobically. This is also true for nitrification versus denitrification. The appearance of phenotypes is a stochastic process and thus is an acceptable unit as a measure of information. The information is the entropy, that is, the measure of the degree of randomness. This entropy continually increases, that is, the system becomes more random.

The information or freedom of choice that is measured is the number of species or a biological parameter such as the biomass of the collection that has been selected (Whilm, 1968). When this measure is compared with the maximum entropy, a figure for the relative entropy can be obtained. If the phenotype is 10% random choice then 1 – 0.1 is the redundancy or that part of the phenotype that is governed by the statistical rules. The lack of meaning in the calculation of the diversity index is exemplified by the fact that both entropy and redundancy are under the control of the environment. Also, we are unable to distinguish the relative influence on each component.

The highly organized system gives very little freedom of choice. A drop in entropy is clearly seen in the stressed ecosystem. Therefore, use of information theory to measure entropy or species diversity of a microbial population is valid. It is the quality of the information that may be suspect. Shannon has called the entropy that is relative to the signal or quality of the information, equivocation and the information, the degree of uncertainty. The measurement of equivocation is the average uncertainty in the information. If we knew the exact size of the genome and its full potential of information we could measure the degree of uncertainty more accurately.

It is not surprising that serious questions were raised on the efficacy of this formula to deal with the complexities of an econiche (Hurlbert, 1971). However, an econiche contains information that can be coded, measured, and compared. An interesting feature of Shannon's index is that the degree of randomness is being measured. In most biological studies, the constraints of sampling impose restrictions on the degree of randomness. As Pielou (1966a) states, in an infinite population the probability that a randomly selected individual will belong to the class A_i is P_i as shown in the formula

$$H' = -\sum p_i \log p_i$$

The formula proposed by Shannon is a measure of the information content contained in a code whose probabilities of occurrence are $p_1, p_2, \ldots, p_n$. H' has its largest value when all choices are equally probable and is zero when one choice reaches unity. Therefore, the uncertainty or information is zero and the diversity is zero. This places a limitation on the use of indices for comparison with other parameters. H' can also be increased by increasing the number of choices. The use of this measure, as occurs in most ecological studies, where the code is based on criteria that are common to the evaluation of each group is mathematically sound, and is based on the laws of probability. The plant population in plots of comparable size would lend itself to this type of analysis. The diversity of corals, another sessile group, also have been demonstrated by the Shannon index (Liddell and Ohlhorst, 1981). The objections of Hurlburt (1971) that there is a lack of scalar dimensions is partially resolved within the biological divisions where each member is evaluated by the same characteristics. In a bacterial study, population selection is not random. The selection process may appear to be random if the colonies are not chosen by criteria that exclude any type. However, the colony isolation procedure is intrinsically restricted by the growth media. This is the first departure from the statistical requirements. In addition, classical speciation is not based on a single set of characters, therefore there is no longer a common code for selecting a genetically defined group. The solution for this may be as described in Section 4.0.

Evaluation of Shannon's index can be improved by calculating evenness by the following formula:

$$J = \frac{H'}{\log S}$$

where S = number of species and H' = Shannon index.

Pielou (1966b) suggests that the calculation of evenness is a necessary adjunct to the Shannon diversity index.

2.7. Brillouin's Index

Pielou (1966c) cites Brillouin's formula as a good example of Type A collection.

$$H = \frac{1}{N} \log \frac{N!}{N!_1 N!_2 \cdots N!_S}$$

where N = total number of individuals and S = number of species.

This formula is theoretically appropriate for small populations of bacteria that can be completely identified. Experiments in bacterial chemotaxis or surface adherance could benefit from this type of analysis. A field experiment that has been reported by Dickman (1969) is one of the earliest examples in which microbial population diversity was analyzed by the Shannon and the Margalef indices. All the algae adhering to glass slides suspended in three temperate lakes over 4 weeks were speciated. This met the criterion of being a well-censused population. This sectored population could have been analyzed by Brillouin's formula, but Dickman properly selected the Shannon index as not every field on the slide was enumerated. Those slides coated with germanium dioxide, which is toxic to diatoms, had a lower diversity index than those not coated with the toxicant.

2.8. Simpson's Index

Routledge (1979) recommends the use of Simpson's index over several of the most commonly used indices to define local diversity and segregation components.

Swift (1975) employed the Simpson index,

$$\Delta = 1 \bigg/ \sum^{2}_{p_i}$$

where p_i = relative frequency of isolation of any species i, to study the change in fungal species diversity during progressive decomposition of branch wood. The rates of decomposition of litter is a powerful determinant in the terrestrial ecosystem.

The structure of the fungal community changed during litter decay. The diversity of the macro community (all samples) decreased but the size of the unit communities (one branch) averaged four species per branch throughout the study. In the terminal stages of decay the species observed most frequently were retained, which implies a greater homogeniety but also that a stimulus to the community had occurred. In the soil samples examined by Swift, fungal diversity decreased with depth. Fungal diversity was lower in the organic and mineral horizons than in the litter layer, which coincided with a decrease in oxygen.

2.9. Discrimination and Indices

The ecological value of diversity measurements is linked to the discriminating character of the index. To be effective, it must distinguish between very similar environments.

In microbiological sampling, repeated samples from the same site vary to such an extent that it is difficult to imagine that the discriminating character of an index can be tested. Analysis of discrimination is rarely reported. Taylor et al. (1976) showed that on repeated samples of moths from a variety of sites in Great Britain, the reciprocal of Simpson's index, which measures species abundance, discriminated between a range of sites. Discrimination was poor for small samples but improved as the species of medium abundance become more predominant. The success of this study was due to the representative quality of the samples. Ohlhorst (1982), fortuitously selected a population that yielded clearly defined diel behavior. Observations on the diel migration patterns of demersal reef zooplankton revealed that the zooplankton rise at variable rates during the night. Migration peaked during the period of least planktivore activity. Diversity values (H') decreased significantly during the night. The real difference was supported by the Kendall coefficient of concordance, (P). Evenness (J') was also calculated and the influence of the dominant species was apparent. The diversity calculation and the careful data collection contributed to the credibility of the conclusions.

3.0. DIVERSITY INDICES EVALUATED

3.1. In Studies of Macrobiota

The annual mean Shannon and Simpson diversity indices of the benthic macroinvertebrates of a Hydrilla infested central Florida lake were calculated by Scott and Osborne (1981) who monitored the Hydrilla biomass, the macroinvertebrates, and 11 water quality parameters for 1 yr. The Shannon index dropped between February and March when a decrease in the number of species richness and evenness. The Margalef (1951) index $d = (s - 1)/\ln N$ was became dominant at that time, which resulted in a high Simpson index. However, there was no significant difference ($p = 0.05$) between monthly mean values of both indices for the remaining months of the year. The annual mean Simpson and Shannon indices were the same for a clean lake and the Hydrilla infested lake. The diversity indices did not contribute to the understanding of the lakes being studied. The species did change with the season and could be related to changes in the environment.

Holt and Strawn (1983) have described the macrozooplankton in Trinity and Upper Galveston Bays, Texas in terms of the Shannon diversity index (DI), species richness and evenness for 3 1/2 yr. Cluster analysis was compared with diversity analysis. The Shannon diversity and species evenness were positively correlated with each other but richness values were often negatively correlated with the DI and the evenness. H' values were higher in the cool seasons when the relative abundance of individuals per taxon was more even and lower in warm seasons when one taxon dominated the collections. The DI varied from year to year in response to changes in abundance. The variation in indices was sufficient to discourage these workers from using the DI. Using discriminant analysis, the site groups could be distinguished from one another on the basis of salinity and temperature. During this 3 1/2-yr study of the estuarine region, macrozooplankton populations were strongly influenced by the river outflow into the bay. Cluster analysis revealed pronounced seasonal and annual communities and responses to salinity and temperature.

Maret and Christianson (1981) surveyed the water quality of the Big Blue River, Nebraska, including the following parameters: pH, temperature, dissolved oxygen, biochemical oxygen demand (BOD), nitrate, ammonia, benthic and planktonic invertebrates, and fecal coliforms. The survey was conducted for 1 yr with samples collected at approximately monthly intervals. The six stations used were at or near point sources of pollution along the river. The river flows through flat agricultural lands. The macroinvertebrate collection was analyzed by the Shannon index. The numbers of individuals (<100) obtained from the benthos by an Eckman bottom sampler was considered too small to satisfy the Shannon formula. Therefore, the index was calculated on the macroinvertebrates found attached to a submerged multiplate artifical substrate. The fecal coliforms and the water quality parameters were indicative of pollution. The indices were low and followed the low diversity, stressed community structure of Odum (1969). However, the physicochemical results of one station were contradictory to the diversity values. Maret and Christianson (1981) concluded that the diversity values must be examined with other features in order to evaluate water quality.

3.2. Comparison of Indices in A Succession Study

Tinnberg (1979) studied the diversity within a phytoplankton community in a eutrophic lake from 1961 to 1975. Five indices were compared according to species richness and evenness. The Margalef (1951) index $d = (s - 1)/\ln N$ was the most sensitive to species numbers. Shannon's (H') index and Brillouin's (H) index were influenced by the most abundant species. Shannon's index was not influenced by species above 10–15 of the most abundant. The Shannon, Simpson, and McIntosh indices all approached a constant value. The study showed an interesting succession of phytoplankton where both cell numbers and individuals were used in the calculations. At the peak of eutrophication *Oscillatoria agardhii* dominated. *Anabaena, Aphanizomenon,* and *Pediastrum* were rare or absent. Species numbers were low before the diversion of waste water from the lake. The diversity increased and previously rare species became apparent. The increase in diversity followed the decrease in pollution. However, *Oscillatoria* remained dominant. The Brillouin and Shannon indices were in good agreement using both cell numbers and individuals. Simpson's index and McIntosh's index approximated Shannon and Brillouin if based on counts of individual cell numbers. Tinnberg (1979) strongly recommends lists of species to accompany the diversity index as the index does not give information on composition or ecology. Tinnberg does not recommend Margalef's index and cautions that Shannon's index is influenced by richness and has pointed out the need to evaluate the information concealed in the index.

4.0. SEQUENTIAL COMPARISONS AND ECOLOGICAL SUCCESSION

Cairns and Dickson (1971) proposed a very simple but useful measure of changing diversity called a sequential comparison index, which compares sequential samples to each other giving a measure of changing species of bottom fauna. The sequential comparison index was used by Larrick et al. (1981) to determine the effects of thermal, heavy and fly ash effluents on aquatic hetero-trophic bacteria. Water samples taken above, at the input of heavy and fly ash basins, and below the point source yielded populations of bacteria that indi-cated a decrease in diversity and heterotrophic activity in the more polluted areas. In addition, chromogenic bacteria and total counts increased at the input of heavy and fly ash basins. This study also revealed that bacterial heterotrophic activity measured by glucose uptake was a more subtle indicator of the changes in the population than bacterial diversity.

Cairns and Dickson (1971) were among the early advocates of diversity indices in microbial population research and recognized the value of the Bril-louin's diversity index and the redundancy expression of Wilhm and Dorris (1969). The expression is presented here as it is rarely seen in detail in the literature. The formula was used by Hood et al. (1975) as described in Section 5.1.

$$r = \frac{\bar{d}_{max} - \bar{d}_{min}}{\bar{d}_{max} - \bar{d}_{min}}$$

where the theoretical maximum diversity $\bar{d}_{max}$ and the theoretical minimum diversity are calculated using

$$\bar{d}_{max} = (1/N) [\log_2 N! - S \log_2 (N/S)!]$$
$$\bar{d}_{min} = (1/N) \{\log_2 N! - \log_2 [N - (S - 1)]!\}$$

the diversity per individual is

$$\bar{d} = -\sum (N_i/N) \log_2 (N_i/N)$$

N is the number of individuals in S species.

5.0. THEORETICAL AND PRACTICAL ASPECTS OF DIVERSITY STUDIES IN MICROBIOLOGY

5.1. Diversity Studies in Microbiology

Reports describing changes in natural populations with an ecological basis have appeared sporadically over the last 20 yrs. Descriptions of bacterial populations that are confined to species identification have provided a wealth of informa-tion of natural populations but have been limited in the ecological interpreta-tion. The rationale for using a measurement of diversity should be to improve our understanding of the econiche, that is, reveal subtleties that are not apparent in the raw data. The premise that low diversity indicates stress and high diversity, a healthy milieu, does hold in some studies. However, the *stressed* environment cannot be defined with the exception of those in the extreme end of the range such as acid mine waters (Dugan et al., 1970), excess nutrient pollution, and organisms imbedded in ice, but it is becoming more apparent that bacteria surviving in nature are not necessarily stressed in their habitat. Arctic waters and the hot springs, the deep sea vents, and the soil at depths of 50 ft or more are the acceptable environments for indigenous organisms. Biologists have categorized environments as stressed based on subjective responses. The capability of the diversity measurement to detect stress should be a serious concern of the advocates of diversity indices. It does not appear that the diversity index can detect subtle changes in the environment.

The use of mathematical diversity indices in ecological research where bacteria are the primary biotic element has begun very tentatively considering the burgeoning literature on the subject in other fields. The first attempt to solve an ecological problem using diversity measurements on samples obtained in the field was reported by Hood et al. (1975) where the bacterial diversity of pristine salt marsh sediment was compared with the diversity found in an oil field marsh sediment. The diversity index of Wilhm and Dorris (1969) was used by Hood to analyze bacterial diversity according to colony types.

The diversity measurement provided another dimension to the study even with the severe limitations placed on the data by the vagaries of bacterial colonial morphology. One of the practical problems associated with bacteria isolated from single colonies is that freshly isolated bacterial colonies from soil and water environments are frequently mixed, which may not be discovered until the isolates are cultivated on single carbon sources. In addition, one species may yield several colonial types on the same plate. This still does not preclude the use of diversity measurements of this type because the colonies appear different. Although colonial morphology meets Pielou's criteria, it is a random event but, at best, it only provides a screening or indication of diversity that should be followed by a more thorough investigation.

Probably the most intransigent feature of bacterial taxonomy from a mathematical standpoint is the lack of correlation between the phenome and the genome. In other words, the phenome becomes the "code" for the genome and each group of biota has a code. Unfortunately, the classification of bacterial taxonomic groups is based to a large extent on different sets of criteria. Many require highly specialized media to force the organisms to express the characteristic being studied. The errors of identification vary from one genus to another. To overcome the lack of evenness in the classification process and provide data that is closer to the desired species unit, several workers have chosen numerical taxonomy clusters formed at the 75, 80, or 85% levels with various interpretations as to their legitimacy as a genetic unit.

Gamble et al. (1977), in a study of denitrifying bacteria in a variety of soils identified the clusters as species or genus and introduced these clusters into the Simpson and McIntosh formulas. This extensive study demonstrated that denitrifying bacteria are more common than previously thought in a variety of soils and sediments and that they cluster at the 75% level. The indices ranged from 0 – 1.0 and agreed in the ranking of the samples. However, the indices did not correlate with the soil properties or the number of denitrifiers. This may have been due to the small numbers in each sample. The error that could have been created by giving equal value to genus and species was offset by using numerical taxonomy clusters. Kaneko et al. (1977) clustered populations from the Beaufort Sea and measured the diversity using the Shannon formula on the clusters formed by single linkage of the similarity coefficient. High species diversity was reported in the winter samples when the population density of heterotrophic bacteria was lower. When the population density was similar to the summer samples, the diversity was lower. The index in this case may have been responding to richness or evenness (equatability). The interest in the use of diversity indices in bacterial research was revived by the Gamble et al. (1977) and Kaneko et al. (1977) reports.

Numerical taxonomy clusters are an improvement over the classical speciation for diversity studies. The strains should be tested on a broad database and clustered at a high level of similarity. The expanded database is required so that each isolate in the mixed population from a natural environment will be tested on the required number of parameters to demonstrate its individual variance. That number cannot be predicted as yet. However, the clusters formed by numerical taxonomy at 75% similarity from natural populations may be phenotypically similar but contain more than one species and even more than one genus as has been demonstrated by DNA – DNA hybridization (Holder-Franklin et al., 1981) and by Sneath et al. (1981). This brings us back to the definition of species or lowest common denominator. There must be some criterion for a distinctive genetic unit to study diversity, particularly when comparing environments that are similar.

The selection of clusters at 75% similarity from a common test base has a varying species selection error rate depending on the bacterial genus. Adhering strictly to the original premise of species, the term species diversity should only be used when the entire census has been speciated. This should apply to any censused community. If a cluster is to be compared with all other strains in the numerical taxonomy analysis, the single member phenons should be included. The strain that represents a single phenon is the representative of a large population when the dilution technique is used for the isolation of colonies. This feature has been stressed in many reports (Holder-Franklin et al., 1978; Bell et al., 1980; Hauxhurst et al., 1981).

The highly similar phenon is a mathematically and ecologically acceptable unit to determine diversity within a collection using the Simpson index or the indices based on information theory. The size of the database and the level of cluster similarity determines the level of discrimination attained by the diversity index. Hauxhurst et al. (1981) stated that an artifact of low diversity may be the result of reducing the level of features such that the true heterogeneity is not detected. In our studies, using a database of 82 tests that had been carefully selected from the original oversized database of 233, low diversity was observed in a pristine stream. After several years and many studies of the St. John River and its tributaries in New Brunswick, Canada, it was apparent that redundant and nondiscriminating tests should be eliminated. Tests removed from the analysis included substrates that were used by < 1% of all strains and those that essentially gave the same information, such as high or low nutrient media. Not all of the tests that were poor discriminators were eliminated as certain tests provide the physiological information valuable in establishing relationships with environmental changes and necessary in the classical identification of species. In spite of the foregoing, a larger database does introduce essential variability into the analysis. But, do the reports in the bacteriological literature satisfy the criteria of richness, evenness, density, and discrimination as described earlier: Those elements that are necessary to elucidate the dynamic of diversity in any econiche or collection (Pielou, 1966a)? Hauxhurst et al. (1981) have addressed the equitability parameter J', the estimate of evenness, and have concluded that the census in their study was incomplete, J' is particularly sensitive to an incomplete census. In addition, correlations could not be found between population size and diversity for the marine bacterial communities being investigated. The samples may not be representative of the econiche. The physiological index, introduced in the Hauxhurst et al. (1981) report, may be very useful in succession studies in a microcosm or limited environment. Each major physiological characteristic was grouped and indexed, for example, nutritional versatility, salt tolerance, and so on, and physiological diversity was observed. Factor analysis of the same multiplicity of variables is a less cumbersome method of calculating this type of variance in a large survey.

The ability of the diversity index to discriminate, a critical but neglected feature of the DI is rarely reported in the microbiological literature. Hauxhurst analyzed the variance of the Shannon indices and demonstrated that a significant difference could be detected. Rarefaction was used to discriminate indices by Tate and Mills (1983) with quite different results. They examined a variety of drained Histosols from the Everglades agricultural area, which were undergoing a period of accelerated oxidation that is common in recovered muck soils. Pahokee muck soils from sugar cane, St. Augustinegrass, and fallow areas were examined for several metabolic parameters. Differences were observed in CO_2 production, succinate metabolism, and population densities but diversity indices did not vary significantly when compared by rarefaction. The soil bacterial indices were as follows: fallow, 2.76, sugarcane, 3.49, and St. Augustinegrass, 3.75. The bacteria isolated were similar in the three soils. A difference in bacterial and fungal activity could be observed and the population density in the cropped soils was higher. The intrinsic diversity was in evidence but was not detected by the Shannon diversity index. The strains were clustered on a reduced database; 38 tests. Mills and Wassel (1980) have demonstrated that diversity can be measured with as few as 11 or 19 tests.

The usefulness of diversity indices in the study of population shifts in our laboratory was evaluated by Bell et al. (1982) by comparing them to other methods and will be described in Section 8.0.

5.2. Hierarchical Diversity: A Theoretical Discussion

The taxonomy of the bacteria in its classical form has been established using different criteria for the designation of the genera. In addition, the species may be classified on any number of varying observations. It is this lack of order that has discouraged species diversity analysis.

Pielou (1966a) overcame the classification problem by including each classification scheme as a subset. The scheme can generate as many sets as there are genera. The species of each set are then calculated separately. First, the genera are classified and there are g genera in the G classification, that is, g is the number of genera. The proportion of the individuals in the community that belong to a certain genus $j = p_j$ ($j = 1, \ldots, g$). Again, using Pielou's designation, the species are placed into the S classification and there are s_j species in the j genus. The proportion of genus j that belong to species $k = g_{jk}$ ($k=1, \ldots, s_j$). The generic diversity is

$$H'(G) = -\sum_{j=1}^{g} p_j \log p_j$$

The species diversity of genus j is

$$H'_j(S) = -\sum_{k=1}^{s_j} q_{jk} \log q_{jk}$$

Therefore, the proportion of the species k that is in the whole community is $p_j q_{jk}$. The two levels of indices are added to obtain the diversity index. Hierarchical diversity is applicable to a bacterial data set as the genus is often a better indicator of true diversity. Distinctive bacterial species may differ from another species in one or two minor features. These features may vary also. There are many one species genera. The suggestion by Pielou (1966a) to utilize the biological hierarchy to measure diversity at two levels, the genus and species, has not been used as yet for microbiological studies. Two of the most practical problems facing the microbiologist are obtaining a complete census and calculating a diversity relationship. The use of the hierarchical diversity concept or measure of subsets could be applied to improve the census of the entire population by a summation of the strains from a series of isolation techniques, which attempt to culture every viable cell in a sample. The first stage, using a general medium to grow all of the predominant aerobic and anaerobic heterotrophs would be followed by a second stage using specialized media to detect autotrophs and species in small numbers. In this manner, some of the diversity hidden by the isolation procedures could be measured and indexed. It is mathematically possible to include many domains and many levels of information into the analysis but they should be analyzed separately as the interpretation is eventually biological.

The measurement of levels of organization may appear to be beyond the techniques available in microbiology, one of these is the concept of alpha and beta diversity. However, ter Braak (1983), as reported in Section 7.2, has addressed the concept of alpha and beta diversity in a unique analysis.

When diversity is measured, the alpha or average diversity within a habitat provides one level of information that can be used to compare large habitats with each other. The beta diversity or the amount of turnover between habitat types provides another level of analysis.

5.3. Sampling Errors in Space and Time

Sampling errors resulting from storage of samples collected from geographically or temporally diverse sites may be appreciable. For example, if aquatic bacteria in a wide geographic area are being sampled, the samples may be held for different times in containers. Wall adherence of fast swimming individuals as the sampling expedition proceeds from point A to point B could introduce a sampling error. After 2 hrs, the inner aspect of the sampling container will show adhered bacteria even on coated or plastic containers. If the time in the container was the same for all samples the loss of diversity may be similar but abundance and density are seriously affected. Marine bacterioplankton could increase significantly. The ratio of culturable cells may change, may increase as reported by Ferguson et al. (1984), or may decrease in fresh water samples from a low nutrient environment. The sampling conditions for diversity studies will vary from one econiche to another and this variance must be included in the research design.

6.0. SUCCESSION STUDIES OF MICROBIAL SPECIES

Succession has been studied in a variety of microcosms. One of the first reports of the use of species diversity indices to study succession of bacteria was reported by Gordon et al. (1969). In a microcosm containing protozoa, an increase in stability coincided with an increase in the heterotrophic bacterial species diversity index. The microcosm included *Chlorella*. The diversity was calculated by a simple formula $D = S/\log(N)$ where diversity (D) equals the total number of species (S) present at a given time divided by the log of the total number of cells (N). Eleven different strains were isolated and characterized at the genus level. The diversity measurements were based on colonial morphology but the population was morphologically distinctive. The species diversity was low in the developmental stages as was the stability. This study provided information on many attributes of a developing ecosystem. The 11 strains of bacteria followed in the microcosm were identified at the generic level, however each could be distinguished as a separate entity and the probes into the relationship between bacteria and algae showed the contribution of each to the maintenance of the microcosm. Thiamin, CO_2, and nitrogen were supplied by the bacteria that in turn metabolized algal excretions.

It is a big leap from a microcosm chamber to the study of succession in the natural environment. The analysis of repeated samples in native ecosystems is demanding. Results do not appear for several months and the final analysis for several more. Laake et al. (1983) have reported the diversity dynamics of planktonic bacteria in an enclosed system where the indigenous bacteria are retained in 1-m bags submersed in a Norwegian fjord. Five of the predetermined dominant types were traced in successive samples by immunofluorescence. The type of planktonic organisms in the surrounding sea were similar but not as abundant as those within the bags, where the productivity could be studied at measurable levels. The diversity calculated by a simplified index, formulated by the authors, was reduced in periods of high substrate availability. The cyclical reduction in total numbers of bacteria could be related to grazing by nanoflagellates.

In our studies on aquatic bacterial diurnal variation where samples were taken 6 hr apart at a monitoring station on the Meduxnekeag River, a fresh water tributary of the St. John River, fluctuations in the predominant bacterial population could be observed in the October, September, and July species but very little change in March samples under ice cover. The database, the test responses of 1258 isolates on 233 tests, was clustered by numerical taxonomy, and the clusters identified. Table 1 shows the number of isolates that clustered in each sampling period. The species identification of each cluster are presented in Table 2 (Holder-Franklin et al., 1976).

In September, *Aeromonas hydrophila* predominated in three samples where the change in species was minimal. A shift occurred between midnight and early morning and *Flavobacterium* sp. became dominant.

The October samples were obtained 2 weeks after the September samples, the temperature of the water remained at 12°C but many of the other 18 water quality parameters had changed. The diurnal variation was more apparent in October. There appears to be a succession effect with *Pseudomonas caryophylli* being replaced by *P. fluorescens* 6 hr later and both disappearing from the predominant population by midnight. A diverse population was cultured from the early morning sample. The March population was very heterogeneous as evidenced by the small number of clustered strains.

Diurnal studies on the Meduxnekeag River prompted a closer look at the changes that could occur over a relatively short time period (Bell et al., 1981). During a 56-hr period in August, 12 samples of water and sediment taken 4 hr apart from a small pristine stream, the Dunbar River, in New Brunswick, Canada were analyzed for bacterial species using 82 tests and numerical taxonomy. Bacterial populations studied were total aerobic heterotrophs grown at 20 and 5°C, total anaerobic heterotrophs, nitrate assimilators and nitrogen fixers, denitrifiers, and nitrate reducers. Sediment samples were analyzed in a similar

TABLE 1. Isolates Tested within each Sampling Time and Percentage That Clustered Each Month

Month	Hour	Total Isolates	Clustered (%)
Sampling Time			
March	1200	75	
	1800	58	
	2400	60	
	0600	72	16
July	1200	95	
	1800	81	
	2400	97	
	0600	99	30
September	1200	67	
	1800	77	
	2400	65	
	0600	71	71
October	1200	97	
	1800	85	
	2400	84	
	0600	71	84

manner. Heterotrophic activity, oxygen saturation, pH, chlorophyll a, temperature, total organic carbon, nitrate–nitrite, and total phosphorus were measured on each sample. The dichotomous test base of 82 tests was clustered by unweighted pair group with arithmetic averaging (UPGMA) and also factor analyzed. The factors were correlated with the parameters cited previously. The Simpson and Shannon indices were calculated on the identified isolates. The numerous variables on each sample provided several approaches for comparison.

The results showed a decrease in oxygen saturation, pH, temperature (6° drop), and in chlorophyll a during the hours of darkness. Heterotrophic turnover oscillated diurnally but V_{max} did not. Percentage respiration remained at 50%. Carbon and phosphorus decreased while nitrate accumulated and the turnover time was stimulated. Against this background, the species diversity was measured. There appeared to be sufficient changes occurring in the bacterial counts on the specialized media to indicate that species diversity could be detected. Furthermore, the highest peaks in the psychrophile sediment counts were observed in the samples of lowest temperature indicating a rapid response of the psychrophiles.

Predominant species, that is, a minimum of four isolates clustered by numerical taxonomy are listed in Table 3. Each group of isolates, that is, from the water and the sediment, was analyzed for diversity according to dark and light periods. The diversity indices and the species abundance and richness all reflect the low diversity between dark and light. The species were different between the water and the sediment but this is not reflected in the indices. The factor

TABLE 2. Predominant Bacteria in Order of Cluster Size[a]

Time	September	October	March	July
Noon	Aeromonas sp. (18) Aeromonas hydrophila (11) Aeromonas hydrophila hydrophila (10) Aeromonas hydrophila anaerogenes (3) Pseudomonas aeruginosa (3)	Pseudomonas caryophylli (74) Xanthomonas campestris (18)	Pseudomonas fluorescens I (6) Pseudomonas stutzeri (2) Pseudomonas lemoignei (2)	Flavobacterium lutescens (4) Flavobacterium aquatile (3) Pseudomonas aeruginosa (3) Flavobacterium capsulatum (2) Corynebacterium sp. (2) Plesiomonas shigelloides (3)
Early evening	Pseudomonas alcaligenes (24) Aeromonas hydrophila anaerogenes (16) Aeromonas hydrophila proteolytica (11) Aeromonas hydrophila (2) Erwinia quercina (3)	Pseudomonas fluorescens II (29) Pseudomonas fluorescens F (24) Pseudomonas caryophylli (2) Flavobacterium aquatile (2)	Pseudomonas sp. (2) Pseudomonas lemoignei (2) Corynebacterium (2)	Flavobacterium breve (4) Pseudomonas alcaligenes (3) Pseudomonas facilis (2)
Midnight	Aeromonas hydrophila anaerogenes (25) Aeromonas hydrophila proteolytica (18) Aeromonas hydrophila hydrophila (2)	Flavobacterium devorans (39) Flavobacterium rigense (13) Flavobacterium breve (2) Flavobacterium aquatile (3) Plesiomonas shigelloides (2)	Pseudomonas fluorescens III (2) Plesiomonas sp. (2)	Cytophaga johnsonae (3) Pseudomonas lemoignei (2) Pseudomonas stutzeri (2) Vibrio sp. (2) Alcaligenes sp. (2) Citrobacter intermedius (2) Gluconobacter sp. (2) Pseudomonas alcaligenes (2)

Early morning	*Flavobacterium rigense* (20) *Flavobacterium devorans* (10) *Plesiomonas shigelloides* (7) *Aeromonas hydrophila anaerogenes* (5) *Flavobacterium breve* (5) *Flavobacterium aquatile* (4) *Aeromonas hydrophila proteolytica* (2) *Pseudomonas aeruginosa* (2)	*Pseudomonas fluorescens* I (18) *Flavobacterium rigense* (9) *Pseudomonas lemoignei* (9) *Aeromonas hydrophila hydrophila* (6) *Aeromonas hydrophila anaerogenes* (5) *Pseudomonas cichorii* (4) *Pseudomonas fluorescens* III (3) *Flavobacterium lutescens* (2) *Pseudomonas stutzeri* (2) *Pseudomonas putida* (2) *Pseudomonas marginata* (2)	*Flavobacterium rigense* (8) *Pseudomonas pseudoalcaligenes* (3) *Pseudomonas acidovorans* (3) *Pseudomonas lemoignei* (2)	*Erwinia* sp. (13) *Pseudomonas* sp. (5) *Flexibacter flexilis* (3) *Flexibacter succinicans* (3) *Azotobacter chroococcum* (3) *Cytophaga fermentans* (3) *Aeromonas hydrophila anaerogenes* (2) *Xanthomonas campestris* (2) *Pseudomonas acidovorans* (2) *Flavobacterium rigense* (2) *Alcaligenes eutrophus* (2) *Pseudomonas solanacearum* (2)
Evenly distributed	*Aeromonas hydrophila anaerogenes* (3) *Plesiomonas shigelloides* (2) *Flavobacterium rigense* (2)	*Pseudomonas caryophylli* (4)	*Flavobacterium lutescens* (2) *Pseudomonas lemoignei* (2) *Alcaligenes* sp. (2)	*Flavobacterium breve* (9) *Aeromonas hydrophila* (6) *Plesiomonas shigelloides* (6) *Flavobacterium aquatile* (5) *Vibrio anguillarum* (3) *Plesiomonas* sp. (2) *Pseudomonas lemoignei* (2) *Aeromonas punctata punctata* (2) *Xanthomonas campestris* (2)

[a]No. of strains in each cluster in parenthesis.

113

TABLE 3. Species Composition in the Water and Sediment

	Dark Period	Light Period
Water Species		
P.fluorescens I	58	58
P.cichorii	1	2
Aeromonas punctata	2	2
Acinetobacter sp.	14	6
Brevibacterium sp.	1	4
Total species	5	5
Total individuals	76	72
Simpson diversity index	0.388	0.344
Shannon diversity index	0.701	0.713
Sediment Species		
P.syringeae	28	27
P.alcaligenes	8	8
P.cepacia	15	2
Gram-negative oxidative rods	2	3
Chromobacterium violaceum	4	1
Aeromonas hydrophila hydrophila	3	7
K.pneumoniae	—	3
Enterobacter aerogenes	22	28
Enterobacter cloacae	3	—
Arthrobacter spp.	2	1
Corynebacterium spp.	—	3
Total species	9	10
Total individuals	87	83
Simpson's diversity index	0.798	0.768
Shannon's diversity index	1.736	1.668

analysis did reveal some diurnal variation in the sediment population but also demonstrated unequivocally the distinctly different composition of the water and sediment populations. The subtle changes occurring during this 56-hr period could not be detected by the diversity indices and succession was also not observed.

Skujins and Klubek (1982) examined bacterial succession in four soil types, meadow, aspen, fir, and spruce of a montane forest sere. The groups of bacteria were determined by counting the organisms on plates grown (1) aerobically, (2) anaerobically, (3) to encourage Actinomycetes, and (4) to encourage fungi (propagules).

These four categories were selected to determine microbial diversity. The physiological diversity increased in the A and O horizons. The taxonomic diversity did increase in the O horizon but decreased or remained the same in the A horizon (Shannon's index). Physiological diversity was measured by counting proteolytic, cellulolytic, lipolytic, chitinolytic, and heteropolycarbohydrate utilizing colonies. The authors concluded that physiological data was a better measure of the diversity and that the diversity index H' had revealed the fundamental error in selection of the taxonomic groups. The overlap in counts between the aerobic and anaerobic plates distorted the index. The information used in the calculation of the Shannon index should be arranged in categories that do not overlap. A strain of bacteria or fungi should be represented only once in the calculation. Theoretically, an index could be formulated to accommodate overlap but none was used in this case. In addition, in most nonparametric data correlations, the data should be in the same domain. Physiological attributes should be grouped separately and taxonomic designations such as actinomycetes or fungi grouped at the same taxonomic level. The interpretation of diversity indices is questionable when analyzing data from mixed domains as it is difficult to determine which attribute contributed the most to the diversity. The study does show an increase in diversity as the soils mature. The physiological diversity followed the increased organic matter content in the soil, a good example of the validation of diversity data by chemical parameters. A regression coefficient of determination (r^2) indicated excellent correlations between organic carbon, nitrogen, the C–N ratio, and the NH_4–NO_3 ratio.

Martin and Bianchi (1980) have compared taxonomy, ecological profiles, diversity (Shannon index), and average catabolic potentiality during two experimental phytoplankton blooms. High diversity was associated with oligotrophic conditions and the phytoplankton exponential growth phase. Diversity decreased during phytoplankton mortality and vibriolike organisms predominated. The clusters were chosen at 90% similarity. The data was also analyzed by the dominance quotient of Travers (1971) to distinguish the bacterial profile. Bacterial diversity increase preceded that of the phytoplankton and continued at a higher rate. Stable states were reflected by high diversity, decreases in diversity were associated with sudden perturbations. The stimulation of bacterial activity by the phytoplankton attained a maximum as chlorophyll *a* reached a plateau. Phytoplankton death stimulates certain other groups of bacteria. The multidisciplinary approach used in this study provided information on the relationships between productivity and growth in bacteria and algae and is an example of the usefulness of the diversity index.

Observations on the succession of bacterial species throughout the year that include seasonal changes may reveal several peaks. There is a minimum amount of information necessary to elucidate features of the econiche and these will not have much meaning unless several facets are examined simultaneously. That is why, in a succession study, equitability should be studied. Species or strain diversity alone is not sufficient to solve ecological problems. Information on the richness, evenness, and variety of the population as well as spatial relationships and ecological succession are needed to extract ecologically relevant facts from a body of data analyzed for diversity.

7.0. FACTOR ANALYSIS

7.1. Environmental Studies Using Factor Analysis

It is clear from the many examples cited that the description of bacterial populations based on physiological and nutritional responses selects an information base that can be related ecologically. The number of variables generated in this type of profile cannot be easily interpreted without a powerful algorithm such as factor analysis or principal components analysis. Reports employing factor or principal components analysis are few. Sundman and Gyllenberg (1967) compared bacterial soil populations using factor analysis. Sundman (1970) related the factors to the environmental conditions. The 44×44 matrix of variables (or bacteriological tests) performed on isolates from four types of soil, produced six factors that described 99% of the variance. The discriminating power of the factors was measured as the squared distance between the factors in the selected six factor space. This report demonstrated clearly that factor analysis was an excellent tool to show diversity in populations without adhering to taxonomic classification and that the entire database could be used. These workers provided the first clear example of the potential for factor analysis in bacterial ecology.

7.2. Factor Analysis Combined with Numerical Taxonomy and Diversity Measurements

Skyring and Quadling (1969) studied four sets of 100 bacterial isolates from 2 different flax rhizospheres and 2 corresponding soil controls by numerical taxonomy and principal components analysis. *Arthrobacter* and *Corynebacteria* were the predominant bacteria isolated from the control soils. The *Pseudomonas* - like organisms were the most numerous isolates in the rhizospheres. Cluster analysis and principal components analysis showed the dissimilarity between rhizosphere and nonrhizosphere groups. Isolates from the control soil demonstrated a greater variety of metabolic activity, but those from the rhizosphere were more likely to be fermentative. The two methods yielded more information than could be obtained by either method alone.

Arfi et al. (1979) studied the comparative distribution of heterotrophic, coliform, and fecal streptococcal bacteria in the sea where the sewage of Marseille is released. The following parameters were also determined: salinity, oxygen, temperature, turbidity, phosphate, nitrate – nitrite, chlorophyll *a*, zooplankton population, carbon, nitrogen, adenylate and anionic detergent concentrations, AMP – ADP – ATP transformations, total aromatic hydrocarbon, phenol, Zn, Ca, Pb and Cu, and the Shannon diversity indices of the phytoplankton population. The principal components extracted from the variance of a 28×28 correlation matrix indicated that the zone where the effluent was released into the sea could be seen in the graphical projection of the major components, the pollution zone and the zone of lower pollution or mixing and the area of least pollution, which followed the projection of high salinity and oxygen. Phenol and detergent appeared to have a lethal effect on the bacteria and were better indicators of pollution than the bacteria. The fecal and other coliforms were close together on the graph, showing very little difference between them. Phytoplankton diversity was related to oxygen levels.

A unique diversity study has been reported by ter Braak (1983) who combined the Simpson diversity index and principal components analysis. Ordination of species was utilized to measure the alpha diversity of sites and the beta diversity of groups of sites measured by the mean squared Euclidian distance. The alpha diversity of the individual sites and the beta diversity of groups of sites are visualized on a distance biplot. Within one biplot, patterns of species composition and abundance as well as diversity are displayed simultaneously. Because the species are loaded on the factors, the proportion of each species can be represented. The success of this method is due in large part to the accuracy of speciating diatoms. This method could be a powerful tool in the comparison of species diversities within and between sites. The report related the decrease in diatom diversity in Dutch moorland pools over 58 yr to an increase in pollution.

In our experience, factor analysis was the preferred method in studies of population shifts of heterotrophic bacteria sampled seasonally in a temperate river system with a watershed covering 465,000 square miles in the Province of New Brunswick, Canada and northern Maine, USA. Study of population dynamics began in 1970 with enumeration of bacteria above and below the effluent of a food processing plant that discharged large amounts of alkaline starch waste (Chalifour, 1974). The first study indicated that the predominant bacteria were, in October, *Enterobacteriaceae*, nonfluorescent *Pseudomonas*, *Chromobacterium*, and *Zoogloea*; in February, fluorescent *Pseudomonas* and *Xanthomonas* species; and in August, *Zoogloea* predominated. The list although limited was of use in planning the database for the next phase of the study when the isolates were tested by numerical taxonomy (Kaneko et al., 1981). Four major groups of physiological responses were tested, 140 substrate utilization tests, in addition to nutritional requirements, metabolic end products, and responses to a range of physical and chemical changes giving a total of 233. The sampling included the river water at the effluent of the food processing plant and the clusters showed clearly that the effluent organisms were very different from the river bacteria. The river strains 1-mile above and 1-mile below the point source were similar and frequently clustered at 75% homology.

Seasonal diversity was clearly shown in the species observed. Growth factor requirement increased with the water temperature and nutritional versatility of the winter isolates was higher. A large and active bacterial population was found under 1 m of ice at 0°C. Seasonal changes were observed in the predominant bacteria, that is, the clustered strains were compared with certain physical features of the water that provided some ecological insight. It was concluded that the bacteria in the effluent were soon diluted but the methods were not sensitive enough to determine if some of the strains survived and became established (Holder-Franklin et al., 1976).

In the Meduxnekeag River study, demonstrable diurnal variation was observed (Tables 1 and 2), which indicated that succession could occur. Noting that the variation of bacterial test responses had been utilized effectively by Sundman (1970) and Toerein et al. (1969) to show the diversity of bacterial populations, the Meduxnekeag River strains were factor analyzed (Holder-Franklin et al., 1978). The homologies established by numerical taxonomy (Table 2) provided a method of identifying the predominant species that had an ecological advantage assuming that the isolation medium did not suppress any of the dominant heterotrophs. Centroid factor analysis was conducted on the intertest correlation matrix determined by a group of 46 reference strains using the fourfold point coefficient. Each sample was analyzed in turn. The factors scores were projected graphically using the SYMVU program (Laboratory for Computer Graphics and Spatial Analysis, Harvard University, Cambridge Massachusetts). A detailed description of the method including computer programs has been published (Holder-Franklin and Wuest, 1983). The factor reference frame projected the coordinates in three dimensions—factor 1 was interpreted as nutritional versatility; factor 2, oxidative metabolism; and factor 3, fermentative metabolism. The spire diagrams represent the species diversity in three dimensional factor space. Each spire represents one strain. The known strains from the ATCC, are displayed in Figure 1. The river isolates in Figure 2.

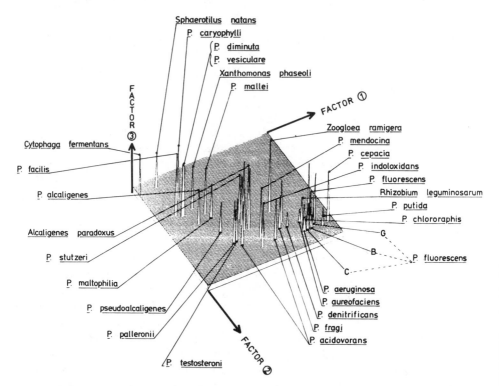

Figure 1. Projection of reference strains in reference factor space. Each spire represents one strain Holder-Franklin et al. (1978). (Factor 1: nutritional versatility, Factor 2: oxidative metabolism, Factor 3: fermentative metabolism.)

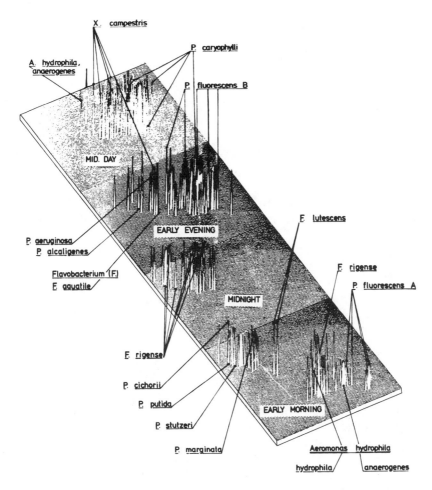

Figure 2. Projection of river isolates in reference factor space Holder-Franklin et al. (1978). Factors are as shown in Figure 1.

The relationship of the strains to each other using a physiological database is very apparent from the diagram. In addition, the diurnal variation of species is shown dramatically where each spire represented a single bacterial isolate. This example has been presented to illustrate the autecological aspect of factor analysis, which is rarely reported.

The same data was analyzed arranged by sampling group, a total of 16 to include the diurnal temporal parameter. The positive feature frequency responses of the group were determined. The analysis yielded a set of factors that were then interpreted. The most important factors were scored. The factor scores were essential in the next phase of the study, that is, to correlate biological factors with the physicochemical factors. The factor analysis of the water quality parameters provided a separate set of factor scores. The ecological information was clearer if the relationships between the factors was calculated before correlating them with another database. Calculation of factor scores is rarely seen in the biological literature.

Correlations made between the bacterial factors and the physicochemical factors indicated that salt tolerance, oxidative metabolism, and nitrification are related to the oxygen concentration of the water. Salt tolerance within the bacterial population is related to the ion concentration of the water. In March, under ice cover, the population was very heterogeneous and did not exhibit diurnal variation. In July, low oxygen levels were linked to nitrate reduction. These factor scores were also used to calculate a cause and effect or path analysis to demonstrate more than correlations, that is, causal relationships (Holder-Franklin, 1984).

The next major study of river bacteria was conducted over 1 yr in the Meduxnekeag and the Dunbar Rivers, Canada (Bell et al., 1980). The Dunbar River represented a pristine woodland stream and the Meduxnekeag River a moderately polluted stream. The first report described the bacterial populations and the physicochemical parameters (Bell et al., 1980). In a succeeding report (Bell et al., 1982), the populations were then analyzed (1) as total heterotrophic counts, (2) as species numbers using numerical taxonomy, (3) by diversity indices, and (4) by factor analysis. Isolates were obtained by plating directly from water samples and by chemostat enrichment. The dichotomous database of 82 tests was clustered using the similarity coefficient recommended by Sneath and Sokal (1973) and the UPGMA clustering using a modified NT-SYS program, NTZ (Rohlf et al., 1971). Clusters with a minimum of four strains were selected for speciation and calculation of the Simpson and Shannon diversity index. The diversity indices for the bacterial strains isolated from the two rivers, arranged by sample date are presented in Table 4. Both indices show the same trend with peaks in the Meduxnekeag River in February and July, that is, heterogeneous populations were observed under the ice cover and in July. These periods of higher diversity were observed in the previous study, however, the indices appear to be reflecting the increases in numbers of species. The indices are low by the recommended medians, which is 3.0 for the Shannon index. If these ecosystems are stressed by the nitrogen limitation observed by Bell et al. (1980), the low indices support the Odum theory.

The correlations observed between diversity indices and other water quality parameters are shown in Tables 5 and 6. The Simpson and Shannon diversity indices in the Meduxnekeag River correlated with ammonium ion, alkalinity, calcium, specific conductance, and color. In the Dunbar River both indices correlated with ammonium ions and temperature; the Simpson index correlated with total phosphous, sulfate, and inorganic carbon. The Simpson index reflected the correlations of the individual species (Table 7).

The predominant species in the Meduxnekeag River were *Pseudomonas aeruginosa*, *P. fluorescens*, *P. alcaligenes*, *P. solanacearum*, *Alcaligenes paradoxus*, *Aeromonas hydrophila*, *Chromobacterium lividum*, *Flavobacterium devorans*, and *Acinetobacter* sp. Most strains correlated with ammonia ion. *P. fluorescens* correlated negatively with ammonia and sunshine. The diversity of

TABLE 4. Diversity in the Bacterial Populations between Samples

Meduxnekeag River	February 7	February 21	March 7	July 25	September 19	October 3
Total individuals	73	101	102	95	73	74
Total species	10	7	7	11	6	6
Simpson diversity index	0.846	0.725	0.570	0.874	0.517	0.491
Shannon diversity index	1.90	1.44	1.21	2.12	1.09	1.02

Dunbar River	February 14	March 1	March 14	September 12	September 26	October 17
Total individuals	75	105	122	104	105	73
Total species	9	5	6	14	7	7
Simpson diversity index	0.616	0.414	0.512	0.880	0.480	0.777
Shannon diversity index	1.35	0.81	1.04	2.27	1.07	1.60

TABLE 5. Correlations between Physicochemical Parameters and Diversity Indices (Meduxnekeag River)[a,b]

	NH$_4$	Alkalinity	Ca	Specific Conductance	Color
		Simpson's Diversity Index			
Correlation coefficient	0.634	0.737	0.734	0.666	−0.674
Significance level (%)	(8.8)	(4.7)	(4.8)	(7.4)	(7.1)
Partial correlation	0.634	0.862	0.793	ns	ns
Significance level	(8.8%)	(6.9%)	(10.4%)		
Variables controlled	—	SC	SC		
		Color	Color		
		Shannon's Diversity Index			
Correlation coefficient	0.765	0.708	0.706	0.607	−0.604
Significance level (%)	(3.8)	(5.8)	(5.8)	(10.1)	(10.2)
Partial correlation	0.765	0.859	0.782	ns	ns
Significance level (%)	(3.8)	(7.1)	(10.9)		
Variables controlled	—	SC	SC	Color	
		Color			

[a]ns denotes not significant.
[b]SC = specific conductance.

122

TABLE 6. Correlations between Physicochemical Parameters and Diversity Indices (Dunbar River)[a]

Simpson's Diversity Index

	NH_4	Temperature (°C)	Inorganic C	C1	Total P	SO_4
Correlation coefficient	0.999	0.612	0.687	−0.634	−0.612	0.732
Significance level (%)	(0)	(9.8)	(6.6)	(8.8)	(9.8)	(4.9)
Partial correlation	0.999	ns	ns	ns	ns	ns
Significance level	(0.4%)					
Variables controlled	SO_4 Total P Inorganic C					

Shannon's Diversity Index

	NH_4	C1	Temperature (°C)
Correlation coefficient	0.853	−0.803	0.797
Significance level (%)	(1.5)	(2.7)	(2.9)
Partial correlation	0.853	ns	ns
Significance level (%)	(1.5)		
Variables controlled	—		

[a]ns denotes not significant.

TABLE 7. Predominant Species in the Meduxnekeag and Dunbar Rivers with Significant Correlations

	Correlations	
	Positive	Negative
Meduxnekeag spp.		
P.aeruginosa	NH_4^+,sunshine	
P.fluorescens[a]		NH_4^+,sunshine
P.alcaligenes	Total P	
P.solanacearum	NH_4^+,temperature	K^+,SO_4^{2-}
Alcaligenes paradoxus	NH_4^+,sunshine	K^+
Aeromonas hydrophila		Chlorophyll *a*
Chromobacterium lividum	SO_4^{2-}	
Flavobacterium devorans	NH_4^+,temperature	
Acinetobacter sp.	NH_4^+,sun,temperature	K^+
Dunbar species		
P.fluorescens[a]	Cl^-	Temp. NH_4^+
P.alcaligenes		DO_2[b]
P.palleronii	NH_4^+,SO_4^{2-} inorganic C	Total P,turbidity
P.flava	Temperature,NH_4^+	Cl^-
Alcaligenes eutrophus	Temperature	
Alcaligenes paradoxus	Inorganic C,Ca^{2+}, Alkalinity	Total P
Aeromonas	NH_4^+,Inorganic C, Chlorophyll *a*	Total P
Flavobacterium devorans	Inorganic C,Mg^{2+} Alkalinity, Chlorophyll *a*	Total P,turbidity
Cytophaga fermentans agarovorans		Ca^{2+},alkalinity,Mg^{2+}, DO_2
C.fermentans fermentans	Total P	Ca^{2+},alkalinity,Mg^{2+}
C.hutchinsonii	NH_4^+,SO_4^{2-}	
Flexibacter succinicans	Temperature	Cl^-
Acinetobacter sp.	Temperature,NH_4^+	Cl^-

[a]Biotype I.
[b]Dissolved oxygen.

the bacterial populations correlated strongly with NH_4 substantiating the proposal that bacterial growth in these two rivers is nitrogen limited (Bell et al., 1980). *A. hydrophila* populations correlated with chlorophyll *a* in both rivers and *C. lividum* with sulfate ion. *F. devorans* and *Acinetobacter* responded to water temperature, however, the *Acinetobacter* was seasonally distributed while the *Flavobacterium* was not. *P. alcaligenes* was the only species to show a high correlation with total phosphorous. In the Dunbar River, *Cytophaga fermentans* was associated significantly with total phosphous. In the Dunbar River, four species correlated negatively with total phosphorus, *P. palleronii, Alcaligenes paradoxus, Aeromonas hydrophila*, and *Flavobacterium devorans*. These four species also correlated positively with inorganic carbon and two with chlorophyll *a*. These species may be favored following an algal bloom. The negative correlation with total phosphorus may indicate that the algae have depleted the meager supply of phosphorus. *Aeromonas hydrophila* was isolated only during the summer and autumn months. In the study reported in Section 6.0, *A. hydrophila* appeared in large numbers during September and October and two species of *Aeromonas* were observed in July. In our experience, *Aeromonas* was rarely observed in the winter or in any samples of water below 5° C.

Four factors emerged which profiled the bacterial community and were common to both rivers. They were, in order of decreasing importance, fermentative metabolism, inorganic nitrogen metabolism, fluorescence–oxidative metabolism, and the lack of starch hydrolysis. The scores of several factors produced significant correlations with a range of physicochemical parameters that were also measured.

The five most important physicochemical factors in each river and their positive and negative correlations are shown in Table 8. In the Dunbar River, the oxidative–fluorescent factor appeared to be inhibited by sunlight as shown in Table 8 (Bell et al., 1982). The summary of significant correlations in Table 9 compares each method in terms of a mathematical correlation with the environment. Factor analysis was the most effective method for revealing correlations between bacterial characteristics and the environmental parameters. However, the use of a variety of methods provided more insight into the ecological aspects.

8.0. CONCLUSIONS

The reports reviewed here indicate that measurements of diversity can be applied to studies of microbial autecology and that the mathematical analysis should be carefully selected to accomplished a clearly defined objective. The Shannon or Simpson diversity index are limited by the size and the representative quality of the sample. The variability in the results and the contribution to verifiable information on the econiche under study leaves the impression that indices provide ecological information only on those communities that have been well censused. For example, in a major study of pollution, the bacterial diversity index drops in an area of high nutrient wastes in response to an increase in certain organotrophs, that is, the number of different species in the predominant population decreases. The grazing protozoa ingest the bacteria of optimal size and the diversity becomes even lower. An algal bloom is in evidence. The first questions are: "What types of algae, bacteria, and protozoa are present?," "How do they interrelate?," and "What role do they perform in the ecosystem?" The example illustrates the essential problem, that enormous resources are needed to attack these highly complex problems. Every environmental study suffers from lack of dimension, from restricting the questions asked. These constraints lead to devising research that shortcuts the necessary elements of ecology.

In planning diversity studies the following suggestions may be helpful:

TABLE 8. Correlations (>0.6 or -0.6) of Bacterial Factor Scores with Physicochemical Parameters

	Physicochemical Parameter	
Factors	Positive Correlation	Negative Correlation
Meduxnekeag River		
Nitrogen fixation	Temperature of water	NO_3^-, Na^+, SO_4^{2-}, DO_2
Fermentative metabolism	Organic carbon	Inorganic carbon
Starch hydrolysis negative	(%) Saturation oxygen	
Oxidative metabolism	Color, turbidity	Na^+, rain, NO_3^-, specific conductance
Levan production	No correlations	
Dunbar River		
Oxidative metabolism	Chlorophyll *a*	
No growth on N free media	NO_3^-	Inorganic carbon, chlorophyll *a*
Oxidase negative Phosphatase +	Color	Na^+, DO_2, chlorophyll *a* Alkalinity, Mg^{2+}, total P
Oxidative fluorescent		SO_4^{2-}, sun, NH_4^+
Starch hydrolysis negative		DO_2

TABLE 9. Summary of Significant Correlations

Analytical Method	Positive	Negative
Viable heterotrophic bacterial counts	Organic C, O_2, rain, NH_4	Sun, Cl
Chlorophyll *a*, chemical analysis	Water temperature	NO_3
Species numbers by numerical taxonomy	Sun, water temp., K, SO_4, P, chlorophyll *a*	NH_4
Species diversity index Simpson Shannon–Weaver	NH_4, alkalinity, Ca Specific conductance color	Cl
Principle factor analysis Meduxnekeag	Chlorophyll *a*, water temperature, organic C, O_2 saturation, turbidity, color, rain.	NO_3, DO_2[a], Na, SO_4, inorganic C, specific conductance
Dunbar	Chlorophyll *a*, NO_3, color	Temperature, inorganic C, chlorophyll *a*, alkalinity Na, Mg, Total P, sun, SO_4, NH_4, DO_2

[a]Dissolved oxygen.

1. The sample should be representative of the ecosystem.
2. In strain diversity studies, the bacterial flora should be identified by numerical taxonomy with a large database to demonstrate variation. The database should be well fortified with physiological tests for correlations with environmental parameters.
3. The physicochemical parameters should be measured.
4. Some parameters should reflect other biota.
5. The biotic group should not be too narrow.
6. The mathematical analysis should be selected before the study begins to ensure that sufficient parameters are introduced into the database.
7. The data must be related by some quantitative method to the environment.
8. The mere presence of certain microbial types is not sufficient in the ecological sense. They must relate to other biota or the environment in a measureable manner.
9. The use of successive samples broadens and strengthens the information base.

Diversity indices are versatile in that any parameter that clearly distinguishes one genetic group from another or one collection from another can be measured. However, they are also limited in that the indices only imply that the sets are different not which of the biological variables are different. The discriminating power of the index is so rarely analyzed that the application of diversity indices as indicators of stress is highly speculative. Ecologically, a numerical taxonomy database with a physiological emphasis is the most beneficial. The clustered strains are physiologically homogeneous and thus form a unit for comparison. The nonclustered strains should be identified for comparison with other databases. The evenness, density, richness, and discrimination components should all be included in the final interpretation. The area that is sadly lacking at this stage is the discrimination analysis to determine if the diversity index is indicative of change. The bias created by the size or distribution of the sample should be explained in each report. When a sample is collected it should not be interpreted as "the" representative. The sample may be an acceptable collection from which to make measurements, but the same hesitation should be employed that one would use in interpreting the findings in a microcosm.

In a fully censused community, the Brillouin index should provide an acceptable analysis that can be compared with other analyses. This ideal situation may not be encountered with microbiological analyses of undisturbed ecosystems.

On the positive side, the indices can be related to their own components as De Jong (1975) has shown or to a series of studies as Tinnberg (1979) has shown. Bell et al. (1981) have demonstrated an ecological relationship by correlating the index with physicochemical parameters. A functional group has been accentuated by Gamble et al. (1977), and succession analysis reported by Cairns and Dickson (1971). Techniques have been developed to overcome the taxonomic conundrum as demonstrated by Bianchi (1980) and Hauxhurst et al. (1981). Diversity indices have their uses and limitations. The change in diversity can be related to an improvement or deterioration in the environment but cannot stand alone. Tate and Mills (1983) have analyzed the significant difference between diversity indices by rarefaction and have shown that an apparent difference can be deceiving.

Use of factor analysis overcomes many of these limitations of data analysis. The database can be test responses of bacteria, measurements of the physical data, or subjective evaluation of responses. The best analyses are conducted on those items from the same domain such as the physiological responses of bacteria. A uniform database yields clearly distinguishable factors and results in the situation that the factor scores of those factors that comprise a high percentage of the variation are excellent products to compare with other factored data sets. The data can be grouped in many ways for the comparisons. Diurnal sampling is a good example. Here individual strains can be observed as they relate to each other in the factor space. For instance, if the oxidative bacteria achieve predominance does this mean that the facultatives are suppressed and if so, what other parameter might assist them to compete?

The factors, by compressing the variance in a large matrix, reveal the most important characteristics of the system. Essential elements of the database are not lost as the significant variance is used to support the major hypothetical constructs. Each variable has a place or weight in the construct.

Diversity studies will continue to add more information on microbiota and how they relate to the environment, but until now the progress in this aspect of microbial autecology has been painfully slow.

REFERENCES

Alexander, M. (1971). *Microbial Ecology.* Wiley, New York.

Arfi, R., A. Bianchi, M. Bianchi, F. Blanc, M. C. Bonin, G. Champalbert, F. Cubizolles, P. David, J. P. Durbec, A. Francois, M. Leveau, M. L. Lizzaragga-Partida, D. Marty, D. Maurer, G. Patriti, J. P. Reys, J. C. Romano, and D. Sautriot (1979). Etude de l'evolution des populations bactériennes d'origine tellurique, entérique et marine dans des systèmes planctoniques soumis à une pollution urbaine, traitment mathematiques des données. *Can. J. Microbiol.,* **25**:1073–1081.

Bell, C. R., M. A. Holder-Franklin, and M. Franklin (1980). Heterotrophic bacteria in two Canadian Rivers. I. Seasonal variations in the predominant bacterial population. *Water Res.* **14**:449–460.

Bell, C. R., M. A. Holder-Franklin, and M. Franklin (1981). "Diurnal variations of the heterotrophic bacteria in the sediment and water of a small woodland stream," in M. A. Holder-Franklin and D. B. Carlisle, eds., *Methods of Studying Population Shifts in Aquatic Bacteria in Response to Environmental Change.* Scientific Series 124. Inland Waters Directorate, Ottawa, (pp. 78–89).

Bell, C. R., M. A. Holder-Franklin, and M. Franklin (1982). Correlations between predominant heterotrophic bacteria and physicochemical water quality parameters in two Canadian rivers. *Appl. Environ. Microbiol.,* **43**:269–283.

Bianchi, M. A. (1980). "Polyphasic study of the Microbial Ecology of bacteria-phytoplankton interactions," in D. Schlessinger, ed., *Microbiology—1980.* American Society for Microbiology, Washington, D.C., pp. 372–376.

Cairns, J. Jr. and K. L. Dickson (1971). A simple method for the biological assessment of the effects of waste discharge on aquatic bottom dwelling organisms. *J. Water Pollut. Control Fed.,* **43**:755–772.

Chalifour, M. (1974). Seasonal variation in the aerobic heterotrophic bacterial population of the St. John River: A taxonomic study. Thesis. University of New Brunswick. Fredericton, New Brunswick, Canada.

Colwell, R. R., M. L. Moffat, and M. D. Sutton (1968). Computer analysis of relationships among phytopathogenic bacteria. *Phytopathology,* **58**:1207–1215.

De Jong, T. M. (1975). A comparison of three diversity indices based on their components of richness and evenness. *Oikos,* **26**:222–227.

Dickman, M. (1969). A quantitative method for assessing the toxic effects of some water soluble substances, based on changes in periphyton community structure. *Water Res.,* **3**:963–972.

Dugan, P. R., C. B. McMillan, and R. M. Pfister (1970). Aerobic heterotrophic bacteria indigenous to 2.8 acid mine waters: Microscopic examination of acid streamers. *J. Bacteriol.*, **101**:973–981.

Ferguson, R. L., E. N. Buckley, and A. V. Palumbo (1984). Response of marine bacterioplankton to differential filtration and confinement. *Appl. Environ. Microbiol.* **47**,49–55.

Fisher, R. A., A. S. Corbet, and C. B. Williams (1943). The relation between the number of species and the number of individuals in a random sample of an animal population. *J. Animal Ecol.*, **12**:42–58.

Gamble, T. N., Betlach, M. R., and Tiedje, J. M. (1977). Numerically dominant denitrifying bacteria from world soils. *Appl. Environ. Microbiol.*, **33**:926–939.

Gordon, R. W., R. J. Beyers, E. P. Odum, and R. G. Eagon (1969). Studies of a simple laboratory microecosystem: Bacterial activities in a heterotrophic succession. *Ecology*, **50**:86–100.

Gyllenberg, H. (1963). A general method for deriving determination schemes for random collections of microbial isolates. *Ann. Acad. Sci. Fenn., Ser. A.*, **4**,69:5–23.

Hairston, N. G., J. D. Allan, R. K. Colwell, D. J. Futuyma, J. Howell, M. D. Lubin, J. Mathias, and J. H. Vandermeer (1968). The relationship between species diversity and stability: An experimental approach with protozoa and bacteria. *Ecology*, **49**:1091–1101.

Hauxhurst, J. D., T. Kaneko, and R. M. Atlas (1981). Characteristics of bacterial communities in the Gulf of Alaska. *Microb. Ecol.*, **7**:167–182.

Holder-Franklin, M. A. (1984). Mathematical analysis of bacterial test responses. Bacteriologie Marine. *Colloq. Int. C.N.R.S.*, **331**:71–77.

Holder-Franklin, M. A., M. Franklin, P. Cashion, C. Cormier, and L. Wuest (1978). "Population shifts in heterotrophic bacteria in a tributary of the Saint John River as measured by taxometrics," in M. W. Loutit and J. A. R. Miles, eds., *Microbial Ecology*. Springer-Verlag, Berlin, Heidelberg, New York (pp. 44–50).

Holder-Franklin, M. A., A. Thorpe, and C. J. Cormier (1981). Comparison of numerical taxonomy and DNA–DNA hybridization in diurnal studies of river bacteria. *Can. J. Microbiol.*, **27**:1165–1184.

Holder-Franklin, M. A., T. Kaneko, and M. Franklin (1976). Numerical Taxonomy of heterotrophic bacteria in a Canadian River. *J. Appl. Bacteriol.*, **41**:4.

Holder-Franklin, M. A. and L. J. Wuest (1983). "Factor analysis as an analytical method in Microbiology," in M. Bazin, ed., *Mathematics in Microbiology*. Academic, London (pp. 139–169).

Holt, J. and K. Strawn (1983). Community structure of macrozooplankton in Trinity and Upper Galveston bays. *Estuaries*, **6**:66–75.

Hood, M. A., W. S. Bishop, S. P. Meyers, and T. Whelan III (1975). Microbial indicators of oil rich salt marsh sediments. *Appl. Microbiol.*, **30**:982–987.

Hurlbert, S. H. (1971). The non concept of species diversity: A critique and alternative parameters. *Ecology*, **52**:577–586.

Kaneko, T., R. M. Atlas, and M. Krichevsky (1977). Diversity of bacterial populations in the Beaufort Sea. *Nature(London)*, **270**:596–599.

Kaneko, T. M. A. Holder-Franklin, and M. Franklin (1981). "An ecological approach to the study of bacteria at the Florenceville site in September and February," in M. A. Holder-Franklin and D. B. Carlisle, eds., *Methods of Studying Population Shifts in*

Aquatic Bacteria in Response to Environmental Change, Scientific Series 124. Inland Waters Directorate, Ottawa, pp. 24–33.

Kempton, R. A. (1979). The structure of species abundance and measurement of diversity. *Biometrics,* **35:**307–321.

Laake, M., A. B. Dahle, and G. Hentzschel (1983). Productivity and population diversity of marine organotrophic bacteria in enclosed planktonic ecosystems. *Mar. Ecol. Prog. Ser.,* **14:**59–69.

Larrick, S. R., J. R. Clark, D. S. Cherry, and J. Cairns, Jr. (1981). Structural and functional changes of aquatic heterotrophic bacteria to thermal, heavy and fly ash effluents. *Water Res.,* **15:**875–880.

Liddell, W. D. and S. L. Ohlhorst (1981). Geomorphology and community composition of two adjacent reef areas, Discovery Bay, *Jam. J. Mar. Res.,* **39:**791–804.

Maret, T. R. and C. C. Christianson (1981). A water quality survey of the Big Blue river Nebraska. *Trans. Nebr. Acad. Sci.,* **IX:**35–47.

Margalef, R. (1951). Diversidad de especies en las communidades naturales. *Pub. Inst. Biol. Appl. Barcelona,* **9:**5–27.

Martin, Y. P. and M. A. Bianchi (1980). Structure, diversity and catabolic potentialities of aerobic heterotrophic bacterial populations associated with continuous cultures of natural marine phytoplankton. *Microb. Ecol.,* **5:**265–279.

Mills, A. L. and R. A. Wassel (1980). Aspects of diversity measurement for microbial communities. *Appl. Environ. Microbiol.,* **40:**578–586.

Mok, W. Y., R. C. C. Luizao, M. do Socorro Barreto da Silva, M. F. S. Teixeira, and E. G. Muniz (1984). Ecology of pathogenic yeasts in Amazonian soil. *Appl. Environ. Microbiol.,* **47:**390–394.

Odum, E. P. (1969). The strategy of ecosystem development. *Science,* **164:**262–270.

Ohlhorst, S. L. (1982). Diel migration patterns of demersal reef zooplankton. *J. Exp. Mar. Biol. Ecol.,* **60:**1–15.

Patrick, R. (1949). A proposed biological measure of stream conditions based on a survey of the Conestoga basin, Lancaster County, Pennsylvania. *Proc. Acad. Nat. Sci. Philadelphia.* **51:**277–295.

Pielou, E. C. (1966a). *An Introduction to Mathematical Ecology.* Wiley-Interscience, New York.

Pielou, E. C. (1966b). Shannon's formula as a measure of specific diversity: It's use and misuse. *Am. Nat.,* **100:**463–465.

Pielou, E. C. (1966c). The measurement of diversity in different types of biological collections. *J. Theor. Biol.,* **13,**131–144.

Pielou, E. C. (1975). *Ecological Diversity.* Wiley, New York.

Rohlf, F. J., J. Kishpaugh, and D. Kirk (1971). NT-SYS numerical system of multivariate statistical programs. Technical Report, State University of New York at Stony Brook, New York.

Routledge, R. D. (1979). Diversity indices: Which ones are admissable? *J. Theor. Biol.,* **76:**503–515.

Routledge, R. D. (1980). Bias in estimating the diversity of large uncensused communities. *Ecology,* **61:**276–281.

Schleifer, K. H. and E. Stackbrandt (1983). Molecular systematics of procaryotes. *Ann. Rev. Microbiol.,* **37:**143–187.

Scott, S. L. and J. A. Osborne (1981). Benthic macroinvertebrates of a Hydrilla infested Central Florida Lake. *J. Freshwat. Ecol.,* **1:**41–49.

Shannon, C. E. and W. Weaver (1959). *The Mathematical Theory of Communication.* University of Illinois Press, Champaign-Urbana. Eighth edition.

Simpson, E. H. (1949). *Measurement of Diversity. Nature(London),* **163:**688.

Skujins, J. and B. Klubek (1982). Soil biological properties of a montane forest sere:Corroboration of Odum's postulates. *Soil Biol. Biochem.,* **14:**505–513.

Skyring, G. W. and C. Quadling (1969). Soil bacteria: Comparisons of rhizosphere and nonrhizosphere populations. *Can. J. Microbiol.,* **15:**473–488.

Sneath, P. H. A. and R. R. Sokal (1973). *Numerical Taxonomy: The Principles and Practice of Numerical Classification* 2nd ed. Freeman, San Francisco.

Sneath, P. H. A., M. Stevens, and M. J. Sackin (1981). Numerical taxonomy of *Pseudomonas* based on published records of substrate utilization. *Antonie van Leeuwenhoek; J. Microbiol. Serol.,* **47:**423–448.

Staley, J. T. (1980) "Diversity of aquatic heterotrophic bacterial communities," in D. Schlessinger, ed., *Microbiology— 1980.* American Society for Microbiology, Washington D.C., pp. 321–322.

Sundman, V. (1970). Four bacterial soil populations characterized and compared by a factor analytical method. *Can. J. Microbiol.,* **16:**455–464.

Sundman, V. and H. Gyllenberg (1967). Application of factor analysis in microbiology.I. General aspects on the use of factor analysis in microbiology. *Ann. Acad. Sci. Fenn. Ser. A.,* **4** 112:3–32.

Swift, M. J. (1975). "Species diversity and the structure of microbial communities in terrestrial habitats," in J. M. Anderson and A. MacFadyen, eds., *The Role of Terrestrial and Aquatic Organisms in Decomposition Processes.* Blackwell, Oxford (pp. 185–222).

Tate, R. L., and A. L. Mills (1983). Cropping and the diversity and function of bacteria in Pahokee muck. *Soil Biol. Biochem.,* **15:**175–179.

Taylor, L. R., R. A. Kempton, and I. P. Woiwood (1976). Diversity statistics and the log series model. *J. Anim. Ecol.,* **45:**255–272.

ter Braak, C. J. F. (1983). Principal components biplots and alpha and beta diversity. *Ecology,* **64,** 454–462.

Tinnberg, L. (1979). Phytoplankton diversity in Lake Norrviken 1961–1975. *Holarct. Ecol.,* **2:**150–159.

Toerien, D. F., W. H. J. Hattingh, J. P. Kotze, P. G. Theil, and M. L. Sibert (1969). Factor analysis as an aid in the ecological study of anaerobic digestion. *Water Res.,* **3:**129–137.

Travers, M. (1971). Diversité du microplancton du Golfe de Marseille en 1964. *Mar. Biol.,* **8:**308–343.

Whilm, J. L. (1968). Use of biomass units in Shannon's formula. *Ecology,* **49:**153–156.

Whilm, J. L. and T. C. Dorris (1969). Biological parameters for water quality criteria. *Bioscience,* **18:**477–481.

6 APPLICATION OF NUMERICAL TAXONOMY PROCEDURES IN MICROBIAL ECOLOGY

E. Russek-Cohen
Department of Animal Sciences
University of Maryland
College Park, Maryland

Rita R. Colwell
Department of Microbiology
University of Maryland
College Park, Maryland

Numerical taxonomic studies have frequently been conducted in an effort to understand the structure of a bacterial community. Whereas numerical taxonomy involves "the grouping by numerical methods of taxonomic units into taxa on the basis of their character states" (Sokal and Sneath, 1963) many of the methods used in numerical taxonomy overlap with, or can be used in microbial ecology. An extensive body of literature now exists that describes the application of numerical taxonomic procedures to microbial ecology problems. Thus, the focus of this chapter is on the interface of the disciplines of microbial ecology and systematics. Specifically, we define, and therefore, restrict, aspects of data collection and analysis to numerical taxonomic studies where the work is part of a larger microbial ecology project. For a more detailed overview of numerical taxonomic procedures, the excellent treatise of Sneath and Sokal (1973) should be consulted.

1.0. NUMERICAL TAXONOMY

Numerical taxonomic research typically involves the analysis of data obtained by performing taxonomic tests and characterizing bacterial strains selected for study. For example, West et al., (1983) studied 216 strains of *Vibrio* for which

Computer time was provided by the University of Maryland Sea Grant College. This research was supported in part by National Science Foundation Grant BSR-84-01397.

151 characters were recorded. The data were used to identify and to classify *Vibrio* spp., as well as to link the incidence of species relative to environmental factors.

The basic rules followed in numerical taxonomy have been that all possible tests should be applied to each strain and that the tests should be weighted equally. Also, taxa are defined on the basis of overall similarity according to results of phenetic analysis based on phenetic characters, rather than ancestry (Colwell and Austin, 1981). The history of numerical taxonomy traces to Adanson (1763) and has been more fully developed in recent years by Sneath (1984) and others. Data analyzed following these rules for numerical taxonomy may, unfortunately, yield taxonomic distinctions that are as much a product of the procedure as of taxonomic differences among the isolates being studied. The conclusion can be greatly influenced by test and strain selection as well as the statistical techniques utilized. Even with these limitations, the successful use of numerical taxonomic procedures is evidenced by the fact that several hundred such studies of bacteria have been reported during the past 25 years (Macdonell and Colwell, 1985; Sneath and Sokal, 1973). Implementation of these procedures into ecological research should be greatly increased in upcoming years in that with the improved speed of computers, investigators are now able to analyze more strains and characteristics in a single analysis.

1.1. Application to Microbial Ecology

In microbial ecology, an investigator is often concerned with interactions among bacterial species or between bacterial populations and higher organisms and the impact of physical and chemical environmental parameters on microbial populations. The approach often followed is first to identify all species present, or to establish those taxa present that are interrelated both taxonomically and ecologically. This usually involves numerical taxonomic techniques (vide infra). An alternative action is to define attributes characterizing strains in a given habitat as compared with those of another site. For example, recently, a study was conducted comparing four sites, two of which were near sewage outfalls, whereas two were located in open waters. The investigators observed that strains collected in the polluted waters more frequently contained plasmids, compared with those for unpolluted waters (Baya et al., 1986). Moreover, a higher percentage of strains in polluted waters exhibited resistance to streptomycin. Other, similar studies have been conducted in which strains in extreme environments such as deep-sea hydrothermal vents (Jannasch and Mottl, 1985) have been examined. Questions asked in ecological research often involve the same or similar tests as are involved with taxonomic work except they employ different analytical, that is, statistical methods. Thus, many of the problems inherent in numerical taxonomic research for taxonomic analysis can also be raised in the ecological applications of the procedures.

1.2. Choice of Strains

Although in many numerical taxonomic studies there are no rules controlling the range of diversity among strains to be examined, common sense dictates that some limitations must be respected, especially in the context of an ecological study (Colwell and Austin, 1981). For example, the microbial strains selected for study ultimately influence the nature of the phenotypic traits chosen for analysis. Traits common to all members of the group obviously are not valuable for distinguishing subsets within the set of strains being analyzed. For example, if only *Vibrio* spp. are studied, the Gram stain will not be a useful characteristic for separating subspecies or biospecies within the genus.

When one attempts to establish the structure of a community, that is, determine the species present, highly nonrandom samples can result in nonsensical conclusions. For example, selecting more samples from one patch of a heterogenous environment than from another patch may lead to the conclusion that more organisms of a given species are present. If 90% of the isolates are from sediment samples and 10% are from surface water, findings that 90% of the samples exhibit the ability to grow anaerobically may be misleading.

Numerical taxonomic results may also be biased because of the physical or temporal heterogeneity of the ecosystem. Common variability observed for soil or water samples may be related to population differences, that is, the depth of the water from where the water sample was taken or location, with respect to soil profile. Thus, when sampling two locations at different depths, pooling across depths may unnecessarily increase the variability of the data. In aquatic systems, animal or plant species may also increase species heterogeneity, that is, sampling more than one host species, such as oysters and mussels, may bias the conclusions. Such variation in the case of soil samples can be related to rhizosphere effects. Thus, one must also consider the habitat of the organisms and/or their host as a factor in a sampling scheme, for example, sampling oysters from less saline waters than that of mussels, with which the oysters are compared can affect the range of species of microorganisms that will be isolated. Clearly, sampling should be done with similar effort for each habitat so that one can distinguish differences arising from habitat versus the host.

Heterogeneity may be temporal in nature. For example, sampling the surface waters of the Puerto Rico trench in January and northern temperature waters off the East Coast of the United States in March will reveal variability, as was observed by Gunn (1981). However, variability noted in such studies may leave open the question of whether the variability arose from temporal or spatial causes. Lack of clarity in interpretation of the sources of heterogeneity often is a problem, or as often referred to in experimental design texts (Cox, 1959), is the confounding of two or more factors.

Heterogeneity, if ignored can occlude patterns that exist by introducing excessive unexplained variability. Heterogeneity can also be introduced by inconsistent methodology in sampling, both in the field and in the laboratory.

Complications may arise in plating samples on a general recovery medium from which colonies are selected for further study. For example, brightly colored colonies may be considered to be more "interesting." But, if only these are selected, one may find the majority to be only of one type, namely, enteropathic organisms. Since the latter are of significant public health concern, the investigator may have been comparing several habitats with the same bias, so that conclusions, suitably restricted to the selected strains, would not be markedly affected. However, if more general aspects of community structure were of interest, the results of such a study can be misleading.

Analytical procedures that define sources of heterogeneity should be employed. For bacterial counts suitably transformed [e.g. to log (counts)] to meet the assumptions, an analysis of variance (ANOVA) quantifying the sources of variation is an excellent approach. ANOVA methods can identify the percentages attributed to, and hence relative importance of, each component of variability estimated. When employing ANOVA or numerical taxonomic methods for the purpose of comparing populations, it may be appropriate to separate the data according to habitat. For example, in aquatic systems, animal hosts such as oysters may represent one habitat and the surrounding water another.

Data collected by one laboratory may be as highly variable as data from two separate habitats, unless a criterion for reproducibility, such as that proposed by Sneath and Johnson (1972), is established. In such a case, a pilot study must be conducted, whereby the laboratories involved employ in each test the same strains for the same attributes. Subsequently, an ANOVA is performed separately for each attribute. The variation may result from variability within the laboratory, among the strains themselves, or from experimental error. If the variation attributable to laboratory differences is statistically significant, the attribute is deemed nonreproducible. The same analysis should also elucidate any significant differences among strains, if only to demonstrate that the sample size employed is sufficently sensitive to establish statistical significance. Since ANOVA methods are primarily applied to quantitative variables, such as bacterial counts, absorption readings, and most area, volume and length measurements, a useful modification of the method of Sneath and Johnson (1972) is to utilize a model properly dealing with two-state response variables. For example, the ability of a strain to produce acid, compared to one that cannot, yields two possible results. ANOVA criteria for determining significance are not always correct for these types of data. Alternative models for such data can be developed by using statistics packages that are now available, such as Statistical Analysis System (SAS) (SAS, 1982). The models that will yield more conclusions that are also reasonably accurate may be a level above elementary statistics and not helpful for the novice.

Ultimately, the objective is to achieve relatively uniform sampling intensities within a given habitat and to compare only those habitats sampled in the same manner.

The overall objective of any study must be considered at the time the strains are selected. If the objective is simply to describe qualitatively the range and type of organisms present, selecting those colonies that are morphologically distinctive might be an appropriate strategy. However, if the objective is to determine the relative importance of strains present in a given environment, an alternative scheme must be employed. A hypothetical example is useful to illustrate this point. Suppose one sample yields 50 colony-forming units (cfu) when plated out on a given medium and another sample yields only 10 colonies. Sampling 10% of each sample will result in 5 strains being selected from the first sample but only 1 strain from the second sample. Each sample may represent the same volume of water, but sample 1 will constitute 83% (5/6) of the isolates selected. Thus, one must consider the definition of "important," in such a case. That is, whether it is to be expressed as a percentage of strains growing on the specific medium or as a percentage of all samples in which the strains can be found.

1.3. Test Selection

Tests can be categorized as two-state or multistate for the purpose of discussion. A two-state attribute is exemplified by the ability or inability to utilize glutamate as a sole carbon source. Such an observation is often coded as 1, or $+$, for the presence of the attribute and 0, or $-$ to indicate absence. Therefore, the attribute is termed "two-state." Multistate attributes include color of the colony, which can be coded as red, white, yellow, and so on. It may also include such attributes as the minimum pH required for growth, with a limited number of pH levels examined as, for example, pH 4.0, 4.5, 5.0 and so on. Quantitative characters may include absorbance readings following the incorporation of a fluorescent marker, or the doubling time of a strain. Whether predominantly two-state or multistate tests are chosen for a given study depends upon the type of test regime that is selected. In general, most numerical taxonomic studies of microorganisms employ two-state attributes.

The choice of which variables, two-state or other are to be measured is important especially for ecological studies, and numerical taxonomic analyses certainly are not an exception. Test selection ultimately should be aimed at two important criteria, accuracy and precision. Accuracy, in the colloquial sense, can be viewed as receiving the "true picture," whereas precision refers to reproducibility of any conclusions that may be drawn. The ideal situation is to have the final results of a numerical taxonomic study to be independent of the tests selected, but that is usually not the case. An excellent discussion of the subject is given by Sneath and Sokal (1973).

Accuracy and reproducibility of the procedures selected for a study can be measured in a number of ways. Pilot studies that include test strains, should also include reference strains obtained from a standardized culture collection, for example, the American Type Culture Collection (ATCC), Rockville, Maryland or the National Collection of Type Cultures (NCTC), London, England. The reference strains can be used as controls, to verify and validate the tests performed in the investigator's laboratory or by all of the laboratories included in a working group. Individual technicians can often create the same type of variation because of variation in test methodology and, therefore, introduce many of the same problems as would be encountered by interlaboratory variation. Statistical aspects of this phenomenon have been discussed by Sneath and Johnson (1972). It is important to recall that frequently more than 50 tests are included in a specific study, therefore even a 5% error rate may be unacceptably high (Sneath and Johnson, 1972). Tests, such as the oxidase reaction, recording of colony or cell shape and size, and gelatin hydrolysis plate tests are not highly reproducible (Sneath and Johnson, 1972) and should be avoided. Each medium must be standardized. Unfortunately variation among brands for a given medium recipe can yield markedly different results (West et al., 1982).

Conventional wisdom in numerical taxonomy implies that the more tests that are done for each strain of a test set, the "better" the results. Many large scale studies, including more than 100 tests on each strain, have been conducted. Frequently, in such large experiments, either an over representation of some classes of tests (vide infra) or large gaps in the data occur, because not all tests are applicable to all strains.

Sneath (1957) proposed the "asymptote hypothesis," whereby if a sufficiently large number of characters are recorded, similarities between each pair of strains will approach a single value. However, this hypothesis works only if one assumes that all characters are selected at random, which is rarely, if ever, true. By preselecting large numbers of traits, that may be biochemically or metabolically related, the similarities may be biased (Sneath and Sokal, 1973). In addition, many multivariate statistical analyses, such as factor analyses, cannot be performed if the number of strains does not significantly exceed the number of tests employed (Rosswall and Kvillner, 1981). Thus, the "conventional wisdom" may be misleading for many applications, not only for numerical taxonomy as applied in microbial ecology.

Tests that are performed are chosen to measure the phenotype. The underlying assumption is that phenotypic similarity approximates genotypic similarity, a more desirable but not yet achievable measure in numerical taxonomy. However, recent advances in sequencing of nucleic acids offer a direct measure of genotype (MacDonell and Colwell, 1985) and may ultimately replace routine phenotypic studies. Since it is genotype rather than phenotype that determines relatedness of two strains, the use of many highly correlated attributes may allow one to measure only a small portion of the genome, that is, causing a weighting in the measure of similarity on that portion rather than on genes elsewhere in the genome. A study of Mallory and Saylor (1984) illustrates some of the problems associated with this assumption. The latter investigators performed two numerical taxonomic analyses using the same strains, but with different characters measured for each analysis. One analysis was more traditional, in that it included 84 characters, 32 of which were carbon utilization tests. The other analysis employed characters based on fatty acid methyl ester composition. The two analyses did not yield the same dendrograms. The suggestion was that using the 32, probably highly related, carbon utilization tests alone would be misleading in determining taxonomic relatedness.

Many catabolic properties may involve only a limited number of biochemical pathways. Statistical examination of such attributes to eliminate those that apparently measure the same metabolic event may be useful, and may also offer insight into how mutations affecting a given pathway may, in turn, also affect the tests employed for phenetic analyses. Strains that cannot utilize a large number of related compounds may, in fact, possess a mutation or deletion influencing earlier steps of the pathway.

Another aspect of test selection relates to taxonomic structure. Some tests may be perfectly adequate for differentiating among families, but may not be sufficient to distinguish genera within families. It is possible that a two-stage approach to the analysis may be useful. The first stage would employ tests selected for the purpose of clustering strains within families. The next stage would be carried out separately, with analysis within each family for the purpose of distinguishing genera. Unfortunately an element of weighting of characters is implied and may violate the principles of Adansonian taxonomy (vide supra). This approach, however, may offer some computational advantages, because the larger data set can be processed using a set of tests that will be useful to separate strains into families.

Data that are not available, because the strains expired before the testing was completed, or the tests were not applicable, and so on, represent a problem that plagues numerical taxonomic analyses. Interpretation of data sets with some of the data missing is often complex, if not impossible. What is often done in such numerical taxonomic studies, when computing similarities, is to do a pairwise deletion of a test if one or both of the strains lack the character, that is, if the data are not available. Inspection of tests and calculation of the frequency of missing values should be made in any numerical taxonomic study. Attributes tested when the strains are run in duplicate presumably are associated with problems in reproducibility if a discrepancy occurs in more than 3% of the strains. Test results that show greater than 3% of the values recorded as missing should be deleted from the analysis. Careful consideration of why a test result is missing from the data set is necessary. If the gaps are nonrandom, any conclusions drawn from the analysis may prove erroneous.

2.0. METHODS USED FOR NUMERICAL TAXONOMIC ANALYSIS

As indicated previously, methods to establish taxa usually include clustering algorithms and discriminant analyses. They are used to validate groupings and to classify new strains into existing taxa or to describe new taxa. The methods that are available will vary in application, according to the type of attributes (see Section 1.3). As stated previously, most of the attributes selected for a numerical taxonomic analysis of data for microorganisms are two-state, which is fortunate, since mixtures of quantitative and two-state procedures are not managed very effectively by existing software. Statistics research needs to be done, so that restrictions on the use of such tests can be eliminated. Work described by Krzanowski (1983) provides a good beginning in overcoming the hurdle.

2.1. Establishing a Taxonomy

In describing how to establish a taxonomy, we restrict ourselves to the analysis of characters included in a test set for the purpose of defining groups at various levels of "similarity," as in a hierarchical cluster analysis. For the present, some of the arguments as to which groups comprise families, genera, or species can be set aside. Hartigan (1975) summarizes many of the algorithms that have been used by investigators doing numerical taxonomy and a review by Blashfield and Aldendorfer (1977) lists software that is available. All of the algorithms, however, require establishment of a measure of similarity or dissimilarity (distance) between each pair of strains selected. In the case of the similarity value, high values are interpreted to mean that two strains are similar, whereas the dissimilarity value measures the opposite. Since the former is more commonly used in bacteriology, it is worth pointing out that more than 25 similarity measures have been defined for pairs of strains in which two-state attributes are used. Fortunately, the two most commonly employed, the simple matching coefficient (S_{SM}) and the Jaccard coefficient S_J correlate reasonably well (Colwell and Austin, 1981).

For a pair of strains, S_{SM} is defined as the percentage of attributes the two strains share. The simple matching coefficient can result in misleadingly high similarity values, if in given reactions the two strains with a large number of attributes in common are absent, that is, both lack the character or are negative in their reaction to the test. Use of the S_J program will eliminate this event from consideration when similar values are computed. The following example is offered. Let p be the number of attributes measured per strain. If each attribute is recorded as $+$ or $-$, then a is the number of attributes for which both strains are positive and d is the number of attributes for which both strains are negative. Then $S_{SM} = (a + d)/p$, while $S_J = a/(p - d)$. S_J is, therefore, sensitive to whichever of the two states is coded $+$ and which is coded $-$, when arbitrary assignment of a positive and negative result is made for a given test, such as spore formation, color, and so on. A new coefficient, falling between S_{SM} and S_J is obviously needed, as this situation is not always consistent in interpretation of metabolic events leading to a negative reaction as the end result. Such a coefficient must differentiate $+$ or $-$ attributes from other two-state attributes. If a^* and d^* are defined as the percentage of double positives (i.e., both strains are $+$), and double negatives, respectively, for $+$ or $-$ attributes only, and b is the number of attributes of the non $+$ or $-$ characters for which both strains are identical in reaction, a possible measure would be $SJ^* = (a + {}^*b)/(p - d^*)$.

This would not be difficult to incorporate into a software package. At the present time we are not aware of any.

When similarities have been defined, taxa or groups are constructed, often via a cluster analysis. Programs are available that contain cluster algorithms, but these vary with computer packages. Readily available packages, such as BMDP (Biomedical Computer Program) (1983) and SAS (1982) do not use those algorithms most frequently employed in bacteriology. The algorithms include the single linkage (nearest neighbor) and unweighted pair group mean algorithm (UPGMA), which are available in NTSYS: a numerical taxonomy and systematics package developed by F. J. Rohlf and R. R. Sokal at Stony Brook, New York and in packages developed by several other microbiologists, including TAXAN6 (University of Maryland Computer Program. Manual for use by R. R. Colwell and J. B. Kaper, Dept. of Microbiology, University of Maryland, College Park, MD 20742). It is recommended that more than one algorithm be tested and the results compared (vide infra). It should also be pointed out that some statistical models based on mixtures of program applications may eventually provide a better approach to the problem. The results of a cluster analysis can be displayed as a dendrogram or as a shaded matrix. Colwell and Austin (1981) and Sokal and Sneath (1963) provide examples.

2.2. Comparing Two Clustering Schemes

To do numerical taxonomic analysis, one may often begin by conducting 100 or more tests. However, at some point it is worth assessing the value of a given test in a clustering scheme. Eliminating tests that do not substantially change the clustering may result in criteria for classification based on fewer tests and less work. The result of the value of a test may also offer insight into the importance of the set of tests selected for a given study and new insight concerning taxonomic relatedness of strains, perhaps a "value-added benefit".

Fowlkes and Mallows (1983) describe the statistical properties of an index, B_k, of similarity between the results of two hierarchical cluster analyses based on n organisms, when each tree has been "snipped" into each of k clusters. The index is based on a matching matrix, consisting of k rows and k columns, where the element (mij) in row i and column j signifies the number of elements in the ith cluster of the first analysis that are in common with the jth cluster of the second analysis. Thus

$$B_k = \frac{T_k}{\sqrt{P_k Q_k}}$$

where

$$T_k = \sum_i \sum_j m_{ij}^2 - n, \quad m_{i.} = \sum_j m_{ij}, \quad m_{.j} = \sum_i m_{ij}$$

$$m_{..} = n = \sum_i \sum_j m_{ij}, \quad P_k = \sum_i m_{i.}^2 - n \quad \text{and} \quad Q_k = \sum_j m_{.j}^2 - n$$

The value of B_k is then computed for k equal to 2, 3, and up to n-1 clusters. The index, B_k, always falls between 0 and 1 for each value of k. Values close to 1 imply similarity and values close to 0 imply a random type of correspondence. Plots of B_k versus k, with a plot of the mean and standard deviation of B_k under a null hypothesis of random correspondence, can be used to compare the ability of two schemes to define groupings at higher and lower levels of taxa.

Within microbial ecology, this technique can be used to compare the results of two separate analyses employing nonoverlapping tests. For example, tests that relate more to habitat interactions, such as salinity, temperature, and pH could be effectively used in one cluster analysis, while biochemical tests dealing with fermentation, carbon utilization, and other metabolic tests could be employed in a second analysis. The comparative ability of such tests to cluster strains would be of interest and may offer some insight with respect to ecological interactions of microbial communities with their environment.

2.3. Classification and Identification Schemes

New species may be identified in a given numerical taxonomic analysis if reference strains are also included in the study. For example, strains that appear in the same cluster with *Vibrio cholerae* would be identified as *V. cholerae*. However, from a statistical point of view, this approach for identifying new strains places too much weight on the few, usually arbitrarily selected, reference strains included in the sample. A much preferred approach would be to use a large, established database that includes many reference strains from each of a wide variety of species.

With such a reference database, the probability of observing a given pattern of characters for each of the isolates tested can be computed. A new strain can then be assigned to the species that generates the highest probability of relatedness, that is, probability for the characters displayed by the new strain. The probability can be further weighted by means of *prior probabilities*. Prior probabilities are most easily defined by example. If all species are viewed as equally likely to occur in the absence of character or test data, then the prior for the jth species is $\pi_L = 1/L$ where L = number of species in the database. If one believes the frequency with which each species is encountered in nature is reflected by the frequency with which it occurs in a database, then π_L is the fraction of times the jth species occurs in the database. Since sampling intensity will vary from species to species, use of this prior is not recommended. Once the priors and the probability distribution function for each species is computed, Bayes theorem can be used to form a rule for classification (Johnson and Wichern, 1981). The theorem states that

$$P(j|\mathbf{x}) = \pi_j P_j(\mathbf{x}) / \sum_i \pi_i P_i(\mathbf{x}),$$

where $\mathbf{x}$ = set of characters observed, $P(j|\mathbf{x})$ = probability of being from species j given $\mathbf{x}$ has been observed, and $P_j(\mathbf{x})$ = probability of observing $\mathbf{x}$ when only looking at species j. Typically, $P_j(\mathbf{x})$ is estimated from sample data (i.e., the established database).

In bacteriology, a common assumption is that the tests observed are statistically independent, that is, uncorrelated. This is done to simplify the computation of $P_j(\mathbf{x})$ to the product of $P_j(X_1) \cdot P_j(X_2) \cdot \ldots \cdot P_j(X_p)$, where X_i represents the outcome of the ith character. The assumption of independence is unrealistic if the traits are related because of sharing the same biochemical pathway. A chisquare test can be used to test for the joint independence of all or any subset of these traits (Bishop et al., 1975). It is interesting and also curious to note that a chi-square analysis of the data is rarely conducted in microbiological numerical taxonomic studies.

Failure to use the correct model (by falsely assuming independence) results in a classification probability that is (artificially) near zero or one (Russek et al., 1983). Since one assigns a strain to the species with the highest probability, the false assumption leads to a false sense of security.

As an illustration of this point, we present an analysis of a data set reported elsewhere (West et al., 1983) on a study of *Vibrio* species. There were 216 strains, with 20 of these run in duplicate in order to assess an overall error rate of ~ 1.5%, using the method of Sneath and Johnson (1972). Since 158 characters were selected, we confined ourselves to those carbon utilization tests in which an amino acid was the sole source. As an illustration of the associations present, we summarize those with glutamate, an amino acid fundamental to the synthesis of other amino acids (Stryer, 1981). These results are presented in Table 1, with entries representing the number of strains exhibiting the ability to use neither carbon source, only glutamate, only the other carbon source, or both. When those associations are significant, an asterisk is noted. A chi-squared statistic was used, except in those cases where expected numbers in a cell were too small; then Fisher's exact test was used (Sokal and Rohlf, 1981).

It should be obvious from the data that strong associations exist and that, as seen in the table for arginine, if 178/216 or 82.4% can utilize glutamate and 101/216 or 46.76% can utilize arginine, a false independence assumption would predict 82.4% $\times$ 46.76% or 38.53% can utilize both. In reality, we observed 45.83% with both. This may explain why systems such as Micro-Is require such high probabilities to indicate a positive identification. With the many characters that are typically employed in these identifications, the probabilities can be totally wrong and may explain why, in some data sets, a substantial number of strains cannot be identified, as reported by Westhoff and Dougherty (1981). It may be that, by not studying the dependencies that exist, we fail to understand what really distinguishes strains, one from another.

3.0. CONCLUSIONS

It is clear that numerical taxonomy is of great value to the microbial ecologist in identifying isolates, describing species composition of microbial communities,

TABLE 1. Associations Among Carbon Utilization Tests: L-Glutamate versus Several Other Amino Acids for 216 Strains of *Vibrio*[a]

	Negative for Both	Negative for L-Glutamate	Positive for L-Glutamate	Positive for Both[b]
L-arginine	36	2	79	99*
L-asparagine	16	22	3	175*
L-aspartate	21	17	98	80ns
L-citrulline	38	0	131	47*
L-glycine	38	0	148	30*
L-histidine	19	19	11	167*
L-hydroxyproline	37	1	169	9ns
L-leucine	38	7	171	7ns
L-ornithine	38	0	145	33*
L-proline	18	20	15	163*
sarcosine	38	0	175	3ns
L-serine	32	6	82	96*
L-threonine	37	1	99	79*
L-tyrosine	38	0	170	8*
L-isoleucine	38	0	177	1ns
L-alanine	34	4	73	105*
D-alanine	37	1	98	80*

[a]Source: West et al. (1983).
[b]ns = not significant.
*$P<.001$.

and in relating occurrence, whether rare or frequent, of species in a given environment. The methods are straightforward, readily applied, and have the advantage of being automated. With the need to monitor genetically engineered organisms released into the environment and the effects, if any, of such species on the environment, including microbial community structure, there is little doubt that autocology will flourish and numerical taxonomy will prove to be the catalyst.

REFERENCES

Adanson, M. (1763). *Familles des Plantes*, Vol. 1, Vincent, Paris.

Baya, A. M., P. R. Brayton, V. L. Brown, D. J. Grimes, E. Russek-Cohen, and R. R. Colwell (1986). Coincident plasmids and antimicrobial resistance in marine bacteria isolated from polluted and unpolluted Atlantic Ocean samples. *Appl. Environ. Microbiol.*, **51**:1285–1292.

Bishop, Y. M. M., S. E. Feinberg, and P. W. Holland (1975). *Discrete Multivariate Analysis*. MIT Press, Cambridge.

Blashfield, R. K. and M. S. Aldendorfer (1977). A Consumer Report on Cluster Analysis

Software (four-part report prepared under NSF Grant DCR No. 74-20007). Pennsylvania State University, University Park, PA.

Colwell, R. R. and B. Austin (1981). *Manual for General Bacteriology*, P. Gerhardt et al. ed. American Society for Microbiology, Washington, DC

Cox, D. R. (1959). *The Planning of Experiments*. Wiley, New York.

Fowlkes, E. B. and C. L. Mallows (1983). A method for comparing two hierarchical clusterings. *J. Am. Stat. Assoc.*, **78**:553–568.

Gunn, B. A. (1981). Distribution and Taxonomy of Gram-positive Cocci in the Marine Environment. Ph.D. Dissertation. University of Maryland, College Park, MD.

Hartigan, J. A. (1975). *Clustering Algorithms*. Wiley, New York.

Jannasch, H. W. and M. J. Mottl (1985). Geomicrobiology of Deep-Sea Hydrothermal Vents. *Science,* **229**:717–725.

Johnson, R. A., and D. W. Wischern (1982). *Applied Multivariate Statistical Analysis*. Prentice-Hall, Englewood Cliffs, N.J.

Krzanowski, W. J. (1983). Distance between populations using mixed continuous and categorical variables. *Biometrics*, **70**:235–243.

MacDonnell, M. and R. R. Colwell (1985). Phylogeny of the *Vibrionaceae* and recommendation for two new genera, *Listonella* and *Shewanella*. *System. Appl. Microbiol.*, **6**:171–182.

Mallory, L. M. and G. S. Saylor (1984). Application of FAME (Fatty Acid Methyl Ester) Analysis in the Numerical Taxonomic Determination of Bacterial Guild Structure. *Microbial. Ecol.*, **10**:283–296.

Rosswall, T. and E. Kvillner (1981). "Principal components and factor analysis for the description of microbial populations," in M. Alexander, ed., *Advances in Microbial Ecology*, Vol. 2, Chapter 1. Plenum, New York.

Russek, E., R. A. Kronmal, and L. D. Fisher (1983). The effect of assuming independence in applying Bayes theorem to risk. *Biomed. Res.*, **16**:537–552.

Sneath, P. H. A. (1957). The application of computers to taxonomy. *J. Gen. Microbiol.*, **17**:184–200.

Sneath, P. H. A. (1974). A study in test reproducibility between laboratories (Report of a *Pseudomonas* working party, Antonie van Leeuwenhoek). *J. Microbiol. Serol.*, **40**:481–527.

Sneath, P. H. A. (1984). "Numerical taxonomy" in *Bergey's Manual of Systematic Bacteriology*. N. R. Kreg and J. G. Holt, ed., Vol. 1. Williams and Wilkins, Baltimore.

Sneath, P. H. A. and R. Johnson (1972). The influence on numerical taxonomic similarities of errors in microbiological tests. *J. Gen. Microbiol.*, **72**:377–392.

Sneath, P. H. A. and R. R. Sokal (1973). *Numerical Taxonomy*. Freeman, San Francisco.

Sokal, R. R. and J. Rohlf (1981). *Biometry*, 2nd ed. Freeman, San Francisco.

Sokal, R. R. and P. H. A. Sneath (1963). *Principles of Numerical Taxonomy*. Freeman, San Francisco.

Stryer, L. (1981). "Biochemistry," in *Biosynthesis of Amino Acids and Heme*, Chapter 21. Freeman, San Francisco.

West, P. A., J. V. Lee, and T. W. Bryant. (1983). A numerical taxonomic study of species of *Vibrio* isolated from the aquatic environment and birds in Kent, England. *J. Appl. Bact.*, **55**:263–282.

West, P. A., E. Russek, P. A. Brayton, and R. R. Colwell (1982). Statistical evaluation of a quality control method for pathogenic *Vibrio* species on selected thiosulphate–citrate–bilesalt–sucrose (TCBS) agars. *J. Clin. Microb.*, **16**:1110–1116.

Westhoff, D. C. and S. L. Dougherty (1981). Characterization of *Bacillus* species isolated from spoiled ultrahigh temperature processed milk. *J. Dairy Sci.*, **64**:572–580.

7 AUTECOLOGICAL STUDIES AND MARINE ECOSYSTEMS

Richard Y. Morita
Department of Microbiology
College of Science and College of Oceanography
Oregon State University
Corvallis, Oregon

1.0. INTRODUCTION

Oceanographers, mainly biological, geological, and chemical oceanographers, do not understand the relationship of marine microbiology to their disciplines. This is due, at least in part, to the fact that they have not been exposed to the subject during their graduate and undergraduate studies. As a result, a black box approach has been applied to many of the processes catalyzed by microorganisms in the oceans. Thus, most marine microbial research currently would be classed as synecology. This is unfortunate in that autoecology would provide an understanding of the basic mechanisms for microbially catalyzed marine processes. Autecological studies are generally not intended to duplicate in situ ecological situations but rather are simple experiments that make it possible to identify operational mechanisms in the laboratory prior to their evaluation under in situ environmental conditions. Since microorganisms are the principal biological catalysts in the ocean, autoecological research must play a larger role in obtaining a complete understanding of the mechanisms involved in the various marine biological processes in the ocean that involve microorganisms. The lack of autecological studies on marine organisms unfortunately leaves great gaps in this presentation, thereby resulting in a nonholistic view of marine microbial ecology. Ecological behavior of individual microbial species must be known so that they can be interrelated to the other components of the environ-

Published as Technical Paper No. 7502, Oregon Agriculture Equipment Station.

ment. Due to the past dominance of the synecological approach of the study of the oceans, this discussion is limited to an evaluation of individual species behavior in relationships to the major environmental factors of the oceans. It is hoped that this review will stimulate more detailed study of the specific behavior of individual microorganisms in marine ecosystems.

Because there are so many microbial problems involved in the marine environment, I have chosen to deal predominantly with the autecology of the most important environmental factors affecting bacteria in the oceans. These are salinity, temperature, hydrostatic pressure, and the availability of nutrients (mainly the lack of energy). These four abiotic factors are associated with the autecology and synecology of all marine organisms. A fundamental understanding of microbial adaptation to these environmental limitations is paramount to the elucidation of marine microbiological processes. In every marine ecosystem [estuarine, open ocean, nearshore, deep sea, sediment–water interface, tropical, polar, aerobic and anaerobic (anoxic), bays, etc.], salinity, temperature, and the energy availability (organic matter for heterotrophs, reduced inorganic substrates for chemolithotrophs, light for photoautotrophs, etc.) play a major role in the functions of the microbes in these ecosystems. Hydrostatic pressure comes into play below the surface of the oceans. The autoecology of microorganisms in environments discussed in other chapters of this book in all probability relate to the marine environment from a comparative biochemical and physiological viewpoint, but salinity, pressure, low temperature, and the dearth of nutrients are, more or less, unique to the marine environment. By far the dominant oceanic ecosystem is cold (5° C or colder), under hydrostatic pressure, fairly constant in salinity, and nutrient poor.

2.0. SALINITY AS AN ENVIRONMENTAL FACTOR

Salinity is defined by marine chemists as the total quantity of solids (in grams) contained in 1 kg of seawater when all the carbonates have been converted to oxide, the bromine and iodine replaced by chlorine, and all organic matter completely oxidized. This is an analytical chemist's nightmare and, as a result, biologists today make either conductivity measurements or refractometric measurements to determine the salinity. The average salinity of sea water is approximately 35 ppt (0/00) but this value varies greatly depending on rain fall, evaporation, and intrusion of fresh water from land. The latter situation is of major impact in bays, estuaries, and salt marshes, due to the outlet of rivers and streams. For most of the oceans salinity is between 33 0/00 and 37 0/00 but higher values are found when there is significant evaporation as in the Red Sea where the salinity may reach 40 0/00 or more.

2.1. Definition of Marine Bacteria

Salinity requirements for marine bacteria were first noted by Fisher (1894) who observed higher bacterial counts of seawater when he employed seawater media. Later, Harvey (1915) found that marine bacteria lyzed when too much distilled water was employed in media. ZoBell and Mitchner (1938) published evidence that the requirement of marine bacteria for seawater or NaCl was not a stable one and that 9 out of 12 isolates for which seawater was required for primary isolation could be grown on freshwater medium after initial isolation. ZoBell and Upham (1944) later found that 56 out of 60 of their marine bacteria isolates could grow on freshwater medium. After prolonged laboratory cultivation or acclimatization procedures, ZoBell and Rittenberg (1938) demonstrated that the marine chitinoclastic bacteria developed an ability to grow in freshwater media; whereas, Stainer (1941) could not adapt marine agar digestors to freshwater media. Hidaka (1965) and Hidaka and Sakai (1964) reported that out of 275 isolates taken from the North Pacific (away from land masses) approximately 50% could be grown on media consisting of polypeptone (0.05%), and yeast extract (0.01%) in distilled water. The pH of the media was 7.8. Varying results have been reported by others. Numerous investigators have tried to define marine bacteria according to their salinity requirements. ZoBell and Upham (1944) classified marine bacteria as those that required seawater upon initial isolation. Due to the difficulty in trying to group marine bacteria in relation to salinity requirements, MacLoed (1965) questioned the existence of specific marine bacteria. Because of these difficulties, most marine microbiologists take a pragmatic approach and state that marine bacteria are those that can grow and metabolize in seawater (any salinity).

The physiological impact of salinity on microbial growth is complex. To a large degree, the salt concentration in seawater provides the proper osmotic pressure for the marine bacteria. Also, some ionic species participate directly in cellular metabolism. But, the requirement for specific cations and anions in seawater varies with microbial species. There is a continuium in the salt concentration of various bodies of water as well as in the various species of bacteria.

2.2. Studies on the Ionic Environment

The specific effect of each major ion on microbial metabolism should be understood. Ions in low concentration may be needed for growth and metabolism since some are directly incorporated into enzymatic proteins; whereas, others (nitrite, ammonia, etc.) are needed in larger concentrations in that they may serve as an energy source for a variety of autotrophic bacteria. The major cations in the ocean are naturally sodium, magnesium, calcium, and potassium; whereas, the major anions are chloride and sulfate. Other functions of inorganic ions are in the activation of enzymes, transport, induction mechanisms, prevention of lysis, and maintenance of intracellular solute concentrations.

Richter (1928) was the first to demonstrate a sodium requirement for marine bioluminescent bacteria. This sodium requirement was also shown by Mudrak (1933) and Bukatsch (1936), whereas Dianova and Voroshilova (1935) demonstrated a large number of marine bacteria had a requirement for sodium that could not be replaced by potassium. Although many investigators have reported the growth of marine bacteria on media not supplemented with NaC1, many of the ingredients used for making media contain sodium. MacLeod and Onofrey (1963) found that agar (1.5%) and trypticase medium contained 0.007 and 0.028 M NaC1, respectively as a contaminant. Because media ingredients contain sodium, growth of many marine bacteria can take place in media prepared without NaC1 or seawater. Nevertheless, the threshold concentration of sodium need by bacteria varies with the species in question. For further discussion of this topic see reviews by MacLeod (1965, 1968, and 1971).

Employing chemically defined media MacLeod et al. (1954) confirmed that marine bacteria required not only Na^+ and K^+ but also demonstrated the requirement for Mg^{2+}, PO_4^{2-}, and SO_4. Some organisms need Ca^{2+} in addition to Mg^{2+} and some required Cl^- (MacLeod and Onofrey, 1956a, 1956b). For maximum population density, the addition of an iron salt was also necessary (MacLeod and Onofrey, 1956b).

A number of studies of salinity effects on marine bacteria can be classified as autecological research. These studies have allowed the determination of the role of seawater cations in marine bacterial metabolism and differentiation of a variety of groups of marine bacteria based on ionic requirements. MacLeod and Onofrey (1957) demonstrate that a marine bacterium (*Pseudomonas* sp.) required 0.2–0.3 M NaC1 for optimum growth and the sodium requirement was highly specific. Only a small component of the function was osmotic, since sucrose was employed to aid the osmotic properties of the medium.

Pratt and Austin (1963) found that, in a *Vibrio* MB 22, a substantial partial replacement of Na^+ could be made by K^{2+}, Mg^{2+}, and sucrose but both Mg^{2+} and sucrose were inhibitory at 0.2 M. After a threshold level of Na^+ was met, K^+ could satisfy the Na^+ requirement. Tedder's (1966) findings suggested that sodium had a specific and nonspecific function. Hence a simple osmotic explanation for the Na^+ requirement is not valid.

Tyler et al. (1960) employing 96 marine isolates found that 19 required Na^+, 25 required Na^+ and K^+, 17 required Na^+ and Mg^{2+}, while 35 required Na^+, K^+, and Mg^{2+}.

Approximately 700 strains and species of Gram-negative marine bacteria were found to require Na^+ for growth (Reichert and Baumann, 1974) but the specific function of Na^+ was found to be required for membrane transport and for respiration.

The lytic susceptibility of a marine bacterium, designated as isolate C–A1, is considered to be the consequence of competition between specific monovalent cations and Mg^{2+} for electrostatic interactions with components of the cell envelope of this organism (DeVoe and Oginsky, 1969).

The uptake of α-aminoisobutyric acid (AIB) (an analog of alanine) was shown to have a requirement for Na^+. Without Na^+ there was no accumulation of the AIB inside the cell (Drapeau and MacLeod, 1963). When unlabeled AIB was added to cells that had a high concentration of radioactive AIB inside the cells, there was a countertransport of the radioactive AIB; the cold AIB replaced the radioactive AIB, this would be expected if a mobile transport carrier was involved (Wilbrandt and Rosenberg, 1961). The optimum level for AIB transport was 200-mM Na$^+$. D-Fucose (an analog of D-galactose) uptake was also found to be dependent upon Na$^+$ for uptake (Drapeau et al., 1967). A role for K$^+$ in substrate transport has also been demonstrated (Thompson and MacLeod, 1971, 1974a, 1974b, Tomilinson and MacLeod 1957 and MacLeod, 1968). Na$^+$ is required for transport of L-alanine and AIB into marine bacterial cells. Cotransport of AIB and Na$^+$ into cells could not be detected, which could be explained by the efflux of Na$^+$ shown to occur in cells (Sprott et al., 1974). Sprott et al. (1974) suggest that there is a mechanism for extruding Na$^+$ from the cells and under normal physiological conditions, when the intracellular K$^+$ concentration is high, Na$^+$ is expelled from the cells as rapidly as it enters as a cosubstrate. Na$^+$-dependent activation in the respiratory chain of *V. alginolyticus* was at the step of NADH:quinone oxidoreductase (Umemoto and Hayashi, 1979).

The marine pseudomonad referred to as B-16 by MacLeod and co-workers has been classified as *Alteromonas haloplanktis* 214 (Gow et al., 1973). *Altermononas haloplanktis* 214 possesses a Na$^+$ dependent D-alanine transport system. This Na$^+$ dependence is not replaceable by K$^+$ or Li$^+$ (Fein and MacLeod, 1975).

Umemoto and Hayashi (1979) found that *V. alginolyticus* grown in the range of 0.2 to 1.5 M NaCl controlled the internal solute concentration, which was always higher than the external solute by about 0.25 os$M$. The concentration of macromolecules (DNA, RNA, and protein) was not affected by the increase in medium NaCl and these macromolecules probably did not contribute to the regulation of internal solutes. However, the K$^+$ concentration accumulated in the cell to about 400 mM when the cells were grown in NaCl concentration from 0.4 to 0.8 M. Both Na$^+$ and Cl$^-$ contribute to the regulation of the internal solute concentration, Cl$^-$ was not as dominant as Na$^+$ in the process. They also found that the accumulation of amino acids in the cells was dependent upon the NaCl concentration of the medium. When the NaCl concentration was high the cells accumulated more amino acids, especially glutamic acid and proline.

Washing of marine bacteria with distilled water greatly reduces their ability to utilize exogenous substrates (Tomalinson and MacLeod, 1957). To maintain the metabolic activity of the organism, Tomalinson and MacLeod (1957) found that Na$^+$, K$^+$, and Mg^{2+} must be present. The organism (designated as B-16) required a concentration of Na$^+$ between 0.1 and 0.3 M and K$^+$ between 0.01 and 0.1 M for optimum oxidation of exogenous substrates. Interestingly, enzymes from marine bacteria in cell-free extracts, do not require the addition of Na$^+$ for activity (MacLeod et al., 1958). This suggests that the impact of the monovalent cations is at the cellular level rather than at the individual enzymes.

All the marine bacteria tested by MacLeod and Onofrey (1957) required or responded to Cl$^-$ in the growth medium. The Cl$^-$ requirement could be replaced by Br$^-$ less readily, but I$^-$ was found to be toxic.

Buckmire and MacLeod (1965) produced evidence that marine bacteria, when placed in distilled water, lysed. The salts added to the suspending solution prevented lysis, not by balancing the internal osmotic pressure of the cells, but by interacting with components of the cell wall.

Marine bacteria do not proliferate in the absence of Na^+ (Webb and Payne, 1971). Cells incubated in media containing mannitol and Na^+ and K^+ synthesized approximately twice the quantity of DNA and RNA as those incubated in mannitol and $0.3\ M\ K^+$ but no Na^+. Both K^+ and Na^+ were found necessary for growth and substrate penetration by Payne (1960).

Recognizing that marine bacteria isolated from seawater require different levels of cations in seawater, Japanese researchers (Hidaka and Sakai, 1964; Daiku and Sakai, 1976) investigated a large number of bacteria isolated from the marine environment in terms of their inorganic salt requirements. Sakai and Sakai (1980) divided the various isolates into four types, based on their ability to grow at two different temperatures and in media made up of various concentrations of salts (Table 1). Furthermore, they state that, even after their studies, no clearcut criteria for differentiation of marine bacteria obtained from marine isolates have been found as yet. The following are the four types of bacteria listed by Sakai and Sakai (1980) with the specific function of cations on their growth and physiology.

1. The marine type (designated M type) is characterized by its inability to be grown in media (see Table 1) comprised of 0.5% NaC1, or 3% NaC1 in distilled water. Growth occurs in media made up with 1/6 strength modified Herbst's artificial seawater and full strength seawater. Hence the M type require Na^+, K^+, Mg^{2+}, and Ca^{2+} for growth at 25°C but little or no growth occurs at 37°C. The M type requires Mg^{2+} and Ca^{2+} for the protection of the cell membrane. These cations appear to activate the cytochrome oxidase and electron transport systems in the cytoplasmic membrane. Both Na^+ and K^+ play extensive roles in the Na^+, K^+ dependent active transport of nutrients into the cells. Na^+, K^+, Mg^{2+}, and Ca^{2+} are required for the growth of this type of marine bacteria.

2. The marine halophilic type (MH type) only require Na^+ for growth at 25°C but does not grow at 37°C. The sodium ion Na^+ plays the same role as in the M type but Mg^{2+} is required for the oxidation of substrates. In addition to these roles for Na^+, Na^+ prevents lysis of the cells and accelerates cytochrome oxidase, the electron transport chain, and ATP formation during oxidation phosphorylation. The MH type requires Na^+ as the sole cation for supporting growth. The potassium ion K^+ is accessorily needed only in the presence of Na^+.

3. The terrestrial halophilic type (TH type) lacks the capacity to grow in the same media as the MH type, grows well at 37°C, and requires a lower concentration of Na^+ than the MH type. The physiological roles of Na^+ in the TH type are the same as in the MH type but a lower concentration of Na^+ is needed to prevent lysis of the cells, the oxidation of substrates, the electron transport system, the cytochrome oxidase, and growth.

4. The T type scarcely requires any cation for physiological roles and is thus

TABLE 1. Method for Differentiating Marine Bacteria from Marine Isolates[a]

Types of Bacteria	Growth at 25°C for 6 Days[b]					Growth at 37°C
	(a)	(b)	(c)	(d)	(e)	(c) and (e)
Marine type (M type)	–[c]	–	–	+[d]	+	–
Marine halophilic type (MH type)	–	– or +	+	+	+	–
Terrstrial halophilic type (TH type)	–	– or +	+	+	+	+
Terrestrial type (T type)	+	+	+	+	+	+

[a]Reproduced with permission from Sakai and Sakai (1980).
[b]Five types of defined media (pH 7.8) containing 0.05% of peptone and 0.01% of yeast extract were dissolved in the following diluents: (a) distilled water, (b) 0.5% NaCl solution, (c) 3% NaCl solution, (d) 1/6 strength modified Herbst's artificial sea water (NaCl, 510 mM; KCl, 9.8 mM; MgCl$_3$, 52 mM; MgSO$_4$, 21 mM; CaCl$_3$, 7.3 mM) and (e) full strength artificial sea water.
[c]No growth.
[d]Growth.

153

capable of growth in all the media listed in Table 1. There are sufficient cations in the media constituents to satisfy the needs of the T-type organisms.

Evidence for an Na^+–H^+ antiporter in *Alteromons haloplanktis* was obtained by Niven and MacLeod (1978). Sodium ions activated the NADH oxidase system; this was not due to the activation of NADH dehydrogenase but resulted from the activation of some other components that were membrane bound. One of the activation components was involved in the 2-heptyl-4-hydroxyquinoline *N*-oxide-sensitive reduction of ubiquinone. However, succinate oxidase was inhibited by high concentration of salt (Ichikawa et al., 1981).

The foregoing studies indicate that the Na^+ requirement is needed for transport of substrate into the cells as well as for respiration of the cells. Hence, we are seeing the dependency of the cell's membrane for Na^+, which in turn reflects ability of the membrane to function in the presence of Na^+. If transport of substrate from the outside of the cell to the inside of the cell is impaired, then its energy source becomes limited or nonexistent.

The inductibility of microbial enzyme systems in marine environments is of prime importance because the sea is inundated with a variety of organic nutrients. Some of these nutrients are the result of freshwater runoff while others may be pollutants, such as pesticides or petroleum. Specific ion requirements have been defined for induction and function of permease systems or inducable enzymes in marine bacteria (Payne 1958, 1960; Rhodes and Payne, 1962, 1967; Drapeau and MacLeod, 1963; Webb and Payne, 1971; Pratt and Tedder, 1974). The ions that have been identified as necessary for induction are K^+, Na^+, and possibly Mg^+. However, Hayasaka and Morita (1978) reported that an exogenous nutrient source was necessary for maximum uptake of a nonmetabolizable thiomethyl-14-β-galactopyranoside (TMG). At optimum salinity, galactose and fructose were the primary inducers but an amino acid was also necessary for induction. Thus, if energy is lacking, it would be difficult to produce an inducable system (permease or enzyme).

3.0. TEMPERATURE IN THE MARINE ENVIRONMENT

Over 90% by volume of the oceans is 5°C or colder. The temperature range in the oceans that covers approximately 70% of the earth's surface is −3 to about 42°C in the tropics. The higher temperatures are found in the tropical surface waters. In the warmer latitudes of world's ocean, the surface temperatures above the discontinuity layer (called thermocline incorrectly by biologists) may be on the warm side whereas, in polar regions, the discontinuity layer may disappear because of the uniform vertical temperature profile. However, high temperatures may exist in such places as the Red Sea where geothermal activity occurs or in the thermal vent areas of the oceans due to tetonic plates pulling away from each other.

It is well known that microorganisms generally grow better in culture at temperatures 10–20°C above the environmental temperature of the ecosystem from which they are obtained. Also, since adaptation to higher temperatures can take place, the ability to transpose laboratory temperature optima data to the natural environment becomes difficult. This is especially complicated in ecosystems where temperatures also influence the chemical and physiological environmental properties. Our understanding of temperature interactions in the marine bacteria may be biased in that much of the research dealing with marine bacteria was performed between room temperature and 28°C. Selection of this temperature range was due to convenience since better growth occurred at these temperatures.

Jones and Morita (1985) demonstrated that the adaptation temperature influences the growth response to various temperatures with a nitrifying bacterium that was isolated from Alaskan waters. Cells adapted to 5°C had an optimum growth temperature of 22°C and a maximum of approximately 29°C. Cell adapted to growth at 25°C had an optimum growth temperature of 30°C and a maximum growth temperature of 38°C. There are also differences in growth response as well as the ability to oxidize ammonium. Cells adapted to 5°C will not grow at any temperatures after being exposed to 30°C for 30 min. This may be the reason why no nitrifiers have been isolated from cold environments.

The general response of microorganisms to temperature, within limits, does follow the Q_{10} rule (Johnson et al., 1954). Temperatures effects on marine microorganisms have been reviewed by Morita (1966) and Oppenheimer (1970). Marine psychrophilic and the ecological aspects of low temperature on microbes (mainly synecology) are discussed by Morita (1975) and Baross and Morita (1978), respectively.

3.1. Marine Psychrophilic Bacteria

It is not difficult to isolate psychrophilic bacteria if source materials are selected that have never experienced warm temperatures, growth media have been precooled to the desired temperatures, and pipets, and so on, are kept cold. Since solar irradiation of snow, ice, water, and so on, can elevate temperatures above those thermally tolerated by psychrophilic bacteria, care must be used to select the right source material (Morita, 1975; Baross and Morita, 1978).

From the data on *Vibrio marinus* MP-1, it has been shown that good growth rates and cell yields can be obtained at the optimum growth temperature as well as near the environmental temperature. For instance, Morita and Albright (1965) recorded a generation time for *V. marinus* MP-1 of 80.7 min at 15°C and 2256 min at 3°C. By employing appropriate media and inocula, it was possible to obtain cell yields of 13×10^{11} at 15°C and 9×10^9 at 3°C cells/mL in 24 hr. This is in contrast with early reports since most of that research was conducted on psychrotrophs inappropriately designated as psychrophiles, thus growth yields were low and generation times were exceedingly long.

Although there is a time–temperature relationship when organisms are exposed to temperatures sufficiently above their maximum growth temperature, thermal death can ensue. Thermally induced lysis occurs in psychrophiles. Autolytic enzymes, which are inactive at low temperatures, are activated at higher temperatures. They cannot be inactivated by returning the culture to the cold environment (Hagen et al., 1964). Lipid phosphorus occurs in the menstrum after the onset of lysis. Temperatures above the organism's maximum cause loss of control of the membrane functions of the cell. As a result, the cells die (Morita and Burton, 1963). Marine psychrophilic bacteria can thermally expire when a cold water mass containing psychrophilic bacteria is upwelled causing the water mass temperature to exceed the maximal growth temperature. Heat exposure can cause cells to lose their membrane control mechanism(s) as evidenced by the leakage of 260-nm absorbing material (Robison and Morita, 1966). This thermally induced leakage material contained protein, amino acids, DNA, and RNA (Haight and Morita, 1966). Malic dehydrogenase is usually thermal labile in *V. marinus* MP-1 (Langridge and Morita, 1966). Lactic dehydrogenase, hexokinase, phosphofructose kinase – glyceraldehyde 3-phosphate dehydrogenase complex, and aldolase are more heat tolerant than malic dehydrogenase, but these activities are inactivated by temperatures of 35 to 40°C for 1 hr (Mathemeier and Morita, 1977; Morita and Mathemeier, 1977). Aldolase from *V. marinus* MP-1 is similar in properties to the Type II aldolases isolated from nonpsychrophilic bacteria but it is inactivated at 32°C (Jones et al., 1979). The amino acid composition of the psychrophilic aldolase was similar to that found in aldolase isolated from a thermophile.

Cell death may result from leakage of cellular material or thermal inactivation of essential enzymatic activities. In *V. marinus* MP-1 cells it originally appeared that leakage of cellular material occurred after 90% of the cell population was rendered nonviable (Kenis and Morita, 1968; Geesey and Morita, 1975). Interpretation of these data is difficult since it is not known how much leakage of cellular material was needed to cause thermal death of the cell. This phenomenon is also complicated by the observation that the amount of leakage also depends upon the temperature at which the bacteria were grown (Haight, J. J. and Morita, 1966). The temperature at which the cells are grown also influences the thermal death time and point as well as the respiratory ability when glucose is used as a substrate.

Physical variations in water column temperatures complicate in situ metabolic estimates. Because there is, in aquatic systems, a vertical temperature profile (except in regions where the upper waters are cold), a temperature discontinuity layer exists. This discontinuity layer acts as an imperfect barrier between the warmer waters and the colder waters below. Organisms falling through the water column experience a decrease in temperature with depth. To circumvent the influence of temperature on microbial activities, most investigators have resorted to the use of in situ temperatures in their studies, especially when employing the heterotrophic activities (potential) method of Wright and Hobbie (1966) for determining the activities of microbes in the environment. This method has also been adapted to sediments (Harrison et al., 1971). (This laboratory generally employs the term "heterotrophic potential" mainly because various radioactive substrates are added to the technique and the addition of the substrates in many cases is more than the quantity that occurs in any ecosystem.)

According to Rüger (1982), in shallow waters, sediment bacteria capable of growing at cold temperatures were less abundant than psychrotrophic bacteria. In sediments of greater depth, true psychrophiles dominated. At about 1500 m, the psychrophilic bacteria of the sediment bacteria was 4.5–9.6 times higher than the psychrotrophic bacteria. These results were supported by INT (2-(p-iodophenyl)-3-(p-nitrophenyl tetrazolium)) reduction to form the red formazan when material was incubated at 2 and 20°C for 2 and 1.5 hr, respectively.

3.2. Salinity – Temperature Interactions

Salinity and temperature variations in marine environment occur mainly where there is a freshwater input into the system such as in bays and estuaries, especially where a salt wedge occurs. However, salinity variation can occur in both polar regions when the ice begins to melt. This interaction between salinity and temperature has been neglected in marine microbiological studies.

A salinity – temperature relationship in terms of the maximum growth temperature of *V. marinus* MP-1 was observed by Stanley and Morita (1968). It was also noted in other marine bacteria. By growing cells at the threshold level of NaCl in the medium, the maximum growth temperature was found to be approximately 10.5°C whereas, at a salinity of 35‰, the maximum growth temperature was found to be 20°C. This large difference between the maximum growth temperatures at two different salinities for *V. marinus* MP-1 should be considered in studies of bodies of water where there is a freshwater intrusion. Unfortunately, in spite of this observation, salinity – temperature regimes in estuarine environment are generally neglected.

To obtain more physiological data relating to Stanley and Morita's (1968) observation, Cooper and Morita (1972) initiated studies on the uptake and synthesis of protein and RNA at various salinity – temperature regimes on the same organism. Again, there was a salinity – temperature interaction in the uptake of proline as well as protein synthesis. At higher salinities and higher temperatures, the cell's ability to take up substrate as well as synthesize protein was retained. The same can be said for RNA synthesis. The data suggest that the effects of salinity – temperature are mainly at the membrane level.

4.0. HYDROSTATIC PRESSURE EFFECTS ON MARINE MICROORGANISMS

In the marine environment, the assumption is that hydrostatic pressure increases 1 atm (14.7 psi) for every 10 m in depth. The deepest areas of the oceans are known as deeps and trenches and all are near island arcs. This assumption is not accurate when there is an increase in the density of the seawater with depth.

The deepest known portion of the oceans is the Challenger Deep [~ 10,480 m, (16,000 psi)]. This is hydrostatic pressure since we are dealing with pressure created by a liquid phase. Although it is a misnomer, pressure created by gasses are referred to as hyperbaric pressure. More details on the effect of hydrostatic pressure on microorganisms were presented by Morita (1967, 1972, 1973).

It was once thought that the deep seas were void of life due to the great pressures that existed at the bottom. Early contrary evidence was collected during the Tailsman Expedition (1882–1883) (Regnard, 1891) when life was demonstrated at depths to 6000 m. Certes (1884) found that various organic substances such as milk, urine, and blood, failed to undergo normal spoilage at 700 atm and that bacterial growth in various types of infusion was retarded. Marine bacteria obtained from depths of 5000 m were found to be more resistant to pressure than terrestrial forms (Certes, 1884). These data obtained from this research indicated that pressure was not the limiting factor for life in the deep sea.

The first microbiological or biological research dealing with the deep sea beyond the continental shelf after World War II was initiated during the Mid-Pacific Expedition of 1950 (Morita and ZoBell, 1955). The microbiological properties of deeps and trenches was first investigated by ZoBell and Morita (1957, 1959) during the Galathea Deep-Sea Expedition (1950–1952). Although the term "barophile" was coined earlier by ZoBell and Johnson (1949), microbiological research aboard the Galathea Deep-Sea Expedition verified the existence of these organisms. Confirmation of the existence of barophile was provided later by Yayanos et al. (1979, 1981), Deming et al. (1981), and others. In all cases barophilic bacteria were found to be psychrophilic. This was the reason ZoBell and Morita (1957, 1959) were not able to isolate the organisms in pure culture. The abnormal thermosensity of psychrophiles was not known at that time. True psychrophilic bacteria were first shown to exist in 1963 (Morita and Haight, 1964; Sieburth, 1964; Hagen et al., 1964).

Pressure effects above the kilobar (1000 atm) range will not be considered since the biosphere does not exceed the kilobar range to any great degree. However, it should be pointed out that we do not yet know how far into the earth's crust bacteria can grow and multiply? Above the kilobar range proteins undergo denaturation (Miyagawa and Suzuki, 1963a, 1963b; Suzuki et al., 1963).

4.1. Growth of Microorganisms Under Pressure

ZoBell and Johnson (1949) demonstrated that hydrostatic pressure retarded the growth of most freshwater and terrestrial bacteria. Marine bacteria that were isolated from shallow marine sources were also inhibited by pressures from 200 to 600 atm (Oppenheimer and ZoBell, 1952). Sudden compression and decompression does not appear to injure the bacteria when no gaseous phase is involved (ZoBell and Johnson, 1949). But, dramatic effects of elevated pressure on cellular morphology have been reported. When *Serratia marinorubra* is subjected to pressure, it grows into long filaments (growth but no division). When the pressure is reduced to 1 atm, these filaments divide into normal size cells (ZoBell and Oppenheimer, 1950). No growth, but elongation of cells of *E. coli* was observed under pressure by ZoBell and Cobet (1964). This elongation of cells due to pressure may aid the filter feeding bacteriovores to obtain microbial cells as food to their increased size.

4.2. Sampling the Deep Sea

When barophiles were discovered in the various trenches and deeps of the ocean, the only means by which they could be obtained was either by use of a coring devise or the use of the J–Z water sampler (ZoBell and Morita, 1959). Unfortunately, these sampling devises did not maintain in situ deep-sea pressure. Furthermore, when the sampling devises were retrieved from the bottom they had to pass through the warmer surface waters. As a result one did not know how many bacteria could not survive the decrease in pressure and/or the increase in temperature.

The first sampling devise that was capable of retaining the in situ pressure up to 200 atm (2000 m) was described by Jannasch et al. (1973). In situ temperature was maintained by the high mass of the metal sampler. Hence, there was no pressure or temperature shock. The sampling devise permitted subsampling (13 mL) with a decrease in pressure. When substrates were employed, there was an initial phase of activity followed by a stationary phase (Jannasch et al., 1976). During the stationary phase virtually no substrate utilization occurs, yet 80% of the substrate available remained unutilized. This unused substrate probably is the result of the unavailability of oxygen in the 13-mL samples. In other words, all the dissolved oxygen is used by the microbes before the substrates are exhausted. All the populations observed that were obtained with this type of sampler demonstrated various degrees of barotolerance.

Employing another sampling devise designed for collecting samples up to 6000 m, Jannasch et al. (1982) demonstrated that most of the isolated microorganisms showed highly barotolerant characteristics, while the remainder (4 out of 15) exhibited barophilic growth in a pressure range 300–500 atm.

Tabor et al. (1982) employed a unique sampling devise that could be used at all depths of the ocean that permitted the sample to remain at the isobaric and isothermic conditions from which the sample was obtained. In addition, subsample volumes up to 150 mL could be transferred without decompression. The ability to transfer a large volume of deep-sea sample without decompression allowed the determination of the uptake of various metabolizable substrates. For instance, samples collected at approximately 5200 m have the ability to utilize $1.0–7.2 \times 10^{-2}\ \mu g$ glutamate $\cdot$ L^{-1} $\cdot$ day^{-1}. This data was obtained over a period of 1–130 days of incubation using subsamples of the original water samples.

Yayanos (1978) describes an amphipod trap for recovery and maintenance of live amiphipods at deep-sea pressures and temperatures. This permitted his group to isolate barophiles that grow better at elevated pressures than at 1 atm (Yayanos et al., 1979, 1981). Success resulted from the capacity to observe decomposition of a dead undecompressed amphipod under pressure and low temperature. Thus, the microbial decomposition had to be due to barophilic bacteria. These barophilic bacteria were subsequently isolated.

4.3. Deep Sea Microbial Studies

Jannasch and co-workers (Jannasch et al., 1971; Jannasch and Wirsen, 1973) have conducted in situ experiments employing the submersible ALVIN or controlled pressure experiments. Such materials as acetate, glucose, mannitol, casamine acids, and agar were employed as substrates. In all studies the incubated samples at 1 atm had higher microbial activities than those under pressure. Thus, all their data indicates that pressure does reduce the activities of the microorganisms substantially. However, it should be noted that many of the substrates employed were readily metabolizable compounds whereas the indigenous organic carbon is not. Much of the organic material in the deep sea is rather refractory.

Foods recovered from the sunken submersible ALVIN (1540 m) were found to be well preserved, probably because they were enclosed (Jannasch et al., 1971). Jannasch reported that the rate of microbial activity on organic matter degradation was 10–100 times slower in the deep sea. But, Sieburth and Dietz (1974) demonstrated that decomposition of food material does occur at 1–3°C and 5200 m within 10 weeks whereas the food in the ALVIN was at the bottom of the ocean for approximately 1 year.

Jannasch and Wirsen (1973) produced evidence for the low rate of activity of bacteria under pressure. However, Morita (1980) concluded that the rate was too fast if one considered the amount of substrate that occurs naturally and the residence time. The slow rate of microbial activity was considered a "blessing in disguise" since a fast metabolic rate would deplete all the organic matter and oxygen from the deep sea and would bring death through starvation for all organisms in the deep-sea ecosystem (Morita, 1980).

4.4. Microflora of Deep Sea Animals

The microflora obtained from the digestive tracts of abyssal scavenging amphipods and a deep-sea holothurian were capable of rapid proliferation at the in situ pressures of 430 and 520 at 3–5°C. Microflora from two different amphipods had doubling times of 5 and 6 hr at isobaric and isothermic conditions of the environment but doubling times of 8 and 6 hr, respectively, at 1 atm. Growth was directly related to the available nutrients. Schwartz et al. (1976) suggested that the intestinal tract of deep-sea animals may be a selective habitat for barophilic bacteria. This is in contrast to the free bacteria in the environment, which do not have a nutrient supply available to them like the nutrient-rich intestinal tract (Deming and Colwell, 1981; and Deming et al., 1981).

ZoBell and Morita (1957) concluded that an abundance of barophiles was associated with the gut or surfaces of many deep-sea animals. Pronounced barotolerant response was observed in bacteria from gut samples of deep-sea fish, echinoderms, and crustaceans when they recompressed (Jannasch et al., 1976). Hessler et al. (1978) formalin fixed contents from abyssal scavenging amphipods retrieved from the Phillipine trench. These samples revealed unusually large concentrations of intact bacterial cells, some dividing cells were also observed. The first study on the barophilic nature of intestinal microbes was that by Schwarz et al. (1976). They isolated several barophilic bacteria, which under proper nutrient conditions and temperature conditions, were not inhibited by the application of pressure. Ohwada et al. (1980) isolated 46 strains of bacteria from intestinal tracts and stomachs of deep-sea macrofauna and showed that there was greater barotolerance among strains isolated from increasing depths. This reaffirms the idea that the habitat of the gut selects for those bacteria physiologically adapted to growth under deep-sea conditions. This was also found to be true with the bacteria associated with the Tanner crab (Morita, 1980).

All of these studies reported that there were many more barophilic bacteria in the gut than in the bottom sediments. Bianchi et al. (1979) estimated that the concentration of barophiles is 50 times higher in the intestinal tract of deep-sea animals than in the deep-sea sediment.

4.5. Barotolerance of Marine Bacteria

Each species has its own barotolerance profile. A survey of the known marine species of bacteria was conducted by ZoBell and Johnson (1949) and Oppenheimer and ZoBell (1952). Some of these organisms had an upper limit of 600 atm for growth but the maximum pressure tolerated clearly varied with the species. In reference to those organisms isolated from the deep sea, most of isolates possessed the capability of growth at 1 atm. For instance, *Pseudomonas bathycetes*, isolated from the Challenger Deep, grew better at 1 atm than at higher pressure. Nevertheless, growth did occur. The culture reached mid-log phase of growth after eight months of incubation. The lag time was long, and its generation time was calculated to be 33 days (Quigley and Colwell, 1968). Varying degrees of barotolerance with other isolates were demonstrated by Jannasch and co-workers as well as Deming et al. (1981).

The first evidence that barophiles grow better under pressure than at 1 atm involved an enrichment culture of sulfate-reducing bacterium (ZoBell and Morita, 1959). This organism was obtained from the Weber Trench (7250m). Evidence of sulfate reduction occurred only after ten months of incubation under 700 atm and 3–5°C. Controls at 1 atm at 3–5°C were negative. Subsequent observations of the controls for a period of 5 yr remained negative. Pure cultures of deep-sea bacteria isolated without decompression of the in situ pressure were performed by Jannasch et al. (1982). The growth rates and substrate uptake of the organisms showed good barotolerant characteristics. Tabor et al. (1981) also recorded substrate uptake by organisms held at in situ pressures with their sampler. Yayanos et al. (1979) isolated a number of barophiles capable of much better growth at elevated pressures than at 1 atm. The barophiles were isolated from amphipods decomposing in a trap specifically designed to retain pressure. Due to the sensitivity of barophiles to temperature the investigators employed a silica gel shake tube (Dietz and Yayanos, 1978).

It should be noted again that all barophiles are psychrophiles. Before the early 1960s, it was commonly held by microbiologists that true psychrophiles did not exist. As a result, no isolation of true barophiles were made in the early studies of the microbiology of the deep sea.

Cell death of a barophile (designed at MT-41) due to decompression has been shown by Yayanos and Dietz (1983). This organism grows only at elevated pressures (pressure greater than approximately 350 atm). One of the interesting points not made by the authors is that death in the presence of growth medium occurs faster than when the cells are suspended in artificial seawater or in filtered seawater. The kinetics of death appeared to be first order for the first 10–15 hr.

Thus, from these studies it appears that barotolerant microbes can be grouped into four categories. These are (1) ability to withstand pressure, (2) ability to grow better at 1 atm, but can also grow at elevated pressures, (3) ability to grow at elevated pressure better than at 1 atm, and (4) those that grow only at elevated pressures.

In addition, *Vibrio* sp. (Ant-300) has the capability to withstand pressure in the starved state (Novitsky and Morita, 1978b). This may be true with most marine surface forms since the amount of energy available in the water column is low during their sedimentation process.

Yayanos et al. (1981) calls barophiles "extreme" psychrophiles due to the equivalence between temperature and pressure. One should be able to offset a change in temperature with a change in pressure and visa versa. This has been done with enzyme systems and growth of organisms (discussed later). Morita (1976) calculated that, with pressure at 1000 atm and the environmental temperature at 2.5°C, the equivalence temperature change would be −28.8°C and therefore would metabolically "freeze" many of the microorganisms sedimenting to the bottom. Employing the same concept, Yayanos et al. (1981) calculated that the optimum temperature for barophiles MP-41 would be −48°C. Hence, they view barophiles as extreme psychrophiles.

4.6. Microbiology of the Hydrothermal Vent Ecosystem

The discovery of the Galapagos Rift thermal vents by Corliss et al. (1979), was followed closely by the discovery of other thermal vents in other rift areas. The presence of thermal vents was a major geological discovery, but during the first research expedition led by Corliss no biologists were present. Their discovery of various macroorganisms caused much excitement. For a more complete discussion of the microbiology of this area, Jannasch and Wirsen (1983) should be consulted.

Since the thermal rift vents are in deep water and no primary productivity in terms of photosynthesis takes place, the primary energy source is the abundant supply of reduced sulfur (mainly hydrogen sulfide) for the chemolithotrophic bacteria. This inorganic energy source producing bacterial biomass is the first trophic level and the driving force behind the biology of the ecosystem. The vesicomyid clams (Turekian et al., 1975; Turekian and Cochrane, 1981) and the mytilid mussel (Rhoads et al., 1981) were judged to have a growth rate of 4 and 1 cm/yr, respectively. These growth rates are 500–120 times faster than that of *Tindaria* and are faster than some shallow-water bivalves (Jones, 1983). These bivalve growth rates are due to the ingestion of microbial cells that are very nutritious as well as being a biological energy source. A chemolithotrophic bacterial symbiont associated with the hydrothermal tube worm, *Riftia pachyptila* (Cavenaugh et al., 1981) was also found.

Probably the most dramatic discovery in the hydrothermal vents was the ability of certain microbes to grow well above 100°C (Baross and Deming, 1983). A titanium growth chamber was employed to grow microorganisms taken from a black smoker at temperatures of 250°C at 265 atm. Trent et al. (1984) claimed that the material observed in the growth chamber after incubation were artifacts. It is hard to visualize that the cells observed by Baross and Deming (1983) were artifacts since the increased incubation periods at the high temperature and pressure did produce increases in the amino acids (Baross et al. 1984). Moreover, only a small amount of amino acids were reported by Trent et al. (1984). Further research will resolve this conflict of views.

One should not forget the pressure applied to the system at 250°C. From the ideal gas law one should expect some protection from denaturation due to the temperature as shown with malic dehydrogenase (Morita and Haight, 1962), inorganic pyrophosphatase (Morita and Mathemeier, 1964), the presence of substrate (Haight and Morita, 1962), and the presence of inorganic ions (seawater) (Mathemeier and Morita, 1964; Matsumura and Marquis (1977).

4.7. Hydrostatic Pressure Effects on Microbial Physiology

The effect of augmented pressure on nonbarophiles has been studied but not the decreased pressure on barophiles. Although various investigators have now isolated barophiles that only reproduce under pressure, it is still difficult to produce a sufficient mass of cells for biochemical studies and to maintain the materials under pressure. Decompression would permit the conformational changes of cellular constituents to take place, especially the macromolecules. Complicating factors such as pH changes, ionization of water and water structure, chemical reaction rates and ionization of inorganic (mainly the salts in marine water) and organic compounds, aggregation of macromolecules, and conformational changes of molecules (see Table 1 and Morita, 1973) must be taken into consideration when studying pressure effects of microbial systems.

The initial study of pH in relation to the depth of the ocean by Buch and Gripenberg (1932) indicates that the pH becomes more acidic with depth. As a result calcereous skeletons are not found below 4000 m. Other studies have also indicated the same results (Distéche, 1959). The degree of ionization of a commonly used buffer phosphate system that has the unusually large volume change of $\Delta V = -24$ cm^3/mole accompanying the dissociated of $H_2PO_4^-$, may be influenced by the pressure (Linderstom-Lang and Jacobsen, 1941). Thus, a phosphate buffer near pH 7.0 would be expected to become about 0.4 of a pH unit more acid under 680 atm. A shift of this order could result in drastic changes in the rate or state of any biological system that happens to be sensitive to pH changes (Johnson and Eyring, 1970). As a result, in most studies, buffers that do not have a large volume change are selected for use in biological systems, such as Tris buffers. To circumvent the changes in pH due to temperature changes, most investigators adjust the pH of the medium, buffer, and so on, at the temperature of the experiment.

Since seawater contains many ions, the solubility of these salts along with the water under pressure must also be taken into consideration (Owen and Brinkley, 1941; Hamann, 1963 and 1964; Distéche and Distéche, 1965; Ewald and Hamann, 1956; Hamann and Strauss, 1965; Pytkowicz and Fowler, 1967). The ionization of water becomes greater under pressure and the viscosity also changes (Horne and Johnson, 1966). Certain structural qualities of water are lost under pressure but some of it is regained due to the presence of sodium chloride (Horne and Johnson, 1966 and 1967). Linderstrøm-Lang and Jacobsen (1941) calculated volume changes associated with ion pairs, amino acid dipoles, and peptide dipoles. How water molecules group themselves around particular cellular molecules, especially proteins, also becomes an important problem.

The theoretical approach to the effect of pressure is presented by Morild (1981). Increased pressures decrease enzyme reaction rates. This effect has been observed with formic, malic, and succinic dehydrogenases (Morita, 1957), urease (ZoBell, 1964), nitrate reductase (ZoBell and Budge, 1965), and phosphatase (Morita and Howe, 1957). In addition to pressure effects on enzymes, macromolecular (protein, RNA, and DNA) synthesis is reduced. Landau (1966) was the first to demonstrate that protein and nucleic acid synthesis was depressed when pressure was applied to the system. In alternate pressurization–depressurization studies, Albright (1969) found that pressure did decrease the synthesis of protein, DNA, and RNA. Marquis (1976) presents a review on this subject. The order of the pressure effect appears to be protein > RNA > DNA synthesis. In terms of galactosidase synthesis by *E. coli* Landau (1967) indicated that induction > translation > transcription was affected by pressure.

There is some conflict in the literature concerning the question of the role of transport in inhibition of macromolecular synthesis in intact cells (Landau and Pope, 1980; Marquis, 1976). Although evidence is presented for both cases, it should be stressed that in the deep sea the availability of substrates are very limited.

5.0. PRESSURE–SALINITY EFFECTS

Although salinity is constant in the deep sea, there are some data concerning pressure–salinity relationships. Within the range 2.5–35‰ growth of *Vibrio marinus* MP-1 (Palmer and Albright, 1970) improves with increased salinity. Growth of *Streptococcus faecalis* under pressure is influenced by the salt concentration of the medium. Two of the major cations in seawater, Mg^{2+} and Ca^{2+} are responsible for this salt effect (Matsumura and Marquis, 1977). In cell-free extracts of *Pseudomonas bathycetes,* specific concentrations of Na^+ and Mg^{2+} were found to be essential for specific barotolerant synthesis systems (Landau et al., 1977).

6.0. PRESSURE–TEMPERATURE INTERACTIONS

Bacterial growth is influenced by a pressure–temperature interaction where the applied pressure increases the capability of certain bacteria to grow better at elevated temperatures, sometime above their maximum growth temperature at 1 atm (ZoBell and Johnson, 1949). A thermophilic *Desulfovibrio* growing at 104°C and 1000 atm was reported by ZoBell (1958). Similarly, bioluminescence enzyme activity is stimulated at higher temperature under pressure (39.4°C and 8000 psi) (Strehler and Johnson, 1954). At the 39.4°C, increasing pressures gave increasing bioluminescence. However, at low temperature (e.g., 3°C), increasing pressures decreased the luciferase activity. With aspartase, Haight and Morita (1962) demonstrated the same principle. The first report of enzymatic activity over 100°C was reported by Morita and Haight (1962). In this case, the enzyme was malic dehydrogenase, which functioned at 101°C under pressure. Inorganic pyrophosphatase is also active at 105°C under pressure (Morita and Mathemeier, 1964). Increases in pressure are predicted to counteract increases in temperature by the ideal gas law. Such observation may help explain the existence of bacteria in the thermal vents.

Elevated temperature brings about the aggregation reaction (hydrophobic bonding) of poly-L-valyl-ribonuclease (PVRNase) (Kettman et al., 1966). This aggregation of PVRNase can be counteracted by application of pressure when it begins to aggregate at 39°C. The calculation for the molecular volume change was 203 mL/mole, which is counteracted by the pressure applied. Other studies dealing with conformational changes are reviewed by Morita and Becker (1970).

7.0. ENERGY AVAILABILITY

Concentrations of available organic matter necessary for support of bacterial growth in most marine environments is lacking. This is especially true for the open ocean where the dissolved organic carbon concentration ranges from 0.3 to 1.2 mg C/L with approximately 0.5 mg C/L in the deep sea (Riley and Chester, 1971). The amount of particulate organic carbon is exceeded by dissolved organic carbon by a factor of 10–20. Other investigators also cite low concentrations of organic matter in the sea and much of the organic matter that is present is rather refractory to microbial degradation. Since phytoplankton growth occurs only in the surface water, the deeper portions of the oceans receive very little organic matter.

When one reviews the lack of energy for the metabolic activities of bacteria in marine environments, most individuals, especially nonmicrobiologists, have a tendency to fail to evaluate the nutrient content especially in terms of essential amino acids, essential ectocrine compounds, energy availability, metabolic availability, and physiochemical nature of the niche in which the microorganism is situated. One of the reasons for not considering these factors is the fact that biological energy is measured in terms of dissolved and particulate organic carbon. A good example is a situation where an organic polymer that can be utilized as energy does not undergo microbial degradation. In this case, it is frequently overlooked that a large amount of energy is required to synthesize the exoenzyme necessary to initiate the enzymatic degradation of polymers; hence, if the bacteria is in the presence of the organic polymer as well as in the presence of a readily available energy source, the polymer would undergo more rapid enzymatic decomposition.

The main point that one must consider in any ecosystem is the availability of various energy sources to the microbial community and that this availability may result in a very long incubation period (residence time) compared to that customarily observed in the laboratory. Therefore, in autecological studies the concentration of available substrates as an energy source must be taken into consideration.

In reference to the amount of dissolved free amino acids and the total amino acids in the deep sea, one must be careful not to conclude that the quantities of total amino acids represent readily metabolizeable amino acids. The combined amino acids are actually adsorbed on or are constituents of small particles of detritus (Lee and Bada, 1975) or may even be microbial cells passing through their filter (use of Whatman GF/C) and then hydrolyzed (Bada and Lee, 1977).

Metabolic availability of the amino acids may also be limited by protein tertiary structure and adsorption of amino acids onto various materials present. Gordon (1979) suggested that particulate organic carbon represents refractory proteins that are slowly converted to bacterial biomass. However, when particulate organic carbon is hydrolyzed, it will serve as a good substrate for bacteria (Seki et al., 1968). When dissolved organic carbon of surface and deep-sea water was concentrated there was a change in the concentration of the dissolved organic carbon by the microorganisms, indicating its resistance to degradation (Barber, 1968). Unfortunately, we do not know the threshold concentration of the various nutrients required by bacteria for maintenance energy, or as energy sources for growth and reproduction. Amino acid availability in deep water may also be reduced by their reaction with other dissolved organic compounds to form humic acidlike substances (Lee and Bada, 1975). Aside from these physical and chemical limitations, microbial metabolism may also be controlled by shortages of essential amino acids, especially methionine, which is needed for translation in protein synthesis. For further discussion of this problem, see Morita (1980).

Many investigators have employed radioactive substrates to evaluate metabolic rates in the deep-sea samples. Remembering that the amount of substrates in the deep sea is minimal (amino acids in nanomoles per liter), the rate of carbon respiration under pressure by samples obtained by Tabor et al. (1981) was 3.8×10^{-1} μg glutamate $\cdot$ L^{-1} $\cdot$ day^{-1} and 1.5×10^{-1} μg acetate $\cdot$ L^{-1} $\cdot$ day^{-1} in undecompressed samples. It also should be noted that the added substrates are readily metabolizable and that in the deep sea, availability of such material may be reduced by adsorption or chemical reactions. This would also imply that there must be a steady input of the substrate employed to the system continuously and replacement of the amount of oxygen in the system. On the basis of a residence time of 1000 yr, even these figures reported by Tabor et al. (1981) may be still too large.

Plant remains have been found in deeps and trenches (Wolff 1976, 1979). George and Huggins (1979) reported the finding of terrestrial plant debris (coconut husts, sugarcane, bamboo, broken branches, twigs of trees, turtle grass rhizomes, *Thalasia, Sargassum,* and *Grassolaria*) in areas of the Puerto Rico trench indicating that microbial metabolic activity is depressed. Muraoka (1971) placed manila hemp and wood in the deep sea only to find that their decomposition was greatly suppressed. Most of the foregoing debris was cellulose rich and reasonably biodegradation resistant. Aside from the effects of lignin content and the wide carbon–nitrogen ratio, a complex enzyme system is required for cellulose catabolism. Since cellulase must be synthesized for the degradation of these compounds, in all probability, the essential nitrogenous compounds are lacking for the microbes to grow, multiply, and synthesize the appropriate enzymes needed to degrade the material. The availability of phosphate or ectocrine compound may also be limiting. Although biological oceanographers and chemists analyze total organic carbon in water samples, a more valid measure would be estimation of metabolizable organic matter. Unfortunately, the state of the art for such measurements is still lacking. Suppression of the indigenous microbial activity due to pressure may only reflect the basic nature of the barophilic bacteria. These effects are considered in terms of the water mass residence time, the rate may be sufficient or in tune with the environment. The lack of all the factors needed for good growth in the deep-sea environment may be a way of controlling the sparse supply of food and thereby depressing the utilization of oxygen. The lack of oxygen would then be harmful to other organisms present.

The barotolerance of organisms appears to be a function of the amount of energy available such as glucose, galactose, maltose, or lactose and the presence of Mg^{2+} and Ca^{2+} (Matsumura and Marquis, 1977). According to Marquis and Bender (1980), there is a reduced yield of bacterial biomass per mole of ATP when cells are grown under pressure.

Barotolerance of a bacterium is also dependent upon its physiological state (Matsumura and Marquis, 1977). Thus, cells designated as Ant-300 survive pressure better in the starved state than did nonstarved cells (Novitsky and Morita, 1978).

7.1. Miniaturization of Bacterial Cells Due to Lack of Nutrients

Generally, most marine ecosystems lack sufficient nutrients to permit active microbial growth. Although there are other factors controlling microbial growth rates, nutrients (energy) and water availability are primary determinants of microbial activity. This nutrient limitation may result in reduced microbial cell size. Microoganisms capable of passing through a 0.45-μm Millipore filter were described by Oppenheimer (1952) and Anderson and Huffernan (1965). Since that time many other researchers (Zimmermann and Meyer-Reil, 1974; Daley and Hobbie, 1975; Morita, 1977; Zimmermann, 1977; Watson et al., 1977; Kogure et al., 1970; Torrella and Morita, 1981, Tabor et al., 1981; MacDonell and Hood, 1982; and Marshall et al., 1971) have noted the existence of small cells that were termed "ultramicrocells" or "ultramicrobacteria" by Torrella and Morita (1981). The ultramicrobacteria have been observed in bays, estuaries, near-shore environments, open, and deep oceans.

Ultramicrobacteria resulting from nutrient deprivation were first observed by Novitsky and Morita (1976). By use of a microculture slide technique, Torrella and Morita (1981) were able to show that many ultramicrobacteria in Yaquina Bay water produced larger cells in the presence of nutrients. Some ultramicrobacteria in the water sample did not increase in size, which may have been the result of not having the proper nutrients on the slide for that particular bacterium and/or other factors such as pH, E_h and so on. Also, in nearshore environments MacDonell and Hood (1982) passed seawater through an 0.2-μm Nucleopore filter. From the filtrate they cultured organisms that were identified as various species of *Aeromonas, Vibrio, Pseudomonas,* and *Alcaligenes.* This definitely indicated that microorganisms < 0.2 μm pass through Nucleopore filter. Carlucci et al. (1976) sampled deep-sea water (1200 m) by means of a pressure vessel in which the material was fixed under pressure with glutaraldehyde. These samples were prepared and observed with a scanning electron microscope and found to be coccoid or rodlike and < 0.4 μm in diameter or width. Some cell diameters were approximately 0.2 μm. Most of the bacteria appeared to be in aggregates or attached to particulate materials but there were many individual cells.

Ultramicrocells have also been found in the deep sea by Tabor et al. (1981). The various genera that were able to pass through the 0.45-μm filters were *Alcaligenes, Flavobacterium, Pseudomonas,* and *Vibrio* as were those retained by the filter. They also demonstrated that cells held under starvation conditions resulted in ultramicrocells.

7.2. Residence Time, and Age and Oxidation of Organic Matter in Deep-Sea Water

Although there have been many papers written on the residence times of various water masses in the ocean, the surface waters generally do not have a long residence time (in terms of years) whereas the deeper portions of the ocean have residence time ranging from 230 to 950 yr (Broecker, 1963). Radioactive dating of the dissolved organic matter in two water samples taken in the Northwest Pacific at depths of 1980 and 1920 m was found to be 2740 $\pm$ 300 yr (Williams et al., 1969). The amount of organic carbon is in the range of 0.05 μg/L and most of it is not readily metabolizable. The oxidation of the dissolved organic carbon was calculated to be 0.1–0.2%/yr or 0.004-mL of oxygen used per liter per year (Craig, 1971). Employing a heterotrophic low nutrient bacterium, Carlucci and Williams (1978) calculated the generation time to be 210 hr (8.87 days), which agrees with the calculations of Craig (1971). The turnover time of dissolved organic matter was estimated by Menzel (1974) to be 3300 yr. The concept of residence time and nutrient limitation is real but the subject has been neglected and warrants much research.

7.3. Physiology of Starved Cells

Not all species will form ultramicrocells when starved. Furthermore, four patterns of starvation–survival have been observed among marine bacteria (Amy and Morita, 1983a; Morita, 1985). With some organisms, there is an initial increase in the number of cells when the culture is placed in a starvation menstruum (Novitsky and Morita, 1977; Amy and Morita, 1983a; Kurath and Morita, 1983; Dawson et al., 1981; Kjelleberg et al., 1982). This increase in the number of cells may be survival mechanism for the species since a large number of cells increases the probability that one of the cells will survive (Novitsky and Morita, 1978a). Ultramicrocells also avoid predation by bacteriovores due to their small size. It definitely aids in its barotolerance (Novitsky and Morita, 1978b). Furthermore, the small size that results provided a larger surface/volume ratio so that they can "see" more substrate in a dilute menstruum. Ultramicrocells have the ability to see glutamic acid at a concentration of 10^{-12} M (Morita, 1984). Another strategy for survival with ultramicrocells is their ability to adhere to surfaces better than cells in other physiological states so that they can utilize the dilute substrates in the water more readily (Dawson et al., 1981; Humphrey et al., 1982). Ant-300 cells do not display chemotaxis until they are starved for at least 24–48 hr (Geesey and Morita, 1979, 1981; and Torrella and Morita, 1982). In low nutrient environment, cells can display a high affinity system for substrates (Geesey and Morita, 1979) as well as display an affinity for scavenging ammonia (Jones and Rhodes-Roberts, 1980).

In the starvation–survival process there are many factors involved in the survival processes, such as culture age, inoculum size, nutrition conditions, and so on (Novitsky and Morita, 1977; Jones and Rhodes-Roberts, 1980).

Nevertheless, long-term survival is possible with certain species. Survival of other species, due to the lack of energy in any ecosystem, does not necessarily entail a long period of time. For instance, it could be seasonal or as short as the time interval required for a microbial pathogen to be transmitted from one host to another. The protein pattern of starved cells in relation to the starvation time changes so that some proteins remain, others disappear, while others make their appearance (Amy and Morita, 1983b). Starved cells will immediately utilize added substrate when cells are undergoing starvation; they probably utilize all the cellular constituents that are not necessary for energy, leaving behind the genome, energy-yielding systems, and so on. When energy becomes available, then the biosynthetic enzymes and other necessary cellular materials needed for growth and reproduction are synthesized by the cell. The longer the starvation process, the longer the lag period of the organisms (Amy et al., 1983a). Thus far the longest time we have recorded for survival due to starvation was 2.5 yr when the experiment was terminated. Because energy is lacking in most environments, Morita (1985) concluded that most bacteria in nature are in some degree of starvation and that this starvation mode was the normal mode for bacteria in the various ecosystems. For further information concerning starvation of microbes Morita (1982, 1985) should be consulted.

8.0. CONCLUSIONS

Studies on the behavior of individual microbial species in situ and in laboratory cultures has shown that the most critical environmental factor in marine environment that influences metabolic and microbial activity, growth, and reproduction of microbes is the nutrient availability (especially energy). Most ecosystems lack sufficient amounts of energy for life processes. In some instances, adequate energy sources are available, but other nutritional factors are lacking, such as ectocrine compounds, essential amino acids, and minerals (especially phosphate). If the nutritional requirements are met in any ecosystem, then microbes will have evolved capable of starvation within that ecosystem. The microbial evolutionary process has occurred for approximately 2.3 billions of years longer than for any other group of organisms. During this evolutionary period, microbes have also developed survival mechanisms so that the survival of the species is insured or further evolved.

In situ autecological research in oceanic ecosystems (oligotrophic, deep, more or less constant salinity, cold temperature, and increasing pressure) is limited. With an increasing understanding of the abiotic properties of this and related marine ecosystems, such studies became more probable. In fact, with the increasing need to open the *black box* commonly used to describe biological process in these ecosystems, an autecological approach to research will become obligatory. It is the author's hope that this abbreviated discussion will accent the needs for such studies and spur the development of this research area.

REFERENCES

Albright, L. J. (1969). Alternate pressurization–decompressurization effects on growth and net protein, RNA and DNA synthesis by *Escherichia coli* and *Vibrio marinus. Can. J. Microbiol.,* **15**:1237–1240.

Amy, P. S. and R. Y. Morita (1983a). Starvation–survival patterns of sixteen isolated open ocean bacteria. *Appl. Environ. Microbiol.,* **45**:1109–1115.

Amy, P. S. and R. Y. Morita (1983b). Protein patterns from growing and starved cells of a marine *Vibrio* sp. *Appl. Environ. Microbiol.,* **45**:1748–1752.

Amy, P. S., C. Pauling, and R. Y. Morita (1983a). Starvation–survival processes in a marine vibrio. *Appl. Environ. Microbiol,* **45**:1041–1048.

Amy, P. S., C. Pauling, and R. Y. Morita (1983b). Recovery from nutrient starvation by a marine vibrio. *Appl. Environ. Microbiol.,* **45**:1685–1690.

Anderson, J. I. W. and W. P. Heffernan (1965). Isolation and characterization of filterable marine bacteria. *J. Bacteriol.,* **90**:1713–1718.

Bada, J. F. and C. Lee (1977). Decomposition and alteration of organic compounds in sea water. *Mar. Chem.,* **5**:523–534.

Barber, R. T. (1968). Dissolved organic carbon from deep waters resists microbial oxidation. *Nature (London),* **220**:274–275.

Baross, J.A. and J. W. Deming (1983). Growth of "black smoker" bacteria at temperature of at least 250°C. *Nature (London),* **303**:423–426.

Baross, J. A., J. W. Deming, and R. R. Becker (1984). "Evidence for microbial growth in high-pressure high temperature environments," in M. J. Klug and C. A. Reddy, eds. *Current Perspectives in Microbial Ecology:* American Society for Microbiology, pp. 186–195.

Baross, J. A. and R. Y. Morita (1978). "Life at low temperatures: Ecological aspects," in D. J. Kushner, ed., *Microbial Life in Extreme Environments.* Academic, London, pp. 9–71.

Bianchi, A., P.-M. Scoditti, and M. G. Bensoussan (1979). Distribution des populations bactériennes heíérotrophes dan les sédiments et les tractus digestifs d'animaux benthiques recuellis dans la faille Vema et les planes abyssales du Demerara et de Gambie, Vol I. Fondation oceanographique Richard, Marseille, pp. 7–12.

Broecker, W. (1963). "Radioisotopes and large-scale organic mixing," in M. N. Hill, eds. *The Sea.* Vol. 2. Interscience, New York, pp. 88–108.

Buch K. and S. Gripenberg (1932). Uber den Einfluss des Wasserdruckes auf pH das

Kohlensaure gleichgewicht in grosseren Meerestiefen. *J. Cons. Conseil Perm. Int. Explor. Mer.* 7:233–245.

Buckmire, F. L. A., and R. A. MacLeod (1965). Nutrition and metabolism of marine bacteria. XIV. On the mechanism of lysis of a marine bacterium. *Can. J. Microbiol.,* 11:677–691.

Bukatsch, F. (1936). Uber den Einfluss von Salzen auf die Entwicklung von Bakterien. *Sbr. Akad. Wiss. Wien, Math.-Naturw. Kl. Abt. I.,* **145**:259–276.

Carlucci, A. F., S. L. Shimp, P. A. Jumars, and H. W. Paerl. (1976). In situ morphologies of deep sea and sediment bacteria. *Can. J. Microbiol.,* **22**:1667–1671.

Carlucci, A. F. and P. M. Williams (1978). Simulated in situ growth rates of pelagic marine bacteria. *Naturwissenschaften,* **65**:541–542.

Cavanaugh, C. M., S. L. Gardiner, M. L. Jones, H. W. Jannasch, and J. B. Waterbury (1981). Prokaryotic cells in the hydrothermal vent tube worm *Riftia pachyptila* Jones: Possible chemoautotrophic symbionts. *Science,* **213**:340–342.

Certes, A. (1884). Sur la culture a liabri des germes atmosphefiques, des eaux et des sediments rapportes per les expeditions due "Travailleur" et du "Tailsman." 1882–1883. *C. R. Acad. Sci.,* **99**:285–388.

Cooper, M. F. and R. Y. Morita (1972). Interaction of salinity and temperature on net protein viability of *Vibrio marinus. Limnol. Oceanogr.,* **17**:556–565.

Corliss, J. B., J. Dymond, L. I. Gordon, J. M. Edmond, R. P. von Herzen, R. D. Ballard, K. Green, D. Williams, A Bainbridge, K. Crane, and T. H. van Andel (1979). Submarine thermal springs on the Galapagos Rift. *Science,* **203**:1073–1083.

Craig, H. (1971). The deep metabolism: Oxygen consumption in abyssal ocean water. *J. Geophys. Res.,* **72**:5078–5086.

Daiku, K. and M. Sakai (1976). Physiological studies on the inorganic salt requirements of marine bacteria. VI. Salt requirements for electron transport chain in the cytoplasmic membrane. *Bull. Jpn. Soc. Sci. Fish.,* **42**:1121–1127.

Daley, R. J. and J. E. Hobbie (1975). Direct count of aquatic bacteria by modified epifluorescent technique. *Limnol. Oceanogr.,* **20**:875–881.

Dawson, M. P., B. Humphrey, and K. C. Marshall (1981). Adhesion; A tactic in the survival strategy of a marine vibrio during starvation. *Curr. Microbiol.,* **6**:195–201.

Deming, J. W. and R. R. Colwell (1981). Barophilic bacteria associated with deep-sea animals. *Bioscience,* **13**:507–511.

Deming, J. W., P. S. Tabor, and R. R. Colwell (1981). Barophilic growth of bacteria from intestinal tracts of deep-sea invertebrates. *Microb. Ecol.,* **7**:85–94.

DeVoe, I. W. and E. O. Oginsky (1969). Cation interactions and biochemical composition of the cell envelope of a marine bacterium. *J. Bacteriol.,* **98**:1368–1377.

Dianova, E. and A. Voroshilova (1935). Salt composition of medium and specificity of marine bacteria. *Mikrobiologiya,* **4**:393–402.

Dietz, A. S. and A. A. Yayanos (1978). Silica gel media for isolating and studying bacteria under hydrostatic pressure. *Appl. Environ. Microbiol.,* **36**:966–968.

Distéche, A. (1959). pH measurements with a glass electrode withstanding 1500 kg/cm^2 hydrostatic pressure. *Rev. Sci. Instr.,* **30**:474–478.

Distéche, A. and S. Distéche (1965). The effect of pressure on pH and dissociation constants from measurements with buffered and electrode cells. *J. Electrochem. Soc.,* **112**:350–354.

Drapeau, G. R. and R. A. MacLeod (1963). Na$^+$-dependent active transport of alpha-aminoisobutyric acid into cells of a marine pseudomonad. *Biochem. Biophys. Commun.*, **12**:111–115.

Drapeau, G. R., T. I. Matula, and R. A. MacLeod (1967). Nutrition and metabolism of marine bacteria. IV. Relation of Na$^+$ activated transport to the Na$^+$ requirement of a marine pseudomonad for growth. *J. Bacteriol.*, **92**:63–71.

Ewald, A. H. and S. D. Hamann (1956). The effect of pressure on complexion equilibria. *Aust. J. Chem.*, **9**:54–60.

Fein, J. E. and R. A. MacLeod (1975). Characterization of neutral amino acid transport in a marine pseudomonad. *J. Bacteriol.*, **124**:1177–1190.

Fischer, B. (1894). Die Bakterien des Meeres nach den Untersuchungen der Plankton-Expedition unter gleichzeitiger Berücksichtigung einiger alterer und neueres Untersuchungen. Ergebnisse der Plankton-Expedition der Humbolt-Strifung. Verlag von Lipsius und Tischer, Kiel und Leipsiz, Germany 4:1–81.

Geesey, G. G. and R. Y. Morita (1975). Some physiological effects of near maximum growth temperatures on an obligately psychrophilic marine bacterium. *Can. J. Microbiol.*, **21**:811–818.

Geesey, G. G. and R. Y. Morita (1979). Capture and uptake of arginine at low concentrations by a marine psychrophilic bacterium. *Appl. Environ. Microbiol.*, **38**:1092–1097.

Geesey, G. G. and R. Y. Morita (1981). Relationship of cell envelope stability to substrate capture in a marine psychrophilic bacterium. *Appl. Environ. Microbiol.*, **42**:533–540.

George, R. Y. and R. P. Huggins (1979). Eutrophic hadal benthic community in the Puerto Rico Trench. *Ambio. Spec. Rep. No.*, **6**:51–58.

Gordon, D. C. (1979). Some studies on the distribution and composition of particulate organic carbon in the North Atlantic. *Deep Sea Res.*, **18**:233–243.

Gow, J. A., I. W. DeVoe, and R. A. MacLeod (1973). Dissociation in a marine pseudomonad. *Can. J. Microbiol.*, **19**:695–701.

Hagen, P. D., D. J. Kushner, and N. E. Gibbons (1964). Temperature induced death and lysis in a psychrophilic bacterium. *Can. J. Microbiol.*, **10**:813–823.

Harvey, E. N. (1915). The effect of certain organic and inorganic substances upon light production by luminous bacteria. *Biol. Bull. Mar. Biol. Lab., Woods Hole*, **29**:308–311.

Haight, R. D. and R. Y. Morita (1962). The interaction between the parameters of hydrostatic pressure and temperature on aspartase of *Escherichia coli. J. Bacteriol.*, **83**:112–120.

Haight, J. J. and R. Y. Morita (1966). Some physiological difference in *Vibrio marinus* grown at environmental and optimal temperature. *Limnol. Oceanogr.*, **11**:470–474.

Haight, R. D. and R. Y. Morita (1966). Thermally induced leakage from *Vibrio marinus*, an obligately psychrophilic bacteria. *J. Bacteriol.*, **92**:1388–1393.

Hamann, S. D. (1963). The ionization of water at high pressure. *J. Phys. Chem.*, **67**:2233–2235.

Hamann, S. D. (1964). High pressure chemistry. *Ann. Rev. Phys. Chem.*, **15**:349–370.

Hamann, S. D., and W. Strauss (1965). The chemical effect of pressure. Part 3—

Ionization constants at pressures up to 1200 atm. *Trans. Faraday Soc.,* **51**:1684–1690.

Harrison, M. J., R. T. Wright, and R. Y. Morita (1971). A method for measuring mineralization in lake sediment. *Appl. Microbiol.,* **21**:698–702.

Harvey, E. N. (1915). The effect of certain organic and inorganic substances upon light production by luminous bacteria. *Biol. Bull. Mar. Biol. Lab., Woods Hole,* **29**:308–311.

Hayasaka, S. S. and R. Y. Morita (1978). Salinity and nutrient effects on the induction of the galactose permease system in a psychrophilic marine vibrio. *Mar. Biol.,* **49**:1–6.

Hessler, R. R., C. L. Ingram, A. A. Yayanos, and B. R. Burnett (1978). Scavenging amhipods from the floor of the Philippine Trench. *Deep-Sea Res.,* **25**:1029–1048.

Hidaka, T. (1965). Studies on the marine bacteria. II. On the specificity of mineral requirements of marine bacteria. *Mem. Fac. Fish. Hokkaido Univ.,* **14**:127–180.

Hidaka, T. and M. Sakai (1964). Studies on the marine bacteria. I. Comparative observations on the inorganic salt requirements of marine and terrestrial bacteria. *Mem. Fac. Fish. Hokkaido Univ.,* **12**:135–152.

Horne, R. A. and D. S. Johnson (1966). The viscosity of water under pressure. *J. Phys. Chem.,* **70**:2182–2190.

Horne, R. A. and D. S. Johnson (1967). The effect of electrolyte addition on the viscosity of water under pressure. *J. Phys. Chem.,* **71**:1147–1149.

Humphrey, B., S. Kjelleberg, and K. C. Marshall (1982). Responses of marine bacteria under starvation conditions at solid–water interface. *Appl. Environ. Microbiol.,* **45**:43–47.

Ichikawa, T., K. Akatani, T. Nishihara, and M. Kondo (1981). The effect of salts on enzymes of the respiratory chain of marine bacterium strain 1055–1. *J. Gen. Microbiol.,* **125**:439–444.

Jannasch, H. W., K. Eimhjellen, C. O. Wirsen, and A. Farmanfarmaian. (1971). Microbial degradation of organic matter in the deep sea. *Science,* **171**:672–675.

Jannasch, H. W. and C. O. Wirsen (1973). Deep-sea microorganisms: in situ response to nutrient enrichment. *Science,* **180**:641–643.

Jannasch, H. W. and C. O. Wirsen (1983). "Microbiology of the deep sea," in G. T. Rowe, ed., *Deep-Sea Biology.* Wiley-Interscience, New York, pp. 231–259.

Jannasch, H. W., C. O. Wirsen, and C. D. Taylor (1976). Undecompressed microbial populations from the deep sea. *Appl. Environ. Microbiol.,* **32**:360–367.

Jannasch, H. W., C. O. Wirsen, and C. D. Taylor (1982). Deep-sea bacteria: Isolation in the absence of decompression. *Science,* **216**:1315–1317.

Jannasch, H. J., C. O. Wirsen, and C. L. Winget (1973). A bacteriological pressure-retaining sampler and culture vessel. *Deep-Sea Res.,* **20**:661–664.

Johnson, F. H. and H. Eyring (1970). "The kinetic basis of pressure effects in biology and chemistry," in A. M. Zimmerman, ed., *High Pressure Effects on Cellular Processes.* Academic, New York, pp. 1–44.

Johnson, F. H., H. Eyring, and M. J. Polissar (1954). *The Kinetic Basis of Molecular Biology.* Wiley, New York.

Jones, D. S. (1983). Schlerochronology: Reading the record of the molluscan shell. *Am. Sci.,* **71**:384–391.

Jones, R. D. and R. Y. Morita (1985). Low temperature growth and whole cell kinetics of a marine ammonium oxidizer. *Mar. Ecol. Prog. Ser.,* **21**:239–243.

Jones, L. P., R. Y. Morita, and R. R. Becker (1979). Fructose-1, 6-biphosphate aldolase from *Vibrio marinus,* a psychrophilic marine bacterium. *Z. Allg. Mikrobiol.,* **19**:97–106.

Jones, K. L., and M. E. Rhodes-Roberts (1980). Physiological properties of nitrogen-scavenging bacteria from the marine environment. *J. Appl. Bacteriol.,* **49**:421–433.

Kenis, P. R. and R. Y. Morita (1968). Thermally induced leakage of cellular material and viability in *Vibrio marinus,* a psychrophilic marine bacterium. *Can. J. Microbiol.,* **14**:1239–1244.

Kettman, M. S., A. H. Nishikawa, R. Y. Morita, and R. R. Becker (1966). Effect of hydrostatic pressure on the aggregation reaction of poly-L-valyl ribonuclease. *Biochem. Biophys. Res. Commun.,* **22**:262–267.

Kjelleberg, S., B. A. Humphrey, and K. C. Marshall (1982). The effects of interfaces on small starved marine bacteria. *Appl. Environ. Microbiol.,* **43**:1166–1172.

Kogure, K., U. Simidu, and N. Taga (1979). A tentative direct microscopic method for counting living marine bacteria. *Can. J. Microbiol.,* **25**:415–420.

Kurath, G. and R. Y. Morita (1983). Starvation–survival physiological studies of a marine *Pseudomonas* sp. *Appl. Environ. Microbiol.,* **45**:1026–1211.

Landau, J. V. (1966). Protein and nucleic acid synthesis in *Escherichia coli:* Pressure and temperature effects. *Science,* **153**:1273–1274.

Landau, J. V. (1967). Induction, transcription and translation in *Escherichia coli:* A hydrostatic pressure study. *Biochim. Biophys. Acta,* **149**:506–512.

Landau, J. V. and D. H. Pope (1980). Recent advances in the area of barotolerant protein synthesis in bacteria and implications concerning barotolerant and harophilic growth. *Adv. Aquatic Microbiol.,* **2**:49–76.

Landau, J. V., W. P. Smith, and D. H. Pope (1977). Role of the 30S ribosomal subunit, initiation factors, and specific ion concentration in barotolerant protein synthesis in *Pseudomonas bathycetes. J. Bacteriol.,* **130**:154–159.

Langridge, P. and R. Y. Morita (1966). Thermolability of malic dehydrogenase from the obligate psychrophile, *Vibrio marinus. J. Bacteriol.,* **92**:418–423.

Lee, C. and J. L. Bada (1975). Amino acids in equatorial Pacific Ocean Water. *Earth Planet. Sci. Lett.,* **26**:61–68.

Linderstrøm-Lang, K. and C. F. Jacobsen (1941). The contraction accompanying enzymatic breakdown of proteins. *C. R. Trav. Lab. Carlsberg. Ser. Chim.,* **24**:1–46.

MacDonell, M. T. and M. A. Hood (1982). Isolation and characterization of ultramicrobacteria from a Gulf Coast Estuary. *Appl. Environ. Microbiol.,* **43**:566–571.

MacLeod, R. A. (1965). The question of the existence of specific marine bacteria. *Bacteriol. Rev.,* **29**:9–23.

MacLeod, R. A. (1968). On the role of inorganic ions in the physiology of marine bacteria. *Adv. Microbiol. Sea,* **1**:95–126.

MacLeod, R. A. (1971). "Bacteria, fungi and glue-green algae," Vol. 1, Part 2. in O. Kinne, ed., *Microb. Ecol.,* pp. 689–703.

MacLoed, R. A., C. A. Claridge, A. Hori, and J. F. Murray (1958). Observations on the function of sodium in the metabolism of marine bacteria. *J. Biol. Chem.,* **232**:829–834.

MacLeod, R. A. and E. Onofrey (1956a). Nutrition and metabolism of marine bacteria. II. Observations on the relation of seawater to growth of marine bacteria. *J. Bacteriol.,* **71**:661–667.

MacLeod, R. A. and E. Onofrey (1956b). Nutrition and metabolism of marine bacteria. VI. Quantitiative requirements for halides, magnesium, calcium, and iron. *Can. J. Microbiol.,* **3**:753–759.

MacLeod, R. A. and R. Onofrey (1957). Nutrition and metabolism of marine bacteria. VI. Quantitative requirements for halides, magnesium, calcium, and iron. *Can. J. Microbiol.,* **3**:753–759.

MacLeod, R. A. and R. Onofrey (1963). "Studies on the stability of the Na^+ requirement of marine bacteria," in C. H. Oppenheimer, ed., *Symposium of Marine Microbiology.* Thomas, Springfield, pp. 481–489.

MacLeod, R. A., E. Onofrey, and M. E. Norris (1954). Nutrition and metabolism of marine bacteria. I. Survey of nutritional requirements. *J. Bacteriol.,* **68**:680–686.

Marquis, R. E. (1976). High-pressure microbial physiology. *Adv. Microb. Physiol.,* **14**:159–241.

Marquis, R. E. and G. R. Bender (1980). Isolation of a variant of *Streptococci faecalis* with enhanced barotolerance. *Can. J. Microbiol.,* **26**:371–376.

Marshall, K. C., R. Stout, and R. Mitchell (1971). Selective sorption of marine bacteria to surfaces. *Can. J. Microbiol.,* **17**:1413–1416.

Mathemeier, P. F. and R. Y. Morita (1964). Influence of substrate-cofactor ratios on partially purififed inorganic pyrophosphatase activity at elevated temperatures. *J. Bacteriol.,* **8**:1161–1666.

Mathemeier, P. F. and R. Y. Morita (1977). Thermolability of dehydrogenases from psychrophilic marine bacterium. *J. Oceanogr. Soc Jpn.,* **33**:90–96.

Matsumura, P. and R. E. Marquis (1977). Energetics of streptococci growth inhibition by hydrostatic pressure. *Appl. Environ. Microbiol.,* **33**:885–892.

Menzel, D. W. (1974). "Primary productivity, dissolved and particulate organic matter, and the sites of oxidation of organic matter," in E. Goldberg, ed., *The Sea,* Vol. 5. Wiley, New York, pp. 659–678.

Miyagawa, K. and Suzuki, K. (1963a). Pressure inactiviation of enzyme: Some kinetics aspects of pressure inactivation of trypsin. *Rev. Phys. Chem. Jpn.,* **32**:43–50.

Miyagawa, K. and K. Suzuki (1963b). Pressure inactivation of enzyme: Some kineteics aspects of pressure inactivation of chymotrypsin. *Rev. Phys. Chem. Jpn.,* **32**:50–56.

Morild, E. (1981). The theory of pressure effects on enzymes. *Adv. Protein Chem.,* **34**:93–166.

Morita, R. Y. (1957). Effect of hydrostatic pressure on succinic, formic, and malic dehydrogenases in *Escherichia coli. J. Bacteriol.,* **74**:251–255.

Morita, R. Y. (1966). Marine psychrophilic bacteria. *Oceanogr. Mar. Biol. Ann. Rev.,* **4**:105–121.

Morita, R. Y. (1967). Effects of hydrostatic pressure on marine bacteria. *Oceanogr. Mar. Biol. Ann. Rev.,* **5**:187–203.

Morita, R. Y. (1972). "Pressure—bacteria, fungi, and blue green algae," in O. Kinne, ed., *Marine Biology—Environmental Factors,* Vol. 1, Part 3. Interscience, London, pp. 1361–1388.

Morita, R. Y. (1973). "Biochemical aspects," in R. Brauer, ed., *Barbiology and Experi-*

mental Biology of the Deep-Sea. University of North Carolina Press, Chapel Hill, pp. 89–105.

Morita, R. Y. (1975). Psychrophilic bacteria. *Bacteriol. Rev.,* **39**:144–167.

Morita, R. Y. (1976). "Survival of bacteria in cold and moderate hydrostatis pressure environments with special references to psychrophilic and barophilic bacteria," in T. G. R. Gray and J. R. Postgate, eds., *The Survival of Vegetative Microbes.* 26th Symposium of the Society of General Microbiologists, Cambridge University Press, Cambridge, pp. 279–298.

Morita, R. Y. (1977). "The role of microbes in the marine environment," in N. R. Anderson and B. J. Zuhurance, eds., *Ocean Sound Scattering Prediction.* Plenum, New York. pp. 445–456.

Morita, R. Y. (1980). Microbial life in the deep sea. *Can. J. Microbial.,* **26**:1375–1385.

Morita, R. Y. (1982). Starvation–survival of heterotrophs in the marine environment. *Adv. Microbiol. Ecol.,* **6**:171–198.

Morita, R. Y. (1984). "Substrate capture by marine heterotrophic bacteria in low nutrient waters," in J. E. Hobbie and P. J. LeB. Williams, eds., *Heterotrophic Activity in the Sea..* Plenum, New York, pp. 83–100.

Morita, R. Y. (1985). "Starvation and miniturisation of heterotrophs, with special emphasis on maintenance of the starved viable state," in M. Fletcher, ed., *Bacteria in Natural Environments: The Effect of Nutrient Conditions.* Academic, New York.

Morita, R. Y. and L. J. Albright (1965). Cell yields of *Vibrio marinus,* an obligate psychrophile, at low temperatures. *Can. J. Microbiol.,* **11**:221–227.

Morita, R. Y. and R. R. Becker (1970). "Hydrostatic pressure effects on selected biological systems," in A. W. Zimmerman, ed., *Hydrostatic Pressure Effects on Cellular Processes.* Academic, New York pp. 71–83.

Morita, R. Y. and S. D. Burton (1963). Influence of moderate temperature on the growth and malic dehydrogenase of a marine psychrophile. *J. Bacteriol.,* **86**:1025–1029.

Morita, R. Y. and R. D. Haight (1962). Malic dehydrogenase activity at 101°C under hydrostatic pressure. *J. Bacteriol.,* **93**:1341–1346.

Morita, R. Y. and R. D. Haight (1964). Temperature effects on the growth of an obligate psychrophilic marine bacterium. *Limnol. Oceanogr.,* **9**:103–106.

Morita, R. Y. and R. A. Howe (1957). Phosphatase activity by bacteria under hydrostatic pressure. *Deep-Sea Res.,* **4**:254–258.

Morita, R. Y. and P. F. Mathemeier (1964). Temperature–hydrostatic pressure studies on partially purified inorganic pyrophosphatase. *J. Bacteriol.,* **88**:1667–1671.

Morita, R. Y. and P. F. Mathemeier (1977). Thermolability of glycolysis enzymes from a psychrophilic marine bacterium. *J. Oceanogr. Soc. Jpn.,* **33**:254–258.

Morita, R. Y. and C. E. ZoBell (1955). Occurrence of bacteria in pelagic sediments collected during the Mid-Pacific Expedition. *Deep-Sea Res.,* **3**:66–73.

Mudrak, A. (1933). Beiträge zur Physiologie der Leuchtbakterien. *Zentralbl. Baktereol Parasitenkd Infektionskr. Hyg. Abt.,* **88**:353–366.

Muraoka, J. S. (1971). Deep ocean biodeterioration of materials. *Ocean Ind.,* 21–23.

Niven, D. F. and R. A. MacLoed (1978). Sodium ion-proton antiport in a marine bacterium. *J. Bacteriol.,* **134**:737–743.

Novitsky, J. A. and R. Y. Morita (1976). Morphological characterization of small cells resulting from nutrient starvation of a psychrophilic marine vibrio. *Appl. Environ. Microbiol.,* **32**:619–622.

Novitsky, J. A. and R. Y. Morita (1977). Survival of a psychrophilic marine vibrio under long term nutrient starvation. *Appl. Environ. Microbiol.,* **33**:635–641.

Novitsky, J. A. and R. Y. Morita (1978a). Possible strategy for the survival of marine bacteria under starvation conditions. *Mar. Biol.,* **48**:289–295.

Novitsky, J. A. and R. Y. Morita (1978b). Starvation-induced barotolerance as a survival mechanism of a psychrophilic marine vibrio in the waters of the Antarctic Convergence. *Mar. Biol.,* **49**:7–10.

Oppenheimer, C. H. (1952). The membrane filter in marine microbiology. *J. Bacteriol.,* **64**:783–786.

Oppenheimer, C. H. (1970). "Temperature. Bacteria, fungi and blue-green algae," in O. Kinne, ed., *Marine Ecology,* Vol. 1, Part 1. Wiley-Interscience, New York, pp. 345–361.

Oppenheimer, C. H. and C. E. ZoBell (1952). The growth and viability of sixty-three species of marine bacteria as influenced by hydrostatic pressure. *J. Mar. Res.,* **11**:10–18.

Ohwada, K., P. S. Tabor, and R. R. Colwell (1980). Species composition and barotolerance of gut microflora of deep-sea benthic macrofauna collected at various depths in the Atlantic Ocean. *Appl. Environ. Microbiol.,* **40**:746–755.

Owen, B. B. and S. R. Brinkley (1941) Calculation of the effect of pressure upon ionic equilibria in pure and salt solutions. *Chem. Rev.,* **29**:416–473.

Palmer, D. S. and L. J. Albright (1970). Salinity effects on the maximum hydrostatic pressure for growth of the marine psychrophilic bacterium, *Vibrio marinus. Limnol. Oceanogr.,* **15**:343–347.

Paul, K. L. and R. Y. Morita (1971). The effects of hydrostatic pressure and temperature on the uptake and respiration of amino acids by a facultatively psychrophilic marine bacteria. *J. Bacteriol.,* **108**:835–843.

Payne, W. J. (1958). Studies on bacterial utilization of uronic acids. Induction of oxidative enzymes in a marine bacterium. *J. Bacteriol.,* **76**:301–307.

Payne, W. J. (1960). Effects of sodium and potassium ions on growth and substrate penetration of a marine pseudomonad. *J. Bacteriol.,* **80**:696–700.

Pratt, D. B. and M. Austin (1963). "Osmotic regulation of the growth rate of four species of marine bacteria," in C. H. Oppenheimer, ed., *Symposium of Marine Microbiology.* Thomas, Springfield. pp. 629–637.

Pratt, D. and S. Tedder (1974). "Variation in the salt requirement for the optimum growth rate of marine bacteria," in R. R. Colwell and R. Y. Morita, eds., *Effects of the Ocean Environment on Microbial Activities.* University Park Press, Baltimore. pp. 38–45.

Pytkowicz, R. M. and G. A. Fowler (1967). Solubility of formainifera in seawater at high pressures. *Geochem. J. (Nagoya),* **1**:169–182.

Quigley, M. M. and R. R. Colwell (1968). Properties of bacteria isolated from Deep-Sea sediment. *J. Bacteriol.,* **95**:211–220.

Regnard, P. (1891). Recherches expérimentales sur les conditions physiques de la vie dans les eaux. Librairie de l'Academic de Medecine. Paris.

Reichelt, J. L. and P. Baumann (1974). Effect of sodium chloride on growth of hetero-trophic marine bacteria. *Arch. Microbiol.,* **97**:329–345.

Rhoads, D. C., R. A. Lutz, E. Revelas, and R. M. Cerrato (1981). Growth of bivalves in the deep-sea hydrothermal vents along the Galapagos Rift. *Science,* **214**:911–913.

Rhodes, M. E. and W. J. Payne (1962). Further observations on effects of cationsa on enzyme inducation in marine bacteria. *Autoine van Leeuwenhoek,; J. microbiol. Serol.* **28**:302–314.

Rhodes, M. E. and W. J. Payne (1967). Influence of Na^+ on synthesis of a substrate penetration mechanism in a marine bacterium. *Proc. Soc. Exp. Biol. Med.,* **124**:953–955.

Richter, O. (1928). Natrium: Ein notwendiges Nahrelement fur eine marine mikroaro-phile Leuchtbakterie. *Anz. Oesterr. Akad. Wiss., Math. Naturwiss. Kl.,* **101**:261–292.

Riley, J. P. and R. Chester (1971). *Introduction of Marine Chemistry.* Academic, New York.

Robison, S. M. and R. Y. Morita (1966). The effect of moderate temperature on the respiration and viability of *Vibrio marinus. Z. Allg. Mikrobiol.,* **6**:181–187.

Rüger, H. J. (1982). Psychrophilic sediment bacteria in the upwelling area off NW-Africa. *Naturwissenschaften,* **69**:450.

Sakai, D. K. and M. Sakai (1980). "Differentiation of marine bacteria: Physiological roles of inorganic salts required for specific marine bacteria," in H. Morishita and M. Masui, eds., *Saline Environments,* Vol. 19. Japanese Conference on Halophilic Mi-crobiology, Tokyo. pp. 135–179.

Schwarz, J. R. and R. R. Colwell (1975). Heterotrophic activity of deep-sea sediment bacteria. *Appl. Environ. Microbiol.,* **32**:46–48.

Schwartz, J. R., A. A. Yayanos, and R. R. Colwell (1976). Metabolic activities of the intestinal microflora of a deep-sea invertebrate. *Appl. Environ. Microbiol.,* **31**:46–48.

Seki, H., J. Skelding, and T. R. Parsons (1968). Observations on the decomposition of a marine sediment. *Limnol. Oceanogr.,* **13**:440–447.

Sieburth, J. McN. (1964). Polymorphism of a marine bacterium *(Arthrobacter)* as a function of multiple temperature optima and nutrition. *Symp. Exp. Mar. Ecol. Univ. Rhode Island Occas. Pub.,* **2**:1111–1121.

Sieburth, J. McN. and A. A. Dietz (1974). "Biodeterioration in the sea and its inhibi-tion," in R. R. Colwell and R. Y. Morita, eds., *Effect of the Ocean Environment on Microbial Activities.* University Park Press, Baltimore, pp. 318–326.

Sprott, G. D., J. P. Drozdowski, E. L. Martin, and R. A. MacLeod (1974). Kinetics of Na^+-dependent amino acid transport using cells and membrane vesicles of a marine pseudomonas. *Can. J. Microbiol.,* **1**:43–50.

Stainer, R. Y. (1941). Studies on marine agar-digesting bacteria. *J. Bacteriol.,* **42**:527–557.

Stanley, S. O. and R. Y. Morita (1968). Salinity effect on the maximum growth tempera-ture of some bacteria isolated from marine environments. *J. Bacteriol.,* **95**:169–173.

Strehler, B. L. and F. H. Johnson (1954). The temperature pressure-inhibitor relations of bacterial luminescence *in vitro. Proc. Natl. Acad. Sci. US,* **40**:606–617.

Suzuki, K., Y. Miyosawa, and C. Suzuki. (1963). Protein denaturation by high pressure. Measurements of turbidity of isoelectric ovalbumin and horse serum albumin under high pressure. *Arch. Biochem. Biophys.,* **101**:225–228.

Tabor, P. S., J. W. Deming, K. Ohwada, H. Davis, M. Waxman, and R. R. Colwell (1981). A pressure-retaining deep ocean sampler and transfer system for measurement of microbial activity in the deep sea. *Microb. Ecol.,* **7**:51–65.

Tabor, P. S., K. Ohwada, and R. R. Colwell (1981). Filterable marine bacteria in the deep sea: Distribution, taxonomy and responses to starvation. *Microb. Ecol.,* **7**:67–83.

Tedder, S. (1966). Replacement of sodium ions by potassium ion in the growth of selected marine organisms. M. S. Thesis. University of Florida, Gainesville, FL.

Thompson, J. and R. A. MacLeod (1971). Functions of Na$^+$ and K$^+$ in the active transport of α-aminoisobutyric acid in a marine pseudomonad. *J. Biol. Chem.,* **246**:4066–4074.

Thompson, J. and R. A. MacLeod (1974a). Potassium transport and relationship between intracellular potassium concentration and amino acid uptake by cells of a marine pseudomonad. *J. Bacteriol.,* **120**:598–603.

Thompson, J. and R. A. MacLeod (1974b). Specific electron dondor-energized transport of α-aminoisobutyric acid and K$^+$ into intact cells of a marine psuedomonad. *J. Bacteriol.,* **117**:1055–1064.

Tomlinson, N. and R. A. MacLeod (1957). Nutrition and metabolism of marine bacteria. IV. The participation of Na$^+$, K$^+$, and Mg^{++} salts in the oxidation of the exogenous substrates by a marine bacterium. *Can. J. Microbiol.,* **3**:627–638.

Torrella, F. and R. Y. Morita (1981). Microcultural study of bacterial size changes and microcolony and ultramicrocolony formation by heterotrophic bacteria in seawater. *Appl. Environ. Microbiol.,* **41**:518–527.

Torrella, F. and R. Y. Morita (1982). Starvation induced morphological changes, motility, and chemotaxis patterns in a psychrophilic marine vibrio. *Deuxieme Colloque de Microbiol.,* Marseille, Publ. Centre National pour l'Exploitation des Oceans **13**:45–60.

Trent, J. D., R. A. Chastain, and A. A. Yayanos (1984). Possible artefactual basis for apparent growth at 250°C. *Nature (London),* **307**:737–740.

Turekian, K. K. and J. K. Cochran (1981). Growth rates of a vesicomyid clam from the Galapagos spreada center. *Science,* **211**:909–911.

Turekian, K. K., J. K. Cochran, D. P. Kharkar, R. M. Cerrato, J. R. Vaisnys, H. L. Sanders, J. F. Grassle, and J. A. Allen (1975). Slow growth rate of a deep-sea clam determined by ^{228}Ra chronology. *Proc. Natl. Acad. Sci. USA,* **72**:2829–2832.

Tyler, M. E., M. C. Bieling, and D. B. Pratt (1960). Mineral requirements and other characters of selected marine bacteria. *J. Gen. Microbiol.,* **23**:153–161.

Unemoto, T. and M. Hayashi (1979). Regulation of internal solute concentrations of marine *Vibrio alginolyticus* in response to external NaCl concentration. *Can. J. Microbiol.,* **25**:922–926.

Watson, S. W., T. J. Novitsky, H. L. Quinby, and F. W. Valois (1977). Determination of bacterial number and biomass in the marine environment. *Appl. Environ. Microbiol.,* **33**:940–946.

Webb, C. D. and W. J. Payne (1971). Influence of Na$^+$ on synthesis of macromolecules by a marine bacterium. *Appl. Microbiol.,* **21**:1080–1088.

Wilbrandt, W. and T. Rosenberg (1961). The concept of carrier transport and its corollaries in pharmacology. *Pharmacol. Revs.,* **13**:109–183.

Williams, P. M., H. Oeschger, and P. Kinney (1969). Natural radiocarbon activity in the Northeast Pacific Ocean. *Nature* (London), **224**:256–258.

Wolff, T. (1976). Utilization of seagrass in the deep sea. *Aquat. Bot.,* **2**:161–174.

Wolff, T. (1970). The concept of the hadal or ultra-abyssal fauna. *Deep-Sea Res.,* **17**:983–1003.

Wright, R. T. and H. E. Hobbie (1966). Use of glucose and acetate by bacteria and algae in aquatic systems. *Ecology,* **47**:447–464.

Yayanos, A. A. (1978). Recovery and maintenance of live amphipods a pressure of 580 bars from an ocean depth of 5700 meters. *Science,* **200**:1056–1059.

Yayanos, A. A. and A. S. Deitz (1983). Death of a hadal deep-sea bactereium after decompression. *Science,* **220**:497–498.

Yayanos, A. A., A. S. Deitz, and R. Van Boxtel (1979). Isolation of a deep-sea barophilic bacterium and some of its growth characteristics. *Science,* **205**:808–810.

Yayanos, A. A., A. S. Dietz, and R. Van Boxtel (1981). Obligately bariophilic bacterium from the Mariana Trench. *Proc. Natl. Acad. Sci. U.S.,* **78**:5212–5215.

Zimmermann, R. (1977). "Estimation of bacterial numbers and biomass by epifluorescence microscopy and scanning electron microscopy," in G. Rheinmeimer, ed., *Microbial Ecology of a Brackish Water Environment,* Springer-Verlag, New York, pp. 103–120.

Zimmerman, R. and L. -A. Meyer-Reil (1974). A new method for fluorescence staining of bacterial populations on membrane filter. *Kiel. Meeresforch.,* **30**:24–27.

ZoBell, C. E. (1958). Ecology of sulfate reducing bacteria. *Prod. Mon.,* **22**:12–29.

ZoBell, C. E. (1964). "Hydrostatic pressure as a factor affecting the activities of marine microbes," in Y. Miyake and T. Koyama, eds., *Recent Researches in the Field of Hydrosphere, Atmosphere, and Nuclear Geochemistry.* Maruzen, Tokyo, pp. 83–116.

ZoBell, C. E. and K. M. Budge (1965). Nitrate reduction by marine bacteria at increased hydrostatic pressure. *Limnol. Oceanogr.,* **10**:207–214.

ZoBell, C. E. and A. B. Cobet (1964). Filament formation by *Escherichia coli* at increased hydrostatic pressure. *J. Bacteriol.,* **87**:710–719.

ZoBell, C. E. and F. H. Johnson (1949). The influence of hydrostatic pressure on the growth and viability of terrestrial and marine bacteria. *J. Bacteriol.,* **57**:179–289.

ZoBell, C. E., and H. D. Michener (1938). A paradox in the adaption of marine bacteria to hypotonic solution. *Science,* **87**:328–329.

ZoBell, C. E., and R. Y. Morita (1957). Barophilic bacteria in some deep-sea sediments. *J. Bacteriol.,* **73**:563–568.

ZoBell, C. E. and R. Y. Morita (1959). Deep-sea bacteria. *Galathea Rep.,* **1**:139–154.

ZoBell, C. E. and C. H. Oppenheimer (1950). Some effect of hydrostatic pressure on the multiplication and morphology of marine bacteria. *J. Bacteriol.* **60**:771–781.

ZoBell, C. E. and S. C. Rittenberg, (1938). The occurrence and characteristics of chitinoclastic bacteria. *J. Bacteriol.,* **35**:275–278.

ZoBell, C. E. and H. C. Upham (1944). A list of marine bacteria including descriptions of sixty new species. *Bull. Scripps Inst. Oceanogr.,* **5**:239–292.

8 AUTECOLOGICAL STUDIES IN MICROBIAL LIMNOLOGY

Charles W. Boylen
Reginald J. Soracco
Fresh Water Institute and Department of Biology
Rensselaer Polytechnic Institute
Troy, New York

Since the observations of Antonie van Leeuwenhoek in the seventeenth century, aquatic habitats have proven to be continuous sources of new and physiologically unique prokaryotes. New species and even new genera are described with each passing year. In this chapter the diversity found in these aquatic ecosystems will be examined in classical ecological terms with respect to the impacts of (1) these ecosystems upon individual populations, (2) individual populations on the physical character of their environment, and (3) populations within an ecosystem upon one another.

The variety in physical and chemical composition of inland aquatic ecosystems has provided ideal habitats for autecological research resulting in major contributions to the delineation of the microbiological role in ecosystem processes. Inland aquatic habitats are one of the more diverse and potentially complex ecosystems for study. This complexity, both biotic and abiotic, is frequently overlooked in the design of most laboratory-based research. Variations in abiotic traits are exhibited by temperature ranges from below the freezing point of water to near boiling, and pH extremes from strongly acid (<1.0) to very alkaline (>11). Moreover, parts of these ecosystems can become seasonally or permanently anoxic, such as wetlands, stagnant ponds, and lake sediments. Anoxic conditions often extend throughout the lower portion (hypolimnion) of stratified lakes. Radiant energy in the form of light to which bodies of water are exposed can vary from that received at the surface of equatorial ecosystems to the perpetual darkness of the hypolimnia of deep lakes and groundwater. In polar regions light energy inputs vary dramatically on a seasonal basis. Seasonal variation may be further complicated by diurnal changes resulting from localized shading. Nutrient conditions in limnologic environments range from those found in pristine mountain lakes and nutrient-poor coldwater streams to eutrophied lakes and anthropogenically polluted rivers. Ionic strength may range from that approaching distilled water to levels over twice as high as open ocean water — not to mention the variety of combinations of ions that exist in between.

This diversity in the freshwater environment has provided the basis for some notable achievements in the study of prokaryotes and, in particular, their autecology. For example, with an increasing interest in biogenic sources of fuels, there has come new understandings of a unique group of aquatic and sediment microorganisms — the methanogens. Isolation of new species has increased the awareness of the ecological function of prokaryotes and demonstrated that present day freshwater environments contain prokaryotes similar to those that first evolved on this planet 2–3 billion years ago (Woese, 1981). Also, the study of cyanobacterial mats in other freshwater habitats has had an important impact on the theories of early microbial evolution (Cohen et al., 1984). Through the discovery and isolation of extreme thermophiles and acidophiles from unusual limnological habitats (Brock, 1978), our understanding of the limits of environmental tolerance of living organisms has expanded. Autecological studies have provided new insights into the varied and essential role of prokaryotes in nutrient cycling and mineralization (Ehrlich, 1985).

Much of our knowledge of the prokaryotes' role in limnology — their ability to alter dramatically their environment as well as their range of physiological adaptation — has been inferred from isolation and study of axenic cultures in the laboratory. Although titles of many articles hint at ecological understanding, such research is not easy to assess in true ecological terms. In the context of the present discussion, it is difficult to know where to give due reference to such research. In an attempt to maintain a true ecological perspective, reference to such studies is minimal; however, some notable examples of this type of investigation are included arbitrarily.

Similar to microbial ecological research in general, primary advancements in the understanding of microbial activity in freshwater ecology have been made using a synecological approach. Traditionally and conveniently, limnological prokaryotes have been treated as a "black box" with little or no regard to taxonomic accuracy or nomenclature. Evaluations of phenomena such as the extent of secondary production, bacterial densities in water columns or underlying sediments, rates of decomposition and mineralization, and contributions to aquatic primary production, typically have been conducted at the microbial community level. Many significant studies address specific physiological activities, for example, methanogenesis or sulfate reduction, but by design result in only determining functional groups. Monospecific populations or those of closely related species are only implied or labeled by some pseudotaxonomic term such as anaerobic sporeformers, caulobacters, or coryneform bacteria. Often ecologists assess populations to a genus level; for example, *Chromatium* spp. or *Oscillatoria* spp., without consideration of individual species or strains. It is interesting to note that many aquatic studies contain precise taxonomic notation of plants, animals, fungi, and even protists, whereas those dealing with the ecological role of prokaryotes usually do not have well-defined taxonomic descriptions.

Since classification beyond the genus level is frequently not necessary or even desirable to achieve experimental objectives and since it is often difficult to relate function to individual genera or species, the term autecology will be used here to include studies of functional microbial groupings. This approach will necessitate the use of the flexible definition given in Chapter 1. There are many studies, however, which are noteworthy in an autecological sense because they specifically address a population of a discrete species in a freshwater setting, for example, the presence of *Legionella pneumophila* in lake water (Fliermans et al., 1981). These studies exemplify autecology in its purest sense.

This chapter is not intended to be an exhaustive review of the current status of microbial autecology in limnology. First, consideration of eukaryotic microorganisms have been omitted entirely. Second, the major focus will be on lake (lentic) ecosystems, reflecting the fact that most freshwater microbial ecology has been centered around these environments. Examples from other limnological environments will be used where appropriate. Of major global importance is the quality of potable water and wastewater—both public and industrial. Although there have been significant autecological studies in these areas, their coverage to any major degree is not possible in the context of this chapter.

1.0. LIMNOLOGICAL ECOSYSTEMS

A brief characterization of freshwater environments will provide the reader with an understanding of the important features of these habitats and the terms used to describe them. More complete and exacting descriptions can be found in standard texts on ecology (Odum, 1971) and limnology (Wetzel, 1983).

Over 70% of the earth's surface is covered by water with more than 97% contained in the oceans. That remaining, loosely referred to as freshwater, is partitioned between the polar ice caps and glaciers (>75%), groundwater (22%), lakes (<0.3%), and rivers (<0.003%) (Goldman and Horne, 1983). Little microbiological research has been conducted on groundwater and even less on permanently frozen freshwater. The bulk of the autecological information about microorganisms present in so-called freshwater ecosystems relates to those inhabiting inland surface waters.

In the strictest sense, the term limnology (derived from the Greek word *limne* meaning pool, marsh, or lake) is the study of still or standing aquatic (lentic) ecosystems located in inland depressions. Today limnology is used to describe the study of flowing aquatic (lotic) ecosystems as well. Together these ecosystems can range in size from swamps and ponds of negligible size and depth to the 420-mile-long Lake Baikal in Siberia with a depth greater than 5000 ft and from ephemeral streams with no more than a seasonal trickle to the Nile, Amazon, and Chang Rivers that are some 4000 miles long and in certain locations over a mile wide.

1.1. Groundwater Habitats

Groundwater is subsurface water that occurs in permeable, saturated rock, sand, or gravel strata called aquifers. Groundwater comprises approximately 4% of the water contained in the hydrologic cycle (Pye, et al., 1983) and is found within 2500 ft of the soil surface. This water is recharged by precipitation, mixes very slowly compared to surface water, and varies greatly in quality. Depending on the concentration of total dissolved solids, groundwater may be classed as freshwater, brackish, saline, or brine (Freeze and Cherry, 1979). Chemical quality reflects its subterranean age as well as the geological formations encountered in its flow history.

Microbial studies of groundwater are not extensive. To a large extent, the observed microscopic diversity has not been duplicated in culture (Balkwill and Ghiorse, 1985; Ghiorse and Balkwill, 1983). The organisms that have been identified are termed as coryneform or arthrobacter types. Nothing is known of their ecological function. Because of their relationship to geological formations associated with fossil fuel deposits, autecological studies of groundwater have dealt most extensively with evaluations of biogeochemical cycles, notably the sulfur cycle (Dockins, 1980; Starkey, 1964).

1.2. Lotic Habitats

Since streams and rivers are flowing water (lotic) habitats, it is difficult for a microbial population to maintain a constant density by a wholly planktonic existence. Therefore, the ability to attach to rocks or other substrata (epilithic) or to the surface of the plants or animals inhabiting these ecosystems (epiphytic) is essential for the persistence of microbial populations in lotic habitats. At low flow rates the possibility exists for planktonic populations similar to those found in lentic (lake) ecosystems to be present. The surrounding terrestrial environments of lotic ecosystems has a tremendous influence on these habitats. With the increased volume and flow of water during and following storm events, planktonic, epiphytic, and epilithic populations may change drastically. The nutrients or toxic substances present in the water may change dramatically due to these natural events or through anthropogenic activities near or upstream of a particular location in the ecosystem.

1.3. Lentic Habitats

It has been long known that there is a great dissimilarity between lakes (Hutchinson, 1957). Their ecological structure is dictated by their morphometry as well as that of their respective drainage basins. Dynamic physical properties such as light, temperature, and water motion (caused by the action of waves and currents) produce an environment that varies by day and by season. Only relatively recently have microbial ecologists realized that such differences have a significant selective power on the individual microbial populations inhabiting these environments.

The influence of the distribution of light and temperature on the physical structure of a lake is diagramed in Figure 1. The photic zone extends through the water column from the lake surface to a depth where the light intensity is approximately 1% of that at the surface. Within this zone, photosynthetic activity normally exceeds respiratory activity providing a net gain of oxygen to the system. The region below this depth (aphotic zone) is characterized by net oxygen consumption due to respiration dominating over photosynthesis as well as occurring in its absence. If respiration demand is greater than the diffusion of oxygen the aphotic zone will become anoxic.

With the exception of those lakes fed by thermal groundwater, solar intensity is the major heat source for lakes. In far northern or southern latitudes, lakes and ponds can be permanently frozen or only briefly thawed. The temperature throughout the water column of lakes in the lower elevations of equatorial latitudes is relatively constant. In temperate latitudes, where most lakes are found worldwide, lentic ecosystems are covered by ice throughout the winter months. During this period, thermal stratification occurs with the warmer water (4°C) in the deeper part of the lake and cooler water (0°C) at the surface under the ice. Upon thawing and warming of the surface waters by the sun's energy, three zones of thermal stratification develop: (1) the upper warmer water, referred to as the epilimnion; (2) the lower colder water, called the hypolimnion; and (3) the demarcation between these regions where the rate of temperature change with depth is greatest termed the thermocline. In many

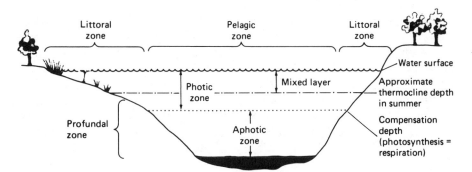

Figure 1. The influence of the distribution of light and temperature on the physical structure of a lake. The zonation is typical of a small temperate lake in summer. The zones vary from lake to lake, are dependent on the chemical and biological clarity of the water column, and will vary seasonally. Reprinted by permission, from Goldman, C. R. and A. J. Horne (1983). *Limnology.* McGraw-Hill, New York. Copyright McGraw-Hill, Inc.

lakes the depth between photic and aphotic and epilimnion and hypolimnion roughly coincide.

Once thermal stratification develops, nutrients are frequently depleted in the epilimnion while accumulating in the hypolimnion. Such partitioning may become a permanent trait of some lakes. With seasonal cooling, the thermal stratification is disrupted in most lakes and the entire volume of lake water is mixed once again bringing the nutrients in the lower waters to the surface.

Knowledge of the roles microbial populations play in primary productivity, detritus processing, and biogeochemical cycling in limnology has come primarily from studies dealing with lentic systems.

2.0. PHYSIOCHEMICAL SELECTION OF PROKARYOTES

Appreciation of the extreme adaptability of prokaryotes has been gained primarily from microbial studies of unusual freshwater habitats. Extremes in the chemical and physical nature of particular habitats eliminate most species diversity often generating essentially a natural pure culture. Numerous situations exist where temperature, pH, anoxia, and light are known to select for particularly adapted prokaryotes.

2.1. Temperature

Studies of the cyanobacterial mats of thermal springs and pools, first characterized independently by Brock (1967a, 1967b), Castenholz (1968, 1969b), and Stockner (1967), resulted in a reformulation of concepts relating to the upper temperature limits for living organisms. These thermal habitats have now been studied worldwide providing a major impetus to the reevaluation of the taxonomy of thermophilic freshwater prokaryotes (Brock, 1968).

Most naturally occurring thermal habitats are aquatic, with their source of heat being primarily telluric. Photosynthetic cyanobacteria grow at constant temperatures as high as 74 °C (Brock, 1967b) and are particularly concentrated in hot-spring waters with a pH greater than six where they form conspicuous mats (Castenholz, 1969a). Many hot springs have a surface effluent that produce thermal gradients ranging from supraoptimal to ambient. Specific differences in growth temperature optima result in distinct species covering different portions of the gradient (Brock, 1969b; Castenholz, 1968, 1984). The biogeography of these organisms have now been characterized on a global scale (Brock and Brock, 1970; Castenholz, 1978, 1984). In some springs, layers of photosynthetic purple sulfur bacteria are found directly beneath the algal cover (Castenholz, 1969a). In others, filamentous photosynthetic flexibacteria have been isolated and studied (Bauld and Brock, 1973; Pierson and Castenholz, 1974). Fluctuating thermal systems set up selective pressures for the development of other types of mat communities whether natural (Mosser and Brock, 1971) or synthetic (Tison et al., 1981). In nuclear plant effluents with shifting thermal regimes, the algal mat communities are dominated at high temperatures (58°C) by *Fischerella* sp. *(Mastigocladus laminosus)*, and *Phormidium* sp. indicating that these communities are similar, structurally, to algal communities of hot springs of Iceland and New Zealand where similar algal communities occur rather than to those found in the Western United States (Castenholz, 1978, 1984).

Upper limits of prokaryotic growth in situ approach the boiling point. Non-photosynthetic prokaryotes such as *Thermus aquaticus* grow at temperatures as high as 95°C (Bott and Brock, 1969; Brock and Freeze, 1969). The conclusion that some bacterial strains can live and grow in boiling water was derived from studies of freshwater thermal pools and springs. Only a few strains have been taxonomically identified. *Thermus aquaticus* (Brock and Freeze, 1969) and *Sulfolobus acidocaldarius* (Brock et al., 1972; Weiss, 1973) have growth optima between 70 and 80°C and can be found in habitats with temperatures as high as 93°C.

These early observations are noteworthy because they have provided the microbial autecologist with the first opportunity to do in situ measurements of biosynthetic rates (Brock and Brock, 1967, 1968), and growth rates (Bott and Brock, 1969) of taxonomically pure populations. Since the early 1970s, temperature tolerance has been examined in a variety of ecosystems. The most notable and promising with regard to high temperature are the submarine thermal vents where elevated pressures and salinities provide a situation in which water remains in the liquid phase substantially above 100°C.

A variety of microbial species have also developed the potential for growth at temperatures near the freezing point of water. Activity of these populations is controlled in part by the existence of free water. Specific examples of this limitation are discussed later in relation to the pathogen *Aeromonas* (Cavari et al., 1981), and the methylotroph *Methylomonas methanica* (Reed and Dugan, 1978). The lower temperature range is not as selective as high temperature, although several psychrophilic or psychrotrophic organisms have been identified.

2.2. Hydrogen Ion Concentration (pH)

Proton concentration or pH in aquatic environments vary by at least 10 orders of magnitude. On the acidic side are the sulfur springs and streams acidified from the oxidation of mine drainage that result in a pH of between 1 and 2 (Brock, 1969a; Darland et al., 1970; Hargreaves et al., 1975; Whitton and Diaz, 1981). At the other extreme are the soda lakes with pH values of 10–11 (Grant and Tindall, 1980; Talling et al., 1973; Tindall et al., 1980). In eutrophic waters, including fish ponds (Rimon and Shilo, 1982) and sewage oxidation ponds (Abeliovich and Azov, 1976), biological activity such as photosynthesis can change the pH within a diurnal cycle by several units (Paerl and Mackenzie, 1977). Prokaryotic adaptations to pH vary. In acidic environments high proton concentrations also results in high concentrations of dissolved metals that may reach toxic levels (Hargreaves et al., 1975). In alkaline environments, low proton concentrations precipitate many essential metals (Langworthy, 1978).

A few autecological studies have been conducted to determine the mechanisms that allow prokaryotes to cope with fluctuating pH extremes. Acidophilic strains of *Bacillus coagulans* have widespread occurrence in hot springs (Belly and Brock, 1974). Most of the research on the microbial distributions in acidic mine waters has focused on the chemolithotrophic action of the iron and sulfur oxidizing bacteria like *Thiobacillus ferrooxidans* and *T. thiooxidans.* Studies have shown these organisms to be prime contributors to the release of the major anions found in acidic coal mine drainage (Ehrlich, 1981). Recent accounts have addressed the distribution in these environments of obligately acidophilic bacterial heterotrophs (Belly and Brock, 1974; Dugan et al., 1970; Johnson et al., 1979; Wichlacz and Unz, 1981). Neither the taxonomy of these organisms nor their ecology is well understood due to poor recovery of obviously distinct species (Johnson et al., 1979; Wichlacz and Unz, 1981). Numerous acidophilic Gram-positive bacteria have been isolated including staphylococci, micrococci, corynebacteria, and *Bacillus* spp. (Dugan et al., 1970; Johnson et al., 1979). However, Gram-negative bacteria, the better characterized strains of which have been designated as *Pseudomonas acidophila* (Manning, 1975), are most often recovered on distinctly acid culture media. Delineation of the role of these acidophiles in nature requires better knowledge of their taxonomic position. This will allow a better understanding of the development of the mechanisms of acid tolerance.

Early ecological studies of acidophiles include the work of Brock and Brock (1970) who first noted that, although cyanobacteria are able to grow at higher temperatures than any other algal group (Brock, 1967b, 1969a), they are not found in very acid waters. In their studies of Waimangu Cauldron, New Zealand, the cyanobacterium *Mastigocladus laminosus* was present only above pH 4.8. This lake provided an ideal situation to study since its acidity originated from the in situ oxidation of H_2S from thermal vents within the lake. The sulfur oxidation resulted in a pH of 3.8 in the main body of water and at the outlet. The presence of alkaline springs flowing into the lake resulted in the development of localized pH gradients. The idea that cyanobacteria are limited to environments with pH values above 4.0 is now in question with the discovery that species can be isolated from softwater acidified lakes with acidities approaching 4.0 (Lazarek, 1980; Singer et al., 1983a).

Many of the extremely acidic aquatic habitats are also temperature stressed (Brock, 1969a). Numerous autecological studies have shown these environments to be a niche occupied by a relatively small number of species worldwide. *Thermoplasma acidophilum, Sulfolobus acidocaldarius,* and *Bacillus acidocaldarius* have been isolated from such habitats having pH values from 1 to 2 and temperatures from 55 to 90°C (Darland and Brock, 1971; Darland et al., 1970). In acid thermal springs, as the habitat pH decreased so did the upper temperature at which bacteria appeared (Brock and Darland, 1970). In these springs (pH 2–3) at temperatures above 60°C, several kinds of bacteria (yet to be identified) were found. Above 80°C, *Sulfolobus* was the only species present.

2.3. Oxygen Concentration

A major variable that controls microbial activities in lentic ecosystems is the concentration of oxygen in the water. Oxygen levels in the water column of lotic ecosystems are usually constant because of the ready availability to and the mixing with the atmosphere. However, anoxia occurs in portions of both these ecosystems, for example, within attached communities, beneath the surface of the sediments, or when there is a high biological oxygen demand in the water. Anoxic conditions commonly occur only a few millimeters below the surface of attached communities and in the sediments of these habitats. In stratified lentic ecosystems, the depletion of oxygen in sediments often extend throughout the hypolimnion. The presence and density of an anaerobic organism like *Peloploca* spp. in sediments and in the overlying water column of a eutrophic lake was shown to be dependent on the oxygen tension (Maiden and Jones, 1984). In groundwater habitats, the biological activity and the organisms present have been shown to be a direct result of the oxygen concentration (Blaszyk and Gorski, 1981).

2.4. Light

There has been considerable study of the relationship between the position of species in the water column and photosynthetic efficiency. Longer light wavelengths (red) do not penetrate the water column as far as the energy of shorter wavelengths (blue light). Prokaryotes containing different photopigments absorb light energy at differing wavelengths leading to a spatial separation of species (Fig. 2). Cyanobacteria of the genera *Aphanizomenon, Anabaena,* and *Microcystis* are usually found at the water surface or high in the euphotic zone (Paerl and Ustach, 1982). Anaerobic photosynthetic bacteria like *Chlorobium* sp. and *Rhodopseudomonas* sp. absorb light in the far red portion of the light spectrum but normally grow at the sediment–water interface, below the planktonic eukaryotic algae and cyanobacteria (Wetzel, 1983). Because these bacteria have only one photosystem they catalyze photophosphorylation more successfully at lower light intensities than do the O_2-producing organisms with two photosystems.

Vertical distribution of photoautotrophs within a lake is also controlled by temperature, oxygen, and H_2S concentrations (Fig. 3). In lakes where the hypolimnion is anoxic, sharp layers of *Chlorobium* and *Chromatium* are found at or slightly below the thermocline (Montesinos et al., 1983). *Rhodospirillum* species, which require reduced organic electron donors instead of sulfur compounds are usually detected lower in the water column where decomposition processes are highest (Caldwell and Tiedje, 1975b; Takahashi and Ichimura, 1970).

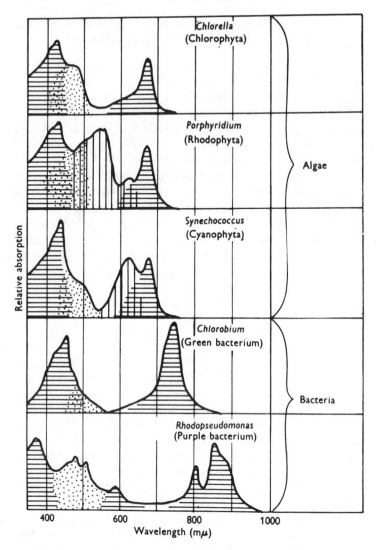

Figure 2. Selectivity within the water column of genera of photosynthetic microorganisms based on the absorption spectra of their photopigments. Ecological advantage provided by niche selection dependent on the penetration of light energies with depth. From Stanier and Cohen-Bazire, 1957; reprinted with permission from Cambridge University Press.

2.5. Attachment

Although not a physical or chemical parameter of the ecosystem, the ability of microcoorganisms to attach to the substratum or other organisms often deter-mines their ability to maintain themselves in a particular habitat. As shown by Costerton and Geesey (1979), the major portion of microbial populations in alpine streams is epilithic. Bacterial counts as low as 2.0×10^3 cells/mL were originally measured in bulk water samples, but when the density of the epilithic community was measured, values as high as 5×10^7 cells/cm^2 were found on submerged surfaces.

The accurate measurement of individual microbial population density, let alone their activities, in an in situ attached community is difficult. Some studies simply lump these organisms together as the "sessile" or attached population (Costerton and Greesey, 1979; Ladd et al., 1979). There have been some in situ

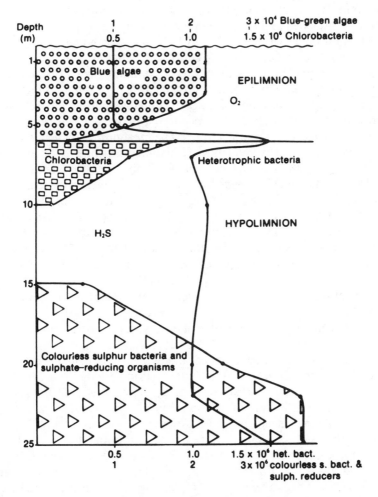

Figure 3. Vertical distribution of bacteria in a lake where the hypolimnion is anaerobic. Cyanobacteria limited primarily to the epilimnion. Anaerobic photosynthetic bacteria found in the upper portion of the hypolimnion where light penetration, oxygen depletion, and H$_2$S concentration all contribute to a narrowly defined favorable niche. Heterotrophs occur in abundance just below the zone of maximal photosynthesis and at the sediment–water interface. Sulfate reducers are abundant in the lower hypolimnion. (From Rheinheimer, 1980; reprinted with permission from VEB Gustan Fischer Verlag.

studies that indirectly show the effect of attachment on the presence and activity of microorganisms in the environment. *Vibrio parahaemolyticus* was found in plankton samples from freshwater habitats (Sarkar et al., 1983). Since this organism is moderately halophilic, it was concluded that the microenvironment provided by the exoskeleton of zooplankton allowed this pathogen to persist longer than might be expected in particular freshwater habitats. In another study of nitrifying activity in a stream receiving geothermal inputs of ammonium, a sharp reduction in nitrifying activity was observed following storm events (Cooper, 1983b). Because these populations are obligately aerobic, they are attached to the surface of the sediment where oxygen is available. The reduction in activity was believed to be due to population dilution as a result of stream bed scouring during periods of high flow. The reestablishment of this sessile population was monitored by measurements of the nitrifying activity that returned to prestorm levels after 12 days. Using this regeneration time of nitrifying activity along with a correction for environmental stress, an in situ growth rate was calculated that was similar to that determined for a *Nitrosospira* sp. isolate in laboratory cultures. The most numerous genus of nitrifying bacteria determined by frequency of isolation from nonenrichment cultures was also *Nitrosospira*. Although not stated directly, it may be assumed that the capability of attachment provided an advantage in this ecosystem. *Nitrosomonas* sp., which was also isolated from this stream had a higher laboratory rate of growth but lower isolation frequency and was apparently less capabel of attachment to stream substrates. In their brief review of nitrofication, Dunnette and Avedovech (1983) concluded that in lotic habitats nitrification was a surface-active phenomena that could be related to the availability of surfaces for attachment of *Nitrosomonas* and *Nitrobacter.*

Most existing studies dealing with attachment and attached communities in "freshwater ecosystems" fall into three general categories: (1) the initial phase of microbial attachment both reversible and irreversible (Costerton et al., 1978; Marshall and Cruickshank, 1973; Marshall et al., 1971; Sjoblad and Doetsch, 1982); (2) studies of the attachment of isolates from a particular ecosystem to a variety of solid surfaces in laboratory systems (Pringle and Fletcher, 1983); and (3) examination of the general morphology of biofilms used in wastewater treatment sometimes identifying morphologically distinct organisms (Alleman et al., 1982; Kinner et al., 1983; McCoy and Costerton, 1982). The stated purpose of the studies of isolates range from determining the effects of surface shear on the attachment of an organism from a culture collection to stainless steel (Duddridge et al., 1982) to testing the influence of different substrata on attachment of selected isolates, for example, from a river (Pringle and Fletcher, 1983). Currently these types of studies have limited autecological value because they are essentially conducted under laboratory conditions and only address early stages in biofilm development. Use of fluorescent antibody labeling techniques (Chapter 2), scanning electron microscopic (SEM) examination of attached microbial populations, and microelectrode measurements coupled with the means to determine the activity of individual organisms in a microbial population (e.g., autoradiography and tetrazolium dye reduction) should provide a way to determine the composition and activities of individual populations within attached communities in situ thereby extending the applicability of this type of research.

3.0. PROKARYOTIC INFLUENCES ON ECOSYSTEM FUNCTION

There is no dispute about the importance of the various roles prokaryotes have in the cycling of nutrients and the flow of energy in all ecosystems. In limnological settings prokaryotes contribution to primary and secondary production, detritus processing, and catalysis of biogeochemical cycles (Ehrlich, 1981, 1985). From an autecological standpoint, we know much about the roles of individual species and populations in many of these activities. Yet for other essential processes little is known about the microbial catalysts.

3.1. Primary Production

With the sun being the earth's primary source of energy, the conversion of solar energy into chemical energy is one of the most significant ecological functions of photosynthetic organisms. The process of storing energy in the form of biomass results in these organisms playing a major role in the cycling of carbon. To a large degree, in many aquatic habitats the cyanobacteria are important primary producers both as components of the planktonic community and as part of extensive benthic surface mats. The photosynthetic bacteria, although almost entirely restricted to anoxic environments, are important producers in certain limnological habitats.

3.1.1. Cyanobacteria and Algal Blooms. An area of limnological ecology often appeared from an autecological standpoint has been that dealing with the cyanobacteria. As prokaryotes they are typically larger than most eubacteria, they are highly piggmented, and they are fairly distinct morphologically. In ecological situations cyanobacteria are often highly visible as water "blooms." Traditionally, they have been studied by phycologists as opposed to microbiologists and consequently elaborate taxonomic schemes based on morphological characteristics are common. Most studies of physiological population dynamics have been conducted on three genera of cyanobacteria that are often responsible for extensive algal blooms: *Aphanizomenon, Microcystis,* and *Anabaena* (Fallon and Brock, 1980; Kellar and Paerl, 1980; Konopka and Brock, 1978; Megard and Smith, 1974; Paerl, 1983; Paerl and Ustach, 1982; Reynolds and Walsby, 1975). In eutrophic freshwaters including rivers (Paerl and Ustach, 1982), reservoirs (Hodgkiss, 1974; Reynolds and Walsby, 1975), and lakes (Fallon and Brock, 1980; Konopka and Brock, 1978; Megard and Smith, 1974), cyanobacterial blooms can easily account for 90 to 95% of the total phytoplankton biomass. The species diversity during periods of blooms are often low

facilitating the interpretation of photosynthetic and other physiological responses of nearly unialgal populations during in situ experimental
manipulation.

In meso to eutrophic dimictic lakes (those with two annual overturns and a
well-developed summer thermocline), cyanobacterial blooms develop after
lake stratification in a regular and recurrent succession of dominant genera. A
typical pattern is illustrated by population shifts in Lake Mendota (Fig. 4;
Konopka and Brock, 1978). *Aphanizomenon flos-aquae* dominates in the early
summer comprising 80–95% of the biomass. This declining population is
replaced by *Microcystis aeruginosa* in the first half of August. From mid-Au-
gust to late September substantial populations of *A. flos-aquae, M. aeruginosa,*
and *Anabaena circinalis* develop in the water column. Through October and
November *Aphanizomenon flos-aquae* again dominates.

Blooms are most often associated with genera capable of fixing nitrogen.
This has been suggested as a primary factor explaining their dominance within
the epilimnia of thermally stratified lakes (Kellar and Paerl, 1980). These genera also contain gas vacuoles that provide buoyancy (Reynolds and Walsby,
1975). Buoyancy regulation is ecologically important to planktonic cyanobacteria that inhabit thermally stratified lakes (Konopka, 1984). For epilimnetic
populations the capacity to migrate vertically throughout the photic zone to

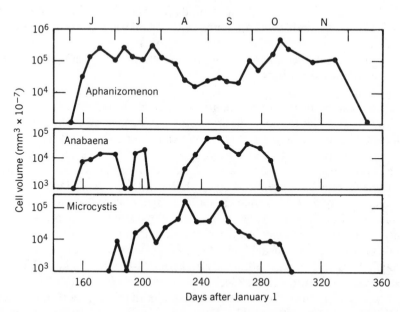

Figure 4. Annual distribution patterns (based on cell volume) of three predominant species of
cyanobacteria in Lake Mendota, Wisconsin (USA): *Aphanizomenon flos-aquae, Anabaena circinalis,* and *Microcystis aeruginosa.* From Konopka and Brock, 1978; reprinted with permission from
the American Society for Microbiology.

optimize photosynthetic activity provides cyanobacteria with a competitive advantage over phytoplankton incapable of such movement.

In low H_2S lakes where the hypolimnion does not become anoxic, populations of planktonic *Oscillatoria* spp. are able to aggregate within the metalimnion during summer lake stratification where the photosynthetic biomass consists almost of a single *Oscillatoria* sp. (Klemer, 1976). Konopka (1980) has studied the physiological ecology of a dense population of *Oscillatoria rubescens* in Crooked Lake, Indiana. These organisms appear to have a preference for low temperature, low light intensity, and have struck a favorable metabolic balance between carbon fixation and nutrient uptake rates.

Fluorescent antibody (FA) techniques have provided a new approach to the autecological study of cyanobacteria. Use of this technique to evaluate lake algal populations is exemplified by the work of Fliermans and Schmidt (1977) with *Synechococcus cedrorum*. Although FA reactive populations varied considerably in density with respect to the seven lakes examined as well as their location with respect to depth in the water column, each lake contained countable numbers of FA-labeled cells ranging from 10^2 to 10^5 per mL at one or more depths.

3.1.2. Anaerobic Photosynthesis.

Phototrophic purple and green bacteria can be found in all aquatic environments and are easily recognized by the formation of sediment surface blooms. The distribution of purple nonsulfur bacteria in mature ecosystems is not as readily apparent since they rarely appear in visible concentrations. Their presence must be evaluated from results obtained by enrichment techniques (Swoager and Lindstrom, 1971; Van Niel, 1971). Early observations of the photosynthetic sulfur bacteria (*Chromatium* spp. and *Chlorobium* spp.) were mainly confined to the surfaces of anoxic sediments such as those commonly found in marshes and highly eutrophic lakes (Wetzel, 1983).

More extensive limnological studies of eutrophic, meromictic (lakes where annual mixing patterns are confined to the epilimnion), and stagnant holomictic lakes have shown dense population of photosynthetic bacteria to occur within the anaerobic hypolimnion or more strikingly within a narrow depth range between the oxidative and reductive zones (Kuznetsov, 1970). Dense populations of anaerobic bacteria can be found layered below the thermocline within the physical confines of a complex interaction between light penetration, light spectral quality, oxygen depletion, and satisfactory H_2S concentrations (Fig. 3). One of the key organisms capable of dense growth under these conditions has been identified as *Chlorobium phaeobacteroides* (Truper and Genovese, 1968).

Because of the differences in the *in vivo* absorption spectrum of cells of various species of *Chlorobium* and *Chromatium,* coexisting groups of populations can be found within meromictic lakes. Montesinos et al. (1983) noted that populations of the brown *Chlorobium phaeobacteroides* were dominant in deep layers whereas green *Chlorobium limicola* dominated in layers nearer the surface or underneath plates of *Chromatium.* Similar patterns of dense populations of morphologically (and taxonomically) unique photosynthetic bacteria have been found sequentially layered below the thermocline of eutrophic lakes (Caldwell and Tiedje, 1975a, 1975b). These populations, severely limited in their movement within the water column, can have an extraordinary impact on the total primary productivity of lakes. As much as 83% of the annual primary production in the meromictic Fayetteville Green Lake, New York was due to these photosynthetic sulfur-oxidizing bacteria (Culver and Brunskill, 1969).

With the isolation and characterization of *Chloroflexus aurantiacus* in thermal environments (Bauld and Brock, 1973; Pierson and Castenholz, 1974), our view of the ecological position of photosynthetic bacteria has enlarged to include those tolerant of oxygen under photosynthetic conditions. The autecology of these organisms in less extreme environments is totally unknown.

The presence of purple nonsulfur bacteria in aquatic ecosystems is largely dependent upon the degree to which the water is polluted by organic matter. Under high light conditions species of *Rhodopseudomonas* become a major ecological force in heavily polluted water such as in sewage lagoons (Cooper et al., 1975; Holm and Vennes, 1970) and organically laden wastewaters (Kobayashi, 1975; Winfrey et al., 1977).

3.1.3. Cyanobacterial Benthic Mats.

3.1.3. Cyanobacterial Benthic Mats. There are numerous limnological situations that promote the development of benthic mats at the sediment–water interface. Those of a predominately cyanobacterial character are usually associated with environmental extremes where one often finds a simple community structure of a single or few readily identifiable producer species (Brock, 1978) and their associated bacterial assemblages of relatively few heterotrophic species, some of which have been identified (Ward et al., 1984). It would appear that in each of the ecological situations to be discussed, the cyanobacterial mat development is favored, in part, by the tolerance of the organisms to particular environmental extremes and, in part, by the absence of bioturbation by benthic animals.

The earliest as well as the most extensively studied mat communities were conducted on the laminated algal–bacterial mats of alkaline hot springs (Brock, 1978; Castenholz, 1978, 1984; Stockner, 1967). A major impetus for the studies was widespread interest in the paleomicrobiology of Precambrian stromatolites (Walter et al., 1972, 1976). These mats comprise a relatively stable in situ experimental system with high population densities and a low species diversity (Brock and Darland, 1970; Castenholz, 1984). These systems are ideal for investigations of the physiology and ecology of naturally occurring microbial populations.

Laminated algal–bacterial mats are of two basic types. The first, which occurs extensively in hot springs of neutral to alkaline pH at temperatures of 55 to 70°C, was described by Brock (1969b). This mat is composed of two different photosynthetic organisms, *Synechococcus lividus* (a unicellular cyanobacterium) and *Chloroflexus aurantiacus* (a gliding, filamentous photosynthetic bacterium) (Bauld and Brock, 1973). These two organisms and their associated heterotrophic bacteria form well-defined laminated mats in which the photosynthetic bacterium is responsible for structural integrity (Doemel and Brock, 1974, 1977).

Brock (1967b) observed that *Mastigocladus laminosus,* a cosmopolitan thermophile, occurred in higher temperature Icelandic hot springs but not in those at Yellowstone where many of the high temperature environments are well colonized by *Synechococcus. Mastigocladus* is present at higher temperatures in Yellowstone only where water flow is very rapid and the unicellular *Synechococcus* cannot be physically maintained (Castenholz, 1969a, 1969b). It is difficult to conclude that temperature is the sole environmental factor affecting the distribution of algae in thermal streams in that Stockner (1967) found a second factor to be interspecific competition for space. In thermal streams at Mount Rainier, *Schizothrix calcicola* (growth range 42–62°C) grows contiguous with *Oscillatoria terebriformis* (growth range 48–52°C). *S. calcicola* grew into the *O. terebriformis* zone when *O. terebriformis* was continually removed around a denuded area but not when *O. terebriformis* was allowed to recolonize. *S. calcicola* appeared to tolerate lower temperatures than its observed minimum but was prevented from colonizing a greater area by *O. terebriformis* due to the latter organism's competitive advantage at lower temperatures.

The second type of laminated mat is that formed by species of *Phormidium* in conjunction with species of *Flexibacteri,* which grow in hot springs at temperatures around 40–45°C (Walter et al., 1972, 1976). These living conophytonlike structures are composed of nearly amorphous silica. In both instances, the taxonomic identification of the principle populations composing these mats has enhanced considerably the physiological delineation within the mat. Studies of population growth rates (Brock and Brock, 1968; Doemel and Brock, 1977), primary production (Brock, 1967a; Brock and Brock, 1967), standing crop (Brock, 1967a), and decomposition (Doemel and Brock, 1977; Zinder et al., 1977) have now been conducted on these mat communities. Recently the development of microelectrodes has allowed an even closer in situ evaluation of the physiological properties of the microbial populations occurring within these mat communities (Revsbech et al., 1981; Revsbech and Ward, 1984a, 1984b).

Cyanobacterial mat formation also occurs extensively in hypersaline lakes and ponds such as the mats found in Solar Lake, Sinai. In winter the mat surface is dominated by unicellular cyanobacteria and the filamentous cyanobacterium *Microcoleus chtonoplastes.* In summer *Phormidium* sp., *Spirulina* spp., and *Johannes baptistii* dominate (Jorgensen et al., 1983). Beneath these species occur species of the colorless sulfur bacteria *Beggiatoa* and *Thiovolum* (Jorgensen and Revsbech, 1983). Microelectrode studies have allowed determinations of oxygen production (Jorgensen et al., 1983; Revsbech et al., 1983) and hydrogen sulfide production (Jorgensen and Revsbech, 1983).

Along with a dramatically high water clarity, a common characteristic of clear-water acidic lakes is the development of a benthic algal mat (Stokes, 1981). The low nutrient concentrations characteristic of these lakes suggests that a relative increase in the importance of benthic productivity may affect the movement of nutrients between the water column and sediments. The feltlike mats that occur in certain acidified lakes in Sweden have been shown to consist of cyanobacteria of the genera *Lyngbya, Oscillatoria,* and *Pseudoanabaena* (Lazarek, 1980). In others, the cyanophytan mat is composed mainly of *Hapalosiphon* spp. (Lazarek, 1982a, 1982b). In Adirondack lakes, the mats are predominantly *Phormidium tenue* (Hendrey and Vertucci, 1980) or *Plectonema* spp. (Singer et al., 1983a) while in Canada, these mats are reported to be *Scytonema* spp. and *Phormidium* spp. (Stokes, 1981).

Because of the extensive growth of cyanophytan mats in acidified lakes, it is suspected that they serve to maintain high total lake productivity even though the phytoplankton and macrophyte communities have been extensively reduced. Unfortunately there are no data to support this hypothesis. At present, the significance of the benthic algal production on various aspects of the acidic aquatic environment is highly conjectural. Nonetheless, mats existing on sediment cores taken from an acid lake in the Adirondacks and incubated under various conditions in the laboratory were highly active in phosphate and nitrate removal (Singer et al., 1983b).

The predominance of the cyanophytan mat in acidified lakes is somewhat an enigma. While the cyanobacteria's position within the planktonic community is much reduced as water pH is reduced, they dominate the benthic community. Basing his observations on acidified waters associated with geothermal activity worldwide, Brock (1978) suggested that pH 4 was the physiological acid limit for cyanophytes and that they would likely be absent in waters of less than pH 5.0. However, as can be seen, acidified softwater oligotrophic waters are relatively new ecosystems to which cyanobacteria have readily adapted.

3.2. Heterotrophic Productivity

The role of nutrient cycling and mineralization performed by prokaryotes is also accomplished by their action on detrital material. Investigations of the attachment and breakdown of this material by prokaryotes will be discussed keeping in mind the importance of these processes in carbon cycling. Other geochemical cycles influenced by prokaryotes in freshwater ecosystems will be discussed mainly based on whether these processes are reductive or oxidative.

3.2.1. Water Column. Of interest to the microbial limnologist is the spatial and temporal distribution of bacteria in the water column. As indicated previously, lakes stratify not only thermally but also chemically with respect to dissolved nutrients and gases. From early examination of bacterial profiles within the water column, we know that bacteria are both spatially and temporally distributed (Henrici and McCoy, 1938; Stark and McCoy, 1938). The use of direct measurements by fluorescent microscopy has provided a more representative determination of densities than the traditional plate count method. For example, Fliermans et al., (1975) showed that pronounced heterogeneity exists in bacterial densities within the water column depending on the presence or absence of thermal stratification. Although turbidity changes in the water column have been correlated with the presence of specific phototrophic phytoplankton populations (Baker and Brook, 1971), the significance of heterotrophic bacteria in microstratification is poorly understood. It is likely that certain bacterial species may predominate at particular depths in the water column due to the structure of favorable microhabitat. We currently know little of the phenomenon itself let alone possess any knowledge of prevalent species that may be involved.

It is clear that autotrophic phototrophs are capable of vertical stratification. Cyanobacteria as well as green and purple sulfur bacteria contain gas vacuoles enabling them to regulate their position in the water column. Heterotrophic gas vacuolated bacteria are common inhabitants of freshwaters (Van Ert and Staley, 1971a, 1971b). But, the extent of their presence in microstratification in lakes is generally unknown. Most of the autecological information collected to date on the occurrence of particular species found within the water column of lakes has come from the meager information associated with the isolation and characterization of unusual prokaryotes (Blakemore, 1975; Collins, 1963; Hirsch et al., 1977; Lewin, 1965; Poindexter, 1981; Starr and Skerman, 1965).

Jones (1975) correlated the presence of *Leptothrix ochracea* in the hypolimnion with total iron concentration in large experimental lake enclosures. In other studies, he noted that in the lake itself a relatively stable consortium of several species was found throughout the year but in the enclosures, heterotrophic communities were often dominated by cycles of single species including those of *Acinetobacter* spp., *Flavobacter* spp., *Moxaxella* spp., *Aeromonas* spp., and corynebacteria (Jones, 1973). There is a striking similarity between these findings and those of Silvey and Wyatt (1977) in their study of the dominant heterotrophs of Lake Hefner. Pronounced cycles of actinomycete–corynebacteria, *Flavobacterium, Brevibacterium,* and *Alcaligenes* population densities were observed in this eutrophic reservoir in the Southwest United States (Fig. 5).

Some autecological studies have been performed on flowing streams (McFeters et al., 1978a, 1978b; Staley, 1971). Over a 1-yr period at several sites, Staley (1971) has shown population shifts between various species of prosthecate bacteria. In many instances these sessile populations are numerically more important than free-living bacteria (Geesey et al., 1978). Furthermore, densities of sessile bacteria associated with the upper surfaces of submerged rocks coincided with fluctuations in epilithic algal biomass.

Most stream and river microbial autecology has centered on the obvious correlation between human waste, and the occurrence of enteric bacteria (Hendricks, 1971; Hendricks and Morrison, 1967; McFeters et al., 1974; McFeters and Stuart, 1972; Stuart et al., 1976). It has been shown that the aquatic environment associated with clear mountain streams supplies sufficient nutrients to support *de novo* growth and maintain populations of enteric bacteria (Hendricks and Morrison, 1967).

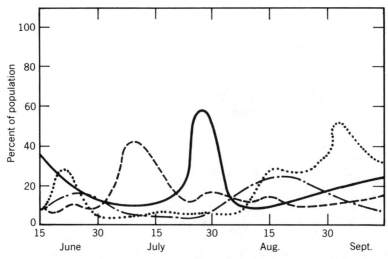

Figure 5. Summer distribution patterns of dominant heterotrophic bacterioplankton in Lake Hefner, Oklahoma (USA). (---), Actinomycetes; (· · ·), *Flavobacterium;* (-··-), *Brevibacterium;* (—), *Alcaligenes.* Reprinted with permission from Silvery, J. K. G. and J. T. Wyatt (1977). "The interrelationship between freshwater bacteria algae, and actimycetes in southwestern reservoirs," in J. Cairns, Jr., ed., *Aquatic Microbial Communities.* Garland Publishing, New York, pp. 161–203. Copyright 1977 Garland Publishing, Inc.

3.2.2. Detritus Processing.

Bacteria and fungi are largely responsible for the decomposition of organic matter in inland waters. Major sites of detrital mineralization and nutrient recycling in aquatic systems are the bottom sediments (Wetzel, 1983). Detritus represents organic carbon arising from "nonpredatory" activities such as reprocessing by ingestion, excretion, secretion, death, and decay (Wetzel, 1983). In small eutrophic lakes where the littoral zone represents a large proportion of the lake bottom, much of the detritus may come from autochthonous sources as compared to deeper oligotrophic lakes with a less developed littoral zone where detritus arises mainly from allochthonous inputs. Not only is there considerable variation in the sources of detritus from system to system but also the total quantities of detritus, as well as its chemical composition, varies. By its definition detritus is present both as particulate organic material (POM) and dissolved organic material (DOM). In most freshwaters, there is about an order of magnitude more DOM than POM (Wetzel and Manny, 1972). Particulate detritus offers opportunities for microbial development quite different from those found in water or sediment since such particles are concentrated sources of food.

Because microorganisms are the initial colonizers of detrital particles, most of the microbial ecological interest has involved observation of those species capable of producing extracellular enzymes that can decompose complex structural organic polymers. Complex detrital microbial populations have been observed microscopically. The bacterial flora contains rods, cocci, filamentous and mycelial forms, and myxobacteria (Rodina, 1963). Usually most microbial activity is observed on the surfaces of individual detrital particles but growth is not limited to particle surfaces. Growth can extend beyond the boundaries of the particles cementing the detrital mass into complex conglomerates. In a study of detritus colonization from six Russian lakes, Rodina (1963) identified high population densities of *Azotobacter* sp., *Cytophaga* sp., and *Sporocytophaga* sp. Surprisingly he found no fungal or actinomycete populations in his detrital samples although these groups are major colonizers of allochthonous terrestrial detritus in lentic habitats (Kaushik and Hynes, 1968; Suberkropp and Klug, 1974). Filamentous sulfur oxidizing species of the genera *Beggiatoa* and *Thiothrix* were common.

Detrital food chains play a significant role in freshwater productivity (Wetzel, 1983). Detritus is used as a major food source by both planktonic and benthic animals. There is growing evidence that the nutritional value of most detritus, in particular, that containing a high residue of recalcitrant allochthonous polymers does not reside in the particle itself but in the associated microbial flora (Levinton et al., 1984). Detritovores consume the particles only to digest the bacteria. The particle is excreted chemically unaltered. Thus, this particle is again available for microbial colonization. Significant autoecological studies need to be conducted to learn more about the microorganisms involved in this cycle. Unlike the aquatic hyphomycete fungi, detrital bacterial communities have never been recognized as an ecological group.

Bacterial decomposition of detritus results in production of a large number of metabolic products, such as simple sugars, amino acids, fatty acids, and so on. Solubilization of these compounds often supports populations of heterotrophic bacteria as dense as 10^{10} cells/g dry weight of detritus, (Fenchel and Jorgensen, 1977). Most of the studies on decomposition processes in freshwaters have dealt more with activities of cellulose and lignin degradation rather than with taxonomic distinctions. Many of these experiments involved assessment of the degradability of major plant polymers by specific prokaryotes, under anaerobic conditions. For example, pectin degradation in anoxic lake sediments proceeds as a result of the metabolic activities of *Clostridium butyricum* and *Bacteroides* sp. (Schink, 1984). Pectin decomposition by anaerobic bacteria in algal–bacterial mat ecosystems has also been observed (Doemel and Brock, 1977). Even a thermophilic species of *Clostridium, C. thermosulfurogenes,* has been isolated (Schink and Zeikus, 1983).

3.3. Biogeochemical Cycling

The autecology of species responsible for biological transformations of inorganic forms of carbon, nitrogen, phosphorus, and sulfur is of considerable interest to the microbial limnologist. Investigations needed to determine the in situ microbial population responsible for these transformations are complex. Such studies usually involve measurements of axenic laboratory cultures of microorganisms from the habitat of interest.

Within freshwater environments, phosphorus is generally recognized as the limiting nutrient (Wetzel, 1983). Organically bound phosphorus is partitioned between living organisms within the water column, dead particulate suspended matter "seston," and sediments (Hooper, 1973). Most inorganic phosphorus is bound within the sediment matrix and serves as the phosphorus reservoir for freshwater systems since soluble inorganic orthophosphate usually comprises less than 10% of the total phosphorus in the system (Hutchinson, 1957). Lake sediments are continuously regenerated by detrital deposition. In deep lakes of extensive area, deposits are produced internally from dead and unchanged organic matter. The available phosphorus in the sediment is dependent on geological cycling between sediment, water, and flora and fauna (Cosgrove, 1977). In shallow lakes, the sediments are formed from material deposited through runoff and erosion within the watershed yielding more available phosphorus than deeper lakes (Goldman and Horne, 1983).

Virtually nothing is known through autecological studies of microbial transformations in the phosphorus cycle in aquatic sediments and overlying waters. Overall, our knowledge of the microbial role in the phosphorus cycle is very uneven (Cosgrove, 1977). Strains of *Bacillus subtilis, B. brevis, B. putrifaciens, B. pumilis,* and *B. polymyxa* have been identified as the active organisms responsible for phosphate solubilization from soil rhizospheres (Paul and Sundara Rao, 1971). These organisms are presumed to be involved in sediment phosphorus release as well. Under acid conditions, the action of sulfuric acid produced by *Thiobacillus* in solubilizing rock phosphate has been shown to occur in situ (Cosgrove, 1977).

Detailed examination of organically bound phosphates in activated sludge implicated *Zoogloea ramigera,* a Gram-negative, floc-forming bacterium commonly found in activated sludge, in removing phosphorus from wastewater (Roinestad and Yall, 1970). This phosphorus precipitation by bacteria is important for the removal of sufficient phosphorus from waste treatment effluents to control algal blooms in rivers and lakes receiving the effluent.

Changes in carbon, nitrogen, and sulfur oxidation states are accomplished by a wide range of microorganisms during the incorporation of these elements into biomass. These assimilatory processes and the simple release of these elements by excretion or degradation of biomass (e.g., ammonification) will not be discussed here, rather the bioconversions of the inorganic forms of these elements used as terminal electron acceptors or as a source of acquiring reducing power will be examined.

3.3.1. Reductive Processes. The reductive portions of the carbon cycle that are of primary importance in freshwater ecosystems are the fixation of CO_2 and the reduction of organic material (usually acetate) to methane with the subsequent recycling of the carbon in the form of CO_2 by microbial oxidation of the methane. Organisms responsible for CO_2 incorporation were discussed previously. We will deal here with those that form methane from organic material.

Methanogenesis occurs in a variety of anaerobic freshwater habitats including the anaerobic muds of lakes, rivers, marshes, swamps, bogs, and flooded soils (Mah et al., 1977; Zeikus, 1977). The methanogens are a morphologically diverse group of prokaryotes whose taxonomic understanding has been elusive (Balch et al., 1979). Physiologically they are a coherent group capable of producing methane through the anaerobic degradation of organic matter. In anaerobic habitats, methanogens are the terminal organisms in the microbial food chain. Most freshwater studies of methanogenesis have been concerned with the detection and quantitation of methane evolution from sediments (Chen et al., 1972; Howard et al., 1971; Winfrey and Zeikus, 1979b). As methane diffuses into the overlying waters, it is metabolized to CO_2 or escapes into the atmosphere (Rudd et al., 1974). Zeikus and Winfrey (1976) have shown the rate of methanogenesis to be severely temperature limited and to vary seasonally. Increased activity correlated with increased methanogen population densities and seasonal temperature maxima. Zeikus and Winfrey (1976) identified several methanogenic genera in Lake Mendota sediments with *Methanobacterium* species predominating. Microbial methanogenesis is not only associated with the polymeric organic material decomposition but can also be detected in habitats where environmental hydrogen originates from geochemical processes. Deuser et al. (1973) have shown in Lake Kivu, an African rift lake, that microbial reduction of CO_2 by volcanic hydrogen accounted for most of the methane formed in the lake.

Most studies of methanogenesis in lakes have been restricted to holomictic lakes where anaerobic activities are limited to bottom sediments. In meromictic lakes where incomplete mixing provides stable anaerobic environments within the lower water column, methane production is extensive within the bottom waters (Winfrey and Zeikus, 1979a).

In anaerobic, freshwater sediments considerable competition appears to exist between the methanogens and sulfate-reducing bacteria. Several chemical parameters of environmental significance influence methanogenic activity in nature. Sulfate is a potent inhibitor of methanogenesis in lake sediments (Cappenberg and Prins, 1974; MacGregor and Keeney, 1973; Winfrey and Zeikus, 1977) as is nitrate (Chen et al., 1972). Sulfide, in contrast, stimulates sediment methanogenesis (Winfrey and Zeikus, 1979a, 1979b). Winfrey and Zeikus (1977) found that sulfate inhibits methanogenesis by altering normal carbon and electron flow during anaerobic mineralization. Because sulfate additions did not cause a significant accumulation of H_2S in the interstitial water, they proposed that sulfate-reducing bacteria assume the role of methanogens in sulfate-containing sediments by utilizing methanogenic precursors. Zeikus (1977) hypothesized that an acetate-respiring, sulfate-reducing bacteria should exist. Recently a *Desulfotomaculum* species that respires acetate has been isolated (Widdel and Pfenning, 1977). Sulfate-reducing bacteria–methanogen interrelationships in freshwater environments appear to be highly dependent on the sulfate concentration. Competitive relationships occur at high sulfate concentrations where sulfate-reducing bacteria dominate by out competing methanogens for common energy sources. In sulfate depleted sediments sulfate-reducing bacteria are not active as shown by Phelps and Zeikus (1984).

Truly autecological studies estimating methanogenic populations have been hampered by difficulties of anaerobic culture techniques, the necessity of prolonged incubation times, and difficulties with the detection of methane. Strayer and Tiedje (1978) prepared an FA for a methanogenic isolate taxonomically resembling *Methanobacterium formicicum*, which was isolated from a pelagic lake sediment. Populations of this single strain in a eutropic sediment ranged from 3.1×10^6 to 1.4×10^7 bacteria/g of dry sediment. Recently, an enzyme-linked immunosorbent assay that holds great promise for further enumeration capabilities for the quantitation of natural populations of methanogens has been developed (Archer, 1984).

Although the existence and techniques for enumerating sulfate-reducing bacteria have been known and available for close to a century, understanding of their autecology is not much different than that of the methanogens. Postgate (1979) points out that much of the data regarding the populations of these organisms in the scientific literature are not reliable because the data were obtained using unsatisfactory culture media. The predominant problem with the growth media resulted from the use of media with an incorrect E_h. Two studies of freshwater ecosystems were cited by Postgate (1979) where increases in the populations of these organisms were satisfactorily documented — one in a river downstream from a paper mill (Desrochers and Fredette, 1960) and another in a lake following the decrease in O_2 concentration (Lighthart, 1963). There have been studies of the sulfur cycle in lakes using sulfur-35 labeled sulfate (Ingovorsen et al., 1981; Stuiver, 1967), which have implications relating to the activity and ecological significance of sulfate-reducing bacteria but presently direct measurements of the contribution of individual species or even genera in this major biogeochemical transformation are not available.

There are three described genera of sulfate-reducing bacteria: *Desulfovibrio*, *Desulfotomaculum*, and *Desulfomonas* (Grant and Long, 1981). However, organisms have been isolated that reduce sulfate, which do not fit any of these genera either morphologically or physiologically. Additional genera have been proposed for these lower fatty acid utilizing organisms, such as *Desulfobulbus* and *Desulfobacter* (Postgate, 1979). The limnological contribution that these, and yet to be described sulfate-reducing bacteria have in particular ecosystems has not been determined and therefore experiments that only examine the rates of sulfate reduction should not be viewed as descriptions of the action of a physiologically distinct group of organisms.

Using lipid fatty acid analysis, Taylor and Parkes (1985) presented data that supports the idea that there are at least two functional groups of sulfate-reducing bacteria in marine sediment environments. These authors were careful to point out how essential the use of fatty acid biomarkers could be in the study of mixed sulfate-reducing bacterial populations in these habitats. There would seem to be a significant potential for the application of this technique to freshwater environments. Also, the interest in the economic impact of sulfate-reducing bacteria on the deterioration of metal (corrosion), provides an impetus for the study of the presence and metabolic processes of these organisms in unique situations. Application and further development of the more recently available methods like fatty acid analysis and various antibody techniques for the in situ detection of these organisms in applied research areas will provide the means to better understand them in natural ecosystems.

There are two significant reductive processes of inorganic nitrogen compounds that occur in freshwater ecosystems. The reduction (fixation) of atmospheric nitrogen to ammonia is often a significant source of available nitrogen in an ecosystem and the processes of nitrate reduction and denitrification can result in a significant loss of fixed nitrogen from an ecosystem. Nitrogen fixation in limnological ecosystems is catalyzed by only a select group of organisms – primarily cyanobacteria but also certain photosynthetic bacteria and even microaerophilic and anaerobic bacteria in the sediments. Nitrogen fixation has been shown to be catalyzed by planktonic (Horne et al., 1972; Horne and Goldman, 1972), epiphytic (Finke and Seeley, 1978), and epilithic (Horne, 1975) cyanobacterial populations. It is also associated with the rhizosphere of freshwater angiosperms (Bristow, 1974) and the roots of nonleguminous aquatic macrophytes (Sylvester-Bradley, 1976). A low rate, but a potentially significant source, of fixed nitrogen production has been shown to be associated with anoxic water and lake sediments (Keirn and Brezonik, 1971). All this information was obtained based on the ability to measure rates of N_2 fixation by the acetylene reduction method. The introduction of the acetylene reduction procedure (Dilworth, 1966; Schollhorn and Burris, 1966) and several subsequent modifications of this technique has (Horne and Goldman, 1972; Paerl and Kellar, 1978; Stewart et al., 1968) provided the capability to quantify rapidly and accurately, nitrogen fixation in situ. In many of these studies, the organism(s) believed responsible for nitrogen fixation were identified, especially in the case of the cyanobacteria, based on their ability to reduce acetylene in laboratory cultures.

Of autecological importance are the studies directed toward determining the physiological characteristics of this process accomplished by frequently dominant cyanobacterial populations. Several of the factors affecting nitrogen fixation and associated processes have been studied in situ. Examples of this type of work are the H_2 production and utilization by *Anabaena* and *Aphanizomenon* (Paerl, 1982), the requirement for iron to maximize the rate of nitrogen fixation by *Aphanizomenon flos-aquae* (Wurtsbaugh and Horne, 1983), the stimulation of the rate of this process by heterotropic bacterial association with *Anabaena* (Paerl, 1978; Paerl and Kellar, 1978), and the dark nitrogen fixation by *Nostoc* (Horne, 1975).

These are excellent examples of autecology, in that, the factors affecting the functioning of a particular organism as well as certain of its physiological requirements were examined using in situ experimentation of nearly unialgal populations of the particular organism of interest. Continued work on the cyanobacteria should provide extensive autecological information on this group of organisms. The function and physiological complexities of the organisms responsible for much of the other nitrogen fixation in other portions of limnological ecosystems will first require the identification of these species and then further investigations into their relationship with their environment.

The study of dissimilatory nitrate reduction in freshwater ecosystems is presently at the stage of quantification of the processes of both nitrate reduction and denitrification (Klingensmith and Alexander, 1983; Vincent et al., 1985). In a recent review of denitrification (Payne, 1981), no freshwater work where the organism(s) were identified as responsible for this process was cited. A variety of bacterial species has been shown to catalyze these dissimulating nitrate reduction processes (Focht and Verstraete, 1977; Horsley, 1978; Payne, 1973). Nitrate reduction and/or denitrification have been assayed in several different types of lake ecosystems such as a temperate, moderately eutrophic lake (Brezonik and Lee, 1968; Keeney et al., 1971), a deep arctic lake (Klingensmith and Alexander, 1983), a subarctic lake (Goering and Dugdale, 1966), and a high-altitude lake (Vincent et al., 1985). However, only cursory mention, if any at all, is made as to the types of microorganisms that are responsible for the process being measured. Methods for enumerating heterotrophic nitrate-reducing bacteria relative to the total heterotrophic population have been described (Horsley, 1978). Other than providing a list of genera of known denitrifiers and application of selective culturing techniques, no satisfactory means have been applied to the in situ study of denitrifiers. But, use of fluorescent antibodies prepared against various denitrifiers appears to be a useful tool for overcoming past limitations to autecological evaluations of denitrifiers. Terai and Yoskioka (1983) used fluorescent antibody staining and serological agglutination reactions to identify denitrifiers in enrichment cultures and isolates obtained from Lake Kizaki during periods of stratification and mixing. The antibodies used in this study were prepared from six denitrifiers previously isolated from the same ecosystem. The main difficulty these investigators encountered was determination of the in situ activity of the organisms they were able to identify. They concluded that the application of a direct counting method would be needed to provide a better understanding of the role of individual species in denitrification.

3.3.2. Oxidative Processes. The oxidation of one-carbon compounds (mostly methane) and the inorganic forms of sulfur and nitrogen have been shown to be mediated by microorganisms, primarily prokaryotes. In most cases, a certain group of prokaryotes has been identified that catalyze the increase in oxidation state of the reduced compounds of these elements. The majority of studies of freshwater ecosystems have focused on the oxidation of methane, hydrogen sulfide, and ammonia. These products of bacterial processes occurring in anaerobic portions of freshwater ecosystems diffuse to the oxic – anoxic boundary (e.g., thermocline, water – sediment interface) where metabolic requirements of aerobic flora are met. Geothermal activity, leaching of mineral sulfides, and other natural phenomenon may also serve as sources of these reduced compounds in the water column and thus support inorganic-oxidizing bacterial populations. In general, most in situ studies have dealt with quantitating these processes with attention devoted to determining the particular population(s) involved only in some special circumstances.

A major substrate for inorganic carbon oxidation is methane. The biogenic production of this compound is equivalent to 15–20% of its ambient atmospheric levels (Higgins et al., 1981). The bulk of this methanogenesis occurs in freshwater habitats (e.g., lakes, marshes, and paddy fields). This estimate, however, refers to the amount of methane evolved from these environments, not the amount produced and subsequently oxidized to CO_2 by methane oxidizing bacteria (methylotrophs). In his review, Hanson (1980) cited data from several investigators (Cappenberg, 1972; Fallon et al., 1980; Harrits and Hanson, 1980; Rudd and Hamilton, 1978) showing that about half of the methane produced yearly was reoxidized by bacteria prior to release. He also proposed that methylotrophs in these ecosystems had not only a significant influence on reducing net methane fluxes but also in causing and maintaining an anaerobic environment in the hypolimnion of these ecosystems through their consumption of oxygen.

This information on the ecology of methylotrophs is based almost entirely on the assumption that the observed methane oxidation results from the population or populations of culturable microbes capable of catalyzing methane oxidation. In some studies, the size and distribution of these populations was estimated by use of various culture techniques (Cappenberg, 1972; Harrits and Hanson, 1980; Lidstrom and Somers, 1984; Rudd et al., 1976). In only a few studies (Reed and Dugan, 1978; Saralov et al., 1984) were the density and distribution of specific species of methylotrophic bacteria measured within a freshwater ecosystem.

Using a fluorescent antibody technique, *Methylomonas methanica* was found at every sampling station in Cleveland Harbor. The density of this organism was inversely proportional to the depth. The distribution of *Methylosinus trichosporium* was similar to *M. methanica,* in that, the greatest densities of this organism occurred at or near the water–sediment interface but it was only detected at two of the ten sites reported. A seasonal variation in the density of *M. methanica* was noted, with the decrease in the density of this organism in the samples obtained in the colder part of the year. This observation correlated well with laboratory results that showed this organism was cold sensitive.

Even though the primary goal of this autecological study (Reed and Dugan, 1978) was to demonstrate the potential of fluorescent antibody techniques in the study of methylotrophs, it confirmed earlier hypotheses about the distribution of these types of organisms and showed that different species have different distributions and seasonalities. This excellent demonstration of the potential for autecological studies of this group of microorganisms, however, caught the eye of only some of the subsequent reviewers of this topic (Higgins et al., 1981) while others (Hanson, 1980; Rudd and Taylor, 1980) dealt mainly with work done on the rates of methane production and consumption with little concern expressed for the microbial population(s) responsible for these transformations.

Another study of the distribution of particular species of methylotrophs was done on several lakes in the Baltic region and the Rybinskoe Reservoir (Saralov et al., 1984). The identification of the various species of methylotrophs was done on the basis of morphophysiological characteristics—that is, the ultrafine structure of the endocytoplasmic membrane system of organisms seen in material sampled from these areas was compared to that of organisms from cultures of a group of methylotrophic isolates that had been obtained from these habitats and previously characterized. A difference in the density of these types of organisms was found depending on the mixing and oxygen tension of the particular environment sampled. In holomictic lakes and flowing waters, the maximum density of methylotrophs was 400–800 cells/mL whereas the microaerobic zones of the metalimnion of stratified lakes had densities of methylotrophs ranging from 500 to 4,000,000 cells/mL. Two groups of predominant species were also noted depending on the mixing and aeration of the water. *Methylosinus trichosporium, M. sporium, Methylocystis parvus,* and *Methylobacter bovis* were found mainly in water that mixed. In the pelagial zone of stratified lakes, *Methylomonas methanica, M. rubrum, M. albus, Methylococcus capsulatus, M. luteus, Methylosinus trichosporium, M. sporium, Methylocystis parvus,* and *Methylobacter chroococcum* were the dominant species. The results of a study like this one are quite impressive in that a distinction between the presence of certain species of a physiological group of organisms was shown to be influenced by the physicochemical conditions in the environment and also in the unique methods used to identify individual organisms.

In comparison to the situation with methylotrophs, evaluation of aquatic nitrification from an autecological view appears to be relatively easy. But, the process is often examined with little regard for the organism(s) involved (Vincent et al., 1985).This is surprising because it is generally accepted that two small and distinct groups of genera in the family of Nitrobacteraceae catalyze the two separate steps of this energy generating process (Belser, 1979). Members of the genera *Nitrosomonas, Nitrosospira, Nitrosococcus, Nitrosolobus,* and *Nitrosovibrio* are responsible for the first step (ammonia to nitrite) and those in the genera *Nitrobacter, Nitrospira,* and *Nitrococcus* complete the transformation (nitrite to nitrate). Many of these genera have been isolated from soil and marine environments as well as from sewage. The two classic genera, *Nitrosomonas* and *Nitrobacter* usually have been detected in freshwater environments. Failure to observe other species may be due to the assumption that *Nitrosomonas* and *Nitrobacter* are the only genera that can cause these transformations (Curtis et al., 1975). Often, they are the only genera for which enumerations are done (Dunnette and Avedovech, 1983). However, when incubation of MPN cultures were allowed to continue longer as suggested by Belser (1979), other ammonia oxidizers were found in the sediments of a stream, that is, *Nitrosospira* (Cooper, 1983a).

The most direct method of enumeration of a specific species—the fluorescent antibody technique—was developed to detect *Nitrobacter* species mainly in soil habitats (Fliermans et al., 1974; Fliermans and Schmidt, 1975; Stanley and Schmidt, 1981). Some of this work was done using samples from freshwater habitats — Mammoth Cave sediments (Fliermans et al., 1974) and Como Lake, St. Paul, MN (Stanley and Schmidt, 1981). Further application of this powerful autecological tool in freshwater environments has not been as extensive as its original potential might have implied possibly due to its high specificity. As pointed out by Belser (1979), to be certain of enumerating all of the nitrifying populations in a particular habitat, fluorescent antibody directed against several genera would have to be applied to samples to detect all the possible organisms responsible for this process. Even with these technical limitations for doing autecological studies, use of fluorescent antibodies would still provide a distinct advantage over cultural methods.

4.0. INTERACTIONS OF PROKARYOTES WITH OTHER ORGANISMS

A barrage of terms results from the descriptions of the various kinds of interactions that exist between two organisms (or population of organisms) inhabiting the same ecosystem. There are a series of considerations required before a particular interaction can be given an appropriate name. First, the effect each of the organisms (or populations) has on the other needs to be determined — is it inhibitory, beneficial, or neutral. Then it must be decided whether the interaction is active or passive (e.g., is the competition by direct interference or over the utilization of a mutual resource). Finally, is the interaction merely favorable or is it obligatory? To accurately identify all these relationships, a great deal of research is necessary, usually requiring an autecological approach.

The most direct relationship to study and describe is that between a pathogen and its host. Due to the dramatic effect that such a relationship can have on the host populations especially with regard to transmission through aquatic habitats, the potential for these kinds of interactions have received a great deal of attention. Also, due to the usual habitat specificity of pathogenic bacteria, considerable effort is devoted to identifying the genus and usually species of these organisms when they are detected in freshwater samples. In most other studies of prokaryotic interactions, very general terms are used to describe the populations of microorganisms in the association. For example, microorganisms involved in such associations are grouped as heterotrophic bacteria, epiphytes, or intestinal flora. Often, it is simply a matter of not having the techniques available, or in cases with complex associations, the time required to do detailed taxonomic studies.

Some selected interactions will be examined in this section. The discussions are not to be interpreted as being exhaustive, rather they are presented to give the reader a feel for the amount of work that is required to obtain an understanding of interspecies interactions and the insight derived from such studies.

4.1. Limnological Reservoirs for Pathogens

With few exceptions, pathogenic prokaryotes do not thrive in environments outside of their primary host. Therefore, studies of pathogens other than when they are associated with their host or in the laboratory are generally relegated to determining the persistence and survival of these organisms when expelled from their preferred environment. This is an important measurement because a primary route of infection is through exposure of potential hosts to water containing pathogen propagules. In a recent series of articles on water pollution (Allen, 1982; Dufour, 1982; Geldreich, 1982; Reasoner, 1982), a tabulation of work done on detection and identification of a variety of these agents was provided (Reasoner, 1982).

Without a doubt, the most commonly performed measurement of bacterial contamination is that for coliforms. The population density of these organisms found in potable and recreational waters is used as a standard to determine the microbiological acceptability of water for public use. Due to the close scrutiny and criticism that accompanies the establishment, implementation, and practical application of any standard method, the techniques for enumerating many of the species that comprise the coliform bacteria have received much attention. Much of the work deals with development or improvement of methods for recovering and enumerating these organisms from environmental samples, for example, see Dufour et al. (1981); LeChevallier et al. (1983); and Sladek et al. (1975). Also, there are many studies demonstrating potential difficulties in accurate determination of coliform population densities in environmental samples (Evans et al., 1981; Kasweck and Fliermans, 1978; Rychert and Stephenson, 1981). However, the autecology of this group of bacteria is not well understood even though this type of information is essential to the use of these organisms as indicators of contamination.

Some investigations of the survival of these organisms, especially *Escherichia coli,* have been done in streams, lakes, well water, and laboratory situations using diffusion chambers (Bissonnette et al., 1975; Fliermans and Gorden, 1977; Gorden and Fliermans, 1978; Kasweck and Fliermans, 1978; McFeters et al., 1974; McFeters and Stuart, 1972). These investigations have provided some information about the capability of *E. coli* to survive and even grow when exposed to these environments (Gorden and Fliermans, 1978). An observation that has major implications relating to estimation of coliform populations in situ is the possibility that a selected laboratory strain of *E. coli* lost the ability to utilize lactose when exposed to thermal stress in a cooling pond receiving thermal effluent from a nuclear reactor (Kasweck and Fliermans, 1978). Since lactose catabolism is used as a selective agent for many enumeration procedures, much of the data relating field population densities could have underestimated the organisms present. Another aspect of coliform survival that has major implications in freshwater systems, is the effect of sunlight on these organisms. Many of these studies have been conducted in marine and estuarine environments (McCambridge and McMeekin, 1981) but some have been done in freshwater (Dutka, 1984). *E. coli* was more sensitive to sunlight than naturally occurring aquatic microorganisms but more resistant than other fecal bacteria, such as, *Streptococcus faecium* and *S. faecalis* (Dutka, 1984; McCambridge and McMeekin, 1981). The majority of survival studies are conducted with washed laboratory grown bacterial cells. Generally laboratory strains rather than recent isolates are used. The differences in results caused by these practices are difficult to assess. Thus, many unanswered questions about coliform autecology and the usefulness of these organisms as indicator bacteria remain.

Besides coliforms, there are several other pathogenic organisms transmitted between hosts through aquatic environments, for example, *Vibrio cholerae* (Johnston et al., 1983), but their existence in these ecosystems also is believed to be only transitory. Another class of organisms referred to as opportunistic pathogens are free-living organisms capable of surviving and proliferating outside their hosts. These organisms only become infectious when a large population comes in contact with a potential host or the host is unusually susceptible through debilitation. Genera representative of the latter group are *Aeromonas, Klebsiella, Pseudomonas,* and *Legionella.*

Autecological studies of at least two of these genera *(Aeromonas* and *Legionella)* are quite extensive. The general distribution and density of *Aeromonas* in fresh and salt waters throughout much of the United States has been determined (Hazen et al., 1978). At almost all (135 out of 147) of the sites sampled *A. hydrophila* was isolated. Of the 12 sites where *A. hydrophila* was not isolated, 7 were stressed environments either by hypersalinity, geothermal inputs, or extreme pollution. These results indicate that *A. hydrophila* is a natural component of the microbial flora of nonstressed freshwater ecosystems. Results of further studies of the distribution of *A. hydrophila* in thermally altered streams and a lake showed that *A. hydrophila* had an in situ temperature optima of 25 to 35°C and a maximum of 45°C (Fliermans et al., 1977; Hazen and Fliermans, 1979). Both survival of pure cultures of *A. hydrophila* placed in the cooling pond and densities of the natural *Aeromonas*-like populations increased when the pond received thermal inputs from a nuclear reactor (Fliermans et al., 1977). Determinations of the densities of this organism along the thermal gradient of two types of thermally altered streams showed slightly (but not significant) different temperature maxima. Attempts to isolate *A. hydrophila* from thermally impacted streams at temperatures above 45°C failed (Hazen and Fliermans, 1979). All these in situ autecological measurements were shown to correlate well with previous laboratory data (Hazen and Fliermans, 1979). Based on the assumption that higher densities of *A. hydrophila* increase its pathogenicity to fish, it was postulated that a high incidence of the resultant "red sore" disease might be expected in fish inhabiting thermally impacted waters.

Ambient water temperature is also a controlling factor in the incidence and densities of *Aeromonas* spp. recovered from divers and their gear (Cavari et al., 1981; Seidler et al., 1980). A correlation was first found between recovery of this genus from divers and *Aeromonas* spp. population densities in the river water column (Seidler et al., 1980). The latter parameter was correlated to seasonal changes in water temperature (Cavari et al., 1981). It was also shown that the general heterotrophic population in the water column and sediments of the river did not follow the same trend in variation of population densities as did the *Aeromonas* spp. population. The population densities of total direct or viable bacteria was two – eightfold higher in the winter months but the *Aeromonas* spp. counts decreased by several orders of magnitude during the same period. Laboratory studies of an *Aeromonas* sp. isolated from the river showed a lower heterotrophic activity at low temperature than the general bacterial population from the river (Cavari et al., 1981). Therefore, it was concluded that low temperatures in the winter months caused the reduction in *Aeromonas* spp. densities and thus reduced the potential for incidences of interactions with divers.

An intensive investigation of a bacterial pathogen followed the identification of the causative agent of an outbreak of pneumonia that occurred after an American Legion convention in Philadelphia held in July of 1976 (Fraser et al., 1977). In response to subsequent outbreaks of the Legionnaires' disease, tests of environmental samples obtained from the vicinity of the outbreak were conducted to determine the presence of the causative agent, *Legionella pneumophila* (Cordes et al., 1980; Dondero et al., 1980; Morris et al., 1979). It became apparent that this organism was prevalent in a variety of aquatic habitats as more samples were obtained and analyzed from areas not related to epidemics (Bopp et al., 1981; Fliermans et al., 1981; Fliermans et al., 1979; Orrison et al., 1981). Because of the great interest shown in this organism, its distribution in limnological ecosystems was fairly well defined within a period of only three – four years.

Due to the difficulty of growing and isolating *L. pneumophila* on standard and many selective laboratory media, recently developed direct microscopic techniques were applied to the environmental study of this organism. Because of the use of direct fluorescent antibody techniques (Cherry et al., 1978) combined with tetrazolium reduction methods for determining bacterial activity (Fliermans et al., 1981), the study of the autecological activity of *L. pneumophila* represents a primary example of how a selected organism can be examined in situ. *L. pneumophila* was found to be a naturally occurring microorganism capable of surviving in freshwater habitats with a wide range of environmental parameters (Fliermans et al., 1981).

Interest in *L. pneumophila* and its autecology still remains quite strong, especially when a disease outbreak occurs. How its place in various aquatic environments influences its potential for infecting man is still not well understood. Many aspects of its survival and growth in aquatic habitats continue to be investigated, for example, its sensitivity to sunlight (Dutka, 1984) and its ingestion by and subsequent intracellular multiplication in protozoa (Barbaree et al., 1986).

4.2. Microbial – Microbial Interactions

The most direct and unmistakable interaction between organisms is the one developed between a host and a parasite – pathogen – predator. This interaction even occurs at the level of the prokaryotes such as phage or *Bdellovibrio* predation on selected bacterial species. However, the extent and ecological significance of many of these interactions is uncertain (Varon and Shilo, 1980). Most ecological investigations have been directed towards the cycling of nutrients — essentially showing the use of the products of one population of organisms by a different population that require the by-product(s) of the first group as a substrate in their own metabolic processes.

For a heterotrophic organism, finding a source of carbon and energy is paramount. The ability of a fastidious organism like *L. pneumophila* to be supplied these requirements in the material excreted by a cyanobacterium, (Tison et al., 1980) provided a possible explanation for this bacterium's proliferation in natural environments. Within freshwater planktonic assemblages, one can readily observe bacteria in association with phytoplankton, primarily in the microenvironments at the algal surface. Mikhayenko and Kulikova (1973) estimated that 97% of the planktonic bacteria are epiphytic. Phototrophic populations create a nutrient-rich microzone through the production and excretion of protoassimilated organic compounds estimated to be as high as 30% of the algal primary production (Wetzel and Manny, 1972). Adhesion processes enable bacteria to proliferate in communities ranging from algal mats in thermal hot springs (Brock, 1978) to cold, oligotrophic waters of mountain streams (Haack and McFeters, 1982; Hendricks and Morrison, 1967; McFeters et al., 1978a, 1978b). Although few such studies have been autecological, a full understanding of the community dynamics will require such an approach. Caldwell and Caldwell (1978) have observed bacteria attached to heterocysts of *Aphanizomenon flos-aquae* and embedded within the mucilage of both *Anabaena flos-aquae* and *Microcystis aeruginosa* in freshwater plankton. Using an autecological approach, they were able to show that the occurrence of one of the bacteria reflected an obligatory requirement for the microenvironment of the mucilage. It was speculated that this was "a new species of *Zoogloea* and of potential importance in phytoplankton ecology." In another autecological study Gallucci and Paerl (1983) showed *Pseudomonas aeruginosa* to be intimately associated with cyanobacterial blooms of *Anabaena* sp. in the Chowan River in North Carolina. Other Gram-negative bacterial species shown to be associated with aquatic cyanobacteria include *Achromobacter, Aerobacter, Flavobacterium, Pseudomonas,* and *Vibrio.*

4.3. Prokaryotic Interactions with Higher Trophic Levels

We are only beginning to understand the complex ecological interrelationships that exist between prokaryotes and other trophic levels in limnological environments. One such interaction is that between aquatic plants and their attached microbial flora. In many aquatic environments, epiphytes have been shown to be an important, productive component of the ecosystem (Brock, 1970; Hickman, 1971; Sheldon and Boylen, 1975). Most of the classical studies have been synecological in nature (Allen, 1971). Currently we know little of the mechanisms by which the periphyton become established on plant leaf and stem surfaces. Greater autecological knowledge will undoubtedly enhance our understanding. Macrophytes as well as eukaryotic algae secrete large amounts of dissolved organic carbon and nitrogen (Wetzel and Manny, 1972). Attraction to a nutrient source would be a major factor in the establishment of a heterotrophic population. In oligotrophic (low-nutrient) waters relatively simple communities of bacteria develop in contrast to the thick slime-layered communities in eutrophic waters where a community of bacteria, algae, protozoa, and small invertebrates is held together in a thick polymeric slime (Costerton et al., 1978; Fletcher and Marshall, 1982). Although there is little direct observation of bacteria in such communities to make quantitative estimates, such information is essential for autecological studies to be developed (Fry and Humphrey, 1978; Hossell and Baker, 1976, 1979).

A few autecological examples of work with epiphytic communities deserve particular mention. In eutrophic shallow ponds many attached communities of cyanobacteria develop. Species of *Gloeotrichia* are primarily responsible for high levels of nitrogen fixation occurring in epiphytic communities attached to *Myriophyllum spicatum* (Finke and Seeley, 1978). Nitrogen fixing heterotrophic bacteria (*Klebsiella* sp.) have also been found associated with duckweed (*Lemnaceae* sp.) mats (Zuberer, 1982). Symbiotic nitrogen fixing organisms are not common in aquatic environments. However, there is a well-known example of this kind of interaction: the cyanobacterium *Anabaena azolae* growing in association with the aquatic fern *Azolla folliculoides* (McKee, 1962).

As secondary producers, prokaryotes are a major source of food for many higher organisms (Ehrlich, 1985). As a base of the detrital food chain, prokaryotes convert this material to cellular biomass that becomes a food source for benthic invertebrates (Levinton et al., 1984). The identification of particular species responsible for these conversions has not been extensive. Another general area of food web interaction — the colonization and commensal relationships of prokaryotes in the intestinal tract of higher organisms — has received some attention (Trust and Sparrow, 1974). As well as colonizing the gut of higher organisms, prokaryotes are also found to take advantage of the special environment provided by the outer surfaces of higher organisms. Many prokaryotes have been shown to be associated with fish and invertebrates utilizing the material excreted by them as a nutrient source.

The use of autecological techniques has provided further understanding of some of these relationships. *Vibrio parahaemolyticus,* a moderately halophilic organism, was isolated by Sarkar et al. (1983) from samples of plankton from various freshwater environments. Although it was concluded that this organism was not part of the autochthonous microbial flora of freshwater systems, this study showed that there was a niche in these environments where this halophile could persist longer than might normally be expected. Some of the most extensively studied associations are those between higher organism hosts and their prokaryote pathogens. The understanding of the infection of bass and humans by *Aeromonas* discussed in Section 4.1 was advanced as a result of autecological studies of this organism.

5.0. CONCLUSIONS

A major point to emerge from the review of material used in preparation of this chapter is that the field of microbial autecology of limnological systems is still in its infancy. There are considerable methodological problems to be overcome before the numbers and activities of key microorganisms in inland waters can be easily quantitated. For the most part, autecological studies have been conducted on unique or unusual limnological environments. These habitats exert tremendous selective forces limiting the number of species able to tolerate their extremes. They provide the potential for interpreting the results of autecological investigations of the dominant organisms based on the observations of the physical parameters of these environments. Unfortunately, the number of in situ conditions permitting numerical dominance is rather limited and only allows for the study of a select few microbial species in a very restricted range of conditions that may only provide a narrow concept of their overall ecology. For example, the morphology of the dominant bacteria observed under such selective conditions has often been found to be remarkably uniform (Caldwell and Tiedje, 1975a, 1975b; Olah et al., 1972). There are, however, some species like *Peloploca* spp., which are morphologically distinct, that can be studied using an autecological approach due to their ease of observation and recognition in samples from several different environments (Maiden and Jones, 1984).

The development and application of what might be considered sophisticated techniques for autecological investigations have occurred when the need to know the identity and density of an organism has had sufficient priority or as a "one-time" demonstration of the usefulness of such a technique. Examples of these circumstances include the use of antibody techniques to detect and measure the activity of *L. pneumophila* in several different environments (Fliermans et al., 1981) and to determine specific methylotrophic populations in a harbor (Reed and Dugan, 1978). Methods based on the selectivity of antibodies and other biomarkers such as fatty acids as well as those relying on morphological characteristics will be needed to augment traditional culturing techniques to provide a more accurate determination of microbial populations and their activities in limnological environments. But these techniques can be both time consuming and expensive and as such will probably only be applied in situations where a significant need for the information can be identified. As the demand for clean and safe supplies of freshwater continues to increase, the need to understand limnological ecosystems, including their microbial populations, will increase. An important part of this understanding will come from auteco-logical study of the microbial populations that play a significant role in the functioning of these environments.

REFERENCES

Abeliovich, A. and Y. Azov (1976). Toxicity of ammonia to algae in sewage oxidation ponds. *Appl. Environ. Microbiol.*, **31**:801–806.

Alleman, J. E., J. A. Veil, and J. T. Canaday (1982). Scanning electron microscope evaluation of rotating biological contactor biofilm. *Water Res.*, **16**:543–550.

Allen, H. L. (1971). Primary productivity, chemo-organotrophy, and nutritional inter-actions of epiphytic algae and bacteria on macrophytes in the littoral of a lake. *Ecol. Monog.*, **41**:97–127.

Allen, M. J. (1982). Microbiology of potable water and ground water. *J. Water Pollut. Control Fed.*, **54**:943–946.

Archer, D. B. (1984). Detection and quantitation of methanogens by enzyme-linked immunosorbent assay. *Appl. Environ. Microbiol.*, **48**:797–801.

Baker, A. L. and A. J. Brook (1971). Optical density profiles as an aid to the study of microstratified phytoplankton population studies. *Arch. Hydrobiol.*, **69**:214–233.

Balch, W. E., G. E. Fox, L. J. Magrum, C. R. Woese, and R. S. Wolfe (1979). Methano-gens: Reevaluation of a unique biological group. *Microbiol. Rev.*, **43**:260–296.

Balkwill, D. L. and W. C. Ghiorse (1985). Characterization of subsurface bacteria associated with two shallow aquifers in Oklahoma. *Appl. Environ. Microbiol.*, **50**:580–588.

Barbaree, J. M., B. S. Fields, J. C. Feeley, G. W. Gorman, and W. T. Martin (1986). Isolation of protozoa from water associated with a Legionellosis outbreak and dem-onstration of intracellular multiplication of *Legionella pneumophila. Appl. Environ. Microbiol.*, **51**:422–424.

Bauld, J. and T. D. Brock (1973). Ecological studies of *Chloroflexis,* a gliding photosyn-thetic bacterium. *Arch. Mikrobiol.*, **92**:267–284.

Belly, R. T. and T. D. Brock (1974). Widespread occurrence of acidophilic strains of *Bacillus coagulans* in hot springs. *J. Appl. Bacteriol.*, **37**:175–177.

Belser, L. W. (1979). Population ecology of nitrifying bacteria. *Ann. Rev. Microbiol.*, **33**:309–333.

Bissonnette, G. K., J. J. Jezeski, G. A. McFeters, and D. G. Stuart (1975). Influence of environmental stress on enumeration of indicator bacteria from natural waters. *Appl. Microbiol.*, **29**:186–194.

Blakemore, R. P. (1975). Magnetotactic bacteria. *Science,* **190**:377–379.

Blaszyk, T. and J. Gorski (1981). Ground water quality changes during exploitations. *Ground Water,* **19**:28–33.

Bopp, C. A., J. W. Sumner, G. K. Morris, and J. G. Wells (1981). Isolation of *Legionella* spp. from environmental water samples by low-pH treatment and use of a selective medium. *J. Clin. Microbiol.*, **13**:714–719.

Bott, T. L. and T. D. Brock (1969). Bacterial growth rates above 90°C in Yellowstone hot springs. *Science,* **164**:1411–1412.

Brezonik, P. L. and G. F. Lee (1968). Denitrification as a nitrogen sink in Lake Mendota, Wis. *Environ. Sci. Technol.,* **2:**120–125.

Bristow, J. M. (1974). Nitrogen fixation in the rhizosphere of freshwater angiosperms. *Can. J. Bot.,* **52:**217–221.

Brock, T. D. (1967a). Relationship between standing crop and primary productivity along a hot spring thermal gradient. *Ecology,* **48:**566–571.

Brock, T. D. (1967b). Life at high temperatures. *Science,* **158:**1012–1019.

Brock, T. D. (1968). Taxonomic confusion concerning certain filamentous blue-green algae. *J. Phycol.,* **4:**178–179.

Brock, T. D. (1969a). "Microbial growth under extreme conditions," in *Microbial Growth, Nineteenth Symposia of the Society of General Microbiology.* Cambridge University Press, Cambridge. pp. 15–41.

Brock, T. D. (1969b). Vertical zonation in hot spring algal mats. *Phycologia,* **8:**201–205.

Brock, T. D. (1970). Photosynthesis by algal epiphytes of *Utricularia* in Everglades National Park. *Bull. Mar. Sci.,* **20:**952–956.

Brock, T. D. (1978). *Thermophilic Microorganisms and Life at High Temperatures.* Springer-Verlag, New York.

Brock, T. D., K. M. Brock, R. T. Belly, and R. L. Weiss (1972). *Sulfolobus:* A new genus of sulfur-oxidizing bacteria living at low pH and high temperature. *Arch. Mikrobiol.,* **84:**54–68.

Brock, T. D. and M. L. Brock (1967). The measurement of chlorophyll, primary productivity, photophosphorylation, and macromolecules in benthic algal mats. *Limnol. Oceanogr.,* **12:**600–605.

Brock, T. D. and M. L. Brock (1968). Measurement of steady-state growth rates of a thermophilic alga directly in nature. *J. Bacteriol.,* **95:**811–815.

Brock, T. D. and M. L. Brock (1970). The algae of Waimangu Cauldron (New Zealand): Distribution in relation to pH. *J. Phycol.,* **6:**371–375.

Brock, T. D. and G. Darland (1970). Limits of microbial existence: Temperature and pH. *Science,* **169:**1316–1318.

Brock, T. D. and H. Freeze (1969). *Thermus aquaticus* gen. n. and sp. n., a nonsporulating extreme thermophile. *J. Bacteriol.,* **98:**289–297.

Caldwell, D. E. and S. J. Caldwell (1978). A *Zoogloea* sp. associated with blooms of *Anabaena flos-aquae. Can. J. Microbiol.,* **24:**922–931.

Caldwell, D. E. and J. M. Tiedje (1975a). A morphological study of anaerobic bacteria from the hypolimnia of two Michigan lakes. *Can. J. Microbiol.,* **21:**362–376.

Caldwell, D. E. and J. M. Tiedje (1975b). The structure of anaerobic bacterial communities in the hypolimnia of several Michigan lakes. *Can. J. Microbiol.,* **21:**377–385.

Cappenberg, T. E. (1972). Ecological observations on heterotrophic, methane oxidizing and sulfate reducing bacteria in a pond. *Hydrobiologia,* **40:**471–485.

Cappenberg, T. E. and R. A. Prins (1974). Interrelations between sulfate-reducing and methane-producing bacteria in bottom deposits of a fresh-water lake. III. Experiments with ^{14}C-labeled substrates. *Antonie van Leeuwenhoek; J. Microbial. Serol.,* **40:**457–469.

Castenholz, R. W. (1968). The behavior of *Oscillatoria terebriformis* in hot springs. *J. Phycol.,* **4:**132–139.

Castenholz, R. W. (1969a). Thermophilic blue-green algae and the thermal environment. *Bacteriol. Rev.*, **33**:476–504.

Castenholz, R. W. (1969b). The thermophilic cyanophytes of Iceland and the upper temperature limit. *J. Phycol.*, **5**:360–368.

Castenholz, R. W. (1978). The biogeography of hot spring algae through enrichment cultures. *Mitt. Int. Ver. Theor. Angew. Limnol.*, **21**:296–315.

Castenholz, R. W. (1984). "Composition of hot spring microbial mats: A summary," in Y. Cohen, R. Castenholz, and H. Halvorson, ed., *Microbial Mats: Stromatolites.* Alan R. Liss, New York, pp. 101–119.

Cavari, B. Z., D. A. Allen, and R. R. Colwell (1981). Effect of temperature on growth and activity of *Aeromonas* spp. and mixed bacterial populations in the Anacostia River. *Appl. Environ. Microbiol.*, **41**:1052–1054.

Chen, R. L., D. R. Kenney, J. G. Konrad, A. J. Holding, and D. A. Graetz (1972). Gas production in sediments of Lake Mendota. *J. Environ. Qual.*, **1**:155–157.

Cherry, W. B., B. Pittman, P. P. Harris, G. A. Herbert, B. M. Thomason, L. Thacker, and R. E. Weaver (1978). Detection of Legionnaires disease bacteria by direct immunofluorescent staining. *J. Clin. Microbiol.*, **8**:329–338.

Cohen, Y., R. W. Castenholz, and H. O. Halvorson, eds., (1984). *Microbial Mats: Stromatolites.* Alan R. Liss, New York.

Collins, V. G. (1963). The distribution and ecology of bacteria in freshwater. *Proc. Soc. Water Treat. Exam.*, **12**:40–67.

Cooper, A. B. (1983a). Population ecology of nitrifiers in a stream receiving geothermal inputs of ammonium. *Appl. Environ. Microbiol.*, **45**:1170–1177.

Cooper, A. B. (1983b). Effect of storm events on benthic nitrifying activity. *Appl. Environ. Microbiol.*, **46**:957–960.

Cooper, D. E., M. B. Rands, and C. P. Woo (1975). Sulfide reduction in fellmongery effluent by red sulfur bacteria. *J. Water Pollut. Control Fed.*, **47**:2088–2099.

Cordes, L. G., D. W. Fraser, P. Skaliy, C. A. Perlino, W. R. Elsea, G. F. Mallison, and P. S. Hayes (1980). Legionnaires' disease outbreak at an Atlanta, Georgia, country club: evidence for spread from an evaporative condenser. *Am. J. Epidemiol.*, **111**:425–431.

Cosgrove, D. J. (1977). Microbial transformations in the phosphorus cycle. *Adv. Microbial Ecol.*, **1**:95–134.

Costerton, J. W. and G. G. Geesey (1979). "Which populations of aquatic bacteria should we enumerate," in J. W. Costerton and R. R. Colwell, ed., *Native Aquatic Bacteria: Enumeration, Activity, and Ecology.* American Society for Testing and Materials, Philadelphia, pp. 7–18.

Costerton, J. W., G. G. Geesey, and K. J. Cheng (1978). How bacteria stick. *Sci. Am.*, **238**:86–95.

Culver, D. A. and G. J. Brunskill (1969). Fayetteville Green Lake, New York. V. Studies of primary production and zooplankton in a meromictic marl lake. *Limnol. Oceanogr.*, **14**:862–873.

Curtis, E. J. C., K. Durrant, and M. M. I. Harman (1975). Nitrification in rivers in the Trent Basin. *Water Res.*, **9**:255–268.

Darland, G. and T. D. Brock (1971). *Bacillus acidocaldarius* sp. nov., an acidophilic thermophilic spore-forming bacterium. *J. Gen. Microbiol.*, **67**:9–15.

Darland, G., T. D. Brock, W. Samsonoff, and S. F. Conti (1970). A thermophilic, acidophilic *Mycoplasma* isolated from a coal refuse pile. *Science,* 170:1416–1418.

Desrochers, R. and V. Fredette (1960). Etude d'une population de bacteries reductrices du soufre. *Can. J. Microbiol.,* 6:349–354.

Deuser, W. G., E. T. Degens, and G. R. Harvey (1973). Methane in Lake Kivu: New data bearing on its origin. *Science,* 181:51–54.

Dilworth, M. J. (1966). Acetylene reduction by nitrogen-fixing preparations from *Clostridium pasteurianum. Biochim. Biophys. Acta,* 127:285–294.

Dockins, W. S. (1980). Sulfate reduction in ground water of southeastern Montana. *Natl. Tech. Inform. Ser.,* 80:221971.

Doemel, W. N. and T. D. Brock (1974). Bacterial stromatolites: Origin of laminations. *Science,* 184:1083–1085.

Doemel, W. N. and T. D. Brock (1977). Structure, growth and decomposition of laminated algal-bacterial mats in alkaline hot springs. *Appl. Environ. Microbiol.,* 34:433–452.

Dondero, T. J., Jr., R. C. Rendtorff, G. F. Mallison, R. M. Weeks, J. S. Levy, E. W. Wong, and W. Schaffner (1980). An outbreak of Legionnaires' disease associated with a contaminated air-conditioning cooling tower. *N. Engl. J. Med.,* 302:365–370.

Duddridge, J. E., C. A. Kent, and J. F. Laws (1982). Effect of surface shear stress on the attachment of *Pseudomonas fluorescens* to stainless steel under defined flow conditions. *Biotechnol. Bioeng.,* 24:153–164.

Dufour, A. P. (1982). Disease outbreaks caused by drinking water. *J. Water Pollut. Control Fed.,* 54:980–983.

Dufour, A. P., E. R. Strickland, and V. J. Cabelli (1981). Membrane filter method for enumerating *Escherichia coli. Appl. Environ. Microbiol.,* 41:1152–1158.

Dugan, P. R., C. B. MacMillan, and R. M. Pfister (1970). Aerobic heterotrophic bacteria indigenous to pH 2.8 acid mine water: Predominant slime-producing bacteria in acid streams. *J. Bacteriol.,* 101:982–988.

Dunnette, D. A. and R. M. Avedovech (1983). Effect of an industrial ammonia discharge on the dissolved oxygen regime of the Willamette River, Oregon. *Water Res.,* 17:997–1007.

Dutka, B. J. (1984). Sensitivity of *Legionella pneumophila* to sunlight in fresh water and marine water. *Appl. Environ. Microbiol.,* 48:970–974.

Ehrlich, H. L. (1981). *Geomicrobiology.* Dekker, New York.

Ehrlich, H. L. (1985). "The position of bacteria and their products in food webs," in E. R. Leadbetter and J. S. Poindexter, ed., *Bacteria in Nature.* Plenum, New York, pp. 199–219.

Evans, T. M., R. J. Seidler, and M. W. LeChevallier (1981). Impact of verification media and resuscitation on accuracy of the membrane filter total coliform enumeration technique. *Appl. Environ. Microbiol.,* 41:1144–1151.

Fallon, R. D. and T. D. Brock (1980). Planktonic blue-green algae: Production, sedimentation, and decomposition in Lake Mendota, Wisconsin. *Limnol. Oceanogr.,* 25:72–88.

Fallon, R. D., S. Harrits, R. S. Hanson, and T. D. Brock (1980). The role of methane in internal carbon cycling in Lake Mendota during summer stratification. *Limnol. Oceanogr.,* 25:357–360.

Fenchel, T. M. and B. B. Jorgensen (1977). Detritus food chains of aquatic ecosystems: the role of bacteria. *Adv. Microbial Ecol.*, **1**:1-58.

Finke, L. R. and H. W. Seeley, Jr. (1978). Nitrogen fixation (acetylene reduction) by epiphytes of freshwater macrophytes. *Appl. Environ. Microbiol.*, **36**:129-138.

Fletcher, M. and K. C. Marshall (1982). Are solid surfaces of ecological significance to aquatic bacteria. *Adv. Microbial Ecol.*, **6**:199-236.

Fliermans, C. B., B. B. Bohlool, and E. L. Schmidt (1974). Autecological study of the chemoautotroph *Nitrobacter* by immunofluorescence, *Appl. Microbiol.*, **27**:124-129.

Fliermans, C. B., P. S. Cain, and E. L. Schmidt (1975). Direct measurement of bacterial stratification in Minnesota lakes. *Arch. Hydrobiol.*, **76**:248-255.

Fliermans, C. B., W. B. Cherry, L. H. Orrison, S. J. Smith, D. L. Tison, and D. H. Pope (1981). Ecological distribution of *Legionella pneumophila. Appl. Environ. Microbiol.*, **41**:9-16.

Fliermans, C. B., W. B. Cherry, L. H. Orrison, and L. Thacker (1979). Isolation of *Legionella pneumophila* from nonepidemic-related aquatic habitats. *Appl. Environ. Microbiol.*, **37**:1239-1242.

Fliermans, C. B. and R. W. Gorden (1977). Modification of membrane diffusion chambers for deepwater studies. *Appl. Environ. Microbiol.*, **33**:207-210.

Fliermans, C. B., R. W. Gorden, T. C. Hazen, and G. W. Esch (1977). *Aeromonas* distribution and survival in a thermally altered lake. *Appl. Environ. Microbiol.*, **33**:114-122.

Fliermans, C. B. and E. L. Schmidt (1975). Autoradiography and immunofluorescence combined for autecological study of single cell activity with *Nitrobacter* as a model system. *Appl. Microbiol.*, **30**:676-684.

Fliermans, C. B. and E. L. Schmidt (1977). Immunofluorescence for autecological study of a unicellular bluegreen alga. *J. Phycol.*, **13**:364-368.

Fliermans, C. B., R. J. Soracco, and D. H. Pope (1981). Measure of *Legionella pneumophila* activity in situ. *Curr. Microbiol.*, **6**:89-94.

Focht, D. D. and W. Verstraete (1977). Biochemical ecology of nitrification and denitrification. *Adv. Microbial Ecol.*, **1**:135-214.

Fraser, D. W., T. R. Tsai, W. Orenstein, W. E. Parkin, H. J. Beecham, R. G. Sharrar, J. Harris, G. F. Mallison, S. M. Martin, J. E. McDade, C. C. Shepard, P. S. Brachman, and The Field Investigation Team (1977). Legionnaires' disease: Description of an epidemic of pneumonia. *N. Engl. J. Med.*, **297**:1189-1197.

Freeze, R. A. and J. A. Cherry (1979). *Groundwater.* Prentice-Hall, Englewood Cliffs.

Fry, J. C. and N. C. B. Humphrey (1978). "Techniques for the study of bacteria epiphytic on aquatic macrophytes," in D. W. Lovelock and R. Davies, ed., *Techniques for the Study of Mixed Populations.* Academic, London.

Gallucci, K. K. and H. W. Paerl (1983). *Pseudomonas aeruginosa* chemotaxis associated with blooms of N_2-fixing blue-green algae (cyanobacteria). *Appl. Environ. Microbiol.*, **45**:557-562.

Geesey, G. G., R. Mutch, J. W. Costerton, and R. B. Green (1978). Sessile bacteria: An important component of the microbial population in small mountain streams. *Limnol. Oceanogr.*, **23**:1214-1223.

Geldreich, E. E. (1982). Microbiology: Water. *J. Water Pollut. Control Fed.*, **54**:931-943.

Ghiorse, W. C. and D. L. Balkwill (1983). Enumeration and morphological characteristics of bacteria indigenous to subsurface environments. *Dev. Ind. Microbiol.,* **24**:213–224.

Goering, J. J. and V. A. Dugdale (1966). Estimates of the rates of denitrification in a subarctic lake. *Limnol. Oceanogr.,* **11**:113–117.

Goldman, C. R. and A. J. Horne (1983). *Limnology.* McGraw-Hill, New York.

Gorden, R. W. and C. B. Fliermans (1978). Survival and viability of *Escherichia coli* in a thermally altered reservoir. *Water Res.,* **12**:343–352.

Grant, W. D. and P. E. Long (1981). *Environmental Microbiology.* Wiley, New York.

Grant, W. D. and B. J. Tindall (1980). "The isolation of alkalophilic bacteria," in G. W. Gould and J. E. L. Corry, ed., *Microbial Growth and Survival in Extremes of Environment.* Academic, London, pp. 27–38.

Haack, T. K. and G. A. McFeters (1982). Microbial dynamics of an epilithic mat community in a high alpine stream. *Appl. Environ. Microbiol.,* **43**:702–707.

Hanson, R. S. (1980). Ecology and diversity of methylotrophic organisms. *Adv. Appl. Microbiol.,* **26**:3–39.

Hargreaves, J. W., E. J. H. Lloyd, and B. A. Whitton (1975). Chemistry and vegetation of highly acidic streams. *Freshwater Biol.,* **5**:563–576.

Harrits, S. M. and R. S. Hanson (1980). Stratification of aerobic methane-oxidizing organisms in Lake Mendota, Madison, Wisconsin. *Limnol. Oceanogr.,* **25**:412–421.

Hazen, T. C. and C. B. Fliermans (1979). Distribution of *Aeromonas hydrophila* in natural and man-made thermal effluents. *Appl. Environ. Microbiol.,* **38**:166–168.

Hazen, T. C., C. B. Fliermans, R. P. Hirsch, and G. W. Esch (1978). Prevalence and distribution of *Aeromonas hydrophila* in the United States. *Appl. Environ. Microbiol.,* **36**:731–738.

Hendrey, G. R. and F. A. Vertucci (1980). "Benthic plant communities in acidic Lake Colden, New York: *Sphagnum* and the algal mat," in D. Drablos and A. Tollan, ed., *Ecological Impact of Acid Precipitation.* SNSF Project, Oslo, pp. 314–315.

Hendricks, C. W. (1971). Enteric bacterial metabolism of stream sediment eluates. *Can. J. Microbiol.,* **17**:551–556.

Hendricks, C. W. and S. M. Morrison (1967). Multiplication and growth of selected enteric bacteria in clear mountain stream water. *Water Res.,* **1**:567–576.

Henrici, A. T. and E. McCoy (1938). The distribution of heterotrophic bacteria in the bottom deposits of some lakes. *Trans. Wis. Acad. Sci. Arts Lett.,* **31**:323–361.

Hickman, M. (1971). The standing crop and primary productivity of the epiphyton attached to *Equisetum fluviatile* L. in Priddy Pool, North Somerset. *Br. Phycol. J.,* **6**:51–59.

Higgins, I. J., D. J. Best, R. C. Hammond, and D. Scott (1981). Methane-oxidizing microorganisms. *Microbiol. Rev.,* **45**:556–590.

Hirsch, P., M. Muller, and H. Schlesner (1977). "New aquatic budding and prosthecate bacteria and their taxonomic position," in F. A. Skinner and J. M. Shewan, ed., *Aquatic Microbiology.* Academic, New York, pp. 107–133.

Hodgkiss, I. J. (1974). Studies on Plover Cove Reservoir, Hong Kong: Composition and distribution of the phytoplankton and its relationship to environmental factors. *Freshwater Biol.,* **4**:111–126.

Holm, H. W. and L. W. Vennes (1970). Occurrence of purple sulfur bacteria in sewage treatment lagoon. *Appl. Microbiol.,* **19**:988–996.

Hooper, F. F. (1973). "Origin and fate of organic phosphorus compounds in aquatic systems," in E. J. Griffith, A. Beeton, J. M. Spencer, and D. T. Mitchell, ed., *Environmental Phosphorus Handbook.* Wiley, New York, pp. 179–201.

Horne, A. J. (1975). Algal nitrogen fixation in Californian streams: Diel cycles and nocturnal fixation. *Freshwater Biol.,* **5:**471–477.

Horne, A. J., J. E. Dillard, D. K. Fujita, and C. R. Goldman (1972). Nitrogen fixation in Clear Lake, California. II. Synoptic studies on the autumn *Anabaena* bloom. *Limnol. Oceanogr.,* **17:**693–703.

Horne, A. J. and C. R. Goldman (1972). Nitrogen fixation in Clear Lake, California. I. Seasonal variation and the role of heterocysts. *Limnol. Oceanogr.,* **17:**678–692.

Horsley, R. W. (1978). "A technique for the enumeration of heterotrophic nitrate-reducing bacteria," in D. W. Lovelock and R. Davies, ed., *Techniques for the Study of Mixed Populations.* Academic, London, pp. 71–87.

Hossell, J. C. and J. H. Baker (1976). The distribution and characterization of bacteria on the surfaces of some river macrophytes. *J. Appl. Bacteriol.,* **41:**14.

Hossell, J. C. and J. H. Baker (1979). A note on the enumeration of epiphytic bacteria by microscopic methods with particular reference to two freshwater plants. *J. Appl. Bacteriol.,* **46:**87–92.

Howard, D. L., J. I. Frea, and R. M. Pfister (1971). "The potential for methane carbon cycling in Lake Erie," in *Proceedings of the Fourteenth Conference on Great Lakes Research.* Inaternational Association for Great Lakes Research, Ann Arbor, pp. 236–240.

Hutchinson, G. E. (1957). *A Treatise on Limnology. I. Geography, Physics and Chemistry.* Wiley, New York.

Ingovorsen, K., J. G. Zeikus, and T. D. Brock (1981). Dynamics of bacterial sulfate reduction in a eutrophic lake. *Appl. Environ. Microbiol.,* **42:**1029–1036.

Johnson, D. B., W. I. Kelso, and D. A. Jenkins (1979). Bacterial streamer growth in a disused pyrite mine. *Environ. Pollut.,* **18:**107–118.

Johnston, J. M., D. L. Martin, J. Perdue, L. M. McFarland, C. T. Caraway, E. C. Lippy, and P. A. Blake (1983). Cholera on a gulf coast oil rig. *N. Engl. J. Med.,* **309:**523–526.

Jones, J. G. (1973). Studies on freshwater bacteria: The effect of enclosure in large experimental tubes. *J. Appl. Bacteriol.,* **36:**445–456.

Jones, J. G. (1975). Some observations on the occurrence of the iron bacterium *Leptothrix ochracea* in fresh water, including reference to large experimental enclosures. *J. Appl. Bacteriol.,* **39:**63–72.

Jorgensen, B. B. and N. P. Revsbech (1983). Colorless sulfur bacteria, *Beggiatoa* spp. and *Thiovolum* spp. in oxygen and hydrogen sulfide microgradients. *Appl. Environ. Microbiol.,* **45:**1261–1270.

Jorgensen, B. B., N. P. Revsbech, and Y. Cohen (1983). Photosynthesis and structure of benthic microbial mats: Microelectrode and SEM studies of four cyanobacterial communities. *Limnol. Oceanogr.,* **28:**1075–1093.

Kasweck, K. L. and C. B. Fliermans (1978). Lactose variability of *Escherichia coli* in thermally stressed reactor effluent waters. *Appl. Environ. Microbiol.,* **36:**739–746.

Kaushik, N.K. and H. B. N. Hynes (1968). Experimental study on the role of autumn-shed leaves in aquatic environments. *J. Ecol.,* **56:**229–243.

Keeney, D. R., R. L. Chen, and D. A. Graetz (1971). Importance of denitrification and nitrate reduction in sediments to the nitrogen budgets of lakes. *Nature (London)*, 233:66–67.

Keirn, M. A. and P. L. Brezonik (1971). Nitrogen fixation by bacteria in Lake Mize, Florida, and in some lacustrine sediments. *Limnol. Oceanogr.*, 16:720–731.

Kellar, P. E. and H.W. Paerl (1980). Physiological adaptations in response to environmental stress during an N_2-fixing *Anabaena* bloom. *Appl. Environ. Microbiol.*, 40:587–595.

Kinner, N. E., D. L. Balkwill, and P. L. Bishop (1983). Light and electron microscopic studies of microorganisms growing in rotating biological contactor biofilms. *Appl. Environ. Microbiol.*, 45:1659–1669.

Klemer, A. R. (1976). The vertical distribution of *Oscillatoria aghardii* var. *isothrix*. *Arch. Hydrobiol.*, 78:343–362.

Klingensmith, K. M. and V. Alexander (1983). Sediment nitrification, denitrification, and nitrous oxide production in a deep arctic lake. *Appl. Environ. Microbiol.*, 46:1084–1092.

Kobayashi, M. (1975). Role of photosynthetic bacteria in foul water purification. *Prog. Water Technol.*, 7:309–315.

Konopka, A. (1980). Physiological changes within a metalimnetic layer of *Oscillatoria rubescens*. *Appl. Environ. Microbiol.*, 40:681–684.

Konopka, A. (1984). "Effect of light-nutrient interactions on bouyancy regulation by planktonic cyanobacteria," in M. J. Klug and C. A. Reddy, ed., *Current Perspective in Microbial Ecology*. American Society for Microbiology, Washington, D.C., pp. 41–48.

Konopka, A. and T. D. Brock (1978). Changes in photosynthetic rate and pigment content of blue-green algae in Lake Mendota. *Appl. Environ. Microbiol.*, 35:527–532.

Kuznetsov, S. I. (1970). *The Microflora of Lakes and its Geochemical Activity*. University of Texas Press, Austin.

Ladd, T. I., J. W. Costerton, and G. G. Geesey (1979). "Determination of the heterotrophic activity of epilithic microbial populations," in J. W. Costerton and R. R. Colwell, ed., *Native Aquatic Bacteria: Enumerations, Activity, and Ecology*. American Society for Testing and Materials, Philadelphia, pp. 180–195.

Langworthy, T. A. (1978). "Microbial life in extreme pH values," in D. J. Kushner, ed., *Microbial Life in Extreme Environments*. Academic, London, pp. 279–315.

Lazarek, S. (1980). Cyanophytan mat communities in acidified lakes. *Naturwissenschaften*, 67:97–98.

Lazarek, S. (1982a). Structure and function of a cyanophytan mat community in an acidified lake. *Can. J. Bot.*, 60:2235–2240.

Lazarek, S. (1982b). Structure and productivity of epiphytic algal communities on *Lobelia dortmanna* L. in acidified and limed lakes. *Water, Air, Soil Pollut.*, 18:333–342.

LeChevallier, M. W., S. C. Cameron, and G. A. McFeters (1983). New medium for improved recovery of coliform bacteria from drinking water. *Appl. Environ. Microbiol.*, 45:484–492.

Levinton, J. S., T. S. Bianchi, and S. Stewart (1984). What is the role of particulate organic matter in benthic invertebrate nutrition? *Bull. Marine Sci.*, 35:270–282.

Lewin, R. A. (1965). Freshwater species of *Saprospira*. *Can. J. Microbiol.*, **11**:135–139.

Lidstrom, M. E. and L. Somers (1984). Seasonal study of methane oxidation in Lake Washington. *Appl. Environ. Microbiol.*, **47**:1255–1260.

Lighthart, B. (1963). Sulfate-reducing bacteria in San Vicente Reservoir, San Diego County, California. *Limnol. Oceanogr.*, **8**:349–351.

MacGregor, A. N. and D. R. Keeney (1973). Methane formation by lake sediments during *in vitro* incubation. *Water Res. Bull.*, **9**:1153–1158.

Mah, R. A., D. M. Ward, L. Baresi, and T. L. Glass (1977). Biogenesis of methane. *Ann. Rev. Microbiol.*, **31**:309–341.

Maiden, F. J. and J. G. Jones (1984). Gliding motility of *Peloploca* spp., and their distribution in the sediment and water column of a eutrophic lake. *Arch. Microbiol.*, **140**:44–49.

Manning, H. L. (1975). New medium for isolating iron-oxidizing and heterotrophic acidophilic bacteria from acid mine drainage. *Appl. Microbiol.*, **30**:1010–1016.

Marshall, K. C. and R. H. Cruickshank (1973). Cell surface hydrophobicity and the orientation of certain bacteria at interfaces. *Arch. Mikrobiol.*, **91**:29–40.

Marshall, K. C., R. Stout, and R. Mitchell (1971). Mechanism of the initial events in the sorption of marine bacteria to surfaces. *J. Gen. Microbiol.*, **68**:337–348.

McCambridge, J. and T. A. McMeekin (1981). Effect of solar radiation and predacious microorganisms on survival of fecal and other bacteria. *Appl. Environ. Microbiol.*, **41**:1083–1087.

McCoy, W. F. and J.W. Costerton (1982). Growth of sessile *Sphaerotilus natans* in a tubular recycle system. *Appl. Environ. Microbiol.*, **43**:1490–1494.

McFeters, G. A., G. K. Bissonnette, J. J. Jezeski, C. A. Thomson, and D. G. Stuart (1974). Comparative survival of indicator bacteria and enteric pathogens in well water. *Appl. Microbiol.*, **27**:823–829.

McFeters, G. A. and D. G. Stuart (1972). Survival of coliform bacteria in natural waters: Field and laboratory studies with membrane-filter chambers. *Appl. Microbiol.*, **24**:805–811.

McFeters, G. A., S. A. Stuart, and S. B. Olson (1978a). Growth of heterotrophic bacteria and algal extracellular products in oligotrophic waters. *Appl. Environ. Microbiol.*, **35**:383–391.

McFeters, G. A., S. A. Stuart, and S. B. Olson (1978b). "Interactions of algae and heterotrophic bacteria in an oligotrophic stream," in M. W. Loutit and J. A. R. Miles, ed., *Microbial Ecology*. Springer-Verlag, New York, pp. 57–61.

McKee, H. S. (1962). *Nitrogen Metabolism in Plants*. Clarendon, Oxford.

Megard, R. O. and P. D. Smith (1974). Mechanisms that regulate growth rates of phytoplankton in Shagawa Lake, Minnesota. *Limnol. Oceanogr.*, **19**:279–296.

Mikhayenko, L. Y. and I. Y. Kulikova (1973). Interdependence of bacteria and blue-green algae. *Hydrobiol. J.*, **9**:32–38.

Montesinos, E., R. Guerrero, C. Abella, and I. Esteve (1983). Ecology and physiology of the competition for light between *Chlorobium limicola* and *Chlorobium phaeobacteroides* in natural habitats. *Appl. Environ. Microbiol.*, **46**:1007–1016.

Morris, G. K., C. M. Patton, J. C. Feeley, S. E. Johnson, G. Gorman, W. T. Martin, P. Skaliy, G. F. Mallison, B. D. Politi, and D. C. Mackel (1979). Isolation of the Legionnaires' disease bacterium from environmental samples. *Ann. Intern. Med.*, **90**:664–666.

Mosser, J. L. and T. D. Brock (1971). Effect of wide temperature fluctuation on the blue-green algae of Bead Geyser, Yellowstone National Park. *Limnol. Oceanogr.*, **16**:640–645.

Odum, E. P. (1971). *Fundamentals of Ecology.* Saunders, Philadelphia.

Olah, J., L. Hajdu, and K. Elekes (1972). Electron microscopic investigation of natural bacterial populations in the water and sediment of Lake Balaston and Lake Belso. *Ann. Inst. Biol.*, **39**:123–129.

Orrison, L. H., W. B. Cherry, and D. Milan (1981). Isolation of *Legionella pneumophila* from cooling tower water by filtration. *Appl. Environ. Microbiol.*, **41**:1202–1205.

Paerl, H. W. (1978). Role of heterotrophic bacteria in promoting N_2 fixation by *Anabaena* in aquatic habitats. *Microb. Ecol.*, **4**:215–231.

Paerl, H. W. (1982). *In situ* H_2 production and utilization by natural populations of N_2-fixing blue-green algae. *Can. J. Bot.*, **60**:2542–2546.

Paerl, H. W. (1983). Partitioning of CO_2 fixation in the colonial cyanobacterium *Microcystis aeruginosa:* mechanism promoting formation of surface scums. *Appl. Environ. Microbiol.*, **46**:252–259.

Paerl, H. W. and P. E. Kellar (1978). Significance of bacterial-*Anabaena* (Cyanophyceae) associations with respect to N_2 fixation in freshwater. *J. Phycol.*, **14**:254–260.

Paerl, H. W. and L. A. Mackenzie (1977). A comparative study of the diurnal carbon fixation patterns of nannoplankton and net plankton. *Limnol. Oceanogr.*, **22**:732–738.

Paerl, H. W. and J. F. Ustach (1982). Blue-green algal scums: An explanation for their occurrence during freshwater blooms. *Limnol. Oceanogr.*, **27**:212–217.

Paul, N. B. and W. V. B. Sundara Rao (1971). Phosphate-dissolving bacteria in the rhizosphere of cultivated legumes. *Plant Soil*, **35**:127–135.

Payne, W. J. (1973). Reduction of nitrogenous oxides by microorganisms. *Bacteriol. Rev.*, **37**:409–452.

Payne, W. J. (1981). *Denitrification.* Wiley, New York.

Phelps, T. J. and J. G. Zeikus (1984). Influence of pH on terminal carbon metabolism in anoxic sediments from a mildly acidic lake. *Appl. Environ. Microbiol.*, **48**:1088–1095.

Pierson, B. K. and R. W. Castenholz (1974). A phototrophic gliding filamentous bacterium of hot springs, *Chloroflexus aurantiacus* gen. and sp. nov. *Arch. Microbiol.*, **100**:5–24.

Poindexter, J. S. (1981). The caulobacters: ubiquitous unusual bacteria. *Microbiol. Rev.*, **45**:123–179.

Postgate, J. R. (1979). *The Sulphate-Reducing Bacteria.* Cambridge University Press, Cambridge.

Pringle, J. H. and M. Fletcher (1983). Influence of substratum wettability on attachment of freshwater bacteria to solid surfaces. *Appl. Environ. Microbiol.*, **45**:811–817.

Pye, V. I., R. Patrick, and J. Quarles (1983). *Groundwater Contamination in the United States.* University of Pennsylvania Press, Philadelphia.

Reasoner, D. J. (1982). Microbiology: Detection of bacterial pathogens and their occurrence. *J. Water Pollut. Control Fed.*, **54**:946–980.

Reed, W. M. and P. R. Dugan (1978). Distribution of *Methylomonas methanica* and *Methylosinus trichosporium* in Cleveland Harbor as determined by an indirect fluorescent antibody-membrane filter technique. *Appl. Environ. Microbiol.,* **35**:422–430.

Revsbech, N. P., B. B. Jorgensen, T. H. Blackburn, and Y. Cohen (1983). Microelectrode studies of the photosynthesis and O_2, H_2S, and pH profiles of a microbial mat. *Limnol. Oceanogr.,* **28**:1062–1074.

Revsbech, N. P., B. B. Jorgensen, and O. Brix (1981). Primary production of microalgae in sediments measured by oxygen microprofile, $H^{14}CO_3-$ fixation and oxygen exchange methods. *Limnol. Oceanogr.,* **26**:717–730.

Revsbech, N. P. and D. M. Ward (1984a). "Microprofiles of dissolved substances and photosynthesis in microbial mats measured with microelectrodes," in Y. Cohen, R. W. Castenholz, and H. O. Halvorson, eds., *Microbial Mats: Stromatolites.* Alan R. Liss, New York, pp. 171–188.

Revsbech, N. P. and D. M. Ward (1984b). Microelectrode studies of interstitial water chemistry and photosynthetic activity in a hot spring microbial mat. *Appl. Environ. Microbiol.,* **48**:270–275.

Reynolds, C. S. and A. E. Walsby (1975). Water-blooms. *Biol. Rev.,* **50**:437–481.

Rheinheimer, G. (1980). *Aquatic Microbiology.* Wiley, New York.

Rimon, A. and M. Shilo (1982). Factors which affect the intensification of fish breeding in Israel. *Bamidgeh,* **34**:87–100.

Rodina, A. G. (1963). Microbiology of detritus of lakes. *Limnol. Oceanogr.,* **8**:388–393.

Roinestad, F. A. and I. Yall (1970). Volutin granules in *Zoogloea ramigera. Appl. Microbiol.,* **19**:973–979.

Rudd, J. W. M., A. Furutani, R. J. Flett, and R. D. Hamilton (1976). Factors controlling methane oxidation in shield lakes: The role of nitrogen fixation and oxygen concentration. *Limnol. Oceanogr.,* **21**:357–364.

Rudd, J. W. M. and R. D. Hamilton (1978). Methane cycling in an eutrophic shield lake and its effects on whole lake metabolism. *Limnol. Oceanogr.,* **23**:337–348.

Rudd, J. W. M., R. D. Hamilton, and N. E. Campbell (1974). Measurement of microbial oxidation of methane in lake water. *Limnol. Oceanogr.,* **19**:519–524.

Rudd, J. W. M. and C. D. Taylor (1980). Methane cycling in aquatic environments. *Adv. Aquat. Microbiol.,* **2**:77–150.

Rychert, R. C. and G. R. Stephenson (1981). Atypical *Escherichia coli* in streams. *Appl. Environ. Microbiol.,* **41**:1276–1278.

Saralov, A. I., I. N. Krylova, E. E. Saralov, and S. I. Kuznetsov (1984). Distribution and species composition of methane-oxidizing bacteria in lake waters. *Microbiology,* **53**:695–700.

Sarkar, B. L., G. Balakrish, B. K. Sircar, and S. C. Pal (1983). Incidence and level of *Vibrio parahaemolyticus* associated with freshwater plankton. *Appl. Environ. Microbiol.,* **46**:288–290.

Schink, B. (1984). "Microbial degradation of pectin in plants and aquatic environments," in M. J. Klug and C. A. Reddy, ed., *Current Perspectives in Microbial Ecology.* American Society for Microbiology, Washington, D.C., pp. 580–587.

Schink, B. and J. G. Zeikus (1983). *Clostridium thermosulfurogenes* sp. nov., a new thermophile that produces elemental sulphur from thiosulphate. *J. Gen. Microbiol.,* **129**:1149–1158.

Schollhorn, R. and R. H. Burris (1966). Study of intermediates in nitrogen fixation. *Fed. Proc.,* **25**:710.

Seidler, R. J., D. A. Allen, H. Lockman, R. R. Colwell, S. W. Joseph, and O. P. Daily (1980). Isolation, enumeration, and characterization of *Aeromonas* from polluted waters encountered in diving operations. *Appl. Environ. Microbiol., 39*:1010–1018.

Sheldon, R. B., and C. W. Boylen (1975). Factors affecting the contribution by epiphytic algae to the primary productivity of an oligotrophic freshwater lake. *Appl. Microbiol., 30*:657–667.

Silvey, J. K. G., and J. T. Wyatt (1977). "The interrelationship between freshwater bacteria, algae, and actinomycetes in southwestern reservoirs," in J. Cairns, Jr., ed., *Aquatic Microbial Communities.* Garland, New York, pp. 161–203.

Singer, R., D. A. Roberts, and C. W. Boylen (1983a). The macrophytic community of an acidic lake in Adirondack (New York, U.S.A.): A new depth record for aquatic angiosperms. *Aquat. Bot., 16*:49–57.

Singer, R., D. A. Roberts, and C. W. Boylen (1983b). "The role of the benthic algal mat in annual nutrient cycling between the sediment and water of an acidic Adirondack lake," in C. D. Collins, ed., *The Lake George Ecosystem.* The Lake George Association, Lake George, NY, pp. 79–84.

Sjoblad, R. D. and R. N. Doetsch (1982). Absorption of polarly flagellated bacteria to surfaces. *Curr. Microbiol., 7*:191–194.

Sladek, K. J., R. V. Suslavich, B. I. Sohn, and F. W. Dawson (1975). Optimum membrane structures for growth of coliform and fecal coliform organisms. *Appl. Microbiol., 30*:685–691.

Staley, J. T. (1971). Incidence of prosthecate bacteria in a polluted stream. *Appl. Microbiol., 22*:496–502.

Stanier, R. Y. and G. Cohen-Bazier (1957). "The role of light in the microbial world: Some facts and speculations," in *Microbial Ecology, Seventh Symposia of the Society of General Microbiology.* Cambridge University Press, Cambridge, pp. 56–89.

Stanley, P. M. and E. L. Schmidt (1981). Serological diversity of *Nitrobacter* spp. from soil and aquatic habitats. *Appl. Environ. Microbiol., 41*:1069–1071.

Stark, W. H. and E. McCoy (1938). Distribution of bacteria in certain lakes of northern Wisconsin. *Zblt. Bakt., 98*:201–209.

Starkey, R. L. (1964). "Microbial transformations of some organic sulfur compounds," in H. Heukelekian and N. Dondero, ed., *Principles and Applications in Aquatic Microbiology.* Wiley, New York, pp. 405–429.

Starr, M. P. and V. B. D. Skerman (1965). Bacterial diversity: The natural history of selected morphologically unusual bacteria. *Ann. Rev. Microbiol., 19*:407–454.

Stewart, W. D. P., G. P. Fitzgerald, and R. H. Burris (1968). Acetylene reduction by nitrogen-fixing blue-green algae. *Arch. Mikrobiol., 62*:336–348.

Stockner, J. G. (1967). Observations of thermophilic algal communities in Mount Rainier and Yellowstone National Parks. *Limnol. Oceanogr., 12*:13–17.

Stokes, P. M. (1981). "Benthic algal communities in acidic lakes," in R. Singer, ed., *Effects of Acidic Precipitation on Benthos.* North American Benthological Society, Hamilton, N.Y., pp. 119–138.

Strayer, R. F. and J. M. Tiedje (1978). Application of the fluorescent-antibody technique to the study of a methanogenic bacterium in lake sediments. *Appl. Environ. Microbiol., 35*:192–198.

Stuart, S. A., G. A. McFeters, J. E. Schillinger, and D. G. Stuart (1976). Aquatic indicator bacteria in the high alpine zone. *Appl. Environ. Microbiol., 31*:163–167.

Stuiver, M. (1967). The sulfur cycle in lake waters during thermal stratification. *Geochim. Cosmochim. Acta.*, **31**:2151–2167.

Suberkropp, K. F. and M. J. Klug (1974). Decomposition of deciduous leaf litter in a woodland stream. I. A scanning electron microscopic study. *Microb. Ecol.*, **1**:96–103.

Swoager, W. C. and E. S. Lindstrom (1971). Isolation and counting of *Athiorhodaceae* with membrane filters. *Appl. Microbiol.*, **22**:683–687.

Sylvester-Bradley, R. (1976). Isolation of acetylene-reducing *Spirilla* from the roots of *Potamogeton filiformis* from Loch Leven (Kinross). *J. Gen. Microbiol.*, **97**:129–132.

Takahashi, M. and S. Ichimura (1970). Photosynthetic properties and growth of photosynthetic sulfur bacteria in lakes. *Limnol. Oceanogr.*, **15**:929–944.

Talling, J. F., R. B. Wood, M. V. Prosser, and R. M. Baxter (1973). The upper limit of photosynthetic productivity by phytoplankton: Evidence from Ethiopian soda lakes. *Freshwater Biol.*, **3**:53–76.

Taylor, J. and R. J. Parkes (1985). Identifying different populations of sulphate-reducing bacteria within marine sediment systems, using fatty acid biomarkers. *J. Gen. Microbiol.*, **131**:631–642.

Terai, H. and T. Yoshioka (1983). Serological study on seasonal and vertical distribution of specific denitrifying bacteria in Lake Kizaki. *Jpn. J. Limnol.*, **44**:81–92.

Tindall, B. J., A. A. Mills, and W. D. Grant (1980). An alkalophilic red halophilic bacterium with a low magnesium requirement from a Kenyan soda lake. *J. Gen. Microbiol.*, **116**:257–260.

Tison, D. L., D. H. Pope, W. B. Cherry, and C. B. Fliermans (1980). Growth of *Legionella pneumophila* in association with blue-green algae (cyanobacteria). *Appl. Environ. Microbiol.*, **39**:456–459.

Tison, D. L., E. W. Wilde, D. H. Pope, and C. B. Fliermans (1981). Productivity and species composition of algal mat communities exposed to a fluctuating thermal regime. *Microb. Ecol.*, **7**:151–165.

Truper, H. G. and S. Genovese (1968). Characterization of photosynthetic sulfur bacteria causing red water in Lake Faro (Messina, Sicily). *Limnol. Oceanogr.*, **13**:225–232.

Trust, T. J. and R. A. H. Sparrow (1974). The bacterial flora in the alimentary tract of freshwater salmonid fishes. *Can. J. Microbiol.*, **20**:1219–1228.

Van Niel, C. B. (1971). Techniques for the enrichment, isolation and maintenance of the photosynthetic bacteria. *Methods Enzymol.*, **23A**:3–28.

Van Ert, M., and J. T. Staley (1971a). A new gas vacuolated heterotrophic rod from freshwaters. *Arch. Mikrobiol.*, **80**:70–77.

Van Ert, M. and J. T. Staley (1971b). Gas vacuolated strains of *Microcyclus aquaticus. J. Bacteriol.*, **108**:236–240.

Varon, M. and M. Shilo (1980). Ecology of aquatic *Bdellovibrios. Adv. Aquat. Microbiol.*, **2**:1–48.

Vincent, W. F., C. L. Vincent, M. T. Downes, and P. J. Richerson (1985). Nitrate cycling in Lake Titicaca (Peru-Bolivia): The effect of high-altitude and tropicality. *Freshwater Biol.*, **15**:31–42.

Walter, M. R., J. Bauld, and T. D. Brock (1972). Siliceous algal and bacterial stromatolites in hot spring and geyser effluents of Yellowstone National Park. *Science,* **178**:402–405.

Walter, M. R., J. Bauld, and T. D. Brock (1976). "Microbiology and morphogenesis of columnar stromatolites *(Conophyton, Vacerrilla)* from hot springs in Yellowstone National Park," in M. R. Walter, ed., *Stromatolites.* Elsevier, Amsterdam, pp. 273–310.

Ward, D. M., E. Beck, N. P. Revsbech, K. A. Sandbeck, and M. R. Winfrey (1984). "Decomposition of hot spring microbial mats," in Y. Cohen, R. Castenholz, and H. Halvorson, ed., *Microbial Mats: Stromatolites.* Alan R. Liss, New York, pp. 191–214.

Weiss, R. L. (1973). Survival of bacteria at low pH and high temperature. *Limnol. Oceanogr.,* **18**:877–883.

Wetzel, R. G. (1983). *Limnology.* Saunders, Philadelphia.

Wetzel, R. G. and B. A. Manny (1972). Secretion of dissolved organic carbon and nitrogen by aquatic macrophytes. *Verh. Int. Ver. Limnol.,* **18**:162–170.

Whitton, B. A. and B. M. Diaz (1981). Influence of environmental factors on photosynthetic species composition in highly acidic waters. *Verh. Int. Ver. Limnol.,* **21**:1459–1465.

Wichlacz, P. L. and R. F. Unz (1981). Acidophilic, heterotrophic bacteria of acidic mine waters. *Appl. Environ. Microbiol.,* **41**:1254–1261.

Widdel, F. and N. Pfenning (1977). A new anaerobic, sporing, acetate-oxidizing sulfate-reducing bacterium, *Desulfotomaculum* (emend.) *acetoxidans. Arch. Microbiol.,* **112**:119–122.

Winfrey, M. R., D. R. Nelson, S. C. Klevickis, and J. G. Zeikus (1977). Association of hydrogen metabolism with methanogenesis in Lake Mendota sediments. *Appl.Environ. Microbiol.,* **33**:312–318.

Winfrey, M. R. and J. G. Zeikus (1977). Effect of sulfate on carbon and electron flow during microbial methanogenesis in freshwater sediments. *Appl. Environ. Microbiol.,* **33**:275–281.

Winfrey, M. R. and J. G. Zeikus (1979a). Microbial methanogenesis and acetate metabolism in a meromictic lake. *Appl. Environ. Microbiol.,* **37**:213–221.

Winfrey, M. R. and J. G. Zeikus (1979b). Anaerobic metabolism of immediate methane precursors in Lake Mendota. *Appl. Environ. Microbiol.,* **37**:244–253.

Woese, C. R. (1981). Archebacteria. *Sci. Am.,* **244**:98–122.

Wurtsbaugh, W. A. and A. J. Horne (1983). Iron in eutrophic Clear Lake, California: Its importance for algal nitrogen fixation and growth. *Can. J. Fish. Aquat. Sci.,* **40**:1419–1429.

Zeikus, J. G. (1977). The biology of methanogenic bacteria. *Bacteriol. Rev.,* **41**:514–541.

Zeikus, J. G. and M. R. Winfrey (1976). Temperature limitation of methanogenesis in aquatic sediments. *Appl. Environ. Microbiol.,* **31**:99–107.

Zinder, S. H., W. N. Doemel, and T. D. Brock (1977). Production of volatile sulfur compounds during the decomposition of algal mats. *Appl. Environ. Microbiol.,* **34**:859–860.

Zuberer, D. A. (1982). Nitrogen fixation (acetylene reduction) associated with duckweed (*Lemnaceae*) mats. *Appl. Environ. Microbiol.,* **43**:823–828.

9 SOIL MICROBIOLOGY AND AUTECOLOGICAL STUDIES

David H. Hubbell
Department of Soil Science
University of Florida
Gainesville, Florida

The objective of soil microbiological research is to achieve an understanding of the form and function of microbial populations in soil ecosystems. Aside from intellectual gratification and the satisfaction of scientific curiousity, the goal of such research is ultimately to manipulate these populations and, hence, their characteristic processes in a manner that is predictably beneficial and not detrimental to the welfare of mankind. Achievement of this broad objective is a formidable task in view of the daunting complexity of the seemingly infinite number of interacting soil microorganisms, soil types, and soil conditions. The problem faced by soil microbiologists is, therefore, primarily that of dealing with this complexity, both mentally and technologically.

Although there have been notable successes in manipulation of soil organisms (i.e., inoculation of legumes with *Rhizobium*), failures have predominated. The final solution to these multifaceted problems lies in the development of a more complete understanding of the microcosms that constitute the macrocosm. To achieve this objective, we must recognize the biological participants (microorganisms), comprehend the nature of their genetically and environmentally determined metabolic potential (biochemistry), and elucidate the necessary conditions for expression of that potential (interrelationships with other microorganisms and chemical and physical factors of the environment). When studied at the species level, these experiments enter the realm of autecology. The intellectual challenge is to devise experiments that will reveal this knowledge in a coherent manner. Development of appropriate technology or methodology has been a constant challenge to ingenuity, and major limitations still exist for many autecological soil studies. However, ideas are perhaps more often a limiting factor than is technology. Research questions must be clearly delineated before we can formulate appropriate ideas and devise sound experiments for their solution. Definition of the research problems clearly depends upon attainment of a certain minimum amount of basic information descriptive of the ecosystem. We must understand ecosystem components in order to evaluate their function as part of the total ecosystem. It is for this reason that autecological research is of paramount importance to soil microbiology.

Autecology, the study of an organism in relation to its environment (as opposed to synecology as the study of populations or processes in relation to the environment), is an artificial discipline. A soil microorganism rarely, if ever, has the luxury of living in pure culture *in vivo*. Thus, since microbial growth and the resultant effects of that growth on ecosystem properties are controlled by both the microbe's biotic and abiotic interactions within the ecosystem, evaluation of microbial activity in mixed cultures rather than pure (axenic) cultures is more representative of the true conditions in the native sample. This complexity of the microbial community limits our success in describing the biotic interactions in a native sample due to the myriad of complex and dynamic interactions occurring between microorganisms and their environment. One approach to reducing this complexity is to dissect the ecosystem into component parts and evaluate their activity individually under varying abiotic conditions. For example, the microbial community could be reduced to axenic cultures of the individual species present. Their growth and survival may then be studied under a variety of defined conditions. Subsequently, these axenic cultures could be combined into well-defined groups and population ratios for a study of their behavior under the same physical and chemical conditions which were used in the axenic studies, except a measurable degree of biotic interactions are allowed. This at least permits us to identify the characteristics of the individual microbial species and to define their genetic limitations or potential for expression of these characteristics under conditions observed in the native sample. By this means we can gradually attain a more complete understanding of the complex interactions in the native soil sample. Such autecological approaches to experimentation in soil microbiology have, in recent years, resulted in noteworthy advances in many areas. However, effort and/or achievement have lagged in many other areas.

The objective of this chapter is to highlight some of the successes and failures in autecological research on soil ecosystems and to explore some possible reasons for the status quo in relation to present and future research. There is no pretension to complete coverage of the appropriate literature in this effort. The topics mentioned are a reflection of personal knowledge, bias, and judgment. The discussions are intentionally of a generalized nature and no attempt has been made to produce a detailed review of the relevant literature. Instead, recent and enlightening books, reviews, and key research papers are cited. Sincere apologies are extended to the many scientists whose excellent works are not mentioned here. This work is largely an amalgam of their ideas.

1.0. SOIL-MICROBE INTERACTIONS

The problem of the relationship of microorganisms to various components of their soil microhabitats is of basic importance. For example, questions of nutrient source and concentrations, foci of plant root infection, survival, colonization, dissemination, and so on, are relevant to microbial growth and survival (Stotzky, 1980). These questions have been frequently addressed and are eminently approachable autecologically. An example of this is Lowendorf's comprehensive review of factors affecting the survival of *Rhizobium* (Lowendorf, 1980). Of a more general nature is the impact of clays on microbial function. Marshall (1975) discussed the effects of clays on microbial activity. He reminds us that even in soil, microbes interact with a system of particulates in an aqueous environment and he indicates specifically how "clays modify the physicochemical status of the microhabitat which, in turn, modifies the microbial balance within the ecosystem."

An example of an economically important clay-microbe interaction was provided by study of a banana wilt disease in Central and South America, caused by *Fusarium oxysporum* f. *cubense,* a soil-borne fungus. Stotzky and co-workers (Stotzky, 1980) have conducted a long and continuing series of autecological studies of numerous facets of this problem. Initial work involved correlation of the spread of the disease (fungus) with clay mineralogical properties. A soil clay, montmorillonite, was shown to promote the growth of disease suppressive bacterial populations. These studies are exemplary in demonstrating what comprehensive and carefully designed autecological experiments can do to place information from laboratory studies in context with field observations and experiments.

The basic information obtained from these autecological studies of clay-microbe interactions may ultimately contribute significantly to an explanation of the development of hydrophobicity of some coarse-textured soils under certain environmental conditions. These sandy soils are characteristically of low clay content. High populations of basidiomycete fungi have been correlated with development of the water-repellent condition, although more recent autecological studies implicate volatile compound(s) from an actinomycete(s) as a contributor to this soil hydrological problem. The water-repellent condition is easily detected under field conditions, but the economic repercussions resulting from poor water penetration (irrigation or rainfall) and consequent drought stress of plants is neither obvious nor well documented. However, data suggest a role for water repellency in the etiology of citrus blight in Florida. Rhoads (1936) observed adverse effects of such "oily" soils on growth of citrus. Subsequently, Jamison (1942, 1946) was able to alleviate the water-repellent condition by amendment of the sands with montmorillonite. The adverse effects of water repellency on soil moisture relations in the root zone of crops may represent a major stress factor inimical to plant vigor, thus predisposing the crop to root infection by opportunistic, normally saprophytic soil-borne pathogens. This problem certainly warrants more extensive autecological study. Both case histories of banana wilt and citrus blight are excellent examples of serious economic problems that demonstrate the need of and potential for autecological studies in solving soil microbiological problems.

A variety of soil properties adversely affect biological interactions. Sandy soils frequently provide an inhospitable environment for the roots of most crops, that is, those not especially adapted. This can generally be attributed to poor moisture and nutrient retention, often accompanied by low organic matter content and poor "biological buffering", that is, low microbial populations and species diversity. In situations where adequate moisture is available from rainfall or irrigation, these barren soils can be made productive by the addition of various amendments such as montmorillonitic clay, humus, or organic matter, such as compost. All of these materials ameliorate the negative properties of the sandy soils in part as a result of their colloidal size and high cation exchange capacity (Gardner et al., 1975). In general, the addition of various soil-modifying amendments has not been extensively studied with regard to real or potential effects on soil microbe equilibria. This is a prime example where commercial soil amendments, which are most likely not only scientifically but also economically unfeasible, have been produced and used in total disregard for, or in most cases, knowledge of their true effect on the soil microbial community. Specific inorganic and organic amendments (Gardner et al., 1975) in liquid or solid form and in varying concentration may be added to soil; this practice should be avoided without some reasonable information regarding probable or possible repercussions in the soil microbial community. Population studies purporting to indicate changes (or lack of change) in broad, nonspecific groups of microorganisms in response to application of such compounds are generally noninformative in their underestimation of numbers and lack of identification of specific qualitative changes in the microflora. Initial autecological studies such as those already mentioned (Stozky, 1980) would be most beneficial.

This discussion of water-repellent soils and soil amendments provides some indication of the impact of variation of soil physical and chemical properties on microbial activity. This topic is discussed in greater detail in a number of reviews (Chapman, 1965; Davey and Danielson, 1968; Ramey, 1965; Hattori and Hattori, 1976; Stolzy and van Gundy, 1968).

1.1. Equilibria of Soil Microbe Populations

Although the complexity of soil-microbe systems makes them difficult to study and understand, there is a redeeming aspect. The more biologically complex or diverse a system is (i.e., the greater the species diversity), the more "biologically buffered" it is. It may be stated that in most soil systems the microbial community is at equilibrium. The microbial populations therein consist of active and inactive propagules. Many of the inactive organisms are viable, but the conditions are not conducive for the expression of their activity. But, as environmental conditions (biotic and abiotic) are altered, inactive propagules may commence active growth and metabolism. Thus, by replacing a previously functional population inhibited by the newly imposed environmental conditions the continuity of biological function is preserved, albeit the actual microbial species catalyzing the process is different. For example, nitrogen fixation catalyzed by *Azotobacter* in aerobic soil is precluded when the soil is flooded if anaerobic conditions are established. However, the nitrogen fixation process may continue, but it is catalyzed by anaerobic *Clostridium* species.

There are numerous other examples of the continuation of a process in a soil system, mediated by different microbial populations in response to alterations in soil conditions that are either conducive or inimical to the growth–activity of one or another component of the soil microflora. One may infer from the ubiquity of this type of phenomenon that the concepts of molecular recalcitrance and microbial infallibility (Alexander, 1965) hold true largely in practice if not in theory, at least in regard to degradation of biologically synthesized molecules. The concept of microbial infallibility means that for each organic compound there exists a microbial population capable of mineralizing it. For many organic compounds a single microbial population capable of total mineralization of the molecular structure does not exist. For such compounds, the metabolic end products of one organism–substrate combination may become the substrate of other microbes as soil conditions change. However, for chemically synthesized molecules, many of which are toxic and highly resistant to biodegradation, the situation is different. In cases where biodegradation pathways for such a compound are nonexistent or inordinately slow, avenues of escape from the adverse and cumulative effects of environmental pollution, such as cometabolism and nonbiological degradation, may not be effective.

1.2. Engineered Organisms versus Natural Isolates

What can we do to reassure ourselves that changing soil conditions and/or substrates will not combine with a soil microflora that is not effectively responsive in terms of biodegradation, thereby leading to toxic accumulations of nonbiodegradable compounds? A solution to accumulation of nonbiodegradable compounds in native ecosystems involves inoculation of the contaminated site with either variants of native populations with the desired metabolic traits or construction of the requisite population through genetic engineering procedures.

In a relatively short period of time, genetic engineering has progressed to the point where genetic information can be moved, almost at will, within and between species of widely varying degrees of relatedness. This superb technology engendered the hope (belief?) that scientists may be able to "engineer" microbes capable of degrading virtually any organic molecule, whether biologically or chemically synthesized. It is frequently assumed from this that the new organism, introduced into a polluted environment in large numbers, will cleanse the system.

The general assumption is at least potentially valid and certainly merits the efforts expended to explore such possibilities. However, this new technology may not always translate into good science. The new or "engineered" organism may do more or less than we expect it to do. In some cases, we may have unwittingly added or deleted more information through modification of the microbe's "genetic machinery" than was intended. In other cases, the alterations may result in disruption of critical relationships between genes. In any event, the variants obtained are predetermined or selected by the defined and controlled conditions of growth imposed in the laboratory. This represents but a single point in the continuum of conditions to which the microbes are subjected in nature. This genetic engineering approach has the greatest possibility for success in relatively discrete or closed systems where alternate or "nontarget" substrates are absent or in low concentration and where environmental conditions conducive to the desired biodegradation process are to some degree amenable to control. Changes in the genetics of a microorganism that are directed, monitored, and understood are often accompanied by unintentional changes that are not obvious in a stable laboratory environment and remain undetected. Upon inoculation into the target soil site, interaction of these unrecognized genetically altered characteristics with the dynamically varying conditions of the soil ecosystems result in rapid death of the introduced organism or a microbial imbalance that creates a new, perhaps unanticipated, problem. In either event, the inoculation is a failure. It is extremely naive to believe that engineered organisms are a current and workable, quick and easy solution to all or even most biodegradation problems. The genetically altered strains resulting from such studies must be stringently characterized in vivo prior to any thought of release. Creation and release of such organisms should be considered a potential economically invaluable possibility, but it must be approached with all due caution in view of potential risks.

The evolution of this type of concern has been concisely documented (Brill, 1985; Baum, 1984) and is exemplified by the controversy over proposed field testing of genetically altered *Pseudomonas syringae* as a biological control agent for suppression of frost damage to crops caused by its ice nucleation-active parent (Federal Register, 1984). Minimizing the potential hazard may be difficult when the parent organism is of a genus that already has some reputation, however slight, as a pathogen of plants, animals, or man.

This is not an attempt to condemn or minimize the aims, achievements, and potential of genetic engineering. It is a reminder that this approach is not a panacea for pollution problems that can be realistically anticipated in the foreseeable future. In the meantime, much valuable information can be obtained using simple, inexpensive methodology, similar to that used to excellent advantage by generations of our predecessors. We do science and society a disservice by ignoring old, simple but successful experimental methods in favor of more "prestigious" biotechnological methodology.

The ordinary procedures of isolation of unique or special organisms by enrichment techniques, followed by mass culture and, finally, inoculation into a particular environment, still retain theoretical validity and practical feasibility. But the success of such approaches depends largely on our basic knowledge of the organism and its environment. This information generally comes most readily from autecological studies.

To increase the probability of a successful inoculation of a soil ecosystem, conventional wisdom indicates that a specific organism desired for reinoculation into a field environment be isolated from that same environment. The rationale for this seems logical; such organisms should be adapted to the idiosyncrasies of that particular environment and, when reinoculated, should encounter less difficulty in surviving and establishing at desired levels. An example might be the selection of *Rhizobium* for tolerance to extremes of pH, temperature, and so on. Although this assumption is reasonable for a specific site or type of ecosystem, its general acceptance or applicability would create problems for development of inoculants for widespread use. Fortunately, this relationship between source and site of intended use is not always observed in the field. For example, most of the *Rhizobium* strains authorized for use as commercial legume inoculants in Australia were isolated in other countries. This underscores our ignorance of what determines a competitive strain of a microorganism. We may ultimately conclude that competitive ability is attributable to different factors or microbial properties under different environmental conditions. In-depth autecological studies using well-characterized microbial strains in combination with well-controlled environmental parameters might improve the success rate of soil inoculation and our understanding of "competition."

Man may choose any environment that he wishes for the introduction of a particular microorganism but the environment ultimately determines the fate of the organism, regardless of the nature of its origin. Natural processes of mutation and selection determine whether the organism does or does not change. These last two variables cannot be controlled through anthropogenic manipulation. Success of a microbe introduced into a new environment may depend on the genetic versatility of the organism. How prone is the organism to alter its genetic program to provide a large number of variants from which the environment may select those fit to survive? An organism carrying several exchangeable plasmids, for example, might prove highly competitive in many different situations. Genetic studies of some soil microorganisms of note are well underway (Beringer et al., 1984; Elmerich, 1984).

Until such time as these concerns can be resolved, we must continue to utilize the time-honored alternative to using genetically altered microbes as a means of biological control of pests, biodegradation of pollutants, and so on. We must accept on faith the concept of microbial infallibility and assume the natural occurrence of at least low numbers of the required microbe. This microbe, "one of Nature's own," is isolated, purified, grown in mass culture, and used to inoculate the problem environment.

In essence, this process uses a microorganism that already possesses the genetic capability of catalyzing a desired process but fails to do so in vivo due to environmental restrictions. Isolation and study of such organisms often results in identification of environmental conditions, such as pH, aeration, moisture, or substrate, which can be changed or imposed to support greater growth – activity of the indigenous, genetically unaltered organism. For example, strains of rhizobia with high ability to infect, nodulate, and fix nitrogen in compatible legume host plants may fail to do so under acid soil conditions; the expected symbiotic association is successfully established in many cases by the simple expedient of liming the soil to a near-neutral pH. The problem is not one of numbers of organisms but of a soil condition (pH), which is critical for establishment – function of the desired process. Obviously, there is no quick and easy cure for microbe-related soil problems. However, with patience and knowledge, the rate of success of such traditional approaches might be much greater than we currently appreciate. Bull (1980) gives a critical and thought-provoking appraisal of autecological approaches to the study of biodegradation.

1.3. Time Constraints

Does time permit any individual microbiologist to deal effectively in the laboratory with problems that have taken or will take many years to materialize perceptibly in nature? Such problems as environmental effects of xenobiotics (Rodriguez-Kabana and Curl, 1980) and the impact of acid rain (Evans, 1984) are prominent examples. Autecological studies of such phenomena are frequently called into question as being too far removed from reality and, therefore, not likely to provide much information of predictive value. The cumulative events of many years in a soil environment are difficult to condense into a laboratory study lasting a few years at best, but we must try. The importance of time as a limiting factor in these approaches can at least be reduced by more stringent efforts to avoid problems. An example of avoidance would be the exercise of care in the release of xenobiotics into an environment that may not be fully prepared, microbiologically, to dispose of them.

1.4. Information Constraints

The extent of our knowledge about the form and function (and numbers!) of microorganisms in natural environments may be the most serious factor limiting our ability to manipulate microbial populations to our benefit. It is axiomatic that soil microorganisms exist generally under stress conditions. Yet there is relatively little information available on the mechanisms by which various microbes persist under such conditions. Evidence indicates that the vast majority of soil microbes are seldom detected or isolated by conventional (and often crude) techniques and, hence, never studied in any regard. We seldom study in the laboratory (autecologically) that which may be of major importance in native soil samples (synecologically). Of what significance are such considerations as form (filterable forms, dwarf cells, minicells, etc.), extremes of one or more environmental conditions, limiting nutrients, and so on? It seems that large numbers of microbes survive in the soil, largely unrecognized and/or ignored (Casida, 1983). Only strong emphasis on autecological approaches, that is, isolation and the study of these organisms under approximate natural conditions, will reduce this critical gap in our knowledge. We cannot hope to control the microbes in their "home" without knowing who is home, how many are home, and what they are doing and/or are capable of doing. The elegant electron microscopy study of in vivo soil and rhizosphere environments by Foster et al. (1983) provides revealing insights for future autecological studies.

1.5. Biological Constraints

Direct alteration of soil microbial equilibria via inoculation has achieved some noteworthy success, such as *Rhizobium* inoculation of legumes, ectomycorrhiza inoculation of a variety of plants, and inoculation for biological control. However, the failures far outnumber the successes. Many such studies fail for reasons that are not intuitively obvious, that is, the inoculated organism merely does not establish and maintain itself at the population density necessary for the desired effect. In other cases, inoculation fails for reasons that should have been obvious beforehand. The early Russian experiments with Azotobacterin and Phosphobacterin are almost legendary examples of such studies. Large populations of *Azotobacter* or *Bacillus megaterium* were added to soils with objectives of increasing nitrogen fixation and phosphorus solubilization, respectively. Although growth parameters of these common soil bacteria were known, the soil environment was not modified so that it would support a high population density of the inoculated organisms. Also, the organisms were already present in the soil in low numbers. Increase in these indigenous populations was previously prevented by the abiotic soil conditions. Thus, data interpretation is complicated by questions of whether amended populations were established or whether indigenous populations were stimulated. Alternatively, plant nutrients may have been derived from the death and mineralization of the soil amendments. To compound the confusion, the few positive results that have proven reproducible are now attributed not to the anticipated nitrogen fixation or phosphorus solubilization, but to production of plant growth-promoting substances. Liberation of these substances in the crop rhizosphere enhanced crop root development and eventually gave increased plant survival and greater yield via enhanced nutrient uptake (Brown, 1974). Interestingly, this entire scenario has been repeated in more recent attempts to achieve agronomically significant nitrogen fixation via inoculation-assisted enhancement of rhizosphere-associated *Azospirillum* (Gaskins et al., 1985). Again, confusion was inevitable due to trial-and-error inoculation methods. Extension of conventional inoculation methods derived from studies of the *Rhizobium*-legume system was largely unsuccessful due to high variability between experiments and absence of basic information on the nature of the system (van Berkum and Bohlool, 1980). As with the *Azotobacter* and *Bacillus* studies cited, use of various autecological approaches has again shown that the occasional beneficial inoculation responses resulted from plant growth hormone production by *Azospirillum.* The erroneous attribution of observable yield increases to nitrogen fixation resulted from inappropriate use of the acetylene reduction assay as a quantitative estimate of nitrogenase activity and nitrogen fixed as a result of inoculation (van Berkum and Bohlool, 1980).

The question of potential application of *Azospirillum* remains controversial, but there is reason for hope. Much pertinent information remains to be obtained from autecological studies of associative nitrogen fixing systems. In the meantime, credible evidence indicates the existence of genetically determined variability between plant genotypes in relative ability to support the establishment of measurably beneficial (agronomically significant) plant root-microorganism associations (Day, 1977; Olsen et al., 1981). Once autecological studies have defined the plant and microbial requirements for establishment of such systems, the plant breeders may proceed rationally in a systematic effort to obtain plant genotypes exhibiting a physiology known to fulfill the requirements of known beneficially associative microorganisms now recognized as normal soil inhabitants.

The consideration of inoculation in a broad context, that is, as related to enhancement of plant – microbe interactions resulting in symbiosis, biological control of disease, and so on, is of paramont importance. The point has been made numerous times that the quality and quantity of rhizosphere microflora of a particular plant is primarily a function of the biochemistry and physiology of the roots of that plant, as expressed under normal growing conditions. The plant root is, in essence, a unique selective medium. The nature of this medium is genetically determined and is consistent with observed differences in the root microflora between genotypes. It follows that the increasingly sophisticated and effective technology of plant breeding and selection should enable us to produce plant genotypes with characteristics capable of enhancing a specific beneficial rhizosphere microflora. Such custom-made rhizosphere populations may circumvent the necessity for inoculation. Identification of these interacting characteristics in plants and their associated microflora will require autecological studies utilizing extensive interdisciplinary cooperation.

The checkered history of inoculation attempts contains many more examples of failure that are similar but, by their nature, less forgivable. This refers to a variety of commercial inoculant preparations, generally referred to as "soil activators," which are characteristically vaguely defined in terms of composition and mechanism of action but lavishly described in terms of their ability to revolutionize agriculture via enhanced crop yields (McAllister, 1983). Some combination of soil microbes, having demonstrated beneficial effects *in vitro,* are frequently implied to be responsible. However, the number of microbes applied at recommended rates categorically mitigates against any lasting effect on plant growth or ultimate statistically significant increase in crop yield. *Caveat emptor.*

In some cases, conclusive, large-scale, field inoculation experiments are generally impossible or impractical due to our inability to grow the microbe in mass culture. An important example is that of vesicular-arbuscular mycorrhizal (VAM) fungi, now known to establish endotrophic symbiotic associations in and on the roots of virtually every known agronomically important crop plant (and most other herbs and shrubs), where they play a vital role in enhancing root uptake of phosphorus in soils that are low in available phosphorus. Analogous to the *Rhizobium*-legume system, the host plant knows more about the nutrition of these fungi than do we. Extensive testing of VAM inoculation awaits definition of their nutritional requirements in vitro. The collaboration of plant physiologists and microbiologists should be most productive.

2.0. PLANT-MICROBE ASSOCIATIONS

Study of the symbiotic nitrogen fixing association between *Rhizobium* species and compatible leguminous host plants presents an interesting case history of successful inoculation. This plant – bacteria system has been successfully manipulated and agronomically exploited for hundreds of years, in spite of the relative absence of extensive basic knowledge of the system and the lack of sophisticated supporting technology. However, the benefits accruing from legume inoculation practices based initially on pragmatic experimentation and, belatedly, on incomplete understanding of the system have reached something of a plateau. The process of isolating a strain of *Rhizobium* and testing it for efficacy (superior nodulation and nitrogen fixing abilities) as a potential inoculant strain is still a laborious process. All too frequently, strains that have proven to be highly infective in laboratory, growth chamber, and greenhouse studies have failed miserably in subsequent field trials. We cannot quickly and reliably isolate *Rhizobium* from a soil or rhizosphere environment using conventional selective culture methods. Embarrassingly, under reasonable plant growth conditions, a compatible leguminous host plant accomplishes this selection with apparent ease. We may take this as a reflection of our general ignorance of critical details of the physiology and biochemistry of host roots and rhizobia and how they interact at this level to achieve a successful association. This information is a prerequisite to our understanding of such questions as how the plant is infected, how nodules are induced, and how the nitrogen fixation process is initiated. The system is quite unique in the realm of biology, and one may infer that certain comparably unique traits govern its establishment. If we could identify these critical traits, we might reasonably expect to devise quicker and better methods for selection and testing of strains of rhizobia without having to rely on the host plant. Some dramatic advances in understanding the molecular basis for the successful establishment — recognition, binding, infection — of plant-microbe associations have occurred in the last ten years (Dazzo and Hubbell, 1982; Keen and Holliday, 1982). This has been due to new concepts, such as the common antigen theory, and to the application of improved sensitive techniques for separation and detection of components (chromatographic, electrophoretic, microscopic, immunological, etc., and their numerous combinations). The development of a simple glass slide culture method, permitting direct microscopic observation of legume root hair infection by rhizobia (Fahraeus, 1957), was instrumental in reawakening interest in this critical process. Since that time the ultimate role of lectins, exopolysaccharides, enzymes, phytohormones, and so on, in the infection process has been studied in some depth (Bauer, 1981). Continued exploration of these questions using defined systems and conditions will surely lead us to a reasonable understanding of and control over this symbiotic system as it occurs in nature.

Another symbiotic nitrogen fixing plant-microbe association, that of the actinomycete *Frankia* with certain nonleguminous plants, has stimulated greatly renewed interest and research activity (Torrey and Tjepkema, 1979). This is due largely to the recent development of methods for the isolation and *in vitro* cultivation of the microsymbiont, *Frankia.* Perhaps one of the most interesting results obtained from these studies is the evidence that one or more "helper organisms," common bacterial rhizosphere inhabitants, appear to assist in the process of root infection by *Frankia,* although the helper itself does not infect (Knowlton et al., 1980).

The overall process of root infection by *Rhizobium, Frankia,* or vesicular-arbuscular mycorrhizal fungi is more than superficially similar. Perhaps the possible role of helper organisms should be studied in depth in all three of these systems, as well as in other important plant root–microbe associations (e.g., pathogenic). Such information could have a major impact in terms of potential improvement in inoculation technology for legumes, biocontrol of plant pathogens, and so on. The existence of such complex interactions should not come as a surprise in view of the diversity of microorganisms compatibly inhabiting the same rhizosphere–rhizoplane habitat. Many of these questions of rhizosphere microbiology can and should be addressed experimentally in laboratory studies using defined systems. Plants may be unwieldy as experimental organisms in the laboratory, but not in all cases. Such techniques as slide culture (Fahraeus, 1957), mist box (Zobel et al., 1976), membrane bag (Brown and Anwar-Ul-Haq, 1984), and tissue culture (Torrey, 1978) have high potential in autecological studies of plant–microorganism relationships.

Autecological studies are invaluable as a means of defining the biological nature and environmental requirements of a soil microbial process but they are not infallible. Laboratory studies of such problems can never do more than represent an approximation of reality. However, they are a necessary prelude to field testing hypothetical solutions to these problems. Such studies are invaluable in determining the nature of the field tests to be conducted. But, laboratory and/or greenhouse tests cannot be substituted for well designed field tests since in a number of cases, strains whose laboratory and greenhouse results suggest they would be ideal for field use, have proven to be dismal failures in the field. Again, a common example is that of field testing of the *Rhizobium* strains isolated, tested, and selected for high ability to infect, nodulate, and fix nitrogen in a host plant. The majority of such strains fail when tested for efficacy as legume inoculants under field conditions. They usually colonize the legume rhizosphere but do not compete adequately with indigenous soil rhizobia in ability to nodulate the host plant. This problem will perhaps be solved when we identify characteristics of rhizobia that are critical for root infection and find ways of screening for these characteristics in the laboratory.

As can be seen by this limited discussion, soil microbe–plant interactions have great economic value. For a more complete discussion of the topic, see the review by Dommergues and Krupa (1978).

3.0. INTERACTIONS BETWEEN MICROORGANISMS

Sustained growth and activity of microorganisms in the soil depends upon the presence of suitable substrate(s) and biotic and abiotic conditions that permit their utilization. Assuming adequacy of these two requirements, the factor most likely to influence soil microbes and processes is that of microbe–microbe interactions, usually discussed ambiguously under the umbrella term of "competition." This term is unsatisfactory in that it includes only negative interactions such as parasitism, predation, antibiosis, and competition for substrate. It ignores such positive interactions as cross feeding. One plausible explanation for this omission may be that the negative interactions are more readily recognized and perhaps more conveniently or definitively studied in vitro (e.g., hyperparasitism, antibiosis). In any event, competition between microorganisms in the soil is not understood, probably because a competitive effect in any one situation is due to a combination of causes not duplicated precisely in any other situation. Therefore, the precise repetition or predictability of any situation is a hopeless prospect. The best that we can hope for is to isolate the microbe(s) involved and study their interaction with a broad range of defined chemical, physical, and biological factors that appear to be most influential in nature.

A practical example of microbial competition in soil involves plant disease. In certain soils, biological and/or abiotic soil properties prevent the development and spread of specific plant diseases. The phenomenon of "disease suppressive soils" has been formalized with a descriptive name and an excellent treatise (Schneider, 1982). Numerous factors, few if any of which may be mutually exclusive, have been implicated in their etiology. They seem to fall into the general category of interactions between microorganisms that result in biological control of plant disease. These interactions are difficult to recognize, define, and study in a natural environment. The role of siderophores, agrocin, and other mechanisms of biological buffering, should be studied autecologically in some detail as a prelude to attempting induction of "suppressive" soils by soil amendment and/or inoculation.

4.0. CONCLUSIONS

Two of the greatest problems facing society today are environmental deterioration and food production. An integral part of both of these problems is the role played by soil microorganisms. The best solution to such problems is to prevent them. That should be the primary charge of science in general and soil microbiologists in particular — to anticipate and thereby circumvent such problems. In a discouraging number of cases it is already too late. Many problems are in full bloom and we must divert a substantial amount of our total scientific effort to the solution of problems that we have created. Can we learn from our mistakes? Truly, if we do not read history seriously, and with understanding, we will repeat it.

A paramount lesson of history is that nature is indifferent to the desires of mankind. Biological systems cannot be manipulated outside of the constraints of genetics and environment. We have historically attempted manipulation of biological systems with little or no regard for either constraint. This lack of regard is based on ignorance. We can no longer afford the luxury of uninformed manipulation. Knowledge of biological systems is the prerequisite to their successful manipulation without concomitant creation of new problems. We must obtain greater understanding of these systems and their relation to the environment before we attempt large-scale alteration of either. We must appreciate from history that we cannot change any one of the chemical, physical, or biological components of the soil ecosystem without changing the others to some degree. The surest means of achieving knowledge and understanding of microbial roles in soil ecosystems is to bring the organisms into the laboratory and study them patiently and thoroughly under controlled conditions of environment reflecting the range of conditions to which they may be subjected in nature. Such is the role and scope of autecology.

REFERENCES

Alexander, M. (1965). Biodegradation: Problems of molecular recalcitrance and microbial infallibility. *Adv. Appl. Microbiol.,* 7:35–80.

Bauer, W. D. (1981). Infection of legumes by rhizobia. *Annu. Rev. Plant Physiol.,* 32:407–449.

Baum, R. M. (1984). Genetic engineering engulfed in new environmental debate. *Chem. Eng. News,* 15–22.

Brill, W. J. (1985). Safety concerns and genetic engineering in agriculture. *Science,* 227:381–384.

Beringer, J. E., N. J. Brewin, and A. W. B. Johnston (1984). "Genetics," in W. J. Broughton, ed., *Nitrogen Fixation* Vol. 2, *Rhizobium,* Chapter 5, Clarendon, Oxford, pp. 167–181.

Brown, D. A. and Anwar-UL-Haq (1984). A porous membrane-root culture technique for growing plants under controlled soil conditions, *Soil Sci. Soc. Am. J.,* 48:692–695.

Brown, M. E. (1974). Seed and root bacterization, *Annu. Rev. Phytopath,* 12:181–197.

Bull, A. T. (1980). "Biodegradation: Some attitudes and strategies of microorganisms and microbiologists," in D. C. Ellwood, J. N. Hedger, M. J. Latham, J. M. Lynch and J. H. Slater, eds., *Contemporary Microbial Ecology,* Academic Press, New York, pp. 107–138.

Casida, L. E., Jr. (1983). Interaction of *Agromyces ramosus* with other bacteria in soil. *Appl. Environ. Microbiol.*, **46**:881–888.

Chapman, H. O. (1965). "Chemical factors of the soil as they affect microorganisms," in K. F. Baker and W. C. Snyder, eds., *Ecology of Soil-Borne Plant Pathogens.* University of California Press, Berkeley, pp. 120–139.

Davey, C. G. and R. M. Danielson (1968). Soil chemical factors and biological activity. *Phytopathology,* **58**:900–907.

Day, P. R. (1977). Plant genetics: Increasing crop yield. *Science,* **197**:1334–1339.

Dazzo, F. B. and D. H. Hubbell (1982). "Control of root hair infection," in W. J. Broughton, ed., *Nitrogen Fixation* Vol. 2, *Rhizobium,* Chapter 9, Clarendon, Oxford, pp. 274–311.

Dommergues, Y. R. and S. V. Krupa (1978). *Interactions Between Non-pathogenic Soil Microorganisms and Plants.* Elsevier, New York, p. 475.

Elmerich, C. (1984). Molecular biology and ecology of diazotrophs associated with non-leguminous plants. *Biotechnology,* **2**:967–978.

Evans, L. S. (1984). Acidic precipitation effects on terrestrial vegetation. *Annu. Rev. Phytopathol.,* **22**:397–420.

Fahraeus, G. (1957). The infection of clover root hairs by nodule bacteria studied by a simple glass slide technique. *J. Gen. Microbiol.,* **16**:374–381.

Foster, R. C., A. D. Rovira, and T. W. Cook (1983). *Ultrastructure of the Root-Soil Interface.* American Phytopathology Society, St. Paul, p. 157.

Gardner, W. R. et al., (eds.) (1975). *Soil Conditioners.* SSSA Special Publication Series No. 7. Soil Science Society of America, Inc., Madison, p. 186.

Gaskins, M. H., S. L. Albrecht, and D. H. Hubbell (1985). Rhizosphere bacteria and their use to increase plant productivity. *Agric. Ecosystems Environment,* **12**:99–116.

Hattori, T. and R. Hattori (1976). The physical environment in soil microbiology: An attempt to extend principles of microbiology to soil microorganisms. *Crit. Rev. Microbiol.,* **4**:423–461.

Jamison, V. C. (1942). The slow reversible drying of sandy surface soils beneath citrus trees in central Florida. *Soil Sci. Soc. Proc.,* **6**:36–41.

Jamison, V. C. (1946). Resistance to wetting in the surface of sandy soils under citrus trees in central Florida and its effect upon penetration and the efficiency of irrigation. *Soil Sci. Soc. Proc.,* **10**:103–109.

Keen, N. T. and M. J. Holliday (1982). "Recognition of bacterial pathogens by plants," in M. S. Mount and G. H. Lacy, eds., *Phytopathogenic Prokaryotes,* Vol. 2, Chapter 9. Academic Press, New York, pp. 179–217.

Knowlton, S., A. Berry, and J. G. Torrey (1980). Evidence that associated soil bacteria may influence root hair infection of actinorhizal plants by *Frankia. Can. J. Microbiol.,* **26**:971–977.

Federal Register (1984). Microbial pesticides; interim policy on small scale field testing. Environ. Prot. Agency U.S., Statement of Interim Policy, **49**:40659.

Lowendorf, H. S. (1980). Factors affecting survival of *Rhizobium* in soil. *Adv. Microb. Ecol.,* **4**:87–124.

Marshall, K. C. (1975). Clay mineralogy in relation to survival of soil bacteria. *Annu. Rev. Phytopath.,* **13**:357–373.

McAllister, J. C. (1983). *A Practical Guide to Novel Soil Amendments,* Rodale, Emmaus, PA.

Olsen, R. A., R. B. Clark, and J. H. Bennet (1981). The enhancement of soil fertility by plant roots. *Am. Sci.,* **69:**378–384.

Ramey, W.A. (1965). "Physical factors of the soil as they affect soil microorganisms," in K. F. Baker and W. C. Snyder, eds., *Ecology of Soil-Borne Plant Pathogens.* University of California Press, Berkeley, p. 571.

Rhoads, A. S. (1936). Blight—a non-parasitic disease of citrus trees. University of Florida Agricultural Experimental Station Bulletin No. 296, Gainesville, p. 64.

Rodrigues-Kabana, R. and E. A. Curl (1980). Nontarget effects of pesticides on soil-borne pathogens and disease. *Annu. Rev. Phytopathol.,* **18:**311–332.

Schneider, R. W., ed. (1982). *Suppressive Soils and Plant Disease.* American Phytopathology Society, St. Paul, p. 88.

Stolzy, E. H. and S. D. van Gundy (1968). The soil as an environment for microflora and microfauna. *Phytopathology,* **58:**889–898.

Stotzky, G. (1980). "Surface interactions between clay minerals and microbes, viruses, and soluble organics, and the probable importance of these interactions to the ecology of microbes in soil," in R. C. W. Berkeley et al., eds., *Microbial Adhesion to Surfaces.,* Chapter 13. Ellis Harwood, Chichester, pp. 231–247.

Torrey, J. G. (1978). *In vitro* methods in the study of symbiosis, in T. A. Thorpe, ed., *Frontiers of Plant Tissue Culture,* Proceedings of the 4th International Congress on Plant Tissue and Cell Culture, University of Calgary, Alberta, pp. 373–380.

Torrey, J. G. and J. O. Tjepkema, eds. (1979). Symbiotic nitrogen fixation in actinomycete-nodulated plants. *Bot. Gaz.,* **140:**(Suppl.)126

van Berkum, P. and B. B. Bohlool (1980). Evaluation of nitrogen fixation by bacteria in association with roots of tropical grasses. *Microbiol. Rev.,* **44:**491–517.

Zobel, R.W., P. D. Tredici, and J. G. Torrey (1976). Method for growing plants aeroponically. *Plant Physiol.,* **57:**344–346.

10 ENVIRONMENTAL MICROBIAL AUTECOLOGY: PRACTICALITY AND FUTURE

Robert L. Tate III

Department of Soils and Crops
Cook College
Rutgers, The State University of New Jersey
New Brunswick, New Jersey

Past advances in microbial ecology attributable to research that could be classed as microbial autecology are obvious from the preceding chapters. Studies of plant or animal pathogen survival under adverse conditions in soils or waters, or evaluation of the behavior of participants in various biogeochemical cycling processes, such as nitrogen fixation or nitrification are of clear economic, health, and/or practical value. Unfortunately, it is also evident that, except in a limited number of exceptional cases, microbial autecological research has been confined to a few microbes possessing easily recognized traits (pathogenicity, unique colonial morphology, etc.). Although the information gleaned from such research has been interesting as well as, in many cases, invaluable, these functionally or physically distinct microorganisms comprise a minor portion of the microbial populations of most ecosystems. We may, in all reality, conclude that total ecosystem stability and function essentially rests upon the growth and development of a vast variety of populations of nondescript microorganisms and that development of a complete understanding of the biotic interactions in most native ecosystems requires greater understanding of the behavior or function of these structurally less distinguishable organisms than is currently available. These latter organisms have not been excluded from study by conscious decision as much as by technical limitations and economic considerations.

This is New Jersey Agricultural Experiment Station Publication No. F-15187-1-85, supported by state funds.

Where economic considerations have made it feasible to gain a better under-standing of a specific organism, such as various rhizobia, methods were devel-oped for their visualization in situ. As will be discussed herein, the methods are now available to overcome past limitations and, perhaps the inertia problems, and to tackle some of the more difficult microbial autecological questions. Thus, the objective of this treatise has been to examine the past contributions of microbial autecology to the general science of ecology and to develop a poten-tially prophetic view of the future of this science. Prediction of the future impact of autecological microbial research must involve an evaluation of past and current technical limitations, the potential to overcome these barriers to ad-vancement of the science through development of new procedures or modifica-tion of existing techniques, and the need for studies of individual microbial populations in situ. As a contribution to meeting these needs, a number of diverse essays were collected in this treatise. In many cases, the procedures presented are currently only slightly applicable to microbial autecological re-search. But, as will be discussed in this chapter, with several of the procedures, the applicability to autecological research has been minimal, either through oversight or as the result of the need to develop data analysis or related proce-dures to make the techniques more practical for autecological research. There-fore, the objective of this concluding chapter is to evaluate those essays in order to derive an overall picture of the role of autecological studies in microbial ecology.

1.0. PAST ACCOMPLISHMENTS, THE CURRENT FOUNDATION

In many instances, the key to the future lies in a keen awareness of past prob-lems and their solutions. Autecological research is no exception to this observa-tion. This science has been limited by (1) an inadequate definition of the boundaries of autecological research, (2) problems of species identification, and (3) lack of sensitive analytical techniques. Basically, autecological science has the objective of answering the questions of who is present in a given ecosystem, what is their contribution to total ecosystem function, and what is the magni-tude of this function? Underlying this reasonably well defined goal is the ques-tion of the identity of the species, for bacterial studies, and of the individual, for fungal autecological research. Before we can really assess the role or impact of individual population(s) on total ecosystem function, we must be able to posi-tively identify and quantify those populations of interest from among all the other millions of microbes present.

1.1. Conceptual Problems, The Species — The Individual

The difficulty of evaluating bacterial species is derived from the mutability of bacteria and the apparent fluidity of bacterial taxonomic schemes. In past years, many bacteriologists were comfortable with the requirements of conducting a few physiological or staining tests and classifying the microbe of interest through examination of a dichotomous key such as Bergey's Manual of Determinative Bacteriology by Breed et al. (1957). The comfort was usually disturbed by the more minor problems associated with finding an "exact fit" between the description of the unknown strain and those listed in the manuals. With the development of modern taxonomic methods, such as the more specialized DNA hybridization procedures, taxonomic specialists generally are needed to positively identify various bacterial species. Thus, the possibility of identifying a bacterial species from a few simple physiological tests is vastly reduced, if it were ever really possible. This leaves the microbiologist wishing to study the individual in situ with a complex problem of truly defining the bacterial strain and readily identifying it in complex soil or water samples. If biotic interactions are included in the study, this taxonomic problem is multiplied severalfold in that it becomes necessary to identify several different microbial species. With the potential for evaluating the concurrent population fluxes of a variety of microbial species in soils and waters, the more readily the individual species can be identified, the greater the quantities of ecological data that can be collected and analyzed. Thus, the microbial ecologist must be trained in taxonomic procedures, study a well-defined group of bacteria, use a limited number of environmental samples, or limit the study to a single or a few microorganisms. The situation today appears to be a mixture of two compromises. If the objective is to develop an overall picture of the populations comprising the microbial community or those capable of catalyzing a given reaction, then the microbial species present in a few discrete samples are defined (e.g., see Gamble et al. (1977) or Chapter 6). Gamble et al. isolated the numerically dominant denitrifiers from 19 soils, 3 freshwater lake sediments, and oxidized poultry manure. Of the over 1500 bacterial isolates capable of growing under anaerobic conditions, 146 were identified as denitrifiers. The denitrifiers were separated by numerical taxonomic procedures into a number of well-defined species. (The numbers of bacterial cultures isolated and physiologically characterized in this study indicate the difficulties that would be encountered in attempting to augment this study by inclusion of an objective of recording changes in the species distribution in the samples with time.) An alternative compromise that provides for collection and analysis of a greater number of samples than does a strict taxonomic procedure, is to group the microbial isolates into physiological or structural groupings known as phena or taxa. This allows for the study of the variation in the ecosystem with time. These phena are groups of bacteria with a high percentage of physiological or structural similarity (Chapter 1 and 2). They may or may not correspond to known bacterial species. At times, a few well characterized bacterial species are included in the physiological analyses and groupings. Thus, the relationship of at least some of the phena to named species or strains is documented. This use of physiological groupings is underlain by a number of assumptions, some of which are

1. The actual species present in the ecosystem studied is not as important as is the physiological niche. The organisms that are active in a given

ecosystem will be the best competitors among those that could potentially occupy the niche. Thus, the identity of the successful competitor is less important than are its overall physical traits and the fact that it is present and active.

2. If a niche is available in the ecosystem, then a microbe will be present capable of filling it. With the extreme variability of microbes, especially bacteria, if life is possible in the site, then a microorganism will be selected capable of taking advantage of the opportunity.

3. Use of phena or taxa in microbial population analyses provides all the information necessary to interpret ecosystem diversity, and thereby, in many instances, ecosystem stability.

The relative merits of true species diversity analyses in opposition to a physiological diversity analytical procedure as an indicator of the effect of biotic and abiotic interactions with microbial populations and the function of the individual therein will be debated long after this book is published. In studies where the organisms of interest are readily grouped into well-defined bacterial species, use of species diversity analysis is most probably superior in that it allows greater comparison of data between a variety of ecosystem studies. But, in many cases, with currently available taxonomic procedures, such analyses are precluded by the excessive technical demands of the taxonomic procedures. In the latter case, the value of defining interactions between individual functional groups to developing a full understanding of the individual microbial behavior in situ must not be sacrificed. Physiological grouping procedures are invaluable, in fact, they are a must.

The problem of defining the individual is of greater concern with fungal populations or species. With bacteria, we can either (1) readily visualize individual organisms through the use of fluorescent antibody procedures or (2) by combination with radiological procedures, assess its metabolic contribution to the ecosystem. But, because of the size of the organisms it is generally the population as a whole that is of interest. A highly active individual bacterium, while having a major impact on the microsite, is most probably going to have a minimal effect on total ecosystem function as compared to the total population of the species or physiological grouping. In opposition, an individual fungal mycelium can be physically immense compared to the bacterium. In theory, it is easy to select the fungal life stage that is of greatest interest in an autecological study, that is, the growing, respiring mycelium. Unfortunately, it is difficult to quantify mycelial mass in a soil containing a mixture of mycelia and spores. The problem in evaluating the behavior of individual fungal species in soil relates primarily to differentiating mycelia from spores. To date, the only feasible solution to this difficulty for general use involves direct microscopic examination of the soil or water sample.

1.2. Technical Problems

Once the functional entity or species has been selected and the sampling procedures evaluated for the field or cultural work, the major limitations to autecological research and interpretation of the data collected therein involve technical problems. That is, what are the best procedures available, and what are their limitations? In the past, many of the studies have been limited to the laboratory because of the lack of valid field techniques to quantify microbial presence and activity in situ. Those projects, which were conducted in the field in many cases, involved overuse of a limited number of procedures or over extrapolation of technically limited analytical techniques. An overview of past work suggests that there may have been some overlooked procedures that could have increased our understanding of microbial activity in the field situation. There are also some definite technical limitations that must be overcome.

1.2.1. The Used — The Overused. There is probably no other microbiological procedure that has been abused as much as the viable plate count techniques. The recording of colony numbers in a data book has introduced more false confidence and outright erroneous concepts into our science than has any other technique. That is not to say that there is no place for plate count procedures in microbial autecology. Indeed there are many situations where such data reveal interactions and concepts that can only be quantified by such techniques (Chapter 2). But, the basic limitations of these methods must be remembered when analyzing the data and developing extrapolations to other systems. Examples of such limitations are derived from complications with the efficiency of extracting microbial cells from soils and the environmental implications of microbial physiological diversity. First, not all organisms in an environmental sample or even the total population of a single species can be cultured on any given single culture medium. Use of several diverse media is inadequate in that overlapping of the selectivity of the two or more media is difficult, if not impossible, to quantify and interpret. Another rarely considered problem relates to the performance of a viable count procedure when used with a variety of environmental samples of different physical and chemical properties. The capability of quantitatively culturing various microbes rests upon the capacity of extracting the propagules from the sample. That is, the recovery of *Escherichia coli,* for example, from a sandy soil may be more efficient than from an organic soil or a heavy clay soil with a high cation exchange capacity where the microbial cell is more likely to become physically attached to soil colloidal particles. Thus, the recovery efficiency for each type of environmental sample for which a given procedure is to be used must be evaluated.

A further complication of plate count data relates to the physiological diversity of microbial populations, especially bacteria. Isolation of a variety of microorganisms on a culture medium capable of catabolizing a selected carbon compound for energy or carbon does not lead to the conclusion that the microorganisms are active in situ and especially does not indicate that the expression of the metabolic trait in the native sample is proportional to the population densities measured. For example, many bacteria and fungi are present in the soil sample in a resting stage. Extraction and plating on a favorable growth medium allows growth of these previously inactive creatures. Thus, the populations detected on selective growth media may overestimate the expression of the specific physiological function in the environmental sample. In contrast, should all organisms not be removed from the native sample, potential activity would be underestimated. Thus, deviation of viable count data from the actual in situ level is not predictable. Plate count data must therefore be interpreted with extreme care.

A popular procedure in use today, in which final interpretation relies upon data derived from direct plating of samples, diluted samples, or extracts on selective media, is the use of antibiotic sensitive mutants (auxotrophs) of bacterial or fungal strains (Chapter 3). Using this procedure solves the problem of identifying nondescript organisms in a complex microbial community but it does not deal with the difficulties associated with quantitative extraction and growth of the microbe on laboratory culture media as required for viable culture procedures. This criticism is of less concern in these studies than with more general viable plate count studies in that it is reasonably easy to measure the percentage of recovery of labeled organisms amended to a soil or water sample. A question that is rarely, if ever, asked relates to the potential for the percentage recovery of the genetically tagged organism to change with incubation time in the sample. This would be of greatest concern with soil samples where physical association of microorganisms with colloidal organic or mineral matter is common. With studies of antibiotic auxotrophs in soils, axenically cultured populations are generally amended to the environmental sample and changes in the populations with time are calculated. Percentage recovery of the population at the initial time is reasonably easily determined in that a viable count may be performed on the inoculum and the freshly amended soil. Most commonly this recovery percentage is assumed to be constant throughout the experiment. But, were it possible for the organisms to interact with the soil in a manner that would decrease the extraction efficiency with time, then viable plate counts would increasingly underestimate population densities with time. Further research is needed to evaluate the potential for this difficulty in microbially amended samples.

Standard plate count procedures have been replaced by direct observation techniques, such as the use of fluorescent antibody singly or combined with viable or autoradiographic methods in some autecological studies. Microbial cells have been examined in situ microscopically for many decades, but use of fluorescent antibody procedures makes species identification as well as general population quantification possible. For example, Fliermans and Schmidt (1975) used both specific fluorescent lables and ^{14}C labeled carbon dioxide to locate and assess the activity of *Nitrobacter agilis* and *Nitrobacter winogradskyi* in pure cultures, a simple mixed culture, and a soil sample. These techniques add a degree of precision that may not even be approachable with the overused culture procedures. Unfortunately, these highly specific procedures are tedious — thereby limiting the number of environmental samples that may be conveniently processed — and, at times, too specific. For example, the antibodies prepared against a variety of strains of nitrifying bacteria are of tremendous value when that specific strain for which the antibodies were produced is examined. Unless the specific organism studied happens to be the predominant or only nitrifier in the sample no measure of overall nitrifier activity in the sample is provided. Although antibodies could be prepared against all strains anticipated to function in a given ecosystem type, this would be laborious. Thus, in spite of the limitations, overall autotrophic nitrifier populations are still generally quantified by most probable number procedures, such as that of Alexander and Clark (1965).

1.2.2. The Overlooked. Two procedures evaluated in this treatise, species diversity analyses (Chapter 5) and numerical taxonomic analyses (Chapter 6) have been used extensively to quantify changes in studies of populations of aquatic microorganisms, as well as in some soil ecosystems. These are generally not classed as autecological research in that the objectives of the studies generally involve evaluation of the organisms present in the ecosystem at a given point of time or comparison of the differences between several sites within a specific time frame. Although numerical taxonomic and species diversity procedures have been used in a number of different laboratories, general usage is limited by the special data analysis procedures required to group the data into taxonomic or functional units. With more limited definitions of microbial autecology, such procedures would not even be classified as autecology in that autecology is considered simply to be the quantification of the individual present in a given microbial community (Chapter 1). With the extension of the definition to include definition of the function of the microbes within the community, elucidation of the interactions with other biotic entities in the ecosystem becomes important. Both of these procedures allow such evaluation of biotic interactions in complex microbial communities, assuming that the microbes present can be isolated and that the isolation method is reasonably quantitative.

The underlying force preventing general application of numerical taxonomic or diversity analyses relates more to the quantities of data that must be collected to provide a representative picture of the population dynamics of the study site and their changes as the result of anthropometric manipulation. Both the physical manipulation of axenic cultures as well as the evaluation of the vast amounts of data become difficult if not impossible. With past limitations in these areas, it is reasonably easy to understand why these two procedures have not been considered under the heading of microbial autecology. But, with the increasing propensity to apply the rapid microbial identification procedures that have been developed for medical microbiology to ecological research and the increased availability of microcomputers with the capability of linking with mainframe computers, it is becoming feasible, and perhaps practical, to evaluate the changes in individual microbial species in relationship with respect to variation in other individual species.

Numerical taxonomic and species diversity analyses have been classified as overlooked procedures in this discussion. This characterization implies not as much of a past omission as a current failure to utilize fully the techniques in light of recent development of computerized data collection and analysis methods. Thus, an overlooked procedure in this discussion includes the implication of immediacy of application rather than past negligence. As the limitations of using these powerful tools of describing ecosystem function and dynamics are relieved, it behooves us to reevaluate these procedures and our definitions of autecology to see how they can be implemented for future scientific advancement.

1.3. The Hope

A perusal of the preceding chapters implies that past studies have in many instances been developed with the view of providing as many answers as possible while keeping the quantities of data collected and numbers of samples analyzed within a manageable range. This was logical considering the degree of automation of most laboratories and the availability of complex data analysis equipment to the average bench scientist. The recent burst of interest in microcomputers and application of these instruments to automation of laboratories has drastically changed the situation. The limitations now appear to relate to: (1) the availability of funds to equip laboratories with the automated equipment; (2) development of more ambitious ideas using the equipment in ecosystem wide studies; and (3) to development of computer software to analyze the data, and in some instances, to automate procedures for which commercial packages are not available. In reality, microbial autecology, as a science, could be said to be standing at the portal to a number of major advances that will change not only the limited concepts of the research area, but will vastly expand our understanding of ecosystem function as it relies upon the microbial community, in general.

2.0. CURRENT STATUS OF AUTECOLOGICAL RESEARCH

In Chapters 7–9, excellent reviews are provided of the status of microbial autecological research in the author's respective areas of expertise. As anticipated, with some ecosystems, such as marine sediments and benthic waters, much of the autecological science has been conducted in the laboratory where as with the more accessible sites, such as soils and shallower surface waters and sediments, evaluation of the behavior and activity of individual microbial populations in situ is becoming more common. Mills (1985) recently described a series of studies on Contrary Creek, Virginia, where microorganisms suspected of being instrumental in recovery of the watershed from acid mine drainage were evaluated. A combination of fluorescent antibodies and electron accepting dyes were used to assess *Thiobacillus ferrooxidans* and *Thiobacillus thiooxidans* activities in the creek waters. The premier example of autecological research in terrestrial ecosystems must be the study of nitrifiers in a variety of agricultural and undisturbed soil ecosystems. These studies rely upon the pioneering studies of immunofluorescence procedures in Schmidt's laboratory in Minnesota (e.g. Bohlool and Schmidt, 1970; Schmidt, 1974; Fliermans and Schmidt, 1975). Both the general applicability and the limitations of the procedures were elucidated through a number of studies conducted over the last several decades.

As was previously alluded to in the discussion of techniques; the striking feature of these chapters is the limitation of the in situ research to a few well studied organisms. In many cases, the underlying force behind development of these studies could be considered to be economic in that the organisms studied were participatory in essential biogeochemical processes (nitrogen fixation or nitrification) or involved in major reclamation problems (acid mine drainage). This is of necessity a symptom of the labor intensive, tedious procedures available for such studies. With the development of greater interest in the basic properties of microbial involvement in total ecosystem function, more incentive is provided to development of methods to overcome the current limitations to a more general application of microbial autecological research.

3.0. THE FUTURE OF MICROBIAL AUTECOLOGY

The scientific benefits of any individual experiment may be debated, but the potential for future impact of microbial autecological studies on microbial ecology and ecology in general are assured. As has been repeatedly demonstrated in the area of biochemistry, tremendous information can be gained by treating the ecosystem as a black box and evaluating the overall processes occurring therein. But, when it becomes necessary to develop an understanding of the control of those processes, to develop fine tuned predictive models, or to increase or reduce the rates of key biologically catalyzed processes, the microorganisms involved and the factors controlling their behavior in situ must be determined. This need is becoming quite obvious as the result of the marriage of biotechnology and microbial ecology, especially in the study of *Rhizobium* behavior in soil ecosystems. Biotechnological procedures have been used quite successfully to produce a number of *Rhizobium* strains that are more effective nitrogen fixers than the original "wild type" isolates. The ultimate objective of strain development is to increase field nitrogen fixation rates. For this to occur, the more effective laboratory developed strains must successfully compete with the indigenous soil strains in nodulating legumes. Again, considerable information can be gained relating to the rates of nitrogen fixation by the inoculated crops, but the cause of this reaction cannot be ascertained until the movement of the cells of the newly developed strain into root nodules is verified. Jenkins and Bottomley (1985) evaluated this problem through examination of indigenous populations of *Rhizobium meliloti* in agricultural soils. Polyacrylamide gel electrophoresis was used to delineate strain differences in the *Rhizobium* isolates. They found that of 32 isolates, 12 and 6 clustered into two major groups, whereas the remaining 14 isolates were each represented by unique protein profiles. In analyses of the same soils after a 2-yr period, they found that 42 of 79 isolates were identical to the 31 previously isolated strains. These studies indicate both a strain variation with time in the soil and a reasonable degree of stability of the population. Any new *Rhizobium* strain introduced into this soil would have to be an effective competitor with these indigenous populations to successfully nodulate legumes and contribute to the soil nitrogen cycle. Pugashetti et al. (1982) demonstrated a variety of microbial populations in soils that were antagonistic towards strains of *Rhizobium japonicum.* The success rate for nodulation of legumes by inoculated strains is rather variable (Koslak et al., 1983). For example, van Rensburg and Strijdom (1985), in their study of *Rhizobium* strain inoculation of *Trifolium* spp., *Medicago* spp., *Glycine max,* and *Lotus penduculatus* observed nodule occupancy by the inoculant strain varied from 17.7 to 100%. Minimal competition effectiveness was observed for a soybean strain, whereas the maximum was observed with the *L. pendunculatus* strain growing in soils that did not contain an indigenous population of its specific rhizobia. Handelsman et al. (1984) have developed a technique using specific bacteriophages as enrichment for more competitive *Rhizobium meliloti* strains. Further autecological research is necessary to determine which cellular traits increase the probability of successful nodulation of legumes by the auxotrophs.

As the demands for more efficient crop production increase and the gains of current emphasis on biotechnological research continues, the need for more intensive study of indigenous as well as exogenously inoculated microbial strains in complex ecosystems is going to increase. This demand for autecological procedures when combined with the increased awareness of environmental problems and their association with ecosystem stability portends a bright future for microbial autecological research. It is the hope of the editor and authors of this short treatise on microbial autecology that the questions raised herein, as well as some of the answers provided, will spur others into expanding the limits of this phase of microbial ecology. Then, as advancement in various biotechnological and environmental sciences are made, the microbiologist will be equipped to apply them to practical needs in the field.

REFERENCES

Alexander, M. and F. E. Clark (1965). "Nitrifying bacteria," in C. A. Black, ed., *Methods of Soil Analysis,* Part 2. American Society of Agronomy, Madison, WI, pp. 1477–1483.

Bohlool, B. B. and E. L. Schmidt (1970). Immunofluorescent detection of *Rhizobium japonicum* in soils. *Soil Sci.,* **110**:229–236.

Breed, R. S. et al. (1957). *Bergey's Manual of Determinative Bacteriology.* Williams and Wilkins, Baltimore.

Fliermans, C. B. and E. L. Schmidt (1975). Autoradiography and immunofluorescence combined for autecological study of single cell activity with *Nitrobacter* as a model system. *Appl. Microbiol.,* **30**:676–684.

Gamble, T. M., M. R. Betlach, and J. M. Tiedje (1977). Numerically dominant denitrifying bacteria from world soils. *Appl. Environ. Microbiol.,* **33:**926–939.

Handelsman, J., R. A. Ugalde, and W. J. Brill (1984). *Rhizobium meliloti* competitiveness and the alfalfa agglutinin. *J. Bacteriol.,* **157:**703–707.

Jenkins, M. B. and P. J. Bottomley (1985). Evidence for a strain of *Rhizobium meliloti* dominating the nodules of alfalfa. *Soil Sci. Soc. Am. J.,* **49:**326–328.

Koslak, R. M. and B. B. Bohlool (1985). Influence of environmental factors on interstrain competition in *Rhizobium japonicum. Appl. Environ. Microbiol.,* **49:**1128–1133.

Mills, A. L. (1985). "Acid mine waste drainage: Microbial impact on the recovery of soil and water ecosystems," in R. L. Tate III and D. A. Klein, eds., *Soil Reclamation Processes: Microbiological Analyses and Applications.* Dekker, New York, pp. 35–81.

Pugashetti, B. K., J. S. Angle, and G. H. Wagner (1982). Soil microorganisms antagonistic towards *Rhizobium japonicum. Soil Biol. Biochem.,* **14:**45–49.

Schmidt, E. L. (1974). Quantitative autecological study of microorganisms in soil by immunofluorescence. *Soil Sci.,* **118:**141–149.

van Rensburg, H. J. and B. W. Strijdom (1985). Effectiveness of *Rhizobium* strains used in inoculants after their introduction into soil. *Appl. Environ. Microbiol.,* **49:**127–131.

INDEX

261